International
Marketing
Strategy

Pergamon Titles of Related Interest

Davis Managing and Organizing Multinational Corporations
Hussey Introducing Corporate Planning, 2nd Edition
Joyner Joyner's Guide to Official Washington for Doing Business
Overseas
Negandhi Functioning of the Multinational Corporation
Wild Operations Management

Related Journals*

Futurics
Long Range Planning
Omega

*Free specimen copies available upon request.

PERGAMON
POLICY   ON BUSINESS
STUDIES

International Marketing Strategy

Revised Edition

Edited by
Hans Thorelli
Helmut Becker

Pergamon Press
NEW YORK • OXFORD • TORONTO • SYDNEY • FRANKFURT • PARIS

Pergamon Press Offices:

U.S.A.	Pergamon Press Inc., Maxwell House, Fairview Park, Elmsford, New York 10523, U.S.A.
U.K.	Pergamon Press Ltd., Headington Hill Hall, Oxford OX3 OBW, England
CANADA	Pergamon of Canada, Ltd., Suite 104, 150 Consumers Road, Willowdale, Ontario M2J 1P9, Canada
AUSTRALIA	Pergamon Press (Aust.) Pty. Ltd., P.O. Box 544, Potts Point, NSW 2011, Australia
FRANCE	Pergamon Press SARL, 24 rue des Ecoles, 75240 Paris, Cedex 05, France
FEDERAL REPUBLIC OF GERMANY	Pergamon Press GmbH, Hammerweg 6, Postfach 1305, 6242 Kronberg/Taunus, Federal Republic of Germany

Library of Congress Cataloging in Publication Data

Thorelli, Hans Birger, 1921-   comp.
  International marketing strategy.

  (Pergamon policy studies on business/international
trade and finance)
  Includes bibliographies and indexes.
  1. Export marketing—Addresses, essays, lectures.
2. Marketing—Addresses, essays, lectures. I. Becker,
Helmut, 1927-   II. Title. III. Series.
HF1009.5.T485 1980   658.8'48   80-14689
ISBN 0-08-025542-6
ISBN 0-08-025543-4 (pbk.)

Printed in the United States of America

Contents

Preface

You are looking at the second, revised edition of a book on international marketing strategy first published in 1973. The first edition has been sold out for some time. The rapidly changing world marketing environment as well as the availability of excellent new writing on the subject prompted a revised edition rather than a simple reprint.

In preparing this book of readings, original editor Hans B. Thorelli has been joined by Professor Helmut Becker as co-editor. Our theme, Strategic Planning in International Marketing, is carried forward from the first edition. In most specifics the contents are changed, however, on the basis of extensive search, sifting, and editing. We can say with confidence that within this compact volume each contribution covers an important topic and each principal article is written by an outstanding expert. Over two-thirds of the readings are new to this edition, and several of the items carried over have been updated.

This edition puts a premium on practical, empirical applications. Thus, about one-fourth of all readings are case studies of actual successes and failures in international marketing, each illustrating the prime points made in the main articles. Many of these, too, are interspersed with concrete examples.

We expect the book to be equally well adapted to executives and students, for reasons detailed in the introduction. It will also be useful to public policymakers who wish to understand the operations and motivations of the companies they deal with in performing their administrative duties. Above all, we expect that readers from all corners of the globe will find ideas and counsel of value to them. We all need to learn from each other – and we all benefit in the process.

Introduction

THE BLOOMING IMPORTANCE OF INTERNATIONAL MARKETING

International trade is blooming as well as important: trade between nations is growing at a rate of 6 percent in physical volume and at twice that rate if inflation is included. The value of world exports now is about 1.3 trillion (1,300 billion or 1,300,000 million) dollars. This figure is similar to the total annual output of all underdeveloped countries in the world. In addition to trade itself, the output of goods and services by multinational companies abroad and marketed in the respective countries where the subsidiaries are located probably exceeds 600 billion dollars. With this broad definition of international marketing it comprises a volume of around 2 trillion dollars.

Many countries are vitally dependent on international commerce. Belgium and Holland derive more than 40 percent of their gross national products from world trade. For most industrial nations the figure is over 20 percent. Traditionally, among Western industrialized countries, the U.S.A. has been least dependent on international trade, which accounts for only about 6.5 percent of GNP. Nonetheless, due to the magnitude of the American economy, this modest share is sufficient to make the U.S.A. one of the largest trading partners of the world. Furthermore, American dependence on international commerce will increase greatly in the next few decades, due to accelerating depletion of domestic national resources and vast growth in luxury imports, reflecting individualization of consumption in affluent economies. Growing international economic dependence in America will also stem from the geometrical progression of technology that simply makes it impossible for any single nation to keep on top in all fields. The original development of steel oxygen technology, miniaturized TV, and supersonic transport in other nations are cases in point.

The Tokyo Round of multinational trade negotiations completed in 1979 may be viewed as a declaration of renewed faith in open international markets. With sustained economic development, international trade will inevitably continue to flourish as long as the principles of these agreements are allowed to operate. Meanwhile, we may well have to face such major dislocations as OPEC in other areas of commodity trade. A net effect of such events on importing nations is to increase the need to develop export marketing skills. These skills are also at a premium in the scramble to prevail on such opportunities as those created by China's half-open door policy.

The EEC is by far the largest trader in the world, followed by the United States — currently being overtaken by West Germany. For a quarter of a century the U.S. share of the world market has been declining for two reasons. First, with more rapid economic development in many other countries it is only natural that the trade of those countries has increased more rapidly than that of the U.S.A. Second, the rest of the industrial world has been catching up with American technology, managerial know-how, and financial prowess. These have been the prime sources of U.S. competitive strength. Paradoxically, American management — the originator of modern marketing concepts and wonderfully adept at implementing these concepts at home — has often been woefully inept in applying them abroad. In view of future U.S. international economic dependence, American business clearly faces an enormous challenge in international marketing.

Different categories of nations have strikingly different shares of the world export market. The industrial West plus Japan accounted for two-thirds of total world exports in the mid-seventies. No less than about one-half of total world exports were from one industrial country to another! OPEC nations at that time still accounted for a modest 13 percent, which, however, was substantially equal to the world export market share of all other Third-World nations (not far from one hundred) taken together. The Communist bloc — including China — accounted for only 10 percent, two-thirds of which represented transactions between bloc members. These numbers lend significance to the great debates about North-South and East-West trading relations in the future.

Clearly, in years ahead international marketing will be even more pervasive than it is today. Indeed, most businesses will be either globetrotters or globewatchers. Globetrotters, an increasing proportion of all firms, are those who engage in export, import, or production abroad; this group is likely to set the pace in most of the economies of the world. Those who elect to stay at home will have to be globewatchers; that is, they will have to face up to ever-increasing competition with overseas firms in their own home market. Even such a trite local venture as the village barbershop will have to follow international fashions on hair colors and hairdos, or face the prospect (hair-raising as it may be) of extinction. Indeed, globewatching in general has great merit: by observing marketing in other cultures the executive (or the student) frequently gains a better understanding of marketing in his own.

WITH THE READER IN MIND

This being a book on marketing, we have attempted to keep the customer in mind. We envisage two groups of readers: seasoned executives and university students of business. The manager should find the book integrated and comprehensive enough to hold its own, whether he personally is a globetrotter or a domestic executive sizing up the international scene. The book also caters to the business student looking for a single concentrated source on international operations. In academic curricula focused on marketing or international business, this collection of readings should find its prime use as a fairly rich supplement to any textbook.

It should be evident, then, that we are assuming some practical or theoretical familiarity with marketing management and at least the rudiments of international trade policy and theory. While the book does specialize on international marketing our selections have been made in full awareness of the fact that in international operations, more than elsewhere, marketing is inextricably intertwined with other management functions. Let it not be forgotten: in nine cases out of ten international business begins with export or import, and the lifeblood of the international firm is marketing abroad.

The treatment here differs from most other books of readings in international marketing. This collection has an integrative framework to both guide and stimulate the reader – and to ensure a useful selection of readings. The overall theme is the adaptation of marketing strategy to the special requirements of international market structures, as outlined below and detailed in Part One. In contrast to other books of readings which deal with differences in domestic operating conditions (comparative marketing), this collection focuses on international marketing. It is more analytical than descriptive – we feel that descriptive material, in these fast-moving times, ages rapidly. To promote integration of materials we have edited and abbreviated a great many selections. In this manner, too, it has been possible to include a greater number and range of contributions. We have also minimized incest by overlap – too many articles are making the rounds of the readings books. By digging further, we are able to present here many valuable contributions not elsewhere reprinted. Finally, in an unorthodox twist, we have resorted to excerpts from books and monographs when no suitable articles were at hand – or tailor-made readings ourselves. In this manner we have dealt with for example international pricing, a vital problem area paradoxically left out of most other international marketing collections.

The level of generalization aimed at is that of the practically oriented and analytically interested executive, as well as of the university student contemplating a career in international marketing at home or abroad. We are avoiding the extreme of generality as found in some background writings on cultural anthropology and international economics as well as the opposite extreme of specificity as encountered in the export-manual type of discussion of bills of lading and letters of credit. The watchword is managerial pragmatism based in sound theory.

Our purpose, then, is to provide an analytical framework in international marketing rather than specific answers for the concrete situation. The objective is to help the reader define the problems he is likely to encounter in international marketing, bearing in mind that defining the problem is the single most important prerequisite to solving it. The executive and the student have a characteristic in common: they are looking for impulses to stimulate their own thinking rather than for a set of patent medicines allegedly curing all maladies. The present collection is intended to meet this need. It should enable the reader to make his own diagnosis of differences and similarities in market structures around the world, and it provides guidelines for the planning of appropriate marketing strategies.

The book should be equally relevant whether the reader (or his company) be European or American, a national of an industrialized or of an industrializing country. If a majority of the selections stem from American sources it is simply because thus far most of the best writings on international marketing have appeared in the United States. We have tried, however, to avoid items looking at the world as a kind of enlarged Yankee playground.

SUCCESS FORMULA: HARMONIZING STRUCTURE AND STRATEGY

Ultimately, the whole field of marketing revolves around a single key question: how to adapt marketing strategy to the prevailing market conditions (i.e., the market structure). Whoever has the answer to this question carries the key to success. In domestic marketing it takes no great discerning skills to see that the marketing of ladies' fashion goods differs from that of Coca-Cola, which in turn differs from the marketing of petro-chemicals or productive equipment for industry. But to note such gross differences is not enough. They are of little interest to a hosiery manufacturer trying to find a niche next to twenty other hosiery manufacturers all catering to the same general market. The rise and fall of firms and brands about which we read daily in the financial pages shows that even subtle variations in strategy may spell the differences between failure and success in the marketplace.

The principal distinction between domestic and international marketing is that as you move from the former to the latter the problem of harmonizing (or "matching") strategy and structure takes on two additional dimensions. One set of complications is encountered in the interface between nations: tariffs, quotas and invisible trade barriers, xenophobia, currency problems, East-West embargoes, UN sanctions, and other manifestations of nationalism and international politics. The second array of complications stems from the very fact that one deals with two or more markets on the international scene. Market structures for a given product may vary appreciably from one country to the next due to such factors as differences in values, styles of life, economic development, government regulation of business, and political stability. The scale of operations apart, Coca-Cola can be successfully marketed in almost the same way in New York and Bombay, but this clearly is not the case with beef hamburgers. The free auto markets of Europe differ drastically from the rigidly regimented ones in most Latin American countries. Superciliously, an economist may tell you that the differences between domestic and international operations are only a matter of degree. Remind him that so is a difference between normal body temperature and one five degrees above (or below).

Unfortunately, marketing as a discipline has not yet developed to the stage where we have scientifically validated prescriptions about what marketing strategies to apply under given market conditions. A pioneering foray is being made around the PIMS (Profit Impact of Market Strategy) data bank by the member companies of the Strategic Planning Institute (see Reading 20). The shortage of valid principles does not mean that it is not worth our while to think about international marketing in a systematic way. On the contrary, the very absence of scientific laws on the subject makes an analytical framework for our thinking all the more desirable. To develop such a framework is precisely what we are attempting in Part One of this book.

HOMOGENIZATION AND HETEROGENIZATION OF DEMAND

One of the most perplexing questions in international marketing is to what extent the emergence of multinational markets (EEC, LAFTA, etc.) and the rapidly increasing communication across national borders will result in greater homogenization (standardization) or greater heterogenization (differentiation, fractionalization) of demand. The corresponding issue for the international marketing strategy planner is whether to capitalize upon (and promote) sameness with its attendant economies of scale, or upon individualized demand which frequently offers a set of profitable niches or submarkets somewhat removed from the hazards of head-on competition. Again, the issue of international market segmentation has not received the attention it deserves in the literature.

Part Five is addressed largely to this question. We observe that people have assumed too uncritically that the EEC and similar creations would result overnight in total regional homogenization. This assumption is far from the case. Studies made by the European Commission have consistently revealed amazingly wide − and persisting − disparities in price on products ranging all the way from refrigerators to detergents as between the common market countries. While this is a reflection of the fact that mobility of economic resources is still far from perfect and that distribution structures and trade margins vary considerably inside the community, there is, of course, a long-term trend towards equalization at work. Part Five makes additional points concerning multinational homogenization of demand by income and lifestyle groupings and about likely future cyclical developments alternating between homogenization and heterogenization of markets.

TRIBALISM IN THE GLOBAL VILLAGE

We hear a great deal about Spaceship Earth and the Global Village. And indeed strong technological and cultural forces are pulling the peoples of the world together. Satellite communications are revolutionizing business communications and, via television, enabling everyman to be on the scene – in real time – in almost any corner of the world. By way of Concorde, transatlantic passage takes only half a working day. Worldwide computer hookups are vastly simplifying the coordination of global concerns; the impact of this single development we have probably only begun to understand. Study and vacation abroad are almost as commonplace to the middle class today as the sojourn at a domestic resort of yesterday.

The links of technology and culture across national frontiers do suggest the nascency of One World. Paradoxically, in the midst of these forces of fusion, man has spawned fission: since the last world war some fifty territories have become independent nations, an increase of more than one-third in the number of suboptimization centers in economic development and international politics. Paradoxically, too, notwithstanding American leadership of the free world, nationalism has become rampant. This is most obvious, and psychologically understandable, in the case of the less developed countries. But the LDCs have no monopoly on nationalism, as witnessed by the policies of a de Gaulle or the writings of a Servan-Schreiber, the restrictions on foreign capital investment in Sweden and Japan, the immigration laws of Switzerland and, lately, the restrictive international economic policies of a somewhat disillusioned United States, itself plagued by trade deficits and balance-of-payments problems. The causes of economic nationalism are many. Common markets and customs unions notwithstanding, in one form or another it will be with us for quite a while.

Economic tribalism is at the root of international dislocations at the level of diplomacy as well as that of international marketing by private firms. Parts Two and Three are intended to provide a basis for a deeper understanding of this situation, as well as of the constraints – and opportunities – it presents to the international marketer.

THE CHALLENGE OF INTERNATIONAL MARKETING

A modern marketing system is indispensable to the smooth functioning of an industrialized economy. Mass production would indeed be inconceivable without mass distribution and mass communication. Customer-oriented marketing is not likely to lose in importance in post-industrial society as that is portrayed in the article on the American market in Part Four. A major challenge of international marketing among developed nations in the future will be to effectuate the exchange of styles of life from one culture to another which will doubtless constitute a cardinal element of the coming individualization among increasingly sophisticated consumers.

Marketing can also play a key role in economic development of industrially backward countries, although this is not yet generally realized. Thus it is that marketing development has been almost completely neglected in UN and other assistance programs. This is because we have accepted too uncritically the notion that in the LDCs you have to start with heavy industry, and you have to have socialist or other autocratic governments, willing to suppress private consumption. Indeed, in this view marketing is really a sort of parasitical activity encouraging waste of scarce resources. Reality is precisely the reverse: only if marketing is given at least as much emphasis as heavy industry, agriculture, and education can nations hope to achieve the twin goals of rapid economic progress and internal political freedom. The key is the motivational effects of modern marketing, which results in a dramatic transformation of attitudes towards work, achievement, savings, family planning and consumption.

Beginning thirty years ago, Sears, Roebuck and Company in Latin America has provided an excellent example of a multinational marketing organization rendering a powerful contribution to local economic development. It does this in many ways, by:

1. Fostering thousands of local suppliers.
2. Introducing new concepts of quality and, not least, of quality standards.
3. Introducing consumer credit.
4. Emphasizing big volume and low margins (the reverse is traditional in less developed countries).
5. Introducing the notion of one-stop shopping.
6. Providing consumer information on an unprecedented scale.
7. Substituting same-price-for-all for wasteful and discriminating haggling.
8. Emphasizing that the customer is king. He is not the means of either merchants or governments.

As indicated by Peter Drucker in Part Eight, perhaps the most important effect of Sears' operations in Latin America has been that of shaking up the established ultraconservative department and specialty stores. These local operators have rapidly adopted — or even carried further — many of these progressive policies, resulting in the overdue arrival of some real competition for the favors of the consumer. Old-time distribution was parasitic and static in outlook. Modern marketing is a prime vehicle of development.

There is enormous challenge in international marketing. From a business point of view, it generally offers greater uncertainty than domestic marketing, but the risks are not necessarily much greater. On the contrary, they may often be reduced by an "international portfolio" approach. The payoffs are often greater than at home precisely because the international marketer brings something new to the situation abroad. From a personal point of view, it offers the satisfaction of contributing to the quality of life and to local economic growth, it broadens our horizons, and, last but not least, it teaches us valuable lessons about how to handle international competition as well as regional and special-group marketing problems in domestic markets.

THE PLAN OF THE BOOK

This collection of readings is somewhat unique in the number of contributions included in a compact volume, as suggested above. To bring this bounty together, all the while minimizing overlaps, it was necessary to excerpt and edit several items. Such an approach was possible only due to the outstanding cooperation of participating authors.

Beyond seeking coverage for relevant areas of subject matter, the selection of readings in the central parts of the book has been guided by two principal concerns. We have tried to provide an integrated mix of survey-type, conceptually oriented articles with quite specific contributions oriented to particular markets or firms. We have also included in most of those parts at least one item on the EEC and one on the less developed countries. It seemed preferable to give these two vital and different areas of the world some special treatment, rather than to follow the law of least resistance encountered in collections with one stray article on each of a dozen countries. Short case stories are used to illustrate particular successes (or failures) in international marketing.

The general scheme is as follows:

Part One deals with the harmonization of market structure and marketing strategy as the key to success in international operations and provides an analytical framework for the parts to follow.

Part Two emphasizes the close linkage between politics and economics in international relations and seeks to project the implications of major developments in this interface between the nations to international marketing.

Parts Three and Four deal with market structures. Part Three deals with the role of public policy in regulating market structures and practices in different countries. Part Four is concerned with international demand analysis and the identification of marketing opportunities. It also deals with the differential availability of market data, transportation facilities, and other aspects of marketing infrastructure.

Part Five is focused squarely on the harmonization of marketing strategy and market structure. Product, pricing, promotion, and distribution strategies in different environments are given special emphasis.

Part Six looks at international marketing from the point of view of the small or medium-sized company, concentrating on factors to consider in going international and means of gaining a foothold abroad.

Part Seven is concerned with the problems of coordination of marketing operations in the large multinational corporation.

Part Eight pulls the threads of the book together. The marketing plan is viewed as the practical means by which market structure and strategy may be harmonized. What is involved in international marketing planning is analyzed both at the conceptual level and in down-to-earth, checklist fashion.

The reader will note that each Part concludes with a "Further Reading" list to complement and reinforce our selections.

International
Marketing
Strategy

I
Success Formula: Harmonizing Structure and Strategy

Introduction to Part I

As stated in the introduction, strategic planning in international marketing ultimately faces only one key question: given our objectives, how do we adapt our strategy to the prevailing market conditions (or market structure) in each country? There are no easy answers to this question. If there were, marketing professionals might as well pack their bags! Yet neither executives nor academics should lose sight of this overriding problem. Whatever he does, the marketer's success ultimately depends on his ability to bring his strategy into harmony with the surrounding market structure.

To be able to attune the two, one needs a good understanding of the concepts of strategy and structure, and some kind of model of how they interact. Reading 1, by Thorelli, seeks to provide such a framework for analysis. It does this by applying an ecologic view, seeing the firm, the marketing strategy, and market environment as an open interaction system. This ecologic approach to problem-solving in international marketing provides the theme for the book. The Reading concludes with half a dozen specific examples of interactive marketing strategy. Readings 2, by Salmans, and 3, by Cooney, provide two additional practical examples of successful harmonization of strategy and structure.

In the trendy ski market, Salmans shows how Skis Rossignol tackled the bewildering cross-currents of cosmopolitan and local fashions, status symbols, and physical skiing conditions by aggressively moving consumer research, marketing, and, in several cases, manufacturing into one national market after another — while still retaining its cosmopolitan image. Discovering that many skiers are also tennis players, Rossignol is also drawing on the benefits of synergy in the end consumer market and sports equipment distribution channels to promote further growth by diversification into tennis rackets.

The Rossignol case also illustrates the extraordinary importance of trust in international marketing. Professional skiers know, and even

3

amateurs sense, that performance and safety vary widely with type of equipment. The fine reputation of Rossignol skis in the winter sports areas around the world has provided a platform of "instant trust" among prospective customers as well as users, representing an important differential advantage for this brand. Western businessmen are often irritated by the practice of Oriental (as well as Russian) executives of spending days or weeks eating, drinking, and talking before getting down to contractual negotiations. Westerners fail to see the function of social intercourse as a means of personal evaluation and building of trust. Once trusting in his Western colleague, a Japanese executive often fails to see the need for the intensely formal and detailed contractual arrangements typically in the mind of the Westerner. Many other examples of the role and means of establishing trust could be given.

Interaction is a two-way street. Cooney shows, step-by-step, how Kikkoman International not only entered the U.S. soy sauce market but in fact largely created and shaped that market single-handedly. Before Kikkoman's arrival, demand had been largely latent. Almost in spite of its basically conservative management, the company became a true change agent on the American scene.

Later parts of this volume will further demonstrate the value of the ecologic or interactive view of marketing as an analytical tool as well as a stimulus in creative market planning. At the end of the book the reader should be able to use – and adapt – this approach for his own purposes.

1 International Marketing: An Ecologic View

Hans B. Thorelli

At least three dramatically different views of marketing are being applied today. The oldest of the current marketing concepts is producer and seller oriented. It is based on the standard that "we sell what we make." This beautifully simple notion derives directly from the industrial revolution: the economies of scale realized in mass production were so great that consumers were more than glad to accept the offering as specified by the producer. This philosophy is still prevalent in many firms dominated by engineering minds, or by the type of sales management which feels that there is something amiss with customers who fail to see the beauty of its product. A variant of the same theme is practiced in the socialist world: "planners know better what is good for the people than consumers themselves."

In affluent and "post-industrial" society with hectic competition between products as well as brands and inhabited by increasingly finicky consumers, the production-oriented idea of marketing has obvious shortcomings. In the fifties, the customer-oriented marketing concept was developed in the United States. In this view, the needs of the customer rather than those of the factory should define the offering (product, price, image, service, etc.) of the firm in the marketplace. The standard is now, "we make what we sell." Customer orientation has since been adopted as the keynote of business policy to varying degrees in most industrialized Western countries.

Certainly, the customer-oriented philosophy of business has great merit. It has called attention to the fact that ultimately firms exist not for their own aggrandizement but to serve the public. It has led to a virtual explosion of marketing research in both theory and practice, such research being the prime vehicle of identifying consumer needs. It has also stimulated much-needed integration of product planning, sales, pricing, advertising, market research, service, and other marketing-related activities in thousands of firms. Without doubt, consumers as well as businesses have been – and are – beneficiaries of this process.

RAILROADS AT BAY

Yet this concept of marketing has at least one major shortcoming. This may be illustrated by one of the examples often quoted in the discussion of producer- versus customer-oriented marketing, i.e. the ailing railroad industry in America. It has been said that the prime reason for the demise of railroad companies has been their producer orientation: they saw themselves only in the business of running trains. Had they but been customer-oriented, so the argument runs, they would have seen their business as that of meeting the transportation needs of the population. Ergo, when buses, trucks, and planes emerged on the scene the railroads should have rushed into these new forms of transport. Superficially, the argument is plausible indeed. But it completely neglects one critical question of entrepreneurship: what are the things we are very good at, and what are the things we are not very good at? Now, there is nothing that prompts us to believe that railroad managers are particularly good at running airlines or trucking companies. Indeed, sociological studies suggest that most railroad executives would lack the flexibility and flair that would be required. Nor is there much evidence that the great physical resources (fixed assets) of the railroads would become much better utilized by the addition of, say, airline operations.

The logic of the situation suggests an entirely different tack. Faced with a long-term decline in the demand for their services, alert railroad managers might more reasonably have asked themselves the question: are there any customer wants we might be good at satisfying besides the need for railroad transport? This would have led them to recall that between 1830 and 1900 American railroads received grants of federal and state lands aggregating the land mass of France to stimulate expansion of the iron roads. These vast domains in large part are still owned by the railroads. What could be more natural than investigating, stimulating, and exploiting the needs of an expanding and affluent population for community developments, recreational facilities, and industrial parks on these lands? The prospect should be especially attractive in that a by-product of these activities would be the generation of additional railroad traffic. And, let it not be forgotten, real estate development is something railroad management has to be good at. Until recent years, however, what had been done by the railroads to develop outlying territories owned by them was unimpressive, with a few notable exceptions.

We have developed the railroad case in some detail because it also illustrates the emerging third approach to marketing: what we prefer to call the ecologic view of marketing. Under this view the marketer's standard becomes "we market what customers need and we are good at." By taking into account both client needs and own resources the ecologic marketing concept in effect combines the producer-oriented and the customer-oriented points of view in a way that yields more meaningful conclusions than those which might be reached by either of the older approaches. Hence the notion of real estate development as a natural extension of American railroads.

MARKETING IS AN INTERACTIVE PROCESS

The ecologic view of marketing provides the theme and outline of this book. It is also an approach to theory by which we can improve our understanding of international marketing. Most importantly, it provides a framework of analysis of direct utility to practical decision-makers. In view of its treble significance, the approach will be developed in some detail.

In common with biological organisms every human being and every company is dependent on its environment for survival. Neither nature nor human civilization are in the end eleemosynary institutions. No one is self-sufficient. The interdependence of the company and its setting stems from the incessant drive towards specialization, or division of labor as the prime means of survival in a world of scarce resources. In effect, what happens in the process of interaction is that the company is obtaining the support of the environment by disposing of some of its differential advantage – or conversely, procuring resources from other organizations where they enjoy a differential advantage. The process of exchange is manifested by a perennial stream of transactions.

The environment consists essentially of a series of input and output markets (for labor, capital, productive equipment, raw materials, end products, etc.) in which the company must transact. For long-term survival the customer market is of paramount significance, as in the end satisfying customer needs is the only reason for the environment to provide the wherewithall (sales revenue) on which company existence depends. This observation is often made to establish the importance of marketing. What is far less clearly realized is that it also establishes that increasing customer satisfaction automatically becomes a key objective of any company with the will to grow.

An ecologic model of the company interacting with its environment is displayed in figure 1.1. There are four critical and interdependent

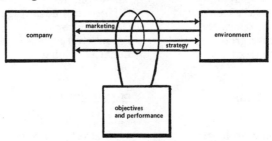

Fig. 1.1. Ecologic view of marketing.

parts in the system: the company, the environment, the marketing strategy governing the interplay between the two, and the objectives at which the strategy is aimed (or, the other side of the coin, the performance actually achieved). Each part actually represents a set of factors or variables distinguishing one marketing situation from another.

The ecologic approach to marketing postulates in effect that a company trying to meet its objectives in a certain environment (market structure) should expect to find some marketing strategies a lot more workable than others. As we are not claiming that there is a single best solution for every situation, it should not be surprising to find several strategies coexisting in a given market environment.(1) This is still a far cry from saying that any random strategy might work. And the more we are able to specify the variables composing each of the four parts of the system, and their likely impact in a given situation, the more adept we shall become in zeroing in on superior strategies. This analytical job is that of the practitioner as much as of the theorist. A point of departure is provided by figure 1.2, which displays a representative selection of variables for each part of the model.

COMPANY CHARACTERISTICS

Our discussion of details in the model is confined to variables of general significance to the planning of international marketing strategy. Clearly, in a given case some variables will be more important than others

Company	Objectives (Performance)
Aggregate size	Survival
Size of local operation	Growth
Resource profile	Customer satisfaction
Headquarter relations	Profitability
Local domain:	Market share
product span	Sales volume
territorial extension	Differential advantage
mode of operations	Data feedback
customer groups served	Productivity
Organization structure	Local vs. global
Leadership	

Marketing strategy	Environment
Product	Layers:
Intelligence and promotion	1. Market structure
Channels of distribution	2. Local marketing environment
Price	3. International environment
Service, before and after sale	See text for further specification
Trust	

Fig. 1.2. International marketing ecology: representative variables.

and some factors not even mentioned here may be of special relevance. Too, different dimensions of a given variable may be significant in different situations. In considering the role of the aggregate size of an international company, for instance, one might have in mind available export capacity in the mother country in thinking about International Nickel, or the ability of the concern to absorb losses in a new venture abroad during a build-up period (Toyota automobiles in Germany in 1970-72), or the strengths and weaknesses of being a large multinational corporation (Unilever, Siemens) versus a small specialty outfit (a maker of paint sprayers, let us say) interacting with the environment in an LDC such as Peru.

That the size of the local operation in a given country is a strong determinant of what strategies may be pursued is beyond doubt. This is also true of the resource profile, notably the proportion of fixed to total assets and of investment to sales, cost structure, manpower skills, patent position, degree of liquidity, and other sources of competitive advantage or disadvantage. In listing headquarter relations we are primarily thinking of the degree of centralization of decision-making about marketing strategy (Readings 37, 39). As an illustration: a few years ago a large American drug maker required that any local price changes be approved by the New York office. When the Venezuelan government invited bids on behalf of public hospitals the company lost out to a nimbler German competitor whose local management was permitted to make price concessions on the spot.

We come next to the local domain. This is an extremely important part of company characteristics. Indeed, together with the set of objectives, the domain defines the mission of the local operation (Thorelli, 1972, p. 290). Every company, every organization may be defined in terms of the four domain dimensions: product span, territorial extension, mode of operations, and customer groups served. Note that the "product" marketed may be a service (dry-cleaning). Territory covered may be confined to a few cities in an LDC, while being nationwide in Britain. The local mode of operations may range all the way from the most modest (marketing a few units through an export agent in the mother country) to the most ambitious (a fully integrated production-marketing operation supplying both the local market and exporting to other countries, see Reading 33). Customer groups served may be distributors, industrial buyers, or end consumers, or specialized subgroups of these. Each clientele will require a more or less unique strategy.

The local domain may be viewed as the niche which the company has carved out of the total environment of a given country. The niche may be quite specifically defined (Volkswagen in America) or it may cover an entire spectrum of products and activities (Nestlé in France). Any domain is likely to change over time, if for no other reason than that the environment is in an incessant flux. In planning for company growth, eco-man (the ecologically-oriented manager) will seek to obtain common economies – or, more fashionably, synergy – between old operations and new. Can any of our existing resources (managerial skills, plant facilities, etc.) be utilized? Does the new product logically supplement the existing assortment? Can the existing sales organization handle the new product? Can we promote it to our existing customers? To capitalize on common economies is especially important in the development of small and medium-sized operations, the paradoxical circumstance notwithstanding that it may be more difficult to find synergistic opportunities in small operations than large.

Organization structure is another critical company characteristic. Of prime significance here is the structuring approach – does the organization setup emphasize product, territory, functions or customer categories? In other words, which dimension of the domain is given priority in shaping the organization? Frequently of equal importance is the allocation of decision-making authority, in other words, the degree of decentralization within the local operation.

Our last company variable is leadership. More than in domestic operations, leadership in international marketing tends to call for skills in perceiving and interpreting environmental signals. For instance, entrepreneurial decisions are typically required more often. The international executive needs the ability to see what the salient similarities and differences are between various parts of the world. He should be able to see when the situation calls for adaptation of his operations and when for the strategy of a change agent. He has to motivate people of a different cultural background than his own and build relationships with them based on mutual respect. Wherever he may find himself in a multinational organization he needs the ability to "think upstream" in global terms rather than with the blinders of local suboptimization. Yet he must have a profound understanding of the tensions inherent in local vs. global perspectives and be ready to strike a workable balance between the two.

The company characteristics discussed here are of special relevance to company strategy. Taken together, they define a profile of the company which largely determines the types of strategies it is capable of pursuing in the short run. In the long run, environmental change will reflect itself in adjustments in strategy which ultimately result in changes in company characteristics. If there is no adaptation, the organization will not survive. Conversely, in the pursuit of company objectives aggressive management may deliberately change company profile and/or strategy in order to affect, or capitalize upon, desirable changes in the environment.

OBJECTIVES

The domain defines the nature of a local operation, but says nothing specific about its intended objectives or actual performance (results). Every firm has a set or a hierarchy of goals, more or less clearly perceived. The goal set of an ecologically-oriented marketer would include the objectives listed in figure 1.2. Any two objectives may be partially overlapping, partially conflicting. Clearly, too, the relative priorities of individual goals will change from time to time.

Of the objectives, survival and growth would seem self-explanatory. Customer satisfaction occupies a key place in ecologic management, as such satisfaction provides the ultimate rationale for the existence of the business. In the ecologic view of the market economy profitability can no longer aspire to be the end-all of business activity. It becomes an objective among others, though still critically important as the vehicle of ensuring survival and growth. As we have said elsewhere, the modern corporation is not in business to earn profits but earns profits to stay in business (Thorelli, 1965, p. 250). Sales volume is an important gauge of viability and growth. An unequivocable finding of PIMS is that market share, once attained, is strongly related to profitability. It is also clear that increases in market share are often bought at the expense of short-term profitability.

Relative to competition any firm has a set of differential advantages (and disadvantages), deriving from its resource profile, niche, and objectives. This differential advantage in the ability to meet customer needs may take any number of forms, such as cost leadership, specialization on a certain clientele or function, high quality, reliable delivery, outstanding service. Like a capital asset, differential advantage is subject to constant change: at any given time the firm is either adding to it or is in the process of using it up. If nothing else, environmental developments inevitably will cause shifts in the differential advantages and disadvantages of competing firms. To identify and maximize differential advantage (while trying to reduce attendant disadvantages) is a major entrepreneurial challenge.

Ecologic marketing requires a great deal of data feedback to establish customer needs, to measure their satisfaction, to keep track of competition, and to forecast changes in the market and in the marketing environment. To ascertain that the company is in tune with its environment, the maintenance of an orderly information flow becomes a natural strategic objective among others. This environmental intelligence operation may take the shape of a Management Information System or simply of personal contacts, analysis of sales data, and other less formal means. In a going concern, marketing research and feedback from distributors and salesmen should provide key elements of feedback, whatever other ingredients may be. Productivity is viewed here as a measure of saleable output relative to the total input of resources, i.e. as an expression of internal efficiency. It is almost tautological to say that increased productivity is an objective of all economic organizations.

In international business operations it becomes necessary to make a distinction between local and overall (global) objectives of the company. In most international concerns top management makes a deliberate effort to harmonize these objectives (see, for example, Readings 41, 43). Due to such factors as nationalism among governments and a tendency of local managers to overemphasize the significance of their particular operations, one must expect to find varying degrees of suboptimization in international marketing. Suboptimization simply means that some of the achievements of a local operation occur at the expense of overall achievement of the concern, such as an increase in sales in country A of high-cost goods made in an inefficient local plant rather than of low-cost goods imported from efficient facilities at headquarters. While perhaps worth striving for, complete synchronization of local and global goals is hardly a realistic proposition.

The spelling out and periodic redefinition of objectives is a critical part of international marketing planning.

STRATEGY AND STRUCTURE DEFINED

Since the key challenge in marketing is to adapt the marketing strategy of the firm to the market structure in which it operates, it is necessary to define these concepts. Market structure refers to all relevant characteristics of the marketplace surrounding the firm, notably consumers, middlemen, competitors, and the product (offering) with which the market is identified. Important consumer characteristics include their number, income distribution, and geographical dispersion as well as the values and attitudes determining their needs and behavior. The same variables apply to distributors and dealers in addition to their classification by size and functions performed. Competing firms may be analyzed in similar terms with market share, and trend therein, as important additions. Also, their profiles of differential advantage and disadvantage are of special interest. So are their strategies; from the viewpoint of firm A the strategies pursued by competitors B to Z constitute a part of market structure, at least in so far as the strategies of B to Z are beyond the immediate influence of A.

Several characteristics of the product (offering) itself are among the determinants of market structure. Physical size and weight of the product may place territorial limits on the market. High unit price may preclude its distribution through such channels as supermarkets, drugstores, and kiosks. A custom-made product faces a different market from a highly standardized one. A complex product, or one requiring special service, will typically have specialized or even exclusive distribution. The markets for industrial products are different from consumer markets, and consumer durable goods markets have little in common with those of foods or household supplies. In many markets the product life cycle represents an important structural feature (Levitt, 1965 and Thorelli, 1967; see also Reading 19). These illustrations could be extended further.

Marketing strategy on the other hand is the approach, or the stance, that the firm adopts in order to cope in the market structure. Ecologically, strategy is the means of harmonizing corporate resources, domain, and objectives with environmental opportunity at acceptable levels of risk. In starkly simplified language market structure may be likened to an arena, while marketing strategy would be the play staged by the home team. Properly conceived, marketing strategy capitalizes on the differential advantages of the firm, while protecting it from unwholesome effects of its differential disadvantages. As strategy refers to the principal means of reaching key objectives, it is often long-range in nature. Hence the current interest in Strategic Planning, a topic with which this book is largely concerned.

The marketing strategy of the firm is reflected in the so-called marketing mix, that is, the particular combination the firm makes of the marketing instruments, notably product, intelligence and promotion, distribution, price, service, and trust (figure 1.2). Note that marketing strategy is a concept going far beyond the marketing mix. Marketing strategy is what makes the elements of the mix work in a coordinated fashion, as a whole rather than as disparate parts. We may say that marketing strategy = marketing mix + synergy among the instruments in the mix. Strategy is a qualitative concept, related to the idea of intermesh and the German notion of Gestalt. To build a house we need a materials mix of bricks and boards, mortar and nails. But without a strategy for putting them together we would more likely wind up with a big pile of rubble than with a house.

Thus, strategy is a scheme or a recipe for applying the means to reach the end in view. Classical marketing strategies include high price-high quality (Rolls Royce autos), low price-mass volume (Ford's old Model T), multi-channel distribution of a standard product with globally homogenized promotion (Coca-Cola). Clearly, the high price and the high quality of Rolls Royce cars fit like hand in glove; the marketing instruments reinforce each other. We may, however, also observe that these instruments to a fair – but always limited – extent may substitute for each other. Rather than to introduce an improved model of our product we may prefer to increase our advertising or to cut price. Yet as time goes by an increasing number of customers will generally switch to the improved models introduced by competition no matter how much we increase promotion or cut price.

The marketing instruments constituting integral parts of Marketing Strategy in figure 1.2 are generally well-known from domestic marketing and do not need redefinition here. Their international implications are developed in some detail in later readings, and especially in Part Five. Only three points need emphasis here. In the context of strategy "product" refers to the specific variant or offering of a firm (Coca-Cola) rather than the generic product characteristics of interest in discussing the market structure in which it is being sold (soft drinks). Commercial intelligence – arranging for data feedback about market structure and broader aspects of the environment – is of special significance in international marketing (Readings 17, 18, 46).

"Trust" has been included for several reasons. In consumer markets it builds store and brand loyalty – especially in the LDCs. The fact that faith in the integrity and reliability of the other party is often a prerequisite to transactions in industrial marketing is familiar to every supplier and purchasing agent. Due to intercultural differences, time lags in communicating, inability to control the other party, and lack of personal contact, trust is a critical ingredient in international marketing strategy. None have realized this more clearly than the Japanese, who have made a heroic and immensely profitable effort to transform prewar international distrust into a strong faith in the quality of their wares and the seriousness of purpose in their commercial dealings.

ENVIRONMENTAL STRUCTURE

Three layers of environment of interest to the international marketer were identified in figure 1.2. These environmental layers reappear in diagram form in figure 1.3. A firm engaged only in domestic marketing may largely confine its attention to the domestic market structure.

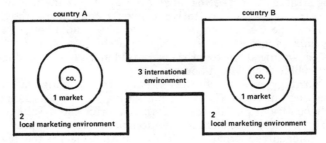

Fig. 1.3. Layers of environment in international marketing.

The international environment is largely irrelevant (at least short-term) and managers generally have acquired an ingrained sense of the local marketing environment as part of growing up in it. The situation is drastically different – and more cómplex – in international operations. Not only must differences and similarities in two or more market structures be recognized: the international marketer must also be aware of the local marketing environment abroad and of salient aspects of the interface between his own country and those others in which his company wishes to operate. Indeed, his ability to see the strategic implications of developments in these two broader layers of the environment will frequently spell the difference between success and failure in multinational marketing. Once again, the ecological view of the field points to the importance of commercial intelligence and environmental scanning in international operations.

Representative variables in the different layers of the total environment are listed in figure 1.4. Market structure has been discussed earlier. The figure also gives a sample of typically important variables in the broader environments. Their relative significance will differ from case to case, and frequently other variables than those mentioned here will be of even greater importance. The identification of relevant factors and the evaluation of their likely relative impact is an important challenge to the international marketer. The successful accomplishment of this task is a logical prerequisite to the design of strategy. In the local marketing environment lack of government stability and predictability of public policy – and attendant risk – is generally of less immediate concern in Western democracies than in the LDCs. Degree

1 Market structure
Consumers
Distributors
Competitors
Product
    (for details, see "Strategy and structure defined" section)
2 Local marketing environment
Government stability
Predictability of public policy
Economic development, stability, and development policy
Government controls:
    competitive practices
    price controls
    state marketing bodies
    health and safety, environmental controls
    product labeling, standardization
Local business culture
Marketing infrastructure:
    data availability
    market research agencies
    advertising media, agencies
    transportation facilities
3 International environment
Relations between countries A and B
Tariffs
Non-tariff barriers
Currency controls
Transportation costs

Fig. 1.4. Market structure and environment: representative variables.

of economic development is an important determinant of market potential. Economic instability – engendered, for example, by excessive dependence on one or a few commodities in export trade or high rate of local inflation (Reading 27) – often means extra risk. Aspects of development policy of key interest include government outlook on the role of marketing and consumer products in general, import substitution policy, local ownership, and minimum local value-added tax regulations. In the same league are inducements to or restrictions on entry into certain trades.

    Government rule-making for domestic marketing is critical in any country. The role and nature of antitrust, consumer protection, and unfair trade practices legislation, as of health, safety, labeling, and standardization requirements and of the direct government engagement in marketing activities (food distribution, agricultural export boards, etc.) varies enormously and somewhat unpredictably around the world (Part Three readings). It is a sobering reflection that in most countries at least some products are subject to some form of price control. Such control may not always be governmentally administered – prices may be set by local cartels too powerful to overcome. Other aspects of the local business culture set the tone of competition and cooperation between firms, define the level of business ethics, the outlook on corruption, and so on. A small operator will often have to take the local culture as given. To the large international concern a major challenge in defining strategy is to decide what aspects of local business customs to emulate and in what respects to be the nonconformist (Readings 43-45).

Marketing infrastructure refers to the relative existence of data and facilitating agencies needed in the course of marketing management activity. Industrialized Western countries generally have a rich and reliable data base maintained by government statistical offices, but the LDCs as a rule are not equally well endowed. Corresponding conditions typically prevail with regard to market research agencies, advertising media and agencies, transportation facilities, mail and telephone systems, etc.

Beyond the local marketing milieu is the <u>international environment</u>, certainly no less important than any other part of the three-tiered setting surrounding the international marketer. The significance of political arrangements and relations between nations to him are illustrated by the European Economic Community and other regional associations (Readings 9-11) and by the special challenges surrounding East-West trade (Readings 7 and 8). While the General Agreement on Tariffs and Trade (GATT) and later rounds of tariff reductions between the major trading nations of the world have lessened the obstructions placed on international economic intercourse by customs duties, the fact remains that tariffs still are far from eliminated and that even highly industrialized nations such as Britain and the United States will reach for import surcharges, "voluntary restraints" on foreign exporters, and other pseudo-tariff devices when in a balance-of-payments pinch. Meanwhile, the role of non-tariff barriers has been rapidly increasing, both relative to tariffs and absolutely speaking (Readings 4 and 12). Not without justice these obstacles are sometimes called invisible trade barriers: their existence and/or significance often is not clear (occasionally not even <u>made</u> clear) to the international marketer until he has already made contractual commitments on the assumption that they did not exist (or would be of but little significance). Neglecting to examine the likely impact of non-tariff barriers on a proposed international marketing venture is simply indefensible. This is also true of the related area of currency controls and exchange rate fluctuations. Less likely to be forgotten in pre-transaction planning are the transportation costs and related risks (war risks, dock and maritime strikes, and so on) in international commerce.

INTERACTIVE MARKETING STRATEGY

Rather widely different strategies may be viable in a given market structure. The ecologic concept of marketing does imply, however, that the superior strategies are those truly interactive. These are strategies based on the fullest possible utilization of differential advantage and/or common economies of the firm in satisfying a well-defined (narrow or broad) set of consumer needs. We will conclude our somewhat abstract discussion of the ecologic approach by a few specific examples of interactive strategy.

Synergy: American Railroads

Relating to the analysis of American railroads at the beginning of this essay, let us restate that one clear cut application of the ecologic concept of marketing in this case involves the diversification into community developments, recreational and industrial parks, and similar large-scale projects based on strong contemporary customer needs and prevailing on the common economies (synergy) derivable from the vast land holdings of the railroads as well as their already existing cadre of real estate oriented management.

Synergy: Multinational Life Cycles

A number of complex products have first been developed in highly industrialized nations and then gradually been diffused around the world, somewhat in tune with local economic development. Growth companies pursuing ecologic marketing strategies will prevail on the scale as well as common economies to be derived from hot pursuit of the international life cycles of these products (Reading 38). A typical example is Ericsson Telephone Corporation of Sweden. While that country has the second highest telephone density in the world, it is obvious that Ericsson would have to be satisfied with modest growth indeed if confined to a market of eight million people. Before the last world war, the company's major thrust of expansion was south and eastwards in Europe — in tune with the natural growth of local telephone demand. After the war the greatest rate (although not always dollar value) of expansion has been in the LDCs. Scale economies occur when export is possible from the Stockholm factories as well as some other West European plants. Common economies occur when the technical, financial, and marketing skills of the company are applied in the LDCs.

Nichemanship: Volkswagen in America

Nichemanship — or market concentration — is the successful application of a strategy of market segmentation or selectivity. Perhaps the single most outstanding example of nichemanship in history is Volkswagen's strategy in the United States from 1955 to 1965. Instead of striving to get 10 percent of the US car market model for model (which would be a catastrophic proposition for a European auto maker) Volkswagen said, in effect, "let us get 100 percent of 10 percent of the US market." This was the niche of the "beetle," the standard VW economy model of which several million units were sold in the period – long before the onslaught of other European, Japanese, and American economy cars. Indeed, Volkswagen even had the stamina to withhold from the American market for years its fastback and four-door models, precisely in order not to clutter its nichemanship image.

In the mid-seventies, when the long-lasting beetle had had its heyday, VW nearly went bankrupt by adopting a broad-scale diversification strategy both in Europe and the US. Appearing at the end of the decade, the Rabbit obviously represented a revival of nichemanship. This time the challenge is greater, however, as there are now both European, Japanese, and American competitors in the same segment. Therefore, while the Rabbit was going strong in 1980, one may doubt that its success will be as durable as that of its legendary predecessor.

Cost and Service Leadership: Hong Kong Tailors

In the past two decades the tailors of Hong Kong made great inroads in the woollen clothing market among male sophisticates around the world. Their simple but effective strategy was based on two elements. Low price (based on low labor cost) without compromising quality of materials was the first element. Personal – custom-tailored is indeed the word – and speedy service was the other. The differential advantage of a rich supply of skilled labor willing to work hard at low wages was utilized to the hilt.

Massive Resources and Homogenization of Demand: Boeing Jets

The differential advantage of Boeing in the jet aircraft market was almost the opposite of the Hong Kong tailors. What counted in the Boeing case was the ability to marshall and manage massive professional manpower, technical resources, and financial strength and then to make maximum use of this type of differential advantage by a strategy of homogenization of carrier demand for jet planes. Only towards the end of the seventies was this strategy being challenged by European planemakers.

Low Profile: The Differential Advantage of
Small Business

Many a small businessman is psychologically overwhelmed by the complexity and risks of international operations, and thus is confined to the domestic market. Small firms which do venture abroad soon discover that they have a natural differential advantage in their low profile. They do not invite aspersions of imperialism, exploitation, or undue influence in local politics. While a large foreign concern is typically expected – or even required – to operate with considerably higher standards than those practiced by domestic enterprise, the small firm typically can avoid this kind of discrimination. The small operation also is a flexible operation. Thus, if it brings a new product, technique or strategy to the market the small international business often has an enviable package of advantages.

The Multinational Corporation as a Change Agent:
Sears in Latin America

In contrast to the small overseas venture, the multinational corporation does not have to take all or most aspects of the local environment as given. It will be able to effectuate changes in the host culture. Indeed, only by a judicious blend of adapting to local conditions and effectuating change in them will the multinational corporation render its most effective contribution to local development. In this manner, too, it is most likely to ensure its own long-term acceptability in that environment. An excellent example of what we are talking about is Sears, Roebuck's operations in Latin America as discussed in the introduction to this book and in the reading by Peter Drucker at the end.

SUMMING UP

The ecologic approach to marketing views strategy as the means of satisfying specific consumer wants for which the resources, talents, and differential advantages of the firm are (or can be made to be) especially suited. Harmonizing structure and strategy is difficult in domestic marketing – even though the international tier of the environment usually will not present any problem and the local marketing environment is familiar and predictable. The special challenge in international marketing is that strategy design must take into account all three layers of the environment: market structure, local marketing environment abroad, and the internation interface. Indeed, merely identifying all the environmental factors of relevance and their relative importance in a given business is in itself a task of entrepreneurial rank.

Complications are many and risks tend to be great in international marketing. But the compensation may be greater than average return on investment and an immeasurable sense of satisfaction from contributing to local growth and development.

NOTE

(1) It would lead off the path to discuss in detail the reasons why several strategies may be viable in a given case. They include the fact that different marketing instruments may serve in either a substitute or complementary relationship to each other, time lags in the interaction process, and the existence of "slack" in both company and environment.

REFERENCES

Ansoff, H.I., Corporate Strategy (McGraw-Hill, 1965).

Levitt, T., "Exploit the product life cycle," Harvard Business Review (November-December 1965).

Thorelli, H.B., "The political economy of the firm – Basis for a new theory of competition," Schweizerische Zeitschrift fur Volkswirtschaft und Statistik (September 1965).

Thorelli, H.B., "Market strategy over the market life cycle," Bulletin of the Bureau of Market Research (Pretoria: University of South Africa, September 1967).

Thorelli, H.B. (ed.), Strategy + Structure = Performance (Bloomington: Indiana University Press, 1972). Especially essays by Thorelli and Preston.

2 Cross Country Skiing*
Sandra Salmans

When French skiers were winning most of the world competitions a decade ago, the manufacture and sale of skis was dominated by Austrian producers. Now the situation has changed. While the French have been overtaken on the slopes by skiers from other European countries and the U.S., it is a French company, Skis Rossignol SA, that now dominates ski sales.

Skis Rossignol emerged as the world's largest ski manufacturer in 1978. With world-wide sales estimated at over $138 million for the fiscal year ending March 1979, the company had 21 percent of the world market in terms of value and, with sales of 1.5 million pairs of skis, 16 percent of the market by volume. Apart from Austria and West Germany, it held the lead in every major national ski market. In all, over 80 percent of the company's revenue comes from foreign sales, and 50 percent of those from the U.S. alone. The domestic French market accounts for less than 20 percent of sales.

The group's impressive growth is due partly to the ever-increasing popularity of skiing. But its dominance of the world market can be attributed to another factor, its multinational approach. While the majority of ski manufacturers have traditionally stayed close to home, centralizing all their production operations, Skis Rossignol has deliberately placed its factories close to its main foreign markets.

When Boix Vives took over Skis Rossignol in 1958 as managing director, the company, based in Voiron near Grenoble, was strictly a provincial operation with a weak position even in the French market. His first task was to increase domestic sales by substituting Rossignol skis for imported ones. As Skis Rossignol came to dominate the French market with a 50 percent share, which it still retains today, Boix Vives

*From Sandra Salmans, "Skiing across countries," International Management (April 1979), pp. 40-42. Reprinted with permission.

recognized that to achieve significant future growth the company would have to penetrate the key markets of the U.S., Canada, Japan, West Germany, Switzerland, Italy, and Austria. Initially, the company sought to do this by increasing exports, setting up commercial subsidiaries in most of its target countries, and improving its distributor network.

Relying exclusively on exports had a number of disadvantages. For one, Skis Rossignol would be extremely vulnerable to fluctuations in foreign exchange rates. Because the franc has risen significantly against the dollar since 1971, for example, French skis exported to the U.S. have become more expensive and less competitive. West German and Austrian manufacturers, whose currencies have appreciated even more and who continue to rely on exports, have suffered accordingly. Other strong arguments against depending on exports were the danger of long delivery hold-ups, by dock strikes for instance, and the threat of protectionist import tariffs. In favor of exporting, on the other hand, was the fact that imported French skis carried a certain status, particularly in the U.S. and Japan. But with the French winning fewer competitions, their prestige had diminished.

Outweighing all other factors, however, was the perceived need to be close to the consumer. As Boix Vives puts it, "we can't learn about foreign markets if we manufacture only in France." And Jacques Rodet, the company's industrial manager, adds that "it is difficult, (for example,) to understand the U.S. from Europe. U.S. skiing trends change quickly, and skiing conditions vary greatly. The mountains in the northeast are icy, while there is deep powder in the Rocky Mountains. With our own subsidiary in the U.S., marketing people could observe trends and conditions more readily, and we could change local production."

In 1965 Skis Rossignol built a factory in Switzerland, and in 1968 it opened another in Italy. In the following years it added manufacturing subsidiaries in the U.S., Canada, and Spain. Although not a primary ski market, Spain was selected partly for its low labor costs.

To support these factories, Skis Rossignol intensified its local marketing effort. In each of its major markets the group hires market researchers to conduct surveys, at least once a year, of both skiers and non-skiers. In addition, the company's own sales staff in each country talks to the retail outlets, as well as to ski instructors. Although the group's research and development (R & D) department is in Voiron, it also operates world-wide. R & D engineers and chemists are sent, for example, to the U.S., Japan, or Germany to keep in touch with snow and skiers throughout the year. Additionally, skis are tested by racers, ski patrols, and even by youngsters belonging to ski clubs.

The information collected by the local sales staffs, market researchers, and company engineers is reviewed at headquarters throughout the year. During the slow summer season, managers from the company's French and foreign subsidiaries plan the next year's production. Manufacture of new lines begins in December, with those skis sent to retailers the following spring. It is generally almost a year between the date of production and the date that the skis reach the slopes.

Despite the long lead time, Skis Rossignol has been able, through its local presence, to recognize and exploit national ski trends. In the U.S., for example, it became aware early of the potential for "free-style" skis, which are shorter than conventional Alpine skis and allow more pivoting. As a result, the group now supplies more than 25 percent of the U.S. free-style market. Similarly, by recognizing the growing interest in cross country skiing in Canada and France, the group has become a major producer in an area normally dominated by Scandinavian manufacturers. To meet the specific local needs, free-style skis account for much of the U.S. production, for instance, while lower priced skis are manufactured in Spain for export to other European countries as well as the U.S. Racing skis are manufactured only in France because of the cachet this carries and because of the greater technical experience of the group's French workers.

The promotion of ski sales is also adapted to the various markets. To gain national attention, Skis Rossignol supplies top ski competitors with equipment and technicians in the hope of becoming associated with a winner. In each country, that subsidiary's marketing department works closely with the national skiing federation and individual competitors, customizing the equipment to improve performance. Such intensive promotion efforts have paid off handsomely, and the Rossignol group has become associated with a number of champion skiers from France, the U.S., Germany, and Switzerland. Thus, French ski enthusiasts identify Rossignol with Jean-Claude Killy and Italians with their own national skiing hero, Piero Gros. At a less glamorous promotional level, the group rents its skis to ski instructors in each country, letting them buy the equipment at discount at the end of the season.

Having moved into a strong lead on the ski slopes, Skis Rossignol in 1976 took its first step toward diversification by entering the tennis market. This was seen as a logical move because the Rossignol name is well known to sports enthusiasts and in the U.S., according to surveys, 80 percent of all skiers also play tennis. The group's international strategy is also being extended to its tennis operations. Skis Rossignol already has one factory in France and two in the U.S., each specializing in a particular kind of racket that is complementary to the others. Though it may be some years before the company becomes a factor in the tennis market (which it perceives as more difficult than skiing and more truly international, involving more countries), the fact that U.S. capacity is double that of France underlines the group's multinational approach. To promote its image on the courts, Skis Rossignol has already begun to look around for tournament-winning tennis players.

3 Top Soy Sauce Brewer in Japan Shows How to Crack U.S. Market*

John E. Cooney

The television commercial has become familiar: A French chef, resplendent in traditional white garb and floppy hat, is cooking hamburgers. "Ah," he says, "you want to know my secret recipe?" Turning a bottle of Kikkoman soy sauce to the camera, he sprinkles some on the sizzling meat. "Add Kikkoman to almost anything," he says.

And add a Japanese company to the list of success stories in American marketing. For two decades, Kikkoman International Inc., a subsidiary of Tokyo's Kikkoman Shoyu Co., has been trying to persuade U.S. consumers that soy sauce is as American as hamburgers. That the company is succeeding was made clear this year: It took over the lion's share of the $20 million-a-year U.S. soy-sauce market after surpassing two well-entrenched American rivals.

The achievement would be just another success story if Kikkoman (pronounced KEE-ko-mon) were American. But in making it big in the U.S., foreign companies such as Kokkoman face far more than a language barrier, no matter how successful they may be at home. They must contend with the diversity of the U.S. population, for example, as well as with the nation's vast geographic sprawl. So "for a foreign company to make it in the U.S., it has to use American marketing techniques," says Emmanuel Demby, chairman of Motivational Programming Inc., an international marketing-consulting firm. These techniques may seem even stranger than the language. Moreover, often the foreign company has to make its product appear as American as possible.

Certainly, Kikkoman's success is all the more extraordinary in view of the difficulties it faced when it founded its U.S. subsidiary in 1957. Kikkoman was selling a product unknown to many Americans. It began

*From The Wall Street Journal, Vol. LVIII, No. 45 (December 16, 1977). Reprinted with permission.

its push at a time when Americans considered Japanese products inferior. And it didn't have any successful models to draw on because few Japanese companies were then operating in a big way in the U.S.

Nevertheless, Kikkoman decided to forge ahead. The company, which had lost its overseas holdings during World War II and was anxious to expand again, viewed the U.S. as a logical market. Kikkoman already had a limited base here; it had been exporting soy sauce to Japanese-Americans since the last century, and it also had been a heavy importer of U.S. soybeans and wheat as ingredients for its product. Finally, many Japanese companies may have a psychological reason for choosing the U.S.; the Japanese, defeated in the war, would look upon business success in America as a "triumph for any Japanese company," says a Stanford University professor who studies Asian companies.

In planning its campaign, Kikkoman moved cautiously. "Our company's basic philosophy has been gradual penetration of the market," says Shinichi Suzuki, currently head of the U.S. subsidiary.

A cautious approach has been a cornerstone of Kikkoman's business philosophy throughout its long history. The company traces its origins back to the 17th Century, when two families, the Mogis and the Takanashis, began a soy-sauce brewing operation. (Soy sauce — or, in Japanese, shoyu — is said to have been used in Japan since the Sixth Century, when Buddhism was introduced there. The new religion prohibited the eating of meat and fish, both of which had been used in making seasonings and sauces. Such traditional flavorings gave way to products made by fermenting vegetables, such as soybeans.)

Gradually, over the decades, Kikkoman Shoyu grew until it dominated soy sauce brewing in Japan. The Japanese industry is a big one: there are some 3,000 soy-sauce brewers; the product, as common as table salt, is delivered door-to-door, and annual per-capita consumption is about 2.5 gallons. In this scramble, Kikkoman has captured 35 percent of the market, and its name is as familiar as Coca-Cola's is here.

"In Japan, we are No. 1, and it's just a matter of keeping up our image," Mr. Suzuki says. Today, that image is maintained through extensive television advertising. However, 20 years ago, when Kikkoman was first entering the U.S. market, the company's promotional efforts at home were largely confined to splashing its name on posters and flashing it out in neon lights. The company also provided free soy sauce to the huge cooking classes attended by young Japanese women about to be married (and it still does so).

This low-key approach was a far cry from the mass marketing of food products in the U.S. So before setting up an American subsidiary, Kikkoman took a close look at how goods are sold here. "Kikkoman studied, studied, studied marketing, marketing, marketing," says Yukio Ike, senior vice president of Yamaichi International (America) Inc., the New York subsidiary of the Japanese brokerage house.

One of Kikkoman's studies found that Japanese-Americans had become so Westernized in their eating habits that they no longer constituted a growing market. Therefore, the study concluded, the marketing target would have to be the American population as a whole.

Another study focused on the competition. The U.S. soy-sauce market, then only $1 million a year, was dominated by two brands, Chung King (now owned by R.J. Reynolds Industries Inc.) and LaChoy (now belonging to Beatrice Foods Co.). Both companies had lines of Chinese foods, which also have long employed soy sauce, and neither promoted soy sauce as anything other than a condiment for the food products. Therefore, the relatively few Americans who knew about soy sauce generally thought of it only in terms of Oriental cookery.

So Kikkoman concluded that to gain a foothold – much less expand – in the U.S. would entail educating Americans about soy sauce and emphasizing its versatility. Earlier, in Japan, Kikkoman officials already had noticed that American occupation troops sprinkled soy sauce on everything from hamburgers to pork chops. And the executives' hunches were backed up by the American advertising agency that they had retained when they first decided to try cracking the U.S. market.

The agency was owned by Richard Guggenheim, now international vice president of Grey Advertising Inc. He recalls urging Kikkoman to stress how "American" soy sauce could be – an approach that fit in with Kikkoman's own studies.

HEAVY USE OF TV

It also was expensive, however, because Kikkoman decided to rely heavily on television advertising. Only in this way, the company believed, could its educational programs succeed. "We had to explain what soy sauce was and how to use it, and what the difference is between our soy sauce and what is made in this country and called soy sauce," Mr. Suzuki says, adding: "What goes under the name soy sauce here would never be called that in Japan."

Therefore, the TV ads emphasized how Kikkoman soy sauce is specially brewed and aged, like beer; the American brands, the ads noted correctly, are made chemically. "Add Quality; Add Kikkoman" was the slogan.

Getting these points across nationwide was Kikkoman's ultimate aim. However, because of the size of the U.S., the company decided to start out regionally. Its first target was San Francisco, where it based its U.S. subsidiary.

In a sense, San Francisco was an easy target. Its large Japanese-American population knew about soy sauce and the Kikkoman brand. But this time, of course, the company was trying to tell not only Japanese-Americans but the rest of the population as well that soy sauce wasn't strictly Japanese and that Kikkoman was the premium product. (The latter claim was buttressed by a decision to price Kikkoman a few cents higher than competing brands.)

REGIONAL INTRODUCTIONS

While it was all a new idea for Americans, it was equally new for Kikkoman. The company, after all, was used to consumers who took its product — and its preeminence — for granted. But the Americans caught on, and so did the subsidiary. By 1959, it was ready to tackle Los Angeles. Over the next 10 years, Kikkoman expanded very gradually on a region-by-region basis. In all cases, the company used food brokers, on the ground that maintaining its own sales force would cost too much; and it still uses them.

So cautiously did Kikkoman move that not until 1970 was the product in nationwide distribution. By 1973, the company had progressed enough to open a soy-sauce plant in Walworth, Wisconsin. By 1976, U.S. sales had grown to $11 million.

And this year, for the first time, the parent company isn't subsidizing the subsidiary's advertising and promotion budget. Last year, the U.S. unit's ad budget totaled $1 million — compared with $5 million spent on advertising by the parent company, whose annual sales are about $350 million. According to Grey's Mr. Guggenheim, the parent company's executives "are still stunned when they see what ad costs for the small subsidiary are."

LONG STRUGGLE

Mr. Guggenheim says Kikkoman now has surpassed LaChoy in soy sauce sales and has taken the overall brand lead. "To build a market took a long time," he observes.

The company also has a long way to go. "There are still some gastronomical wastelands in the country that don't respond well, such as Pittsburgh and Detroit," the advertising man says. "They are areas that are reluctant to try new foods." By 1974, however, a study undertaken by the agency found that two-thirds of all U.S. households had tried soy sauce and that 61% of them are "users," that is, they buy more soy sauce when they run out.

Eventually, Kikkoman's cautious campaign may have every corner of the U.S. awash in soy sauce. Meanwhile, the company's success hasn't been lost on its competitors. Although Chung King and LaChoy still have done little to single out their soy sauces from other products in their advertising campaigns, both have borrowed one leaf from Kikkoman's promotional book: they now are advertising how "American" their Oriental product lines are.

FURTHER READING – PART ONE

Boddewyn, J.J. and Hansen, D.M., "American marketing in the European Common Market, 1963-1973," European Journal of Marketing, Vol. 11, No. 7 (1977), pp. 548-63.

Chisnall, Peter M., "Challenging opportunities of international marketing," European Research, Vol. 5, No. 1 (January 1977), pp. 13-24.

Keegan, Warren J., "Strategic marketing: International diversification versus national concentration," Columbia Journal of World Business, Vol. XII, No. 4 (Winter 1977), pp. 119-30.

Van Dam, André, "Scarcities, lifestyles, waste management and international marketing," European Journal of Marketing, Vol. 12, No. 4 (1978), pp. 306-15.

Wiechmann, Ulrich E. and Pringle, Lewis G., "Problems that plague multinational marketers," Harvard Business Review, Vol. 57, No. 4 (July-August 1979), pp. 118-24.

Wind, Yoram and Perlmutter, Howard, "On the identification of frontier issues in multinational marketing," Columbia Journal of World Business, Vol. XII, No. 4 (Winter 1977), pp. 131-9.

II

Inter-Nation Interface: The Fusion of Politics and Economics

Introduction to Part II

In international relations politics and economics are inextricably inter-twined. It is probably still true that a majority of world trade can be explained by the operation of the classic economic principle of compar-ative advantage, the principle that nations as well as firms possess differential advantages (and disadvantages) being exchanged in a grand international division of labor by means of trade. But this magnificently simple view of things is vastly complicated by political factors oper-ating on the international scene. Nationalistic, military, ideological, and idealistic considerations all have played their roles in the emer-gence of such political measures as the Marshall Plan, the General Agreement on Tariffs and Trade (GATT), East-West trade "freezes" and "thaws," and aid to the LDCs. The liberal ideas behind the Marshall Plan and the GATT have more recent manifestations in the Tokyo Round agreements and, at least in part, in economic communities and other regional market arrangements, while crass – and in many respects reactionary – nationalism motivates commodity cartels such as OPEC. Part Two deals with the impact of international politics on inter-national marketing in some areas of high interest in the eighties.

Reading 4, by Thorelli, depicts the Tokyo Round agreements as the 1980 update of the GATT. These agreements will truly constitute the Magna Charta of international marketing in the 1980s if they are implemented in spirit as well as letter by the major trading nations of the world and gain the expected acceptance and adherence of a major number of LDCs. Reading 5, by Shultz, illustrates the fusion of politics and economics in international relations by the "light-switch" diplomacy applied by the U.S. government in a specific, large-scale transaction between Dresser Industries and the Soviet Union. Former Secretary of the Treasury of the United States and chief executive of Bechtel Corporation, Shultz shows the dangers of on-again, off-again govern-ment intervention in international marketing. He also stresses a key point of this volume: the extraordinary importance of trust in inter-national transactions.

Reading 6, by Becker, analyzes what may well be "the international marketing deal of the twentieth century": the General Dynamics campaign to ensure the adoption of the F-16 as the key fighter of the NATO countries in the eighties. The number of firms, governments, and considerations involved staggers the imagination.

Readings 7, by Lange-Elliott, and 8, by Teske-Kravalis-Lenz, deal with East-West trade. While Eastern countries (including China) have had some success in Western consumer markets, economic and political conditions in Communist countries do not yet permit much consumer goods importation. In industrial marketing the Western trader can reach the potential user by advertising in trade magazines and displaying at trade fairs, but the final go or no-go decision is still being made in all Eastern countries by the mighty Foreign Trade Organizations (FTO). The Western marketer (seller or buyer) should be aware that the state trading monopolies tend to play one competing Western firm against another. Lange-Elliott go well beyond the confines of East-West trade in their examination of various types of barter and compensation arrangements – old types of trade which are being strongly revived by Communist and LDC traders. (The sponsorship is no accident, as these types of trade could not survive in open markets.) Teske-Kravalis-Lenz analyze prospects for trade between China and the Western world (including Japan) from a macro perspective. Much will depend on the sincerity – and effectiveness – of China's modernization program.

Reading 9, by Koopmann, with a postscript from the Wall Street Journal, constitutes a re-examination of the first decade of the Andean Pact. The philosophy of the Pact – developed in some detail – may be taken as representative of many types of regional economic integration, ranging from free trade areas to tightly-knit economic communities. The challenges typically encountered in the practical implementation of such multinational integration are also illustrated. Relations with the more broadly based though less integrative LAFTA are somewhat unique. It seems fair to say that among the dozen or more regional economic groupings of any significance the performance record of the Andean Pact to date is at least average.

4 GATT and the Tokyo Round: The Magna Charta of International Trade
Hans B. Thorelli

This brief summary of the principal agreements establishing the global framework of international marketing is focused on the so-called Tokyo Round agreements of 1979. These agreements (to which U.S. legislation was aligned by the Trade Agreements Act of 1979) were negotiated under the auspices of the General Agreement on Tariffs and Trade in Geneva (GATT). The 99 nations participating in the four years of negotiations under the Tokyo Round represent well over 90 percent of the total volume of international trade.

Actually, the Tokyo Round was the seventh "round" of multinational trade negotiations of which the GATT agreement itself was the first in 1947. Most rounds have centered on negotiating reductions in individual tariff rates of participating nations. The GATT and Tokyo Round agreements stand out in laying the very groundrules of trade. The basic philosophy underlying these agreements is that freedom of international trade is in the best long-term interest of all nations. Free trade is seen as a powerful vehicle of economic growth and development. In this respect it is natural to view GATT and the Tokyo Round as the Magna Charta of international trade.

It should be emphasized, however, that many (perhaps most) less developed countries (LDCs) do not share this view. They feel that insufficient allowance has been made in the agreements for their special needs for "import substitution," "protection of infant industries," stabilization of raw materials and commodity markets (which they tend to think can best be achieved through cartel-type commodity agreements), privileged access to the import markets of the industrialized countries, and so on. At the time of writing a number of these countries have failed to ratify the agreements. (Some of the nonsignatories may still find it to their advantage to abide by the rules established by nations representing the lion's share of international trade.) In fairness, it should also be stated that both GATT and Tokyo Round agreements carry a number of special provisions and exemptions in the interest of the developing countries.

The LDCs have found a forum to vent their grievances in UNCTAD, a permanent United Nations agency named after the first UN Conference on Trade and Development in 1964. UNCTAD has been promoting additional international commodity agreements. It has also attempted to persuade industrialized countries to grant tariff concessions to the LDCs on a non-reciprocal basis, in order to permit the LDCs to expand their exports of manufactured goods. Clearly, the GATT and UNCTAD philosophies are in sharp contrast. Thus far, the unilateral concessions UNCTAD has wrung from the industrialized nations are relatively modest.

GATT

The GATT agreement commits each member to general adherence to the most-favored-nation principle with respect to other members. Thus, nondiscriminatory treatment is the rule: a concession granted one member should automatically extend to all others. A few exceptions to the rule are specified. Thus, regional free trade areas and common markets may be established by members, provided they do not result in increased discrimination against outside GATT members.

GATT aimed at the liberalization of trade primarily by gradual reduction of tariffs and such other direct barriers to trade as import quotas and licenses. In later "rounds" great accomplishments have been made in tariff reduction. But endeavors to reduce import quotas and licensing have been weakened by exceptions permitted countries in balance-of-payment difficulties, with special domestic agricultural programs, or attempting to industrialize through protection of infant industries. Another significant achievement of GATT has been the spread of more unified procedures and nomenclature in customs evaluation and antidumping measures among members.

The original GATT agreement was relatively weak in its attempts to deal with more indirect obstacles to trade, often referred to as nontariff or invisible trade barriers. Never unimportant, these barriers have gained greatly in relative significance as tariff barriers were reduced and as nations for a variety of reasons have introduced additional indirect restrictions. Some of these restrictions are in clearcut contravention of the spirit of GATT, such as various forms of subsidization of export industries. Others may or may not have their origin in a desire to reduce imports (or protect domestic industry), such as the so-called "technical" barriers involving minimum product standards and such ancillary regulations as packaging, labeling, and inspection requirements. Even if a standard originated in a concern with safety – such as the complex Swedish electrical products regulations – or with the environment – such as the demanding American automobile exhaust provisions – their effect on international trade may clearly be detrimental.

THE TOKYO ROUND

Concerned with the rapidly growing jungle of indirect barriers, the members of GATT made them the major focus of the Tokyo Round. As a result, this new set of agreements lays down a number of codes of member behavior to restrain, or at least normalize, the use of indirect barriers as well as countervailing measures individual nations have taken against them.

Government Subsidies and Countervailing Measures

This code spells out rules on how nations should deal with increasingly difficult international trade problems resulting from the use of direct and indirect government subsidies.

In imposing countervailing duties to offset foreign government subsidies, the code requires all countries to consider "simultaneously" the technical issues involved in foreign government subsidies and their injury to domestic industries. More generally, the agreement specifies that the countervailing, or penalty, duties will not be imposed in an amount "in excess of the subsidy" provided by a foreign government.

The countervailing duties are similar in many respects to traditional antidumping measures also covered by the code. They are to be of limited duration, remaining in force only as long as necessary to counteract the subsidy abroad that is causing the injury to a domestic industry. Although the code doesn't attempt to ban the use of subsidies entirely, it says each country will "seek to avoid" injuring other nations and their industries through the use of export bounties and other types of subsidies. The agreement sets detailed procedures for conciliation, dispute settlement, and authorized countermeasures when such measures are appropriate.

For developing nations, the countervailing steps and subsidies agreement has somewhat easier rules. But in dealing with the subsidies provided by state-controlled economies, where prices are fixed by governments and trade is carried out largely through state monopolies, open-market countries could use "any reasonable basis" in determining the existence and amount of subsidies.

Import Licensing Restrictions

In effect, this code recognizes (though it does not formally legitimatize) that "the particular trade, development and financial needs" of the LDCs have induced most of them – and, occasionally, industrialized countries as well – to impose import licensing restrictions. The center of attention here is so-called nonautomatic licensing. As many traders in the LDCs have experienced, the possibilities of abuse in this area are legion.

The code provides that licensing procedures adopted for the administration of quotas and other import restrictions "shall not have trade restrictive effects on imports additional to those caused by the imposition of the (original) restriction." There are also several significant provisions for publicity and information. Any foreign nation or firm shall be able to obtain information regarding licensing procedures and imports of the licensed goods accounted for by country of supply and, in addition, a firm denied a license is given the right to have the reasons for the denial.

An obvious weakness of the code is that it makes no attempt to restrain the use of import licensing. In effect, the adoption or nonadoption of this practice is left to the discretion of member countries. Strictly speaking, the whole practice rhymes poorly with GATT.

Customs Valuation

The agreement provides that the customs value for imported goods shall be the "transaction value" – that is, the price actually paid for the goods when sold for export. This provision reflects the need for a fair, uniform, and "neutral" system for valuing goods moving in international trade and for rules that "preclude the use of arbitrary and fictitious customs values."

Even if an exporter and an importer are related business ventures, the agreement provides for the use of the "transaction value" for goods if such valuations closely approximate those in transactions involving identical or similar goods between unrelated sellers and buyers.

Technical Barriers to Trade

In developing and enforcing technical standards and regulations, including packaging, marking, and labeling requirements, each country will assume obligations under this code to bring its government standards into line with internationally accepted rules. This includes their application in a nondiscriminatory manner, with most-favored-nation treatment.

The agreement stresses that governments will "ensure" that their technical regulations or standards do not create "unnecessary obstacles to international trade." Further, the code says that imports "shall be accorded treatment no less favorable" than domestic products subject to the technical standards. Access to testing methods and certification systems is to be granted to all suppliers on an equal basis.

Again, the technical standards code recognizes that "special and differential treatment" must be allowed for developing countries.

Government Procurement

This code, which seeks to end discrimination against foreign bidders for government contracts, applies to "any procurement contract" with a value of at least 150,000 Special Drawing Rights, or about $193,500. It requires that countries provide potential foreign suppliers with "treatment no less favorable" than that "accorded domestic products and suppliers."

Under the agreement, technical specifications won't be "prepared, adopted or applied with a view to creating obstacles to international trade nor have the effect of creating unnecessary obstacles to international trade." Procurement agencies will prescribe technical specifications "in terms of performance rather than design" and such specifications will be "based on international standards, national technical regulations or recognized national standards."

More specifically, government agencies "in the process of qualifying suppliers shall not discriminate among foreign suppliers or between domestic and foreign suppliers." The code then spells out rules covering such matters as notification of proposed purchases, submission, receipt and opening of tenders, and awarding of contracts, increased public information flow being the thrust of these provisions.

Parties to the agreement are also required, in setting up government procurement procedures, to "facilitate increased imports from developing countries," especially the poorest nations.

Commercial Counterfeiting

This code carries provisions to curb international trade in "counterfeit merchandise." The term is defined as any article to which a "spurious" trademark or trade name has been affixed; it could include, for example, French perfumes and American-made branded blue jeans. Trade in counterfeit goods is especially widespread in the LDCs. The counterfeit products, under the code, will be seized by customs officials in various countries, usually upon the written request of the trademark or trade-name owner.

Agriculture

Agricultural products have traditionally been a problem child in international trade. This is due to the fact that for various reasons (such as the political power of the farm bloc) domestic agriculture is heavily regulated – and often subsidized – in most countries. To make domestic regulations "stick," governments have commonly found it necessary or convenient to restrict imports and, sometimes, to subsidize exports in various ways.

Major exporters of agricultural products are typically countries with high productivity, as Denmark in bacon and dairy products, Argentina in beef, and the United States in grains and broiler chicken. Among industrialized nations the continental European countries have typically been most restrictive, which from time to time has soured the climate of trans-Atlantic trade negotiations.

The Tokyo Round attempts but a few modest steps in the direction of liberalizing international trade in agricultural commodities. Beef-exporting and -importing countries will participate in an International Meat Council, a group that will seek the "progressive dismantling" of trade restrictions involving beef products and live cattle. To monitor world trade in dairy products and attempt to maintain prices at "equitable levels," the agreement calls for creation of a GATT-sponsored international dairy products council.

With regard to agriculture in general the Tokyo Round calls for an "improved level of international cooperation" to ensure the efficient functioning of international farm commodity agreements and to anticipate changes in world production, consumption, prices, stocks and trade in agriculture commodities. An international agriculture advisory council, sponsored by GATT, is to address some of these tasks.

IN CONCLUSION

The Tokyo Round has not solved all the international trade problems in an increasingly interdependent, yet ever more competitive, world economy. It has been negotiated against a backdrop of global economic turmoil: energy shortages, sluggish economic growth, inflation, unemployment, and resulting pressures for trade protectionism. The increasing strain on the international monetary system should also be mentioned in this context.

The weaknesses of the Round are abundant. For example, agreement still has to be reached on a draft code in the so-called safeguard area, dealing with temporary emergency actions such as import quotas or tariffs, designed to protect industries that are suddenly threatened by a large volume of imports. The purpose of a safeguard code of conduct would be to reduce the trade-distorting effect of such emergency actions. Pending the adoption of such a code, it is likely that many emergency actions inconsistent with GATT will continue to be taken as "undercover" operations.

One may also doubt that the growing number of state-owned companies, such as Airbus Industrie, the Chilean Copper Trust (CODELCO), and Renault, will be effectively reined in, though nominally covered by the codes. Not least disquieting is the fact that many LDCs thus far have refused to sign the agreements.

Nevertheless, considering world economic and political turmoil, and the vastly differing domestic political and economic systems represented in GATT, the Tokyo Round is a remarkable achievement. It reaffirms the basic faith of the world's great trading nations in the merits of open markets for all and extends the implementation of liberal trade philosophy into the jungle of nontariff trade barriers. The language employed frequently is as broad and vague as that of Magna Charta and other great constitutional documents. It is all the more important for the future health of international trade that the spirit of free access and non-discriminatory treatment guide the conduct of member nations in years ahead.

5 Light-Switch Diplomacy*
George P. Schultz

An extra element has been injected into international trade: a political dimension overlaid on commercial transactions. This political element is a vigorous and flamboyantly administered initiative that uses foreign trade as a tactical instrument of foreign policy. I call it light-switch diplomacy.

There is apparently a belief in our government that individual trades can be turned on and off like a light switch to induce changes in the domestic and foreign policies of a host government. As a result, the position of U.S. goods in world markets is eroding as our trading partners increasingly see evidence that we cannot be counted on as a reliable supplier.

Take the field of nuclear energy. There are nuclear plants all around the world that we sold on the explicit guarantee that we would supply enriched uranium – the enrichment process is a government monopoly in the U.S. – to fuel those reactors. Only a few years ago, the U.S. government viewed these supply contracts as a big plus in our balance of trade.

At that time, enriched uranium was a virtual U.S. monopoly in the non-Communist world. But the Europeans, particularly the French, are now very much on the move in this area. They are rapidly developing their capability to reprocess spent fuel and to build the fast-breeder reactor on a commercial scale. As recently as 1972, the U.S. had 100 percent of the nuclear power export market outside the Communist bloc. By 1978 the U.S. share had shrunk to 14 percent.

*Reprinted from the May 28, 1979 issue of Business Week by special permission, ©1979 by McGraw-Hill, Inc., New York, N.Y. 10020. All rights reserved.

POTENTIALLY UNRELIABLE

In any event, given the past and present dependence on the U.S. for enriched uranium, our government's suggestion that uranium might be withheld from our trading partners – as a friendly persuader to go along with the President's policies opposing spent-fuel reprocessing and the fast-breeder reactor – came as a shock. Because of concerns about the diversion of nuclear materials into weapons use, the President felt these developments should not go forward – a sharp departure from earlier government policy. Whatever the merits of the President's view, this approach to the persuasion of others has caused widespread resentment, even disbelief, in the nuclear power community. And it has been one of the important ways in which our government has placed a chill on exports in general: the threat of denial has given us the reputation of being a potentially unreliable trading partner, and it has enhanced the determination of other countries to eliminate their dependence on the U.S.

Examples of light-switch diplomacy abound in other areas as well. Take this chronology involving Dresser Industries' $150 million contract to build a drill bit plant in the Soviet Union. As a way of demonstrating our protest to Soviet treatment of dissidents, various Presidential advisers urged the President to veto the sale.

- July 17: The President places all American exports of oil technology to the Soviets under government control.
- Aug. 9: The Commerce Dept. (reportedly with the President's blessing) approves Dresser's export license, enabling the company to go ahead with the sale.
- Aug. 25: A special review panel convened at the request of the Defense Secretary advises against the "technology transfer."
- Aug. 30: The President's senior advisers vote by a 3-to-2 margin to stop the deal.
- Sept. 6: The President reaffirms the decision to allow the sale.

The light goes on, the light goes off, the light flickers, the light goes on. I don't know whether it is going to stay on or not, but in the meanwhile it is hard to see that these manipulations have had any impact on the nature and operation of Soviet society.

MARKET EROSION

Against this background, we must realize that our dependence on world trade has increased sharply. Yet our share of world exports has been steadily declining. Our market share of exports of manufactured goods, for instance, has fallen almost 30 percent since the late 1950s. Meanwhile, our appetite for imports has been voracious. These imports are not just a matter of taste and convenience. We have come to depend on many of these imports to provide us with key commodities; oil is only the best-known example.

Under these circumstances, we can welcome the President's statement expressing his determination to "place a higher priority on exports." Our need to do so is apparent. But we must recognize that major commercial relationships cannot be turned on and off like a light switch; they have to be built up and sustained over a period of time. It takes a long time to go abroad, get positioned, and learn about how to do things there. A considerable investment is made on both sides of the transaction, and there emerges a certain interdependence that necessitates confidence in the continuing good faith of both sides. In this process of investment, a company develops what the government may regard as a bargaining chip. But if our government then takes that bargaining chip and spends it, where does that leave the company? The company has lost out, and its commercial relationship deteriorates. Who wants to deal with an unreliable supplier, especially when the supplier is not the only game in town?

With this in mind, let us look at the section of the President's statement entitled "Export Controls for Foreign Policy Purposes." The object of the section seems to be to ensure that "export consequences" are taken "fully into account when considering the use of export controls for foreign policy purposes." But a quite different message is hard to miss: Even in a statement designed to bolster exports, the President puts us on notice that trade is to be regarded as a hostage to foreign policy, which nowadays covers the domestic as well as foreign policies of other governments.

Frosting is applied to this cake with an added sentence: "Weight will be given to whether the goods in question are also available from countries other than the U.S." What is the point here? Where we have a lock on the market for some reason, temporary or not, can that leverage then be used, or at least can we threaten to use it to achieve our foreign-policy objectives? If that is what the President means, what a beautiful tool he hands to our foreign competitors who are seeking a foothold in those few markets where we are still dominant!

We can predict, even observe, that light-switch diplomacy as it is used more and more becomes a wasting asset. Increasingly, when the diplomat flicks the switch, the light will not go on. It will not go on because private firms cannot afford the cost, cannot make the investments, to create the bargaining chips and then have the bargaining chips used. And self-respecting trading partners will not put up with it.

PREDICTABLE RULES

If light-switch diplomacy is turning off our trading partners, what then is the proper relationship between trade and government policy?

(1) Governments should provide a stable and predictable set of rules under which trade can take place on individual and corporate initiative, as free as possible from the uncertainties inherent in the ad hoc exercise of government authority. Rules instead of authorities – rules that we can read; rules that are predictable.

(2) Traders, individual or corporate or government, must keep their bargains, and government must not place private parties in the position of breaking a bargain properly arrived at. We cannot ignore the essential importance of trust, confidence, and continuity.

Certain products and countries may require special treatment on grounds of national security. But here, as elsewhere, rules are essential. If there is some product we should not sell, it should be specified. Just because a product is in an area linked to security does not mean we should just leave the whole thing open to the discretion of an ever-changing cast of characters who have access to the light switch. Outside the security-related area, rules should be kept to a minimum, be clear and consistent, and be as free as possible from the need for interpretation by government authorities.

If our government adheres to these principles, then U.S. companies can develop and uphold their reputation as reliable suppliers, a reputation essential to their success in export markets. When our government turns away from these principles, it correspondingly undermines our competitive position abroad.

6 The Ultimate International Marketing Case: Where Business Meets Politics
Helmut Becker

In the heated battle for air supremacy that culminated in January 1975, General Dynamics, Inc., of Fort Worth, Texas, finally won the right to build the United States Air Force's (USAF) new generation lightweight fighter plane. This opened the way for the company to strike some international business deals that must certainly rank among this century's biggest and potentially richest. The award could ultimately mean for General Dynamics (GD) multiple thousands of aircraft sales domestically and internationally worth more than $20 billion. The case reveals a telling story of intricate political and diplomatic maneuvers at highest corporate and governmental levels intertwined with exhaustive transatlantic business negotiations to win lucrative contracts in the international weapons market.

GD's single-engined air combat fighter, the F-16, won over its competition (mainly Northrop's heavier, twin-engined F-17) because of superior performance and lower costs. With better marks in agility, acceleration, turn rate, and endurance, the F-16 could execute attack missions 500 miles away and return without refueling, fly at twice the speed of sound (Mach 2.0 plus), and outmaneuver enemy aircraft in dogfights. The cost range of $4.6 million to $6.7 million (at 1975 US dollars) per copy was also lower than anything the competition could offer. Because the F-16 was designed with the same Pratt-Whitney engine that powered McDonnell-Douglas' F-15 air superiority fighter, GD achieved enormous scale economies in research and development and in production too. In addition, the plane was far more fuel-efficient than competing aircraft designs (especially the two-engine version), potentially saving the USAF $1.5 billion in operating expenses over 15 years according to original estimates. (At 1980 fuel prices – still rising – savings could be well over triple that amount.)

Armed with such convincing selling points GD, with the help of the USAF and the United States Department of Defense (DOD), set out to market the F-16 to several of America's NATO allies shopping for suitable replacement for their aging Lockheed F-104 Starfighter fleets. The group involved Belgium, The Netherlands, Denmark, and Norway, with the possibility of Germany joining at a later time. The pooled requirements for the initial four countries alone was 350 planes, and the international competition for such profitable stakes was predictably fierce as the British, French, and Swedes all vied for a share of the huge market.

Though the United States may still enjoy a certain differential advantage in aviation technology, other nations have advanced sufficiently to demand and get pieces of the F-16 action to support and further develop their own aerospace industries. From the beginning the philosophy of the project was to get the NATO countries involved as early as possible. To accomplish this, GD had to identify and assemble a consortium of over a hundred companies in the United States and in the four European partner-countries (Belgium, The Netherlands, Denmark, and Norway) to further develop, finance, and produce the fighter plane for both their own and third-country use. In so doing the company was faced with far more than an international marketing problem: it had to develop and make work a complex offset program by which all participants could share in the market for parts, castings, sub-assemblies, and aspects, and ultimately in the profits of the program, in a manner satisfactory to all of them. GD took indeed a management task of gargantuan proportions upon its shoulders.

The package proposal was originally presented to the four-country consortium by a team consisting of representatives from the USAF, DOD, and GD itself, whose permanent European F-16 headquarters were established in Brussels. The flyaway price of $5.16 million (in 1975 dollars) for each aircraft included tooling costs for two production and assembly lines in Belgium and Holland and an 11 percent GD management fee. Not included were the costs of spare parts and ground equipment that were estimated to add another 20 percent and 15 percent, respectively, to the unit price.

Parts, castings, and sub-assemblies were to be produced in all four consortium countries. On the basis of a 40-10-15 offset formula the European nations would supply about 40 percent of the parts for the aircraft they purchased, along with 10 percent of parts for all aircraft ordered by the USAF and 15 percent of parts for third country sales. Including assembly in Belgium and Holland, GD's program offered a total offset of 88 percent to the NATO countries based on an "initial" run of 1500 fighters: 650 for the USAF, 350 for the consortium's four member countries and 500 for other countries. If and when sales would reach 1800 units GD was even willing to extend a 100 percent cost retention offer to its partners.

Offsetting deals or reciprocal purchases are nothing new in international marketing, but there has never been anything like the F-16 deal in terms of magnitude and intricacy. With ultimate worldwide sales projected to reach as many as 4000 planes in 15 years and with replacement sales stretching far into the 1990s the Europeans could stand to earn a substantial return on their more-than-$2-billion investment in the F-16 program. To reduce some of the financial risks for the partner countries, the deal even incorporated an escalator clause tied to the inflation rate in each country to be reviewed every six months.

Decisions to finalize the contracts rested heavily on political considerations and on nationalistic desires to retain a strong, self-sustaining aircraft industry in the participating countries. Thus, a group of some 66 European and over 50 American major contractors and subcontractors was assembled to bring together the parts, engines, and sub-assemblies in GD's Fort Worth assembly plant and in those located in Holland and Belgium. At any of the three assembly locations parts were to be brought in from either European or American suppliers or from both. Therefore, all parts, whether manufactured in the U.S. or in any of the four European consortium countries, had to be perfectly interchangeable, and the final product had to be identical.

- BELGIUM − Aft fuselage, wing box, vertical fin, and aircraft assembly and flyout in the structure category. Fan and core module and engine assembly for the Pratt-Whitney F100 engine. Radar data processor, signal processor, and receiver/exciter.

- DENMARK − Major parts in the avionics/equipment field, including accessory gear box, flight control computer, electronic component assembly, pilot display unit for the head-down display, integrate fire control/navigation panel, primary, secondary, and regenerative heat exchangers, emergency power unit, leading edge flap drive, jet fuel starter with Norway, speed brake actuator, chaff and flare dispenser, channel frequency indicator, fire control computer, head-down display electronic unit, radar altimeter, instrument landing system, flight control panel assembly, and manual trim panel. Danish companies also to construct pylons, assembly inlets, and composites as well as gear box module.

- HOLLAND − In the structural area, the center fuselage leading edge flaps, flaperons, aircraft assembly and flyout, and main and nose landing gear. In avionics and equipment, radar antenna and transmitter, pilot display unit for the head-up display, generators, and fuel quantity measuring system.

- NORWAY − The 600-gal. and 370-gal. tanks and engine fan drive module. In avionics and equipment, head-up display electronic unit, digital scan converter, rate gyro, central air data computer, jet fuel starter with Denmark, inertial navigation set, air/ground receiver-transmitter and mount, head-down display rate gyro, threat warning interference blanker, stores management, ammunition handling system, wheels and brakes, anti-skid system, turbine compressor, and pneumatic sensor.

Fig. 6.1. Country assignments for F-16 coproduction.

With all these companies in different countries on two continents supplying parts for and assembling F-16 fighter planes, GD's task of coordinating the action is monumental, and the opportunities for disruptions and mistakes are equally large. Many experts believe that the Europeans are paying a premium for asserting their significant role in the overall project. Higher labor costs, additional management and transportation charges, and occasionally less efficient production methods are likely to raise the final price tag above that originally projected. Nevertheless, even if costs or other aspects of the project diverge more or less from their planned schedules, the consortium deal that GD was able to strike with its F-16 fighter aircraft may well be the forerunner of things to come in international marketing-business-political relationships with and between the countries of this earth.

Meanwhile, Northrop is continuing efforts in marketing its two-engine F-17 air combat fighter independently. Germany's Luftwaffe, for example, will need replacement for its F-104 aircraft too. As a result of a series of crashes and losses of pilots, the Luftwaffe is particularly receptive to the idea of a twin-engine plane. Though the Germans may eventually need up to 400 fighter aircraft, "independent" marketing of such complex weapon systems may ultimately prove difficult. As Grumman and other American military aircraft manufacturers had to learn, every huge foreign sale from now on is likely to include the Pentagon.

7 East-West Trade and Barter*
Irene Lange
James F. Elliott

BARRIERS AND INCENTIVES TO TRADE EXPANSION

Structure of Foreign Trade

One of the principal difficulties in assessing the direction and future potential of East-West trade is that policy decisions are frequently based upon political – rather than economic – considerations. This is true to a certain extent for both sides, but especially in the East where it reflects the structure of foreign trade in the East European countries.

In the Soviet Union, foreign trade is a monopoly of the Foreign Trade Ministry, and it is administered through foreign trade organizations (FTOs), each of which is the sole organization that is authorized to import or export products of a given category. At present, most of the FTOs are under the direct control of the Foreign Trade Ministry; but there have been reports of a reorganization that would move some of the organizations out of the Ministry and place them under the control of the industries that they serve. This is viewed in the West as a positive reform since it would put the officials who purchase equipment in closer touch with the end users.

The dominant feature of the Soviet foreign trade system, as it now operates, is the centralization of the decision-making process. The five-year plan – and its annually amended edition – is formulated by Gosplan (the State Planning Commission); and the Foreign Trade Ministry operates within these parameters, issuing permits for imports and exports and supervising the settlement of the subsequent transactions. The Foreign Trade Bank handles all the necessary banking transactions involved in foreign trade.

*From Irene Lange and James F. Elliot, "U.S. role in East-West trade," Journal of International Business Studies (Fall/Winter, 1977), pp. 5-16. Reprinted with permission.

The objectives of foreign trade, as set by GOSPLAN, reflect not only the economic but also the political goals of the Soviet Government. Imports are made for the purpose of supplementing areas of inadequacy in Soviet production as well as for the modernization of Soviet industry. Exports, on the other hand, are not viewed as a possible means of expanding domestic production, but rather, for the purpose of earning hard currency to pay for imports, or to meet bilateral commitments to the Council for Mutual Economic Assistance countries and to developing countries. The latter two are, to a large extent, political objectives.

In discussing the structure of foreign trade in Eastern Europe, the tendency is to deal primarily with the Soviet system, presenting that as a model for the systems in the other countries. This is valid to a point, but there have been significant modifications in some of the more progressive of these countries.

All of the other East European countries have experimented with some form of decentralization of foreign trade, and this may have influenced the reported reorganization of Soviet foreign trade alluded to above. Bulgaria, after rejecting its experiments, remains closest to the Soviet model. East Germany is generally regarded as one of the most rigidly centralized economies, but it permits large enterprises – those involved in export production and sales enterprises attached to industrial associations – to engage in foreign transactions. In addition to this, there are foreign trade enterprises controlled directly by the Ministry of Foreign Trade. Czechoslovakia, like East Germany, permits enterprises whose production is most important for foreign trade to engage in foreign transactions. The central authorities, however, still retain significant control in both East Germany and Czechoslovakia (Movit, 1977).

The remaining three countries – Poland, Romania, and Hungary – are the leaders in East European economic reform, and this is reflected in their foreign trade systems. Poland permits selected producing enterprises to sell – but not purchase – abroad. This is true for Romania, also, which permits certain industrial combines to conclude agreements directly with foreign firms and to maintain marketing facilities abroad. Hungary has gone further than all the others in that it attempts to conduct foreign trade on a profit-making basis and allows a fairly large number of enterprises to both buy and sell abroad. Romania and Hungary have been participating with Western firms in joint ventures for several years. Poland in 1976 passed similar legislation, but it was more restrictive than that of Romania and Hungary.

Eastern Nontariff Barriers

The structure of the nonmarket economy and the foreign trade system in Eastern Europe are, to a large extent, responsible for creating considerable nontariff barriers to market penetration from the West. Although Eastern tariff structures have not been a significant obstacle to trade from the West, the five-year plans, which have the force of law, determine what can be imported and in what quantity, and they can be viewed, therefore, as import quotas.

The centralization of import decisions removes them from the end users of the products and puts them in the hands of the central bureaucracy. This situation creates a whole series of problems for the Western businesses, which are accustomed to marketing products or services directly to their customers.

Financing imports is a priority issue for the East Europeans because of the inconvertibility of their own currencies and their chronic shortage of hard currencies. They have found themselves in the crunch between their need to import Western plants, equipment, and technology, and their difficulty in exporting sufficient Eastern goods to pay for those imports. The situation is less severe for the Soviets than for most of the other Eastern European countries because, heretofore, they could export energy and other raw materials. However, the Soviets could become net importers of oil by the early 1980s, and this would seriously impair their hard currency earning potential.

At least two aspects of this problem act as barriers to trade. The greatest obstacle to trade is the growing pressure on American businesses to engage in countertrade – a financing tool to offset hard currency needs to pay for Western imports by stipulating purchases of Eastern products in the transactions. The other aspect is the Eastern European countries' growing debt to the West.

From 1971 to the present, the total debt of the East European countries has grown from negligible levels to $48.8 billion at the end of 1976. Western European banks, with officially guaranteed credits, account for the largest shares. This may also explain the dominance of Western European countries in this marketplace. In general, both U.S. and Western European bankers consider the East European debt manageable, and they remain ready to extend credit. This appraisal stems from several assumptions: that the Soviet Union with its vast resources is a good credit risk; that the Soviet Union will help out the other Eastern European countries; and that, through central planning, the USSR can control its consumption. Poland has the second largest debt, but many analysts see in Poland a great potential for growth in terms of its many resources; many of the loans are used for import substitution or to produce hard currency exportable goods. However, these arrangements and intra-CMEA trade commitments make it difficult to appraise their ability to generate hard currency exports to meet their debts. Given the magnitude of debt and the service ratio, some of these loans are used to alleviate balance of payment problems. In addition, certain export-generating projects have not come up on stream and those that did were subject to fluctuating Western demands.

Western Nontariff Barriers: The U.S. Case

The limit of governmental credits available to communist countries, however, is one of the most frequently cited nontariff barriers to trade on the U.S. side. The Export-Import Bank Amendments of 1974, along with the Trade Act of 1974, make the extension of credits to Eastern Europe (excluding Poland) conditional upon a country's emigration practices. The Soviet Union is further singled out: there is a $300 million ceiling on loans for the four-year authorization period; and fossil fuel projects involving $25 million or more in Export-Import Bank loans would require notification to the Congress before finalization. American businesses in many cases are forced to initiate deals through their subsidiaries in Western Europe in order to take advantage of available government credits in those countries.

The Export Administration Act of 1969, as amended in 1972, 1974, and 1977, authorizes the Department of Commerce to use export controls to the extent necessary to oversee the export and reexport of commodities and technology transfers deemed of strategic importance. Types of technology, types of transfers, and their control, are key issues for U.S. policy makers and businessmen. In addition to the commodities controlled unilaterally by the United States, all NATO countries (excluding Ireland) and Japan cooperate in the international strategic control system through the Coordinating Committee (COCOM). The export controls, although eased to a considerable extent, still limit certain high technology exports.

Lack of universal standards for health, safety, quality, labeling, and processing act as additional nontariff barriers. A working party of the General Agreement on Tariffs and Trade (GATT) and the United Nations Economic Commission for Europe both have completed drafts on codes of standards definitions to be used in multilateral trade negotiations. The most problematic area within this broad category is the quality standards of Eastern manufactured goods. Established product standards in the U.S. may make it difficult for Eastern European countries to export certain goods to this country. But, in many respects, the problems are commercial rather than legal. The design, quality, and reputation of their manufactured products often impede access to Western markets and thus impair the potential for Eastern Europe to earn hard currencies. This problem is also one of the reasons that Western businessmen are, on the whole, reluctant to engage in countertrade with Eastern European countries (Taylor, 1977).

Furthermore, the U.S. maintains a number of measures to protect itself from possible dumping or market disruption. These measures include the general escape clause of Title II of the 1974 Trade Act, antidumping provisions in the Anti-Dumping Act of 1921 (amended in Section 321 of the 1974 Trade Act), countervailing duty provisions in the Tariff Act of 1930 (amended in Section 331 of the 1974 Trade Act), and a market disruption provision applied solely to communist countries in Section 406 of the Trade Act of 1974. Application of these measures has not been frequent due to the low level of imports to the U.S. from the East European countries, but it could become significant if this trade flow increases. The centrally planned economies are particularly vulnerable to charges of dumping, however, since the test is whether a given country is selling abroad at a price below cost of production. But it is extremely difficult for the centrally planned economy to establish its cost since costs are not accumulated in the same way as they are in a market economy.

Indicators for Assessing Market Potentials

There is a strong relationship between market potential and central planning. It is not how much the market can absorb, but how much importance is attributed by the central planning officials to that product or industry, which has to be established. However, given the following conditions — that centrally planned economies rely on a system of controlled prices, set for the most part by planners; that prices do not necessarily have a relationship to the relative scarcity of the particular product or to production costs; and that export prices have a general relationship to world market prices, but are adjusted for what the traffic will bear — the analyst is stymied when trying to use the prices for meaningful interpretation.

Since all aspects of investment, growth, production, and development have been tailored by the Government and recorded in comprehensive planning documents, one might suppose that centrally planned economies would offer an easy task to the analyst. It would seem, in other words, that one should need to study only five-year and annual plans to derive import and export plans. However, published plans indicate only the general guidelines for domestic economic growth. The data on total consumption, which would include import and export plans, are not published. In some research studies attempts have been made to extrapolate import needs based on past production data, exports, and imports. This may be useful for vertically integrated industries, but for products or systems where their use is horizontal, this approach is of limited use. Given different nomenclatures in the reports of the end users, the use of statistics further complicates rather than simplifies this assessment (Marer, 1977).

Published annual plans, reflecting yearly changes in allocations and targets are more current and detailed than the five-year plan; but inspection of even these reveals that this information is presented in only the broadest terms, making it barely useful for substantive market analysis. However, reviews of annual plans may suggest underfulfillments, which, in turn, may be used to estimate incremental import needs. But even in the case of underfulfillment, the central planners may decide to reduce consumption and avoid importing due to other constraints, including shortages of hard currency or problems in obtaining foreign credit (Brock and Tarullo, 1977).

"Shopping lists" generated in Eastern Europe have also been used for purposes of analysis. They indicate particular needs and priorities in terms of specific items and technology. These lists may suggest "substitutability" or "complementarity" for other needs, but because of limited disclosures of needs and capacities, the lists may serve as only limited indicators.

Assessments of these markets also need to be reviewed in terms of CMEA integration activities. Reflecting past performance, Western business cycles, and terms of trade, projected economic growth rates of Eastern European countries are lower in the current five-year plans than in the previous ones. Instead of pursuing integrated economic plans, every country is intent on solving its own regional problems, promoting bilateralism, and establishing trade and financial relations with the West.

Nevertheless, as a result of Western inflation and Eastern Europe's (with the exception of the Soviet Union) dependence on imports of raw materials and energy, some integration is necessary, and so joint projects to supply the area's needs have become important.

Since prices are set differently in each of the countries, plans for multilateral trade within CMEA and currency convertibility are limited. Under these conditions, bilateral trade is considered both desirable and essential to central planning; thus, it predominates not only in intra-CMEA trade but also with Western countries.

Because of the increased prices for petroleum and other raw materials charged by the Soviet Union to the other CMEA countries, most of these countries have had to increase their exports to the Soviet Union to pay for their imports. This, of course, has put more of a burden on them in their efforts of servicing their Western debts. Since oil exports are the major source of hard currency for the Soviet Union, more pressure will be placed on the other member countries to look for additional sources and to diversify their export base.

Finally, in assessing market potential, an analyst should study decision-making in Socialist countries by identifying key incentives and forces acting upon officials. What targets in the five-year plans, for example, will be most influential in decisions concerning the country or producer from which the product or technology will be purchased? Is there a pattern in decision-making regarding what types of products will be bought from the West instead of CMEA countries? The trend over the last ten years was for most East European countries to allocate two-thirds of their trade to the CMEA countries but this has been changing, as evidenced by increasing debt to the West. Trade patterns continue to differ by individual country and by product. Given current trade composition and inflexibility of plans, major shifts may be difficult to attain in the near future. However, with increasing numbers of institutional reforms, industrial cooperation may provide additional opportunities (Lenz and Kravalis, 1977).

NEW FORMS OF TRADE

The problems experienced by the centrally planned economies of Eastern Europe due to the inconvertibility of their currencies and their chronic shortages of hard currency have resulted in part from the difficulty for their manufactured products to enter Western markets. Several factors have acted as barriers: poor quality controls, lack of marketing expertise, inflexibility to respond to Western demands, and various Western restrictions. These problems are becoming more acute as the level of industrialization of these countries rises, thus increasing their need for Western technology.

A major Eastern European approach to solving the problems of earning hard currency and gaining access to Western markets has been that of industrial cooperation. On the whole, the Eastern perception of industrial cooperation has been that Western firms should supply the basic technology and know-how to assist Eastern enterprises in developing production. The extent of cooperation includes forms of sale of complete production systems or "turnkey" plants, licensing, franchising, coproduction, joint ventures, and other variations. Due to the magnitude of some of these projects, multinational firms have been dominant in this market (Holt, 1973). In the context of East-West trade, the development of industrial cooperation has been impeded to some extent by the great reluctance of the Eastern Europeans to allow Western equity and real management participation in socialist enterprises located within CMEA. Although joint ventures are now allowed in Romania, Hungary, and Poland, the Eastern partner always retains control, even while allowing Western participation in profits and management.

Usually, at least a portion of the products resulting from industrial cooperation projects in Eastern Europe are to be marketed eventually in the West to pay for the original investment and to earn additional hard currency. Western firms, however, have been reluctant to enter into agreements under which their remuneration, in part or in whole, depends upon the marketing of products in the West, the quality of which they cannot control and which, traditionally, has not met Western standards.

Heretofore, the solution for the USSR has often been that the products marketed in the West have not been manufactured but rather raw or semiprocessed materials for which it is much easier to find buyers. With the exception of Poland, this solution, however, has not been possible for the other Eastern Europeans due to their general paucity of raw materials. It is not a satisfactory solution for the Soviet Union either, and in the 1976-80 five-year plan period, all indications are that there will be a strong push for payment arrangements involving manufactured products.

As the use of industrial cooperation as a commercial arrangement has evolved, a financial provision to offset hard currency shortages has been instituted. With the exception of barter, most forms of industrial cooperation between the Eastern European and Western firms require upfront financing via Western credits. Countertrade is the financial proposition which frequently provides a basis for repaying at least part of those credits (Matheson, McCarthy, and Flanders, 1977).

The simplest but least frequently used form of countertrade, is barter. This is a one-time, direct exchange of goods, with no money or credit required, and without the involvement of a third party. It was common after World War II when the shortage of convertible currencies was most acute and before more satisfactory marketing channels were reestablished. Pure barter in East-West trade is now quite rare.

Switch financing is another form of East-West countertrade which is sometimes associated with barter. It differs, however, in many significant ways. Switch deals involve at least three parties, usually a Western firm, Eastern Europe, and one of the less developed countries (LDC). The need for switching arises when one party to a bilateral agreement cannot take his full quota of goods, leaving him with a nonconvertible dollar balance which cannot be used for all possible purchases in his partner's country. A third party has to be found who is willing to take the unwanted merchandise and pay hard currency for it, invariably at a considerable discount. Although ten years ago some sources estimated that as much as one third of East-West trade may have involved a switching, most agree that the use of this complex process is now much less than that and is steadily declining (Morgan, 1973).

Although straight barter and switch financing are no longer significant in East-West trade, counterpurchase (also referred to as parallel barter) is currently the most frequently used form of countertrade. In this kind of transaction, two contracts are signed — one in which an Eastern buyer purchases Western products for hard currency (usually supplied by Western credits) and one in which the Western partner agrees to purchase certain goods within a set period (normally no longer than five years). These goods are normally "nonresultant"; that is, they normally are not derived from the first contract (Matheson, McCarthy, and Flanders, 1977).

A variation of counterpurchase occurs when the Western partner receives only partial payment in hard currency and agrees to purchase, for hard currency, Eastern products equal to the remaining value of the contract. This is regarded by many as a poor deal for the Western partner because his full remuneration is deferred until he sells the Eastern goods. As with other forms of countertrade, however, the contract price of the original exports is often set in anticipation of this condition.

Compensation arrangements (also known as buy-back) are regarded as the most rapidly growing form of countertrade, especially with the Soviet Union. The period of the agreement is usually long-term (ten years or longer is not unusual), and the dollar value of the contract is larger than in the other forms of countertrade. Two contracts are signed providing for the Western partner to supply plant, technology, or equipment for hard currency, and in return to purchase, over a period of years, products which most often result from the Western supplied plant or technology. The value of the products purchased over the life of the second contract often equals or exceeds the value of the Western export. A variation of this form permits the Western partner to purchase both resultant and nonresultant Eastern products.

Precise statistics on the proportion of East-West trade which involves some form of countertrade do not exist, but most sources estimate about 20 percent at present. By 1980, this could be as high as 40 percent.

Lease financing is another form of East-West trade financing which is now being considered as a possible way to overcome the lending limits of both private U.S. institutions and of the Export-Import Bank. This approach provides for a long-term (10-15 years) lease with fixed payments. Although the lessee enjoys full use of the equipment, ownership is retained by the lessor until the end of the lease period, when it is transferred for a nominal sum. The retention of ownership in the West is paradoxically one of the principal advantages and, at the same time, a disadvantage. It provides the possibility for financing without being subject to any legal lending limits to communist countries. On the other hand, the centrally planned economies (CPEs) are reluctant to have capital equipment that belongs to a Western company. Some proposals have advanced the possibility that the lessor could be a joint venture with controlling interest held by the CPE, but the question is still unresolved. The Soviets regard lease financing as a more expensive way to do business, and as long as other sources of financing are available, they probably will not use leasing extensively.

Even with the more conservative five-year plans, future projections seem to suggest that imports of Western technology will continue to be important. Given their large debts, credit limitations, and balance of payment difficulties, countertrade may overcome some of these problems since it may offer entry into Western markets for their products and facilitate technology acquisition and update. The countertrade transactions specify future commitments and are self-liquidating; and these aspects are especially acceptable to central planning. In general, industrial cooperation with the financing and marketing aspects of countertrade encourage bilateral balancing, which is desirable for central planners. However, this puts more financial pressure on Western firms which, in turn, may hamper future growth by creating potential competitors and complicating the task for Western firms of marketing Eastern products.

The use of an industrial cooperation agreement by the Western firm to facilitate entry into other CMEA countries may, however, be limited: Eastern partners often stipulate that resultant products must generate hard currencies. Since most forms of industrial cooperation have a countertrade provision, the price valuation placed on the goods that are accepted as payment is especially critical for the Western partner and his competitors. In the event of low prices, most West European countries and the United States have several measures to protect themselves against any market disruptions. Should pricing in these arrangements present problems, official Western participation in these bilateral arrangements may occur. Even with some of these difficulties, industrial cooperations – which are especially adaptable to large or multinational firms – can facilitate the exchange of goods, the mobility of technology, and the flow of capital and managerial know-how.

CONCLUSIONS

The future development of East-West trade depends most significantly upon Eastern Europe's plans for economic growth and its management of indebtedness to the West. This argument assumes, in turn, flexibility on the part of Eastern European countries to make internal adjustments in the form of institutional changes and economic directives.

An analysis of the five-year plans of Eastern European countries (1976-80) uncovers several interesting trends in their efforts to solve long-term development problems. Although specifics vary from country to country, some of the key underlying economic trends common to all or most include the following: the plans call for a more balanced overall growth in an attempt to increase the material standard of living of the population, with special attention to energy, technology-utilization, agriculture, and consumer goods production. It is expected that a stronger emphasis on exports will alleviate the increasing trade deficits with the West. Concomitant with this trend is a greater susceptibility to Western market conditions that is unlikely to be reversed. Import strategies will attempt to minimize the fluctuations of Eastern Europe's interdependence with the West. Alternatives to accomplish this include import substitution, long-term trade agreements to smooth out fluctuations, and the upgrading of purchases during favorable periods. Poland, Romania, and Hungary plan to contribute to this effort by continuing the encouragement of Western capital investment through various types of cooperation agreements, including joint ventures.

Reduction in imports, however, does not appear to be an economically or politically viable alternative. Due to continuous problems in economic performance, imports must continue to increase. Adjustments to the debt will have to come, instead, from hard currency generating exports. On the demand side, the accessibility of Western markets is especially critical. Even without any governmental restrictions, the quality, after-sale service, and general marketing approaches are important to the considerations of export expansion. Internally, the ability to satisfy these conditions is contingent on the nation's commitment to the development of Western markets. This consideration also assumes increased flexibility and, perhaps, decentralization in the planning process.

Although a trend toward decentralization is evident in many Eastern European countries, it is not uniformly evident. Because of inconvertible currencies, shortages of hard currency, and balance of payments problems, some forms of control will remain. Bilateral trade agreements will continue to play a large role in foreign trade patterns.

Even though bilateral agreements are the main instruments for facilitating East-West trade, the actual conduct is changing since the concept of industrial cooperation is developing new flows of business. For the Soviet Union, turnkey projects, with long-term agreements for repayment, seem to be most desirable. For the other Eastern European countries, industrial cooperation takes a variety of forms, and, as with the Soviet Union, these arrangements are used to facilitate investment and technological developments. To Eastern Europe, countertrade arrangements are of special importance, both as financial instruments and as a means of access to Western markets and to marketing know-how. The long-term aspects of countertrade agreements are especially suitable to central planning whereas the short, self-liquidating contracts are used to correct specific problems. Industrial cooperation agreements encourage bilateral balancing which is desirable for central planners. Unless alternative forms of financing become available, industrial cooperation agreements and their countertrade components will likely continue to be used to facilitate trade.

REFERENCES

Brock, John J. and Tarullo, P. Ronald, "Estimation of incremental import potentials in the Soviet Union," Journal of International Business Studies (Fall/Winter 1977).

Garland, John S., Financing Trade in Eastern Europe: Problems of Bilateralism and Currency Inconvertibility (New York: Praeger, 1976).

Lenz, Allen J. and Kravalis, Hedija H., "An analysis of recent and potential Soviet and East European exports to fifteen industrialized Western countries," in East European Economies post Helsinki, Joint Economic Committee Compendium of Papers, U.S. Congress (U.S. Government Printing Office, 1977), pp. 1055-1132.

Holt, John B., "New role for Western multinationals in Eastern Europe," Columbia Journal of World Business, Vol. 8 (Fall 1973), pp. 131-9.

Marer, Paul, "Toward a solution of the mirror statistics puzzle in East-West Commerce," in F. Levick (ed.), Internationale Wirtschaft: Vergleich und Interdependenz (1977).

Matheson, Jenelle; McCarthy, Paul; and Flanders, Steven, "Countertrade practices in Eastern Europe," in East European Economies post Helsinki (1977), pp. 1277-1312.

Morgan, John P., "The financial aspects of East-West trade," Columbia Journal of World Business, Vol. 8 (Winter 1973), pp. 51-6.

Movit, Charles H., "Organization and conduct of East-West trade by non-market economies," in East-West Trade: Managing Encounter and Accommodations, an Atlantic Council Policy Paperback (Boulder, Colo.: Westview Press, 1977), pp. 59-60.

Taylor, Karen, "Import protection and East-West trade: A survey of industrialized country practices," in East European economies post Helsinki (1977), pp. 1132-75.

Wolf, Thomas, "Progress in removing barriers to East-West trade," in Nemschak, ed., World Economy and East-West Trade (New York: Springer-Verlag, 1976).

8 Trade with China: Prospects through 1985*

Gary R. Teske
H.H. Kravalis
A.J. Lenz

China – with its enormous land mass, vast natural resources, and a billion people – has embarked on an ambitious ten-year modernization program. In addition, Chinese borrowing capacity is essentially untapped – due largely to past conservative borrowing/debt policies – in the face of considerable Western bank liquidity.

Given these facts, the temptation is to conclude that China must offer a vast market for Western exports. In fact, such conclusions already have been drawn. Recent news articles project that Chinese imports will soar from $8.5 billion in 1978 to $50 billion in 1985. However, it is unlikely that such scenarios will develop. Any nation's ability to import is limited essentially to the earnings from its exports of goods and services plus the capital made available from foreign borrowings and direct foreign investment. Moreover, while debt and equity capital may be of very great importance in Chinese strategy to expand imports, all imports inevitably must be paid for by exports. The gap between current imports and current exports cannot grow too wide without impairing borrowing ability or driving up credit terms.

PRC EXPORT CAPABILITIES

China's current exports are composed of a variety of foodstuffs, textiles, raw materials, and light manufactures. In 1977 exports to hard currency destinations amounted to $6.6 billion, and in 1978 probably reached $8.2 billion. The 25 percent export surge in 1978 stemmed mainly from sharp gains in Chinese sales of textiles and other light manufactured goods.

---

*Excerpted from "U.S. Trade with China: Prospects through 1985," Business America, Vol. 2 (February 12, 1979), pp. 3-7, with permission.

It is not likely that Peking can maintain such a growth rate for the remainder of its 10-year plan (1979-85). China's ability to rapidly increase exports during the 10-year plan faces a number of problems, including:

● Demands of its population for higher living standards are likely to keep a tight rein on the growth of foodstuffs exports (China's major hard currency export earner);
● In an atmosphere of sluggish Western economic growth and rising protectionism – particularly within textile industries – it is doubtful that China will be able to escape the effects of Western import restrictions;
● Domestic demand pressures and inadequate production capacity will limit the growth of light industry manufactured exports; and
● The long lead time necessary to get new heavy industry plant and equipment in production, as well as substantial domestic demand, will inhibit rapid growth of heavy industry exports.

Peking's current strategy appears to aim at exploiting its oil and mineral deposits. Many see oil as the commodity which will significantly boost Chinese hard currency earnings, particularly in light of the long-term agreement with Japan. The potential for exports through 1985, however, is uncertain. Although oil reserves are estimated to be about three times greater than U.S. reserves, rising domestic demand – largely due to an ambitious modernization program – and the need to acquire Western equipment and technology to tap the reserves may hinder export growth. In addition, Chinese oil will be hard to market because of its heavy wax content. Chinese facilities to eliminate the heavy wax are not expected to come on stream until the mid-1980s.

Japan, constructing its own refineries with this capability, is, therefore, the only viable major market for several years. Under the long-term agreement (1978-85) Chinese oil and coal exports are to total $10 billion. However, due to the limited capacity of Japanese refineries to process Chinese crude, there is some doubt whether Tokyo will be able to absorb all the Chinese crude contracted for after 1982. Consequently, at least through 1985, revenues from oil exports will be significant, but inadequate in themselves to support China's import drive.

Another large and growing source of hard currency is new earnings from invisibles (tourism, Chinese business activities in Hong Kong, shipping, and remittances). Tourism is expected to generate substantial earnings as China opens the country to growing numbers of tourists. The recent signing of contracts with Western firms for hotel construction should significantly boost China's facilities for accommodating tourists. Income from activities in Hong Kong – that is, income from profits of PRC-controlled banks, insurance companies, shipping agencies, retail outlets, and real estate holdings – should grow rapidly as part of China's international economic expansion. The continued growth of China's merchant fleet also could provide Peking with significant earnings. In the case of remittances, their relative importance is expected to decline as relations between overseas Chinese and their mainland relatives tend to weaken over time.

Given the hard currency shortage that almost certainly will develop from China's modernization program, the volume of credits extended by Western governments and banks will be an important determinant of Chinese purchases from the West. Peking currently is easing its conservative financial policies to permit the use of longer term credits and other forms of borrowing. As a result, China – because of its excellent credit rating – will be able to secure the necessary financing to support a substantial capital goods import program. Peking recently signed its first major credit deal for $1.2 billion over 5 years with a multi-bank British consortium. In addition, China presently is negotiating on a number of other large credit deals.

One banking source stated that China could secure enough financing to push its hard currency debt from $1 billion in 1978 to $30-$35 billion in 1985. China's willingness to incur that much debt, however, is uncertain. Additionally, while $30-$35 billion of PRC debt by 1985 may seem viable in the current environment of highly liquid Western capital markets, these conditions may not persist through 1985.

In addition to credits, China could tap alternate forms of financing for capital goods imports. Continued use of barter arrangements would provide China with essential imports and markets for some of its exports that otherwise would not be marketable. Compensation agreements might help boost Chinese borrowing and export capabilities by having the supplier accept payment from the output of the newly constructed plant. Such agreements may have a major impact on Chinese exports before 1985. Finally, there is some indication that the Chinese will enter into joint-equity projects in China by allowing Western firms to acquire a minority interest in a project.

ALTERNATIVE SCENARIOS

Projecting potential levels of Chinese trade with the West is a tenuous process. Nevertheless, rough orders of magnitude essential to analysis of the issue can be developed from 1) current Chinese economic plans; 2) appraisals of China's export capabilities; 3) rough estimates of potential Western bank lending to China; and 4) estimates of China's willingness to allow its hard currency debt (and possibly equity capital intakes) to grow. Hopefully, the following scenarios will assist in placing potential PRC-Western trade in perspective, so as to avoid unjustified euphoria that could lead government policymakers and business officials to incorrect expectation and decisions.

Given previous assumptions about Chinese export capabilities, a 10 percent annual growth in real exports is a plausible target that the Chinese can shoot for over the 1979-85 period. Export growth could, however, be higher after 1985 when production facilities acquired as part of the modernization program could come into full swing. U.S.

Commerce Department analysis indicates that current Chinese modernization plans require a "minimum" annual growth in real imports of 15
percent if the projected growth in the economy is to be achieved. The
PRC already has reached agreements on contracts totaling about $27
billion (Japan $10 billion, France $7 billion, West Germany $4.6 billion,
the United States well over $2 billion, and the United Kingdom and
Netherlands about $1 billion apiece). It is expected, however, that
China's import growth will surge in 1979-80 and then taper off towards
1985. Such a trailing off in the growth rate would probably be necessary
because China will need time to absorb the capital goods purchased in
the earlier part of the period.

Table 8.1. PRC Hard Currency Trade and Debt
Estimates, 1978-85
(millions of dollars)

	1978	1981	1985	1978-85
Imports	8,500	14,100	22,500	122,800
Exports	8,200	10,900	16,000	92,800
Balance of trade	-300	-3,200	-6,500	----
Year-end debt	1,000	4,300	20,700	----
Debt/export ratio	.12	.39	1.3	----

Assumptions: Average annual real export growth is 10 percent; average
annual real import growth is 20 percent in 1979-80, 15 percent in 1981-
83, and 10 percent in 1984-85; average annual real invisibles growth is
10 percent in 1979-80, 15 percent in 1981-82, and 20 percent in 1983-
85; average interest rate on borrowings (government and private bank)
is 7.5 percent.

Given the above, Table 8.1 presents a realistic, albeit "conservative," estimate of an export/import/debt scenario for the 1978-85
period. Real exports were assumed to grow 10 percent annually. Real
imports were allowed to grow by 20 percent annually in 1979-80 and
then gradually reduced to 10 percent in 1985. The average annual
growth in imports over the period, however, is 15 percent. Separate
estimates for equity capital infusions have not been included, since they
could be only relatively minor by 1985.

In the scenario presented in Table 8.1, imports from hard currency
countries would total $123 billion during 1978-85. (Because of the
difficulties in forecasting inflation rates, all projections are made in
1978 prices). Of this amount, China's capital goods import requirements
could run on the order of $60-$80 billion and total hard currency debt
would reach $21 billion by 1985 – an amount China could service, and
probably would be willing to incur to support its modernization plans.

An alternative, more "optimistic," scenario of China's export capabilities and the leadership's willingness to incur higher levels of hard
currency debt assumes that China will be able to boost exports by 12.5

percent annually – the highest rate sustainable over the period in our view – and that Peking allows imports to grow by 20-25 percent annually in 1979-81 and then gradually reduces the growth to 10 percent by 1985. Under this scenario, imports would total $136 billion. Of this amount, capital goods import requirements could approach $90 billion. China's hard currency debt would reach $27 billion by end-1985.

Additional import/export/debt scenarios, under various alternative export/import growth rate assumptions, have been developed. However, assuming that the best possible growth in Chinese exports is 12.5 percent annually, higher import growth rates that would result in total 1978-85 imports significantly in excess of $140 billion would result, in our opinion, in intolerable debt levels.

Projections of trade levels through 1985 should, of course, be treated with caution, since each is only as good as the assumptions on which it is based. It can only be said with assurance that the degree to which China's imports from the West in 1979-85 will match current Chinese plans will in large measure be dependent on (1) China's actual export performance, (2) willingness of the West to lend large amounts to China and a willingness of the Chinese leadership to accept growing hard currency debt levels, and (3) the rate at which China's economy can absorb the imported technology.

9 Ten Years of the Andean Pact: A Reexamination*

Georg Koopman

On May 26, 1979, the heads of state of five Andean countries – Bolivia, Colombia, Ecuador, Peru, and Venezuela – celebrated in Cartagena (Colombia) the tenth anniversary of the so-called Cartagena Agreement, which forms the legal base of economic integration within this Latin American subregion. (As of October 30, 1976, Chile had withdrawn from the Andean Pact while Venezuela has been full member of the group only since January 1, 1974.)

The Andean approach to integration goes far beyond the typical integration scheme applied by developing countries. This is true with regard to both objectives and mechanisms of integration. Integration is understood by the Andean countries as a main vehicle to facilitate self-sustaining development and strengthen the bargaining position vis-à-vis third countries. What is more, special emphasis is laid on a balanced distribution among the member states of the benefits to be derived from integration.

SHORT-COMINGS OF LAFTA

As far as mechanisms are concerned, the Andean countries learned from the experiences with the Latin American Free Trade Association (LAFTA) that mere trade liberalization tends to accentuate intercountry polarization. (Apart from the five Andean Pact countries, which are special status members, LAFTA comprises Argentina, Brazil, Chile, Mexico, Paraguay, and Uruguay.) The main winner of trade liberalization within LAFTA has been Brazil, whose share in intraregional exports increased from 16 percent in 1962-64 to 26 percent in

*Slightly abbreviated from Intereconomics (May/June, 1979), pp. 116-22, with permission.

1976, whereas the corresponding import share declined from 35 percent to 27 percent. In contrast to this the Andean countries (including Chile) participated by 40 percent in LAFTA exports in 1976 as against 43 percent in 1962-64, and the subregion's share in intrazonal imports rose from 33 percent to 45 percent.

A second criticism raised against LAFTA concerns the role of transnational corporations (TNCs) in Latin American integration, which in many cases have affiliates with largely identical production programs in various LAFTA countries. As a consequence the LAFTA meetings on tariff reductions were often dominated by representatives of foreign subsidiaries, which in many cases belonged to the same parent company. This may be regarded as a main contributing factor to the slow progress of trade liberalization within LAFTA since the mid-sixties, because established foreign companies are showing little propensity to real-locate production the more so as integration between politically un-stable countries is associated with high risks. Foreign newcomers on LAFTA markets, on the other hand, have a strong preference for the larger market and more advanced countries in the region, in this way aggravating the polarization tendencies referred to above.

ANDEAN RESPONSE

In response to the short-comings of LAFTA the Andean Countries agreed upon a far more ambitious scheme of economic integration:

- trade liberalization is conceived as automatic, irreversible, and extensive, in sharp contrast to the product-by-product negotiations within LAFTA;
- a common external tariff (CET) is to be implemented, whereas LAFTA is designed as a mere free trade area;
- a substantial share of total tradeable merchandise is earmarked for so-called Sectoral Programs for Industrial Development (SPID), by which the decision of where to invest within the subregion is taken away from the market mechanism;
- policies regarding foreign capital, trade-marks, patents, and licenses are to be harmonized among the member states;
- a coordination of planning, rural development, infrastructural, fis-cal, financial, and monetary policies is envisaged, though the Cartagena Agreement remains vague on these issues;
- the least developed countries of the subregion, Bolivia and Ecuador, are awarded preferential treatment;
- an independent community institution with the power of proposal, the Junta, and an inter governmental supranational institution with the power of approval, the Commission, are established.

In terms of integration theory, the Andean Pact may thus be characterized as a customs union with some degree of policy harmoni-zation and an LDC-specific element of developmental nationalism. (In addition to a customs union, which is a free trade area with a common

external tariff, the Andean integration scheme contains elements of a
common market, where restrictions on factor movements are abolished,
and an economic union, where a considerable degree of policy harmonization is achieved. (See Moravetz, 1973, p. 3).) The following analysis
examines the constitutive elements of the Andean integration scheme,
i.e., trade liberalization, industrial programming, and common treatment of foreign direct investment.

TRADE LIBERALIZATION

The economic rationale underlying trade liberalization within the
Andean Group is simple and evident. The domestic markets of the
member countries are too small to permit plants of an efficient size to
be built. In 1977 population and gross domestic product in the five
Andean states were on an average only 10 percent of the corresponding
figures for Brazil. The combined Andean economic potential, on the
other hand, as measured by population and GDP, is as strong as that of
Mexico, the second largest Latin American market (cf. Table 9.1)

Table 9.1. Selected Indicators of Andean and Other
Latin American Economies

	Population		Gross Domestic Product		GDP per capita		Share of Manufacturing in GDP (%)	
	1000 pers.	(a) 1973/77	Mill. $ 1977	(a) 1973/77	$ 1977	(a) 1973/ 1977	1960	1976
Bolivia	4,788	2.5	2,321	5.9	485	3.4	12.7	14.6
Colombia	24,762	2.7	15,136	5.0	611	2.3	17.4	19.5
Ecuador	7,083	2.9	4,383	8.4	618	5.5	15.6	17.1
Peru	15,358	2.8	14,548	4.0	889	1.2	20.0	26.0
Venezuela	12,737	3.1	26,532	6.7	2,083	3.6	14.2	17.4
Andean Group	65,733	2.8	69,920	5.7	957	2.9	16.5	19.9
Argentina	26,056	1.8	44,841	1.6	1,721	-0.2	31.1	36.7
Brazil	113,208	2.8	123,431	7.3	1,090	4.5	24.9	28.9
Mexico	64,404	3.5	63,851	3.7	991	0.2	22.6	28.2
Latin America	319,229	2.8	340,239	4.9	1,066	2.1	22.6	26.6

(a) – Average annual growth rate.

Source: Inter-American Development Bank, Economic and Social
Progress in Latin America, 1977 report, Washington, 1978; author's
calculations.

Trade liberalization is also expected to favor a reallocation of existing industrial activities according to comparative cost advantages, the more so as a considerable scope for intraindustry specialization among the Andean economies is said to exist, prevented from materializing only by high tariff and non-tariff barriers to subregional trade.

This appears, however, to be a rather optimistic view given the striking similarities of industrial structures resulting from import-substitution policies, to which the Andean countries devoted themselves in the post-war area. The conditions for trade liberalization to stimulate industrial growth are, therefore, less favorable in the Andean area than, for example, in the EEC or EFTA region.

The Cartagena Agreement provides that all intrazonal trade restrictions are abolished by December 31, 1980, at the latest (Article 45). By the same date the CET would be implemented. This schedule proved, however, to be too tight. It has therefore been extended in various protocols modifying the Cartagena Agreement, the last being the Protocol of Arequipa, signed on April 21, 1978, which postponed the deadline for completing the customs union to December 31, 1989.

In spite of the delays the progress made until now in trade liberalization is considerable. According to information by the Andean Pact Junta, non-tariff barriers have already been eliminated by Colombia, Peru, and Venezuela for products actually traded within the subregion and not included in SPIDs, i.e. 65 percent of intrazonal trade. For 70 percent of these commodities tariff barriers to trade between the three countries have been reduced to between 1 and 20 percent, the highest tariff rate for the remaining 30 percent being 38 percent (Bundesstelle, 1979 and Moravetz, 1973).

The reduction of trade barriers gave rise to the strong performance of subregional trade as evidenced in Table 9.2. In 1968 internal exports amounted to only $75 million, i.e. less than 2 percent of the Andean Group's exports to third countries. Until 1977 internal exports increased to more than $800 million, thus exceeding by one-fourth the deliveries to the rest of LAFTA and reaching nearly 6 percent of total exports to third countries.

The increase in subregional trade is predominantly accounted for by manufactured products, whereas primary commodities remain directed towards traditional markets in advanced industrial countries. Between 1969 and 1974 the growth rate of intra-Andean trade in manufactures has been about three times as high as that in raw materials (Ffrench-Davis, 1978).

A dynamic intratrade pattern in manufactures does, however, not automatically enhance self-sustaining industrial growth. Firstly, the significance of reciprocal trade in total industrial activities remains low. In Colombia, for example, which is most important in intra-Andean trade, the share of manufactured exports to the remaining Andean countries is less than 5 percent of the country's industrial value-added. Secondly, much will depend on the level and structure of the CET. If the latter would turn out protectionistic in such a way, that inefficient capital intensive industries are promoted, the shortcomings of preintegration national import-substitution policies might be repeated on a regional level: Moreover, the countries to suffer most from trade diversion would presumably be Bolivia and Ecuador, which do not have substantial intermediate and capital-goods industries and would thus be forced to redirect the corresponding imports from suppliers outside the subregion to more expensive intra-Andean sources.

Table 9.2. Intratrade within the Andean Group 1968-1977
(mn $; %)

	Mill. $	Intratrade as % of:	
		total exports to third countries	exports to third countries within LAFTA
1968	75	1.6	37.7
1969	94	1.9	42.9
1970	119	2.2	54.6
1971	142	2.8	62.8
1972	156	3.0	55.9
1973	223	2.9	54.4
1974	459	3.0	55.5
1975	440	3.5	59.5
1976	647	4.9	90.1
1977	803	5.5	125.9

Source: UN, Yearbook of International Trade Statistics, various issues (figures for 1968 to 1975). Deutsch-Südamerikanische Bank, Kurzbericht 1979, No. 1; 1978, No. 2 (figures for 1976 and 1977); author's calculations.

In recent years the criteria have been redefined, according to which the CET is to be structured. Labor intensive activities and activities contributing to technological development are to receive preferential protection. If these criteria prevail in the final draft of the CET to be adopted until December 31, 1989 conditions may improve considerably for developing industrial activities in the Andean region, which are both less dependent on foreign inputs and competitive on international markets (Ffrench-Davis, 1978).

INDUSTRIAL PROGRAMMING

To establish efficient industries showing strong linkages with the domestic economies on a viable technological base is a central objective of industrial programming within the Andean Group. Industrial programming is the chief instrument to secure an equitable sharing of industrialization benefits between the member states. In the first five years of the Andean Pact, when trade liberalization was already under way while industrial programming was only on paper and in negotiation, the main beneficiary of intra-trade expansion had been Colombia which belongs to the more advanced countries in the subregion. Since 1973, however, Colombia's share in intrazonal exports has been stagnating, whereas especially Ecuador experienced a strong upward trend. The latter is to a certain degree due to overproportionate oil price increases and a preferential treatment of Ecuador in trade liberalization, but may also be explained by the program for industrial development in metalworking, which is in force since August 1972.

In its final stage industrial programming is to cover nine key industrial sectors and assume an overall significance amounting to 11 percent of subregional industrial value-added as projected by 1990 (Vaitsos, 1978).

Of the three SPIDs adopted so far the metalworking and automobile programs appear to be more adequate from a developmental point of view than the one relating to the petrochemical industry, since the latter is highly capital intensive, provides only little scope for subregional intra-industry division of labor, and does not give rise to substantial technological spillovers to other sectors.

The metalworking and car industry program, on the other hand, may contribute significantly to job creation and the development of skills and know-how, the use of which can spread throughout the rest of the economy. In addition to this, the technical nature of production and the wide range of sub-products and sub-activities in these industries, e.g. foundering, forging, machining, and tooling, permit an exchange of parts and components, in which all member countries, including the small and backward ones, can participate. Bolivia and Ecuador may thus, at least in theory, enjoy substantial benefits from the metalworking and automotive agreements, while in the absence of planning mechanisms these countries would possibly get nothing.

In reality, however, dissatisfaction prevails. One of two firms in Bolivia, which took up production within the metalworking program, has closed down operations and in both countries the assignments made in the car industry have come under heavy attack. In Ecuador, for example, the anti-motor industry groups argue that Ecuador does not have the capacity to train the skilled labor force needed by the motor industry in the short term, that no real study of investment alternatives has been made nor any analysis of who stands to gain, and that the money ($250 million) would better be invested elsewhere, e.g. in the agricultural sector.

As far as the outstanding SPIDs are concerned, the approval of the chemicals, pharmaceuticals, fertilizers, and electronics programs has been delayed until December 1979, whereas the shipbuilding and steel plans are to be adopted only in the eighties. It may, however, be doubted that even the revised schedule can be met, if it is called to mind that the Junta as early as 1973 submitted an automotive industry program to the Commission. The agreement was finally signed in September 1977, but the struggle for models as well as parts and components continued.

In negotiating and implementing the SPIDs the Andean planning authorities are facing a complex set of difficult choices and severe constraints. Not only is a workable balance between market and nonmarket elements to be established so as not to run into too costly economic inefficiencies, but opposition by powerful private interest groups must be overcome, which have been for a long time established in one or more of the member countries. Furthermore, technological and financial bottlenecks must be widened: if the industrial programming is to get ahead according to the schedules $33 billion are needed.

Apparently, this sum cannot be raised on the domestic capital markets nor is the basic technological infrastructure in the subregion developed sufficiently to carry out the ambitious industrial projects. As a consequence, the Andean countries must to a considerable extent rely on capital and technology from abroad, including direct investments by transnational corporations.

It is not intended to maximize foreign factor inflows, but to attract them under conditions, which in general secure a more balanced distribution of benefits between investors and host countries than has been experienced in the past, and in particular guarantee that the gains of integration are not enjoyed overproportionately by foreign-based firms.

To a good deal, the unsatisfactory developmental performance of direct foreign investment observed in the fifties and sixties may be attributed to a weak bargaining position vis-à-vis foreign companies. The Andean countries had to offer only limited markets and were facing intercountry competition in attracting foreign capital. Moreover investment policies were subject to frequent and substantial modifications in connection with general political reorientations. As a result foreign companies predominantly engaged themselves in investment projects with short payback periods.

The above considerations suggest, that foreign capital flows might be stimulated and at the same time directed in accordance with the receiving countries interests and priorities, if intercountry competition were abolished, integrated markets created and international rules established, which are less sensitive to national political changes.

Based on this reasoning, the Andean states agreed upon a common code on foreign capital and technology, whose implementation started in June 1971.

COMMON TREATMENT OF FOREIGN INVESTMENT

The Andean Code goes far beyond regulations applied in most other LDCs in that it pertains not only to balance-of-payments transactions, but touches upon almost the whole range of foreign investment aspects relevant to economic development.

The main rules are contained in Decision 24, which was adopted by the Andean Pact Commission on December 31, 1970 and subsequently modified several times though its basic nature did not change (see

Oswald, 1977). With regard to economic integration among the member states the most important provision concerns the transformation of foreign subsidiaries into mixed companies and national firms according to a fixed timetable. Until December 31, 1968 (in the case of Bolivia and Ecuador December 31, 1993) all foreign investors, existing ones as well as newcomers, which want to enjoy the advantages of trade liberalization within the Andean Group, must give Andean investors an equity share of at least 51 percent and a corresponding participation in the company's management (Vaitsos, 1978).

Decision 24 aroused harsh criticism and pressure, especially from North American Business circles where it was qualified as an "accident of history" and from foreign subsidiaries already established in the subregion. West European and Japanese investors, on the other hand, as well as newcomers showed a more flexible attitude. As a matter of fact, investment applications decreased in "critical" years, as has been demonstrated for Colombia, which was considered the "weak link in the nationalistic stance of the Andean Pact." In subsequent years, however, the decrease has been more than compensated for by additional applications. To a certain degree this may be explained by apprehensions on the part of US-investors to lose market shares against West-European and Japanese competitors. Inter-company rivalry and the prospects of growing markets appear thus to be stronger than objections against stricter rules of the game.

After almost eight years of implementation the Andean Code on foreign investment has at least proved to be fairly resistant against political changes in the member states. Moreover, the swift adoption of the modifications to Decision 24 following the withdrawal of Chile from the Andean Pact shows a remarkable ability to flexibly adapt provisions to changing circumstances and reveals a considerable extent of agreement on the issue. This contrasts positively to the lengthy negotiations about industrial programming and trade liberalization. The common treatment of foreign capital, therefore, turns out to be the most important contributing factor to the Andean Group's cohesiveness and the viability of the approach to integration chosen by these countries.

THE ANDEAN PACT – A POSTSCRIPT

The Wall Street Journal in 1978 (October 14) said that General Motors Corp. had been awarded the right to negotiate a contract with Venezuela to build V-6 engines for the five Andean Pact nations. GM had edged out Ford Motor Co. in competitive bidding. GM said that the proposed agreement meant it would be the supplier of V-6 engines for most vehicles assembled in Venezuela and a major portion of those built in Ecuador, Colombia, Peru, and Bolivia.

The Pact assigns different phases of vehicle manufacturing to each country to take advantage of economies of scale in production for the expanded five-country market. Experts in Caracas estimated that construction of such an engine plant would cost over $100 million. Under Andean Pact rules, local investors must provide at least 51 percent of the capital.

Ford produces about 40 percent of all cars assembled in Venezuela. A company spokesman acknowledged that it would have to use GM V-6 engines under a Pact award to GM. However, Ford said the Pact also had opened another round of bidding for rights to build a second V-6 engine for the trading block, in which it invited Ford, Chrysler, and Renault to participate.

REFERENCES

Bundesstelle fur Aussenhandelsinformation, Struktur und Entwicklung des Andenpaktes (Structure and development of the Andean Pact) (Köln 1979), p. 2.

Ffrench-Davis, R., "The Andean Pact: A model of economic integration for developing countries," in J. Grunwald, ed., Latin America and the World Economy (Beverly Hills, Calif., 1978), pp. 173-7.

Milenky, E., "Developmental Nationalism in Practice: The problems and progress of the Andean Group," Inter-American Economic Affairs, Vol. 26, No. 4 (1974), pp. 49-68.

Moravetz, D., The Andean Group: A case study in economic integration among developing countries (Cambridge, Mass. and London, 1973), pp. 3 and ff.

Oswald, H., Die auslandischen Direktinvestitionen in der Industrialisierungspolitik des Andenpaktes (Foreign direct investments in the industrialization policy of the Andean Pact) (Diessenhofen, 1977).

Vaitsos, C., "Crisis in regional economic cooperation among developing countries: A survey," World Development, Vol. 6 (1978), pp. 730-62.

FURTHER READING – PART TWO

Business International Corporation, Operating in Latin America's integrating markets: ANCOM, CACM, CARICOM, LAFTA (New York: Business International Corporation, 1977).
Brunner, James A. and Toaka, George M., "Marketing and negotiating in the People's Republic of China: Perceptions of American businessmen who attended the 1975 Canton Fair," Journal of International Business Studies, Vol. 8 (Fall/Winter 1977), pp. 69-82.
Fayerweather, John, "A conceptual scheme of the interaction of the multinational firm and nationalism," Journal of Business Administration, Vol. 7, No. 1 (1975), pp. 67-89.
Hibbert, E.P., "The cultural dimension of marketing and the impact of industrialization," European Research, Vol. 7 (January 1979), pp. 41-7.
Kaikati, Jack G., "The reincarnation of barter trade as a marketing tool," Journal of Marketing, Vol. 40, No. 2 (April 1976), pp. 17-24.
Kravis, Irving B.; Heston, Alan; and Summers, Robert, International Comparisons of Real Product and Purchasing Power (Baltimore and London: Johns Hopkins University Press, 1978).
Kugel, Yerachmiel and Gruenberg, Gladys W., "Criteria and guidelines for decision making: The special case of international payoffs," Columbia Journal of World Business, Vol. XII, No. 3 (Fall 1977), pp. 113-23.
Richman, Barry, "Sino-American economic relations: Constraints, opportunities and prospects," California Management Review, Vol. XXI, No. 2 (Winter 1978), pp. 13-28.
Sethi, Prakash S. and Post, James E., "Infant formula marketing in less developed countries: An analysis of secondary effects," in Subhash C. Jain (ed.), Research Frontiers in Marketing: Dialogues and Directions, 1978 Educators' Conference (Chicago, Ill.: American Marketing Association, 1978), pp. 271-5.
Szuprowicz, Bohdan O. and Szuprowicz, Maria R., Doing Business with People's Republic of China (New York: John Wiley & Sons, 1978).
Stowell, Christopher, Soviet Industrial Import Priorities, with Marketing Considerations for Exporting to the USSR (New York: Praeger Publishers, 1976).
Weigand, Robert E., "International trade without money," Harvard Business Review, Vol. 55 (November-December 1977), pp. 28-30 ff.

III

Local Environment: Public Policy Sets the Scene

Introduction to Part III

Public (i.e., government) as contrasted to private (i.e., business) policy assumes an increasingly dominant, not to say domineering role in national as well as international marketing decisions. Though individual cases may differ, the government's influence on business conduct is clearly on the rise, not only in the LDCs and the developing countries, but particularly also in the industrially advanced countries. At the international level, public policy intends to regulate business and economic relationships between countries. At the national or "local" level, public policy is primarily concerned with regulating business within a country. Two sets of local public policy factors must be considered by the international marketer: those pertaining to the home country and those pertaining to the host country. Part Three deals mostly with the latter, that is with governmental influences on the local environment as they impact on international marketing strategy in the host country.

The nuclear role in all cultures is played by the "rules of the game" in the marketplace as defined by public policy on competitive practices. Between cultures, these rules range from the strongly pro-competitive antitrust laws of the United States all the way to compulsory cartelization to government owned and operated industries in socialist economies. Closely related are regulations concerning misleading advertising and deception, games, premiums and trading stamps, mail-order and door-to-door selling, product safety, informative labelling, and other measures to protect consumers. In parallel with growing government worldwide is the trend toward industry self-regulation, sometimes more rigorous than the governmental variety, in a belated effort to blunt the impact of an ever more restrictive public policy. And intertwined with public policy and self-regulation are the rules of conduct prescribed by local business culture and by politics. These are reflected by local views of competition and cooperation, morality and business ethics, attitudes toward corruption, nepotism and reciprocal dealings, respect for contractual obligations, and the regard with which commercial activities are held in general.

Reading 10, by Jones, provides a comparative analysis of the U.S. antitrust laws and the laws of competition of the European Economic Community. While clearly inspired by the American model, the EEC laws have their own distinct features. For example, in Europe a parent company can assign territories to and set prices for a subsidiary which is at least 51 percent parent-owned, and certain "good" cartels are permissible. Such practices are per se illegal in the United States. Licensing agreements and mergers are also less restricted in the EEC. In pointing out major similarities and differences between the American and European approaches, Jones furnishes a useful executive antitrust guide to the multinational marketer. However, he does advocate expert advice for the more subtle, legal differentiations. Reading 11, by Permut, is a simplified, tabular overview of consumer product warranty legislation of the main partners of the EEC. It illustrates the accelerated growth of market legislation in response to consumerism in recent years.

Reading 12, by Preston, deals with governmental controls on marketing in the LDCs. Such controls are analyzed in the context of local economic development policies. While indirect regulation of markets still tends to be the rule in the industrialized countries, the regulatory arsenal in the LDCs characteristically also includes more direct and detailed market intervention – such as price and quality controls – and market participation by public enterprise. The contribution of many conventional LDC marketing regulations to economic development is quite doubtful, but it would clearly be foolhardy for the international marketer to ignore their existence. At the same time, the framework of regulation in LDCs is generally more flexible than in industrialized nations. The larger the firm and the more desirable its activities in the local scale of priorities, the greater the probability that it may strike a bargain with local authorities exempting the company from certain restrictions or introducing special regulations in its favor.

Reading 13, by Carson, develops a decision framework for incorporating political factors into multinational strategies. Although the article is based on the author's research on 41 sub-Saharan nations, the methodology and analysis are applicable to other countries and areas as well. As the ongoing social unrests, revolutions, and undeclared wars in many parts of the world demonstrate, multinational planning for alternate political scenarios as suggested by Carson is bound to become even more critical in the future as we turn into the 1980s.

Reading 14, by Mayer, describes how the exchange process has evolved in a socialist economy. He draws interesting parallels between Western-style marketing and the way individual "marketing" functions are conducted by state-owned organizations under conditions of central economic planning. In the absence of the free market mechanism and competition generated by it, Mayer finds the pricing variable most different from Western practices, in turn giving rise to various barter arrangements in dealing with foreign nations (see Reading 7). On balance, the insights gained from the article are invaluable to the multinational marketer bent on doing business with and in Eastern bloc and other socialist countries.

10 Executive's Guide to Antitrust in Europe and the U.S.*
Robert T. Jones

All over the world, from Australia to West Germany, antitrust laws are being revised, extended, and strengthened. This trend is making business increasingly complicated and bewildering for the multinational corporation. While the intricacies of antitrust have become a special field for specialist lawyers, executives making the deals that antitrust is concerned with can hardly afford to ignore the subject. At the least, it is necessary to know the high spots of the law so that a problem can be identified when it arises.

There is a positive side. The antitrust rules are intended to better the business environment for all concerned. Their very existence in the sky overhead, quite apart from their enforcement, helps keep the competition and the game "honest."

Antitrust can also be a tool for the sophisticated negotiator. In negotiating a deal in the United States, one frequently encounters the "antitrust ploy." That is, one side will argue that the other must do this or that "because of the antitrust laws." Unless a negotiator himself has a knowledge of antitrust or has his legal counsel at his side, he is likely to be floored by this tactic. In the European Economic Community (EEC) the antitrust ploy can be used to advantage, too.

Let us begin with a look at the antitrust systems of the United States and Europe. We can then turn to some marketing, licensing, and merger problems.

*Reprinted by permission of the Harvard Business Review. Adapted from "Executive's Guide to Antitrust in Europe and the U.S." by Robert T. Jones (May-June 1976). Copyright © 1976 by the President and Fellows of Harvard College; all rights reserved. Mr. Jones is an American attorney practicing in London with Messrs. Crane & Hawkins.

OUTLINES OF U.S. ANTITRUST

There are three main federal antitrust statutes in the United States:

1. The Sherman Act of 1890, aimed at restraints of trade and monopolies.

2. The Clayton Act, originally enacted in 1914, which expands on the Sherman Act and regulates mergers.

3. The Federal Trade Commission Act, enacted in 1914 also and directed toward unfair and deceptive trade practices.

Of these, the Sherman Act is the most fundamental. It has two essential provisions that have become a model for antitrust legislation the world over. First, according to Section 1 of the Sherman Act, every contract, combination, or conspiracy in restraint of trade among the states or with foreign nations is illegal. In other words, this section outlaws restrictive agreements by two or more persons acting in concert. Second, under Section 2 of the Sherman Act, every monopoly, attempt to monopolize, combination, or conspiracy to monopolize any part of U.S. trade or commerce, interstate or international, is illegal.

Note that all three of the U.S. statutes were enacted at the turn of the century when raw laissez-faire capitalism held sway in American economic life. Those were the days of the "robber barons," who by their skill and cunning acquired ownership or control of whole sectors of American industry – people like Andrew Carnegie in steel, John D. Rockefeller in oil, and J.P. Morgan in finance. In many cases, they organized combines through the medium of that peculiarly English device, the trust. That is, legal title to shares and other assets was committed to trustees who managed the assets in the interests of the various monopolistic groups. The excesses that were committed by these trusts led to a popular reaction at the grass roots level, hence the term "antitrust."

The philosophic essence of the U.S. laws is the belief in free and open competition fairly conducted. The idea is that business is better conducted by a large number of smaller entities competing against one another than by one or a few large entities. In this sense, bigness is equated with badness.

Are the U.S. Laws Obsolete?

Some people argue that laws designed to meet the problems of America at the turn of the century are not suitable to the economic conditions and policies of the 1980s. Business has grown too complex, it is said, to be forced into the Adam Smith model of many small companies competing in local markets. Moreover, businessmen argue, the laws are so vague as to permit antitrust attacks on such long-standing business practices as the licensing and franchising of know-how. Huge stakes are involved, and companies do not know where they stand. One also hears complaints that the rigorous U.S. antitrust laws hamstring American companies competing abroad, while Japanese and other companies are not subjected to these restraints.

Despite these criticisms, all indicators suggest that U.S. antitrust is likely to become harder before it becomes softer. Proof of this trend lies in the toughening of criminal sanctions passed by Congress in 1974. Antitrust violations are now a felony instead of a misdemeanor. They are punishable by jail for three years and fines of up to $100,000 for individuals and $1,000,000 for companies.

Do not forget that antitrust is as much a political as a legal phenomenon in America. For example, when the oil crisis came along, a first reaction of the administration was to start an antitrust investigation of major oil companies and to set up an "energy unit" in the Antitrust Division of the Justice Department.

Another political use of antitrust is to keep out the "damned foreigners." The United States is open to foreign investment with no prior right of government approval, as in France and the United Kingdom. But antitrust, whether enforcement officials admit it or not, is an effective keep-out weapon, as British Oxygen, Burmah Oil, British Petroleum, and other foreign companies have recently found.

How the Laws Are Enforced

Over the years, antitrust enforcement in the United States seems to have had two essential purposes, which are related but operative on different levels. The first is to maintain and foster competition; the second is to ensure fairness and prevent competitive excess.

On the first level, the antitrust authorities are attempting to create and maintain competition in various industries and markets and to ensure that it is not eliminated by cartels or restrictive agreements. The authorities are particularly concerned with the structure of markets and industries. The objective is to procure the right conditions and ensure enough participants for viable competition to exist. Indeed, in recent merger-monopoly cases, where divestiture has been ordered, the Justice Department has gone out of its way to make sure that the divested company remains healthy and does not fold up.

The classic examples of the concern with market structure were the 1911 cases breaking up the Standard Oil and the tobacco trusts. We see the same purposes at work today in the Justice Department's attempt to break up IBM, AT&T, and Xerox. There is little concern with evil intent on the part of companies or individuals at this level; the aim is primarily to increase competition as such.

On the second level, antitrust officials attempt to regulate competition to ensure that it is not excessive or cutthroat. The idea is to promote competition, but not "too much" or "too raw" a type. Here the attack is on unfair trade practices such as price discrimination, refusal to sell, and boycotting. This aspect of U.S. policy is more concerned with how people behave than with larger questions of market structure. The focus is on predatory activities in the marketplace. Concomitantly, there is great concern at this level with the degree of wrongful intent of those accused of violations.

A twofold standard has been developed by the courts for judging antitrust issues. These are the concepts of per se illegality and the rule of reason. Under the per se concept, certain kinds of activity, such as horizontal price fixing between competitors and tying agreements (deals whereby the sale or supply of one product is conditioned on the sale or supply of another product) are considered illegal, no matter how one carries them on or what their impact on the market may be.

For conduct that is not illegal per se, the rule of reason applies. This entails judging activities in their economic context to see whether they significantly and unreasonably restrain competition. Although it is very vague and can take one into a never-never land of economic speculation, the standard does impart needed flexibility by ensuring that only the most important restraints are caught by the legal authorities.

The Justice Department and the Federal Trade Commission share primary antitrust enforcement responsibility in the United States. Other agencies dealing with specific industries also have antitrust responsibilities. These agencies have at their disposal a wide range of enforcement remedies, ranging from the power to bring suits for injunction or cease and desist orders to the power to make criminal prosecutions.

The most unique aspect of the U.S. system is the right of action given to private parties. A private party injured by the action of another private party in violation of the antitrust laws can bring a suit either for injunction or for damages. In a conscious effort to promote these suits, the law gives successful plaintiffs an automatic tripling of their damages. The tripling can have dramatic results. Witness the original judgment obtained by Telex against IBM (since reversed), which, after tripling, resulted in an award of some $352 million. In another pending case, no less than $13 billion of damages arising from well-publicized incidents in Libya is claimed against a major oil company. There has been an explosion of private suits in the past few years. In 1973, for example, the Justice Department filed only some 45 antitrust suits, but 1,152 private cases were filed.

HIGHLIGHTS OF EEC ANTITRUST

In the law of competition in the EEC, the counterpart of the Sherman Act is Articles 85 and 86 of the Treaty of Rome. The approach is the same as that of the Sherman Act. Restrictive agreements are treated separately from monopolies. In addition, the wording of the articles is very similar to that of the Sherman Act.

Paragraph 1 of Article 85 prohibits agreements or concerted practices between enterprises to prevent, restrict, or distort competition and affect trade among member nations. Two parties acting in concert are needed for an Article 85(1) violation, as is true for violation of Section 1 of the Sherman Act.

Article 86 echoes Section 2 of the Sherman Act: if it holds a dominant position that affects trade among member nations, an enterprise cannot abuse its power. Article 86 does not apply to companies that lack a dominant market position or are not seeking one by abusive means.

Both Articles 85 and 86 require an effect on trade between member states before the articles can apply. The terms of the articles are not concerned with purely local intranation restraints on trade. This requirement has a precise parallel in the American antitrust statutes, which have as their jurisdictional prerequisite that a practice affect interstate commerce. This parallel exists because both systems are federal. Under the U.S. Constitution, the states retain base-line regulatory power over internal affairs and it is only interstate commerce that is delegated to federal regulation. The same applies to the relationship between the EEC member nations and the EEC itself.

There has been a marked tendency in the United States over the past 100 years to increase the scope of centralized federal power. The courts have assisted in this increase by giving the interstate commerce clause in the antitrust statutes an ever wider interpretation to the point that almost anything one does is deemed legally to be a transaction in interstate commerce. One sees the same trend in the EEC. For example, in the recent case of a cement cartel operating only in Holland, it was held that there is an effect on trade between member states simply because the cartel covered a significant part of the internal Dutch market.

The interstate trade clause has also been expanded in the EEC to embrace trade with third countries. For instance, a recent Article 86 case involved a small drug company in Italy that traded only with North Africa. The drug company was supplied with raw materials by an Italian affiliate of the American Commercial Solvents Corporation, which had a dominant position as far as the raw material was concerned. When Commercial Solvents suddenly decided not to supply any more, the drug company complained on the basis of Article 86. The European Court upheld this complaint. Despite the fact that the drug company traded only with North Africa, and not within the EEC, the court's rationale was that if the Italian drug company were forced out of business by failing to receive the supplies, the competitive structure in the EEC would be changed. As theoretical and minimal in its incidence upon EEC commerce as this effect was recognized to be, it was sufficient to satisfy the legal requirement of an "effect on trade between member states."

Some Contrasts with U.S. Law

A jurisdictional requirement of Article 85 is that two or more enterprises must participate in the violation. The term enterprise has been defined to mean an independent economic entity. One result of this definition is that a parent and its wholly owned subsidiary cannot violate Article 85 because they are not independent.

This is a very useful doctrine for managers of large international groups to bear in mind. For example, without fear of Article 85 consequences, a parent company can feel free to set prices and to assign sole territories or customers among its subsidiaries as long as they are at least 51 percent parent-owned and controlled.

In the same vein, the EEC authorities have also taken the position that an agent – such as a sales agent – of a company is not an independent enterprise because, under European national law, an agent is deemed auxiliary to and dependent on the principal. Thus in marketing through dependent agents, an enterprise need not be concerned about violating Article 85.

The situation is the opposite in the United States. In contrast to the "enterprise entity" doctrine, as it is known in the EEC, the U.S. law has the "bathtub conspiracy," or "intra-enterprise conspiracy," doctrine, which holds that two corporate members of a group, or indeed two officers of the same company, are guilty of conspiring to violate the antitrust law if their actions adversely affect outside parties.

Another contrast arises from Paragraph 3 of Article 85. This section creates the possibility of exemption from the antitrust prohibitions for "good" cartels as distinguished from "bad" ones. In Article 85(3), cartels are defined as "good" if they contribute to improving the production or distribution of goods or to the promotion of technical or economic progress, allow consumers a fair share of the resulting benefit, do not impose restrictions unnecessary to the attainment of these objectives, and do not allow elimination of competition. American law has nothing comparable to this exemption.

Guidelines and Procedures

Only the European Economic Community Commission (EECC) has power to grant an exemption to a "good" cartel. To obtain such an exemption for some contemplated agreement or restrictive practice, management must formally notify the EECC. Once such notification has been made, the agreement is immune from fines and other sanctions until the EECC makes a decision. Agreements the EECC is not notified about and that violate Article 85(1) are made null and void as of the time drawn up.

Thus a threshold question in any potentially restrictive agreement with another company is whether to notify the EECC or not. The question is one for management's judgment. Relevant factors include the importance of the agreement, the likelihood of an exemption being granted, the nuisance of having the EECC look into company affairs upon a notification, the danger of the EECC imposing conditions on its grant of exemption, the likely magnitude of fines, and the possibility that the agreement will come to light.

Soon after the notification procedure was introduced as the sole means of obtaining the exemption for benign cartels (Regulation 17 of 1962) the EECC found itself subjected to a crush of thousands of notifications. In order to reduce this work load and also to provide guidance to businessmen, the EECC began granting group exemptions. These are in the form of regulations giving the benefits of Article 85(3) automatically and without need for notification to agreements that conform to certain criteria.

So far, group exemptions have been issued for exclusive distributorship agreements and for so-called specialization agreements aimed at rationalizing production or marketing efforts of small and medium-sized companies. An example of the latter might be an agreement between two radio manufacturers whereby the one shall cease making radio cases and concentrate its production on the "inside" (electronics), the other shall cease making the insides and focus only on the cases, and each shall supply his "specialty" to the other.

Anticompetitive though such specialization agreements may seem at first blush, they find their justification in the criteria of Article 85(3) in terms of promoting economies of scale, avoiding needless duplication, and offering other advantages. Specialization agreements would not stand a chance if measured under U.S. antitrust rules. The exemption illustrates that, parallel with its objective of promoting competition in the sense of American antitrust, the EEC also seeks to develop effective European companies of a size and scale that can meet and best the American and Japanese MNCs in world markets.

The two group exemptions issued to date have proved very useful, and it is expected that other group exemptions will follow, particularly in the fields of licensing and formulating uniform standards and types. In addition to the group exemptions, the EECC has also published several notices in the form of guidelines as to how to make and how not to make agency, cooperation, and other types of agreements.

Obviously, the EECC is making efforts to bring certainty and predictability to its competition law. In this respect, the EECC is ahead of U.S. authorities, who, despite their long antitrust history, have no such thing as group exemptions or guidelines of the clarity one finds in Europe. In the United States, the task of predicting antitrust consequences is left pretty much to the private antitrust lawyers. The U.S. lawyers charge their clients accordingly: legal costs on both sides in a recent antitrust case involving ownership of a U.S. flag airline, for instance, approached $20 million.

On the other hand, the European system is open to serious criticism in that only the EECC, and not the national courts, has the power to grant a Section 85(3) exemption to a "good" cartel. Different substantive legal rules apply, depending on whether a case is before the EECC or the courts, and the courts' judgments are restricted by the lack of flexibility that the EECC enjoys.

What about private suits against companies? So far, the EEC national courts have not dealt with any cases in which private litigants have sued for damages resulting from violations of Article 85 or 86. While there would be no American-style trebling of damages in such an EEC case, most legal commentators accept that such a right of action exists. It remains for some ambitious litigant to make legal history on this point.

One does not find a clear-cut dichotomy between per se illegalities and the rule of reason in the standards of interpretation applied in the EEC. With the possible exception of contractual export restrictions, no equivalent of the per se illegality rule used in the United States has emerged. However, the EEC approach is rather close to the rule of reason in the sense that the ·cases teach one to judge restrictions in their economic context and in relation to their actual impact on trade.

Agreements that have small economic impact are disregarded. If the aggregate sales of both parties to an agreement are less than $15 million to $20 million, there would ordinarily be no risk of violating Article 85. Note that in both the United States and the EEC what actually happens in the marketplace is what counts. Brave and self-serving recitations in a contract − for instance, "Nothing in this contract shall be considered violative of any antitrust law" − are worthless.

Competition Policy as a Means to Unification

In contrast to the laissez-faire tradition of the United States, the European tradition has been mercantilistic, paternalistic, and protectionist. There was practically no antitrust law on the books of any European country prior to 1945.

The draftsmen of the Rome Treaty had one overriding and very noble purpose − to create a common market and common economic system that would unite the countries of Europe and prevent still another holocaust. This purpose led to the customs union and the dismantling of tariffs and other official barriers to trade. At the same time, however, it was necessary to ensure that private barriers would also be removed. These included the traditional practice of sealing off each national market and treating it as an economic unit. In short, the primary objective of Articles 85 and 86 was the same as that of the Rome Treaty itself − to create a common market and favorable conditions for trade between member nations. Thus there are really two themes in the law of EEC competition. The first is to unify the market and do away with anything that is a barrier to that goal. The second is to maintain and foster competition in the American fashion.

The first theme received far more attention in early enforcement efforts. Consider, for example, the first great case of EEC competition, the Grundig-Consten decision. Grundig had appointed Consten, a French company, as its exclusive distributor for France. The agreement provided for absolute territorial protection in the sense that Consten was prohibited from exporting from France, while all other Grundig distributors in other countries were contractually prohibited from exporting from other countries. In addition, the distribution agreement had an exclusive trademark license in favor of Consten for the Grundig trademark in France. Any imports into France would be infringements of the trademark. In combination, the two devices gave Consten what is known as "absolute territorial protection."

Both of these devices were held violative of Article 85 by the EECC, and this ruling was affirmed by the European Court. Since then, there have been a host of other examples of enforcement of competition law against arrangements that seal off national territories.

Now that the law on territorial protection can be regarded as clear and well settled, the EECC is turning its attention to cases more in line with the second theme of maintaining and fostering competition. Witness the EECC's attack on a merger alleged to be an "acquisition of a monopoly" in the <u>Continental Can</u> case. This case was wholly concerned with the competitive structure of industry in the EEC, and it suggests that future enforcement in Europe is increasingly likely to reflect U.S.-style concern with market structure. Let us turn next to a comparison of the U.S. and EEC laws in three especially important areas – marketing, licensing, and mergers.

MARKETING: EEC FOLLOWS U.S. LEAD

Without requiring any proof that they have adversely affected competition, U.S. law makes certain marketing practices violations. These "per se violations" include horizontal price fixing between competitors, market division by agreement between competitors, and restriction placed on a buyer of goods as to how he may dispose of them after purchase (for example, a restriction on the kind of customer to whom the buyer might resell). Restriction placed by a seller on the price at which the buyer might resell, that is, resale price maintenance, is illegal per se. Price discrimination is also prohibited subject to a vast welter of complications under the Robinson Patman Act.

Other practices that are virtually illegal per se are (a) refusals to sell, when the purpose is to coerce customers to behave in a certain way, and (b) tying arrangements, which may be permissible if necessary to maintain quality standards but not if made to coerce customers.

These U.S. rules are followed fairly closely by the EEC. However, the EEC is more generous than the United States in allowing exclusive supply arrangements and restrictions on the buyer's freedom to compete with the seller. EEC law has established a clear-cut distinction between agencies and distributorships. <u>Agents</u> are deemed auxiliaries of their principal. They act for the benefit of their principal, do not take the economic risks of the transactions they make for the principal, and are usually paid by way of percentage commission. As such, they are not independent, and contracts between principal and agent are not covered by Article 85.

In contrast, distributorships are independent enterprises. A distributor buys goods for his own account, resells them, and takes his profit on the sales. Since a distributor bears the economic risks of his own transactions, distributorship contracts are covered by Article 85.

Restraints on Distribution

Following the lead of antitrust in the United States, EEC officials realized early on that exclusive distributorships are by their very nature restrictive; the supplier is limited in those to whom he can sell. The EEC approach has been to sanction such distributorships as long as their additional restraints on competition are fairly minimal.

The criteria for restraints on competition are laid down in Regulation 67/67 a block exemption granting the benefits of Article 85(3) to exclusive distributorships. If you are ever involved in making an exclusive distributorship contract for Europe or if your company has distributorship contracts that need review, Regulation 67/67 is the essential tool. Any agreements should be tailored to meet it.

Can the supplier dictate the distributor's selling price? Illegal in the United States, there have been no EEC decisions on the point so far, but most commentators agree that the authorities are only waiting for the opportunity to bring a case against this practice and that when they do they will prevail. Resale price maintenance has been illegal in France for many years, has recently been outlawed in Germany, is very much on its way out in Holland, and is illegal with some exceptions in the United Kingdom. The future trend is certainly against it. Accordingly, the most a manufacturer should do in distribution contracts is to suggest or recommend a price, but not back it up with any sanctions.

Recently there has been an interesting development in what is known as "selective distribution." A selective distribution system consists of a whole network of exclusive distributors in a territory. The system is most appropriate to high-quality products such as watches and automobiles. The classic case concerns Bavarian Motor Works (BMW):

Management appointed a series of wholesalers with responsibility for various territories, who in turn, subject to approval by BMW, appointed retail dealers. Both the wholesalers and the retailers were obligated not to sell BMW motorcars to anyone other than private customers or other authorized dealers. This meant that BMW had complete vertical control down through its chain of distribution for all its cars. No authorized dealer was allowed to sell to an independent or unauthorized dealer. Was the system permissible?

Among the arguments urged in favor of this system was the idea that BMW cars required special know-how for their sales and servicing and that the improper performance of these functions by pirates would not only impair BMW quality but might even put dangerous cars on the road. Although it had rejected a similar argument in an earlier case, the EECC accepted this argument for use in the case of BMW. Since the BMW case, the EECC has also accepted selective distribution in the case of Omega watches and Rochas perfumes. Executives interested in selective distribution of this kind are encouraged to take a look at the BMW decision. The EECC went to a great deal of trouble in that decision to establish a model for a selective distribution contract.

Controls Over Pricing

EEC law does not require a company to sell its goods at the same price throughout Western Europe. What is required is that an EEC buyer be able to buy his goods wherever the prices are lowest and take them back for resale to his home country.

The classic case on this point was the Kodak decision. Kodak sold its cameras in Europe through wholly owned subsidiaries located in each country. The products were sold subject to uniform conditions of sale. These conditions allowed the products to be sold to customers located anywhere in the EEC, but it was provided that the customer be involved by the local Kodak subsidiary in his home country at the local price. This provision meant that a customer in, for example, Germany could buy in France, but he would still pay the German price in deutsche mark. The EECC insisted that this condition be removed so that the customer could practice price arbitrage by buying where the prices were lowest. The EECC felt that the economic laws of supply and demand would eventually lead to prices falling to the approximate level of the subsidiary with the lowest prices. This approach was followed in the BMW and the Omega cases decided by the EECC.

LICENSING: EEC TAKES DIFFERENT ROUTE
FROM U.S.A.

In the United States, restrictive provisions in industrial property licenses are subject to both the antitrust laws and the general equity rules on fairness. The fairness rules are premised on the notion that he who seeks enforcement by way of injunction of a patent or other right must come to the court with clean hands. If he has exceeded the scope of the privileges lawfully given to him, his hands are unclean. Moreover, since the famous 1969 case of Lear v. Adkins, licensees have been free to attack their licensors' patents and indeed can recover royalties paid under invalid patents that they successfully attack. As for know-how, it, too, can be licensed, and the licensor can impose secrecy conditions.

The following contractual restrictions are per se violations in U.S. law:

- Restrictions on resale – For example, in a selling license, it is illegal to forbid one's licensee to resell in bulk and to require that he sell only individual items.
- Mandatory package licensing – A company cannot require its licensee to take a package of licenses in order to get the one or two licenses that he might want.

- Mandatory sales royalties – Unless the licensee requests it, the licensor cannot impose a royalty on total sales the licensee makes of all his products instead of on sales of licensed items alone.
- Postexpiration royalties – The licensor cannot demand royalties beyond the life of the licensed industrial property.

There are other "virtually per se" restrictions. These are so close to being per se violations that they should always be regarded as "no-no's," but for historical or other reasons the law has never got around to denominating them as flatly illegal. In this category are the tie-in clauses, reservation by the licensor of the power to fix the licensee's selling prices, and maximum quantity restrictions on the licensee's sales, among other prohibitions.

Other licensing restrictions are subject to attack under the "rule of reason." Two tests must be passed: (1) Is the provision justifiable as necessary and ancillary to a lawful main purpose? The lawful main purpose in a license is normally the public interest in spreading the use of the patent or property. (2) Are less restrictive alternatives available that are more likely to foster competition?

For example, some licenses give a licensee permission to operate in a defined field and no other. Thus a license might be given to manufacture and sell for home but not for commercial use. Such a restraint can cause problems. The classic case is United States v. Fisons, the British drug company. Fisons licensed a new drug to two competitors in America; one licensee was to supply it for human consumption, the other to supply it to veterinaries for animal consumption. The Justice Department attacked this restraint on the ground that since the two licensees were competitors in both fields, an artificial classification had been created that was not necessary under the rule-of-reason test. In short, the licensor must be able to show that carving out a field of use is rational and no more restrictive than necessary in order to persuade the licensee to take the license. Territorial restrictions are also a problem. They cannot be used as a means of carving up a market among competitors.

Special Problems in EEC

The EEC is wrestling with a very difficult problem in the field of industrial property rights. In Europe, these rights are creatures of the member states and confer territorial monopolies within the states in which the rights are issued. Until a few years ago, it was considered a natural part of these monopolies that they carry with them the right to exclude imports of similar products from abroad, even from countries where the seller himself had valid patents or other rights.

Obviously, to the extent that industrial property rights are used as keep-out weapons to seal off national markets, they are contrary to the EEC's overriding purpose of unifying the European market. The EECC is attacking this problem on two fronts: (1) reform of industrial property laws to comply with treaty objectives and (2) application of the competition law.

As for law reform, the solution adopted by the proposed Common Market Patent Convention envisions that, once a company has marketed a product with the protection of its patent right in one EEC country, it shall have exhausted that right. The goods can thereafter flow anywhere in the EEC, and the company cannot assert its rights in any other EEC country. Most of the cases to date that have been premised on the free-movement-of-goods principle have relied on the "exhaustion doctrine."

U.S. law also recognizes the exhaustion doctrine in the sense that, once one has marketed goods under patent, he has used up his rights and cannot raise the patent again. The difference is that, in Europe, sale in one country exhausts rights in other EEC countries, whereas in America the exhaustion by first sale only affects U.S. patent rights.

MERGERS: MORE OPPORTUNITIES IN THE EEC

In the U.S. the Sherman Act tests also apply to mergers. In addition, the Clayton Act bears on mergers. This act goes beyond the Sherman Act to make unlawful any acquisition that "in any line of commerce in any section of the country may substantially lessen competition or tend to create a monopoly." One merger — by Alcoa of a small company known as Rome Cable — was struck down under the Clayton Act even though the acquired company only had 1.3 percent of the relevant market.

There are several points to bear in mind where the Clayton Act is concerned: It reaches mergers that may restrict competition. The idea is to nip potentially restrictive mergers in the bud before they actually produce anticompetitive effects. The act reaches vertical as well as horizontal mergers. An example is the 1972 Ford Motor case, in which Ford, with the idea of self-supply, bought a spark plug manufacturer. Since this purchase would foreclose sales to Ford in the future on the part of other independent spark plug manufacturers, it was judged to be a violation.

The act also reaches conglomerate mergers. On its face, the building of a conglomerate might not seem anticompetitive since the various parts of such an enterprise are in different industries. One conglomerate merger has been struck down, however, because it created the opportunity for reciprocity. That is, the acquiring company would be likely in the future to take its supplies only from its newly acquired subsidiary or to buy only from its old independent suppliers if they in turn sent business to the new subsidiary. On the other hand, the "toe hold theory" is beginning to receive some recognition. This is the idea that it is permissible for a large company to buy a small competitor in another geographic area in order to gain a toehold in the market and enable the acquiring company to become a competitive force in the new territory.

Varying Approaches

The approach to mergers in the EEC differs according to whether the Coal and Steel Treaty or the Rome Treaty applies. Coal and steel mergers are subjected to prior review by the EECC under Article 66 of the Coal and Steel Treaty. A generous policy favoring mergers has been followed to help in the nationalization of these problem industries and to encourage concentration and the economies of scale that they require.

Under the Rome Treaty the only case is the one involving the American Group, Continental Can. The group acquired a Dutch company that produces metal lids and cans for meat and fish. Through its German subsidiary, Continental already had about 70 percent of the German market for these items. The Dutch company that was acquired had most of the market in Holland.

The acquisition was attacked by the EECC as an abuse of a dominant position. No other abusive behavior was alleged. Much of the argument centered on whether a merger — that is, the acquisition or extension of a dominant position — was an "abuse" under Article 86. The real issue was whether the authority of Article 86 by its terms was adequate to let the EECC control mergers or whether the EECC needed a further regulation or Rome Treaty amendment in order to do this.

The European Court decided in favor of the EECC on the legal issue in the Continental Can case. The EECC does have power to challenge mergers under Article 86. However, the court felt that the EECC had not proved its case on the facts. The EECC's definition of what the relevant market was in terms of cans for meat and fish was too narrow. There was nothing unique about meat or fish cans, and the EECC should have concerned itself with the light metal container market in general. The same was true of the metal closure market; substitutes such as corks should have been considered.

In the final analysis, it seems the EECC has won the opening skirmish but lost the battle and the war. It took the Continental Can case no further and since then has brought no other merger cases. Officials have said privately that before they can proceed much further in the field, they need a regulation authorizing them to police mergers and setting out policy criteria.

A draft regulation was issued in 1973. It calls for mandatory prior notification of mergers involving companies with aggregate sales of over $1 billion; in the case of companies with sales between $200 million and $1 billion, prior notification of a merger may be given if management wants to do so. In that regulation, the term merger is defined as taking control, and it includes joint ventures. There has been no progress recently toward final issuance of this draft regulation. In view of the weak state of European merger law, the present is obviously a good time to make mergers in Europe. Joint ventures present more of a question. Article 85 does apply to joint ventures, but there has been little experience in its application.

11 Product Warranty Laws in Europe: A Simplified Comparison

Steven E. Permut

(Ed. note: The table on pages 96-97 is included for two reasons. It demonstrates the new and vital importance of consumer policy in all affluent countries, and it illustrates the fact that legislation relevant to international marketing is still far from harmonized within the European Community.)

TOPIC	BELGIUM	DENMARK	FRANCE
1. Formal distinction between actual & latent defects in the law?	YES	NO	YES
2. Right to have price reduced for defective good?	YES	YES	YES
3. Right to demand repair? Right to demand replacement?	NO NO (unless specified in contract)	Possibly Possibly	NO
4. Right to claim damages? (see notes below)	YES[a]	YES[b]	YES[a]
5. Length of time for a buyer to raise a claim for latent defect? (Time starts from the discovery of defect except where noted otherwise.)	"Within a short time" (determined by court on case-by-case basis).	One year. Seller must be notified "forthwith" i.e., without delay.	"Within a short time."
6. Is warranty variation of seller's liability possible under existing law? (subject to "the seller's bad faith" clause almost universally.)	YES (subject to no gross misconduct by seller); modification of warranty time and specifics can occur if agreed to by buyer at time of sale.	NO (subject to "unreasonableness" as viewed by courts); the Marketing Practices Act guarantees buyers rights and cannot be waived without buyer's agreement.	YES (subject to no gross misconduct by seller); courts tend to view any modification narrowly; often disregarding them; prior agreement to such clauses required.

[a] particularly if seller acted in bad faith, or gross misconduct
[b] damages awarded if false promise of quality or defect are fraudulently concealed
[c] not allowed in addition to contract dissolution or price reduction

*Excerpt from "Consumer product warranty legislation in Western Europe," Multinational Product Management, Proceedings American Marketing Association/Marketing Science Institute Research Workshop, August 1976, Report No. 76-110, Marketing Science Institute, with permission.

TOPIC	G. BRITAIN	ITALY	GERMANY	NETHERLANDS
1. Formal distinction between actual & latent defects in the law?	NO	YES	NO	YES
2. Right to have price reduced for defective good?	NO	YES	YES	YES
3. Right to demand repair? Right to demand replacement?	NO NO	NO	NO (not a "right") YES	NO
4. Right to claim damages? (see notes)	YES[c]	YES[a]	YES[b]	YES[a]
5. Length of time for a buyer to raise a claim for latent defect? (Time starts from the discovery of defect except where noted otherwise.)	Unspecified (determined by courts on case-by-case basis; any claims must be brought at least within 6 years from purchase).	"Within one year after delivery"; must also be notified within 8 days of the defect's discovery.	Within six months for "movable" goods where seller maliciously failed to disclose a defect 30 years for claim is specified.	"Within a short time" from the moment of reasonable discovery by a vigilant but not expert buyer
6. Is warranty variation of seller's liability possible under existing law? (subject to "the seller's bad faith" clause almost universally.)	NO (subject to "fundamental breach of contract," in return seller agrees to make good on all defects); "implied buyers rights" cannot be nullified as of 1973 Implied Terms Act.	YES (subject to actual concealment of defect by the seller), and where such clauses are clearly unambiguously expressed.	YES (valid clauses vary by type of goods & type of transaction); exclusion of buyer rights must provide the right to obtain repair to be held valid.	YES

12 Market Control in Developing Economies*
Lee E. Preston

In most of the developing countries, and in such countries scattered throughout the political spectrum from capitalism to communism, internal trade is primarily conducted through controlled markets. The specific character and function of controls vary widely, but the line between market socialism and controlled capitalism is thin; whereas the difference between both of these and, on the one hand, unrestricted markets and, on the other, purely administrative coordination systems, is evident to even the casual observer. In controlled markets, whether embedded in a capitalist or socialist economic structure, public authorities operate continuously not only to establish specific limits on market outcomes, but also to influence the direction and purposes of market activity. However, in contrast to administrative coordination systems, controlled markets leave a significant scope for independent action and individual flexibility.

Examples of market control activities may be gleaned from almost any study of a developing economy. However, in such examples, the unique circumstances of the individual case tend to dominate, and the common elements and alternatives among control activities are obscured. This tendency to see market control in terms of unique cases is also characteristic of control administrations. The division of control authority over different industries and market levels among different, and often rivalrous, ministries and agencies serves to hide, rather than reveal, the basic similarities and inherent inter-relationships of many control activities, and thereby stimulates the development and persistence of inconsistent and even mutually offsetting policies.

The purpose of this paper is to identify domestic market control as a significant aspect of development planning and administration, quite

*Reprinted from L.E. Preston, "Market control in developing economies," Journal of Development Studies, Vol. 4, No. 4 (1968), pp. 481-96, with permission.

apart from the particular ideological context or product/industry setting in which the controls may operate. To this end, we characterize the principal objectives of market control and the methods used to achieve them: we then touch on the problem of evaluating control effectiveness. Throughout the paper, examples are cited in order to draw attention to both the contextual diversity and the underlying similarity of control activities.

MARKET CONTROL: WHAT AND WHY

For purposes of this discussion, a market may be defined as any exchange relationship in which the trading parties exercise a range of choice with respect to their selection of trading partners, products, prices, or quantity purchased or sold. The range of choice may include, of course, the alternative of abstaining from trade entirely. The general term market is intended to include such disparate phenomena as the assembly of agricultural products from primary producers and the distribution of manufactured goods to consumers, as well as the purchase and sale of materials and products within the industrial sector. Market control is not simply demand control; supply management activities may be of equal or greater concern.

Market control may be aimed at any or all of the results of market activity — the character and quality of merchandise and services exchanged, their volume and prices, and the distribution of sales and purchases among potential sellers and buyers. An essential aspect of control administration is the inter-relation among the several results, and the appraisal of control effectiveness rests on the comparison of results achieved with those that might have occurred under unrestricted market activity or administrative direction.

A preliminary question arises: why have so many developing countries, capitalist as well as socialist, chosen market control over either free markets or comprehensive administration as a principal form of domestic supply and demand coordination? The answer appears to lie in both ideological and practical considerations. A preference for markets reflects, in part, the sheer difficulty and cost of providing a satisfactory administrative substitute. Although the relatively small size and industrial simplicity of many developing countries would appear to facilitate the use of administrative mechanisms, these advantages are as a rule offset by the absence of essential information and of the skills and social habits necessary for administrative efficiency. As a result, small and simple developing countries are as difficult to coordinate administratively, for economic as well as political purposes, as large and complex developed ones. Further, the task of economic coordination without markets becomes more rather than less difficult as the development process proceeds, because of the increasing variety of products and services available and the widening range of choice among economic and noneconomic activities. On the ideological side, political recognition of the value and strength of individual preferences provides an additional rationale for the use of markets. This recognition is particularly important in countries where a large traditional sector continues to exist alongside a developing core of urban industry. If the fruits of development are to be made available to village populations, then products, services and distribution arrangements must be adapted not only to traditional requirements but also to the opportunities for experimentation and gradual change that arise as development continues.

These practical and ideological considerations account for the use of controlled markets in circumstances that might otherwise favour more centralized planning and administration. In private ownership economies, adoption of controls over markets otherwise free is primarily intended to bring the activities of private owners and purchasers into conformity with basic development goals and to achieve specific welfare objectives. The need to maintain low food prices for an industrial labour force or to prevent profiteering from temporary shortages are obvious examples. In addition, market controls are intended to curb the mercantile psychology prevalent in many developing societies, in which the maximum gain on the immediate transaction is preferred to long-term market expansion. In these circumstances, one feature of market control is to substitute the long-term production and sales goals of the Western capitalist for the short-term view of the traditional merchant. In addition, of course, rapid development of poor countries typically requires some centralized administration of primary investment decisions, foreign exchange, and basic subsistence supplies, no matter what the form of government or pattern of property ownership. And such administrative activity frequently generates a network of supplementary controls with varying impact on domestic markets.

MARKET CONTROL OBJECTIVES

Market controls are not ends in themselves but are intended to facilitate the accomplishment of basic development goals – stimulating domestic production and consumption, conserving foreign exchange, and improving human welfare. Specific market control activities can rarely be conducted or appraised by direct reference to these goals, however, because of the many factors involved in achieving any major goal and because of the multi-dimensional character of the goals themselves. Thus, specific market control activities must be aimed at more specific objectives, which in turn contribute to the long-run development strategy. Unfortunately, failure to specify these objectives and to observe the inter-relations among them has been characteristic of both the analysis and the practice of market control in the developing countries.

Marketization

A major characteristic of traditional economies is the relative weakness or absence of markets. Not only are subsistence households and communities commonplace, but – much more important – sizeable production and demand potentials exist side by side but separated by ignorance, institutional barriers, or high marketing costs. A substantial increase in output, and the wellbeing of both producers and users, may be achieved if all the potential trading parties can be made aware of the exchange possibilities and drawn into a market relationship.

Marketization typically involves both organizational change and educational or promotional activity; it may require facilities for investment as well. Constructing public market places, establishing buying or selling agencies to act as market intermediaries, and introducing regular storage and communication-transportation facilities are typical activities aimed at this objective. The primary purpose of these innovations is to make the exchange possibilities apparent, and to lower the cost of contact among market participants. At the same time, however, marketization monetizes both costs and revenues that were previously accounted, if at all, only in real terms. Great inconvenience and ignorance may be overcome by means of relatively small money expenditures – as in the payment of market participation fees or taxes – or by the adoption of fairly simple standard operating procedures or standards. But these expenditure and operating changes are readily observable, whereas the unmonetized real costs, which perhaps prohibited exchange altogether, and traditional operating procedures are accepted as normal. Marketization therefore frequently appears to involve increases in costs and inconvenience for potential market participants, rather than the reduced costs or improved cost/return ratios which are its goal. To overcome these difficulties – often summarized as "these people don't know what's good for them" – an element of compulsion may be required, in addition to systematic educational and promotional effort. It may also be necessary to introduce a variety of auxiliary control elements aimed at assuring the trading parties specific benefits from market participation, and – perhaps of equal importance – of demonstrating that the benefits promised are actually received.

Marketization may also be an essential preliminary to other more specific types of control activity. For example, the formal market reorganization associated with the establishment of marketing boards in the agricultural countries of the Sterling Area has been primarily justified as creating conditions for market stabilization. The idea is that the institutional and regulatory system of the boards would make possible the conduct of stabilization policies. Critics, such as Bauer and Yamey (1954), have charged that this power to stabilize involved too great an interference with other aspects of market activity. More recently, one careful analysis has raised considerable questions about the ability of the boards to achieve any significant stabilization results (Helleiner, 1966). Another example is the susceptibility of markets to redistributional techniques such as price manipulations and rationing; in the absence of markets, redistribution of goods – as, for example, of food supplies – may be attainable only through confiscation or forced collectivization.

Increased Volume

Marketization implies an increase in the volume of goods flowing into trade channels. It is therefore quite compatible with the broader control objective of increasing the volume of goods produced and consumed. Increased output may come from both previously operating and new sources, and increased consumption may be aimed at welfare goals (increased total consumption) or at the diversion of demand from imports (increased consumption of domestic products). Whatever the detailed problem, the obvious strategies are to stimulate output by price increases, and to stimulate use by price reductions. Evidently, when the intent is to increase both domestic production and use of the same product – the typical case – these two strategies are in direct conflict.

The simultaneous increase of buying and decrease of selling prices requires either that intermediate trading margins be narrowed, or that subsidies be provided from the general treasury. Intermediate trading margins may fall for two reasons: (1) the cost of intermediate activities, such as central market trading, financing, transport and storage, is reduced; or (2) intermediate monopoly positions exist and can be eliminated. Both of these may be real possibilities, but both are apt to require considerable expenditure of funds and considerable managerial skill on the part of control authorities. By contrast, increasing production and use through price manipulations appears relatively easy, and subsidies thus become common features of volume expansion programs. As a result, one evidence of the success of such programs, at least in the short-run, in accomplishing their output and use objectives is their increasing money cost; the greater the increase in volume, the greater the subsidy required.

Subsidy costs can be reduced, and the impact of price manipulations sharpened, when specific price incentives are linked to specific producer or user characteristics or behaviour. For example, advantageous selling prices may be established only for over-fulfillment of marketing or production quotas, and low buying prices made available only to specific industries or to households in accordance with employment status or family needs. These selective techniques make it possible to apportion the total increase in volume among specific sources and uses, and may also reduce subsidy costs substantially as compared to a general subsidy program. However, selective programs also require a much more detailed administration and present innumerable opportunities for abuse, both by control authorities and by subsidy receivers.

Inflation Control

Increased investment and rapid urbanization in the course of economic development, as well as specific subsidies for output and consumption referred to above, commonly tend to generate inflationary pressures, particularly in consumer goods lines. Although fundamental adjustment to these pressures must lie in some combination of taxation and increased output, a certain amount of direct control over the price level is characteristic of almost all developing economies. If effective, such control may avoid the spread of an inflation psychosis throughout the economy, and thus facilitate the accomplishment of fundamental development goals. Stringent short-run price controls may also avoid the necessity of downward price adjustments when a more nearly balanced market situation is attained. However, the simple control of explicit prices, whether or not accompanied by systematic rationing, familiar in the developed countries as a wartime emergency measure does not provide a model for inflation control in economies experiencing a substantial amount of "permanent" inflationary pressure in the course of development. Three essential differences stand out:

1. Control environment and administration: Inflation control in the advanced countries is generally a temporary and fairly simple addition to an already well-articulated public and private market information system. In the developing countries, no such system exists. Little reliance can therefore be placed on established reporting practices or routine self-policing devices. Nor can appeals to patriotism or emergency requirements be expected to have effect over the long term. On the contrary, where basic supply and demand imbalances remain uncorrected, exceptions to the basic control pattern tend to multiply, leakages expand, and the need for compulsion increases. Crucial to the success of any control system is that the policies announced be, in fact, carried out, and that control administration be honest and open, in appearance as well as in practice. The personnel, procedures, and knowledge required for efficient price control are rare enough in advanced countries, and inevitably lacking in less-developed ones.

2. Diverting inflationary pressures: As important as the selection of items and prices to be controlled is the availability of activities into which inflationary purchasing power can be diverted. The alternative of accumulating liquid savings or securities is seldom viable, because savings and investment institutions themselves are not generally available or accepted as reliable, because liquid savings are peculiarly susceptible to taxation or confiscation, and because of the inflation psychosis. Traditional means of hoarding, such as the purchase of jewels and precious metals, usually provide a sufficient outlet only for small savers. A major outlet for savings in the non-communist countries in recent years has been urban real estate, particularly housing. Although speculative booms in construction

have been frequently criticized as diverting resources from primary development tasks, they are probably preferable to black market financing or simple capital flight. The high labor content of construction results in the diffusion of purchasing power among lower income groups, and construction typically uses large proportions of domestic rather than imported materials. For these reasons, the maintenance of an outlet, such as private building, for inflationary pressures may be a significant element of inflation in other sectors of the economy.

3. Decontrol: The idea that inflation control contributes importantly to the development process implies that controls can be relaxed as development proceeds. Again, unlike wartime control systems, this relaxation is not likely to occur all at once, or as a result of changes in external or economy-wide factors, but rather gradually and selectively as particular development goals are attained. It is a particular danger of price control systems that they will not be abandoned when their immediate purpose is served, but will rather live on to serve other purposes. In many countries – not all of them particularly underdeveloped – vestiges of post-World War II price control systems may be observed still in operation, but with their purposes changed to maintaining high and stable prices for some particular industry or trade rather than holding prices down and rationing short supplies.

Product Quality

The most numerous type of market controls in the advanced countries are those concerned with merchandise quality. Standardized grades and labels, minimum health and safety standards, regulation sizes and packages are pervasive throughout both industry and agriculture, and provide a basis in law and language for long-term market development among diverse suppliers and users separated by great distances. The developing countries, by contrast, have been slow to perceive the value of standardized quality for its own sake, and quick to note the high, but frequently once-for-all, costs associated with standardization.   Such controls as do exist in the developing countries arise primarily from the demand of foreign buyers. For example, developing countries coming into association with the European Common Market are compelled to grade and standardize their raw material and agricultural exports in order to obtain favorable market access conditions. The success of Israel and Lebanon in the export of fresh produce, chiefly to Western Europe, has been based very firmly on high and uniform product standards, established and enforced by joint government and private controls. By contrast, a substantial element in the deteriorating world market position of Egyptian cotton has been the virtual collapse of the classification and grading system within the country.

With rare exceptions, the potential contribution of quality standard-ization to domestic market expansion in developing countries has not as yet been perceived. When such controls are found, they are frequently directed at maintaining low rather than high quality items in domestic consumption, either as a protection device for specific industries or as an element of price control. For example, in many countries controls over commercial baking that were originally established, at least in part, as a consumer protection device have been gradually transformed into a system of varying the quality of bread so that the price can be maintained constant in money terms. Another feature of the general neglect of quality maintenance within market control systems is that imbalances among prescribed market results – e.g. volume, prices, etc. – may work themselves out in the form of quality changes, typically unfavorable and, in the end, expensive.

Redistribution

Quite apart from increasing the extent of market utilization, changing the volume of goods, prices or quality levels, market controls may aim at the redistribution of goods and income among various classes of market participants. Redistribution is usually thought of in terms of the availability of consumption goods and services to particular economic or social groups, especially those that have been historically disad-vantaged or for whom a particularly strong economic stimulus is desired. However, redistribution applies equally well to the supply side of the market, where it involves changes in the opportunity to make sales, particularly under favorable selling conditions. In addition, al-tering marketing arrangements so as to remove the monopoly position of middlemen or credit sources is also a redistributional policy.

The standard means of changing the distribution of a flow of goods among potential suppliers and users is to impose a licensing or rationing system which limits, or even eliminates, the participation of individual sellers and buyers in the market. Rationing, in effect, adds a second medium of exchange – the ration card – to the primary medium of money. Either both may be required to effect a transaction, or the card may substitute for money in making limited quantities of merchandise available at special prices. Redistribution may also be accomplished by the compulsory channelling of particular supplies of (or demands for) merchandise into new directions, or by prohibiting certain classes of traders from buying, selling, or otherwise participating in the market.

Miscellaneous Welfare Goals

A large number of specific market control activities have as their objective the protection of individual groups of consumers, producers, traders or professionals from the rigors of competition or the pressures of economic and social change. Controls of this type seem to be more prevalent in the upper range of developing countries, where certain minimum standards of life have been achieved by particular groups in the population and where the rate and direction of development has not been such as to assure these groups of their continued good fortune. As a result, protective restrictions designed to freeze patterns of doing business or trade conditions in the interest of specific groups are enacted. Although numerous in detail and annoying in operation, controls of this type are probably of limited long-run effect. Their principal impact may be in the rate of adaptation of the economy and its socio-political character. For example, the political power of small shopkeepers and their landlords has had obvious effects on the speed and pattern of introduction of mass retailing in most countries, but does not seem to have prevented it in any instance. Indeed, in spite of opposition, mass retailing in many countries appears to have been introduced more rapidly than demand conditions warranted.

MARKET CONTROL METHODS

Three principal methods are used, either separately or in combination, in the developing countries in order to attain these control objectives. They are: (1) centralizing some key marketing function or activity in a state agency for control purposes; (2) establishing state enterprises to compete with private firms, or among themselves; and (3) supervising and regulating private marketing activities directly.

Key-function centralization is characteristic, for example, of foreign trade, and of domestic trade in raw materials and fresh produce in many countries. The function itself may be an essential element of the marketing process – as in the case of state-monopoly export trading companies, publicly administered central markets, or credit and storage facilities – or may be an additional function created purely for control purposes – as in the case of licenses, permits and taxes. In any event, key-function centralization provides a device for monitoring the entire flow of market activity and influencing the broad pattern of market results, without regulating them in detail. The most obvious variable subject to control is the total volume passing through trade channels; however, auxiliary regulations may easily alter merchandise quality and allocation among sources and uses as well. A particular strength of this control method is that prices and procedures at any centralized market level tend to become reference points for prices and procedures at other levels. Thus, by exerting control over the reference price, quality, or volume, authorities can influence the entire marketing structure without concerning themselves in detail with its individual elements.

Like key-function centralization, market control through the competition of state and private enterprises also relies considerably on unrestricted market activity to work out results in specific detail. The role of the state enterprise is to provide a competitive alternative to the offerings of private traders; the latter are then brought into conformity by the forces of competition. This conformity may not, of course, involve identical behavior by private and public enterprises. Rather, the public enterprises offer a norm against which the different quality, service, location and other features of the private firms can be evaluated. This type of market control is attractive because it avoids both compulsion and inspection. Its effective operation requires, however, that the market alternatives of the public enterprises be readily accessible throughout the market, and that customers be skilled in discovering and evaluating alternatives. The effectiveness of this type of control is limited by (1) the ability of the state enterprises to manage their own operations successfully in open competition, which is no mean task; and (2) the ability and willingness of private firms to conform to the control system rather than leave the market entirely. Evidently, the latter implies that controlled market results will not generally deviate very far from those that would otherwise occur. However, one of the special strengths of the state enterprise is that it can vary its activities from time to time and market to market in such a way as to offset particular adverse developments in the short-run. The massing of available supplies in order to maintain price stability in areas temporarily subject to shortage or excess demand is a particular example.

Direct regulation of market results through supervision and enforcement by government agencies, who in fact perform no essential marketing function themselves, is undoubtedly the most common market control method. Even in developing countries where most production activity is concentrated in state-owned enterprises, a formal structure of price and related controls over some substantial part of domestic trade is usually found. In addition, elaborate systems of permits and licenses, and other ad hoc regulations, are characteristic. Many of these control activities are directly related to foreign trade, either preventing high prices for scarce imports or maintaining low prices for import substitutes. Also, these regulatory systems constitute a kind of reserve force; they may be without appreciable effect on market activity at any moment of time, but they can be invoked on short notice if the need should arise. An important feature of such regulations is that they are subject to a considerable amount of administrative variability, which allows their effects to be somewhat more selective than their formal structure might indicate. For example, although formal two-price systems, whereby particular classes of buyers or sellers enjoy a favorable (unfavorable) position relative to others, are difficult to justify and maintain, de facto two-price systems can be easily operated by uneven enforcement of price controls.

The formal and administrative selectivity of direct controls are, however, the source of their greatest disadvantages as principal means of economic coordination. Detailed regulation requires close supervision and elaborate record-keeping, and thus control administration becomes expensive and onerous, even if desirable results are obtained. Further, the multiplication of exceptions and instances of uneven administration may eventually neutralize the effects of the system entirely. Finally, the very specificity of direct controls requires the fragmentation of control authority, with increasing possibilities of conflict and inconsistency among objectives and results.

APPRAISING CONTROL EFFECTIVENESS

Given the multiplicity of control objectives and the complexity of techniques, it is little wonder that the effectiveness of market control activities is seldom carefully appraised. Operating authorities are generally satisfied with an "it works" kind of evaluation, and – when control is obviously not working – to recommend the revision of objectives rather than of control methods. Although this approach can be easily criticized, it is difficult to specify criteria for appraising the effectiveness of controls in a development context, even at the conceptual level. If the combination of development effort and control is successful in changing underlying economic conditions, then a comparison of pre- and post-control market results does not provide an appropriate basis for judgement: the two situations will be different in too many important respects. A similar problem arises in the comparison of contemporaneous transactions taking place within and without the control system, since the results outside the system are likely to be influenced by it nonetheless. For example, uncontrolled prices may follow controlled prices because of the pressures of market competition, or, as in the case of black markets, may differ from them in direct proportion to the effectiveness of control. (That is, black market volume is small and price high <u>because</u> controlled market volume is large and price low.)

It is, in addition, misleading to think that market control systems can be evaluated entirely within a simple supply-and-demand context. Marketing activities are heavily institutional, and thus strongly condition the way in which basic supply and demand forces come into being and interact. Market controls therefore change not only the specific results of market activity but also the way in which these results are obtained. Market operations also involve a dynamic mechanism, so that a unique and nonreversible sequence of results is generated over time. As a consequence, even short-lived controls may produce long-term effects, both desired and otherwise.

A final problem in appraising control effectiveness is that market controls comprise a part of the total political and social policy structure, and generate overtones and reactions within that structure. In a society politically committed to the principle of strong central administration, even relatively ineffective market controls may perform some function as elements of a comprehensive scheme of economic planning. By contrast, in less centralized societies, even fairly effective market controls may prove to be social and political liabilities.

REFERENCES

Bauer, P.T., and Yamey, B.S., "The economics of marketing reform," Journal of Political Economy, Vol. 62 (1954), pp. 210-35.

Helleiner, G.K., "Marketing boards and a domestic stabilization in Nigeria," Review of Econonomics and Statistics, Vol. 48 (1966), pp. 69-78.

13 Political Factors as Managerial Decision Elements in Formulating Multinational Strategies: Sub-Saharan Africa*

D. Carson

Few regions of the world have experienced the fundamental political shifts during the last two decades as has sub-Saharan Africa. Because of the socio-economic diversity of its peoples and of its nations – including their politics – the region in many respects can serve international managers as a model for choice of strategies in facing rapid political change.

Africa may be divided into three areas: (1) the five nations bordering the Mediterranean Sea, primarily Arabic in language, culture, and international orientation; (2) eight off-shore political entities ranging from the "postage-stamp"-size Comoro Islands to Malagasy (formerly Madagascar), roughly equivalent to Sweden in population but larger in area; and (3) the 41 Continental states located in and south of the Sahara, variously known as sub-Saharan or Tropical Africa. This paper concentrates on the third area, by far the largest in terms of size and population, although it has intimate political, economic, and cultural ties with the first two areas.

STRATEGIC ALTERNATIVES

In view of the diversity of opportunities for investing in sub-Saharan Africa, the present or potential investor must consider the individual characteristics and situations existing in the nations and project them for the future, but the area's rapidly shifting political scene makes this difficult.

Several scales of political stability have been formulated by political scientists. Although of some value for the international manager, they generally lack direct application for specific situations, products, individuals, and opportunities. The most comparable schema directly

---

*From Management International Review, Vol. 19, No. 1 (1979), pp. 71-79. Reprinted with permission.

related to international management was published over ten years ago, but was never meant to be more than a conceptual approach. MNCs which attempt to apply a wide range of quantitative data to basic decisions relating to environmental conditions in specific nations commonly report that difficulties in obtaining reliable, comparable, current information make these efforts merely supportive and peripheral to nonquantitative considerations.

A systematic scheme toward approaching strategic investment decisions is illustrated in Table 13.1. Naturally, decisions are modified by such considerations as the existence and size of investments in a nation; the degree of risk related to potential for profit (including the likelihood of recouping existing investments); synergistic considerations with other nations in the area or within the firm, or even with LDCs (less developed countries) throughout the world; and the availability within a nation of such particular managerial facilities or institutions as efficient, cooperative distribution channels.

Table 13.1. Strategic Positions Toward Investing in Tropical Africa

Position	Positive	Neutral	Negative
Dominant considerations	Maximize control	Maintain flexibility	Minimize risks
Preferred actions	Enter Expand	Holding position	Decrease position Withdraw
Time span	Long-term	Medium-term	Short-term or immediately
Arrangements	Own branches, and distributorships	Licensing Management contracts Joint ventures	Import Export Management contracts

MAJOR POLITICAL DIRECTIONS

The current political systems and trends of the 41 sub-Saharan nations are predictably diverse, but the vast majority nevertheless appears to follow six directions to some degree: (1) moves toward federation, (2) national fragmentation, (3) the effects of external (often worldwide) political ideological drives, (4) particular types of governmental styles, (5) a considerable degree of instability, and (6) a decided trend toward Africanization. Seemingly opposite tendencies are frequently observed in these nations, accounting to some extent for the pervasive instability in the area.

The remainder of this paper will describe the principal elements of the six major political directions noted in the area, applying the three strategic positions presented in Table 13.1 to each of these elements. The scheme for the six parts of Table 13.2 (a through f) has been based upon an analysis of the experiences of several scores of multinational firms in sub-Saharan Africa.

1. <u>Federation</u>. Table 13.2a delineates the elements of the first of the six political directions, federations. "High" indicates a likelihood that an element <u>would</u> lead to a strategic position; "Low" indicates little likelihood of its doing so. For instance, the first element under "Federation" is "Homogeneous in language, ethnicity, religion." If such homogeneity is strong ("High") in a nation, it tends to support federation with the country. The element would, moreover, encourage investors to assume a positive stance (as described in Table 13.1) toward investment in that nation. Should this element be weak ("Low"), the investor would be likely to adopt a negative position.

Table 13.2a. Selected Elements Influencing Adoption of Strategic Position(s): Moves toward Federation.

Position:	Positive	Neutral	Negative
Homogeneous in language, ethnicity, religion	High	Medium	Low
Ethnic, tribal groups all contained within national boundaries	High	Medium	Low
Adherence to viable regional organizations, blocs, customs unions, etc.	High	Medium	Low
Wide usage of international languages	High	Medium	Low
Strong economic infrastructure	High	Medium	Low
Strong traditional marketing networks	High	Medium	Low

During the latter half of the 1950s and the early 1960s, when political sovereignty was attained by a majority of the sub-Saharan nations, a high priority was set on unifying peoples separated for centuries by approximately 1,000 distinct languages, by religions (principally Christian, Moslem, or local traditional), by numerous ethnic cleavages, by small political (tribal) units, and by rigid socio-economic classes. Efforts toward unification benefited from fresh memories of opposition to colonial rule, by a newborn fervor for pan-Africanism, and by the use of languages spanning wide geographic, ethnic, and social sectors. French, English, and Portuguese were pragmatic legacies of former colonial powers. And for centuries, several African tongues had served as common means of commercial and political communication for vast territories. Swahili, Fulani, Hausa, and Kikongo are still in wide usage.

Current political boundaries between the various states were drawn in general during the latter part of the 19th century by the European colonial powers in their haste to expand their empires, without a shred of concern for the lives that were disrupted by the new borders. Considering the centrifugal pressures inherited by the contemporary states, the survival of so many is remarkable.

Nigeria is a salient example, for since its founding in 1960 there has hardly been a year when the Federal Republic was not being torn asunder. The Biafran sessionist war of 1967-1970 was only one of such serious threats, but by mid-1978 Nigeria remained a viable federated nation.

2. Fragmentation. Table 13.2b illustrates elements of fragmentation. Contemporary sub-Saharan political history is rife with examples of territorial fragmentation: the splitup of the Mali Federation into the Republics of Senegal and Mali; the ineffectiveness of the brief union between Ghana and Guinea; the demise of the East African Common Market; the dismemberment of the federation of Rhodesia and Nyasaland into Zambia, Malawi, and Rhodesia; and attempts to wrest the Shaba (Katanga) Province from Zaire soon after Zaire's independence from Belgium in 1960, and again in 1977 and 1978, presumably with Angolan, Cuban, and Soviet support (Hull, 1977).

Table 13.2b. Selected Elements Influencing Adoption of Strategic Position(s): National Fragmentation

Position:	Positive	Neutral	Negative
Serious disputes with neighbors	Low	Medium	High
Ethnic, tribal groups extending beyond national boundaries	Low	Medium	High
Usage of international languages	High	Medium	Low
Maldistribution of assets, incomes, by class, by ethnic groups, by geographic district	Low	Medium	High

Somalia's armed attempts to annex the bleak Ogaden region of Ethiopia in 1977 alerted Kenya, since Somalis predominate in its Northeast territory, and alarmed Djibouti (formerly French Somaliland), about half of whose people are Somalis. The tenet of the inviolability of territory espoused by the OAU (Organization of African Unity) and the UN conflicts with the Somali drive to bring together a people homogeneous in terms of language, religion, and culture, but long separated by the imposition of political borders.

3. Ideologies. Elements of political ideologies are listed in Table 13.2c. Although the sub-Saharan nations have nominally liberated themselves from colonial dominance in one sense or another; political ideologies which originated elsewhere still exert a powerful influence on the region. France continues to provide political direction — along with cultural and economic aid — to most of its former territories, as does Britain in several of its one-time vassal states. And even the U.S.A. retains a special relationship, however altered, with Liberia. Although political cords to the "Motherlands" have been formally snipped, many of the economic ties remain firm, and their accompanying political messages are unmistakable.

Table 13.2c. Selected Elements Influencing Adoption of Strategic Position(s): Political Ideologies

Position:	Positive	Neutral	Negative
Marxists active, vocal	Low	Medium	High
Ties to international Marxist groups	Low	Medium	High
Ties to major (non-Marxist) industrial nations	High	Medium	Low
Ties to traditional Arab nations	Medium	Medium	Low

Marxist influence, emanating largely from the Soviet Union and its satellites, was until recently merely a threat to sub-Saharan Africa. During the past several years, however, Soviet-type Communism has been officially espoused by Mozambique, Somalia, and Benin; and more recently Guinea, the Congo Republic, Angola, and Ethiopia have followed suit in practice, if not in name. China's influence has been more limited politically as well as geographically. Even nations of such differing political persuasions as Nigeria and Tanzania have adopted some facets of socialism or, at the least, given lip-service to them.

Links to North Africa and to other Arab nations, until recently historical curiosities except for territories abutting Arab states (e.g., Sudan, Mauritania), have of late been reinforced. The 22-nation Arab League, financed to a large extent by its oil-rich members, has been making unmistakable inroads into Mid-Africa. Thus in summer 1977, when Kenya found it impossible to conduct trade as usual with most of its immediate neighbors, the Arab League encouraged Kenya's establishment of commercial relations with the Middle East. The ideological implications of these connections are clear (Leger, 1977).

Increasingly sub-Saharan Africa is being swept into the mainstream of the world's major ideological currents.

4. Government Styles. Major governmental styles in the area are enumerated in Table 13.2d. At least half of the African nations are ruled by military or by civilian-military cliques, and government and

business corruption is believed to be rampant. International smuggling and profiteering are customary. Yet public and private investments continue to flow to the Continent, attracted by economic opportunities. From 55 to 80 percent of government budgets are commonly earmarked for salaries for the military and police forces, and for the civil service. "Show" projects such as superhighways or elegant public buildings are often favored over more fundamental social or economic improvements.

Table 13.2d. Selected Elements Influencing Adoption of Strategic Position(s): Government Styles

Position:	Positive	Neutral	Negative
Authoritarian	Low	Medium	High
Socio-political tradition of authoritarianism	Low	Medium	High
Government highly centralized	Medium	Medium	High
Wide sharing of power	High	Medium	Low

The elevation of Bokassa, President of the Central African Republic for 11 years of adroit political maneuvering, to "Emperor" of the Central African Empire in December 1977 is an example of an extremely repressive regime. Despite the liquidation of the central bank, and dire mass poverty reflected in annual per capita income of somewhat over $100, Arab and French interests were not deterred in exploring further investment opportunities in the "Empire." Even Nigeria, among the politically freer countries in the area, professed increased social justice as a national goal while many of its major newspapers remained government-owned.

The move to totalitarianism is by no means one way, however. In 1969 Ghana, after being ruled by Kwame Nkrumah and later by a junta since its founding in 1960, returned to a civilian government. In summer 1977 the military regime which assumed power in 1972 announced a timetable for another return to civilian rule by mid-1970. Admittedly, unlike the typical African nation, Ghana has a broader middle class to support a democratic regime, and a larger body of highly-educated civilians.

5. Relative Stability. Major factors influencing political stability in the area appear in Table 13.2e. The reasons for political instability are manifest – poverty and gross maldistribution of income, raging inflation (especially since 1973), unprofessional and inexperienced public and private management, and endemic tribal animosities. The wonder is that governmental coups and seizures, and outbreaks of violence, have not been more frequent. Not atypical is Dahomey which experienced no fewer than six military coups from 1963 to 1972.

Table 13.2e. Selected Elements Influencing Adoption of Strategic
Position(s): Relative Stability

Position:	Positive	Neutral	Negative
Standard of living, broad distribution of income	High	Medium	Low
Broad middle class	High	Medium	Low
Educational levels	High	Medium	Low
Level of industrialization	High	Medium	Low
Ratio of exports in crops, raw materials	Low	Medium	High
Socio-economic ferment	Low	Medium	High
Prevalence of forced/violent political change	Low	Medium	High

Yet forced turnovers of national regimes are not by themselves solid measures of political instability. Sekou Touré, who became head of the Guinean Government in 1958, was still the undisputed ruler by mid-1978 – with the strong help of the military forces, the gendarmerie, and other trappings of a police state.

Major international powers – all of which offer obeisance to "freedom of conscience," "democracy," and "human decencies" – often support severely repressive regimes when it is in their geopolitical and economic interests. France is one of the more blatant examples of such practices in Africa.

6. <u>Africanization.</u> Crucial elements related to Africanization are noted in Table 13.2f. Even before the African nations were granted their independence, most colonial powers and their home-based business firms introduced programs to train Africans to perform highly skilled tasks and to assume managerial positions. With the assumption of power by the new regimes, requests for such assistance frequently turned into government edicts. The next step, the take-over of many foreign enterprises (in part, or through outright expropriation), seemed inevitable.

For instance, even before Nigeria achieved its independence from Britain in 1960, considerable effort was exerted to train Nigerians for higher positions in the public sector. Similar measures were also taken in the private sector. But until 1972 company ownership in the private sector by foreign interests generally continued essentially unchanged. The "Nigerian Enterprises Promotion Decree" proclaimed in 1972, and amended in 1976, formalized the proportion of equity to be held by Nigerians. Ownership was specified for individual branches of the private sector (e.g., oil extraction, banking, manufacturing). Some flexibility has been evident, however. When eight major multinational oil firms curtailed exploratory drilling and the inflow of fresh capital in early 1977 in response to what they considered harsh disincentives, the Nigerian government responded by altering certain provisions in order to spur the MNCs to higher levels of involvement and performance. Nonetheless in Nigeria – as elsewhere in the area – the specter of expropriation looms.

Table 13.2f. Selected Elements Influencing Adoption of Strategic
Position(s): Africanization

Position:	Positive	Neutral	Negative
Cordial relations with former colonial rulers	High	Medium	Low
Prevalence of Marxist ideologies	Low	Medium	High
Openness to foreign investment	High	Medium	Low
Threats or actual expropriation of foreign investments	Low	Medium	High
Potential among Africans for advanced training	High	Medium	Low

CONCLUSION

In view of the rapidly changing sub-Saharan political scene and the differences in specific situations, each current or potential investor must make his own application of this scheme toward decision making. The elements in Table 13.2 were selected for their importance to sub-Saharan Africa and may not be equally appropriate when applied to other regions. But in view of the great diversity of the political environment in Tropical Africa, the basic approach may be adopted by MNCs and by other international management groups in formulating their own policies toward foreign investments on a global scale.

REFERENCES

Hull, Galen, "Internationalizing the Shaba conflict," Africa Report (New York) (July-August 1977), pp. 4-9.
Leger, Richard R., "The Arab Connection: Kenya sets up trade links to the Mideast to help surmount its border difficulties," The Wall Street Journal (October 12, 1977), p. 48.

14 Marketing in Eastern European Socialist Countries*

Charles S. Mayer

Eastern European Socialist countries have recently "discovered" marketing as an important tool to bolster their economies. While their form of marketing is not identical to that practiced in the West, its emergence is important for three reasons. First, it raises the question of why marketing surfaced in an economy that viewed it as a "non-productive cost." Second, socialist marketers are attempting to develop practices consistent with their philosophy of what is socially desirable at a time when western marketing is under attack for its lack of responsiveness to social needs. Third, the emergence of marketing in a socialist world gives the semblance of closure between two competing forms of economic organization. How real this closure is, and how far it will progress is important to future relationships between East and West.

This paper will discuss the emergence of marketing from a historical point of view and the various aspects of socialist marketing which show the path of development.

MARKETING IN A FREE ENTERPRISE SOCIETY

In order to compare socialist marketing to our western system, it is important to extract the essence of marketing as we practice it. There seem to be five fundamentals in western marketing:

1. The central organizing principle of production and distribution is consumer satisfaction (the marketing concept).
2. Consumer satisfaction is derived from both goods and services.

---

*From University of Michigan Business Review, Vol. 28, No. 1 (January 1976), pp. 16-21. Reprinted with permission.

3. The market is composed of different segments, each with its own needs and wants.
4. The profit motive brings forth new goods and services.
5. The standard of living of an individual is uniquely determined according to the satisfaction of his needs and wants.

MARKETING IN A TRADITIONAL SOCIALIST ECONOMY

Marketing has a completely different starting point under traditional socialism. The teachings of Marx, Engels, and Lenin offer some insight into the role of marketing. Their views seem to be in direct contrast with the five fundamentals of western marketing:

1. Supply creates its own demand (Say's Law).
2. Only goods have labor content value: services and other marketing activities add nothing (Labor Theory of Value).
3. Consumer communes are viewed as uniform.
4. The output of society is distributed to its members not in relation to productivity, but according to needs.
5. The standard of living is determined and administered centrally.

The goals of the socialist economy are implemented through central planning. When particular problems manifested themselves under a rigidly-conceived central plan, the resulting dissatisfaction led to many of the marketing changes discussed in this paper.

DEVELOPMENTS IN THE SOCIALIST SYSTEM

In 1930, the GOSPLAN (the central planning agency in the Soviet Union) dealt with but a few hundred products. By the early 1950s, this number had risen to about 10,000 with at least 5,000 listed in detail in the annual plan. Needless to say, the planning process had become very complex and difficult to manage centrally.

A form of regional decentralization was attempted by Kruschev in 1956. However, that solution was not satisfactory and was abandoned eight years later. During this time, the USSR had arrived at the stage where consumers were becoming restless about their nonparticipation in the productive benefits of their economy. Some attention had to be paid to producing a variety of consumer goods. But what goods to produce?

With the "luxury" of discretionary consumer income, inventories of undesirable goods began to accumulate. Thus, some attention had to be paid to the requirements of the market. Prices could not be used to clear surpluses because they were based on labor content. Yet, the emergence of shortages and black market prices of scarce, desirable goods, and the simultaneous emergence of excess inventories of other goods, clearly indicated that prices should reflect both production costs and consumer preferences. The need to estimate carefully the consumer demand in those fields which were deemed socially acceptable became an important aspect of production planning.

State trading companies became more insistent that manufacturers' obligations not end when goods were delivered to the trading company. The insistence surfaced in the emergence of contractual agreements with the productive enterprises, including, in the case of dissatisfaction, contractual penalties to be assessed against the manufacturers. In other words, the responsibilities of the manufacturer were expanded from meeting production quotas to the level of sales and sometimes beyond.

The need for adaptive behavior at the manufacturing level became clear. These enterprises had to respond rapidly to changes in the marketplace to correct flaws in the plan — more rapidly than was possible under central planning.

Growing foreign trade also created problems in planning. With increased trade among the socialist countries and between East and West, prices could no longer reflect the labor costs in one country; they had to be comparable to trading block or world prices. For this reason, emphasis on internal cost reduction began to surface. To this point, there had been little incentive at the enterprise level for cost reduction, since this would only result in price reduction, not volume sales increases. Now, lower costs were the only means of obtaining foreign contract sales. All these factors underscored the need to decentralize some of the decision-making to the manufacturing level.

THE NEW MECHANISM

A new rationale was adopted between 1965 and 1970 by all socialist countries: profitability was the new yardstick of enterprise efficiency. Under this yardstick, the central plans could be more aggregated and operate through regulatory means. Individual enterprises would be able to determine how they wished to operate within centrally-defined "socially desirable" constraints. Enterprise efficiency could be measured by profits. "Profit" calculations under the socialist system do not include rents for capital, productive resources or land, nor does depreciation form any part of productive costs.

The main change under the new mechanism was the end of detailed planning by the central agency and, in its place came more detailed, locally-determined planning. The overall control of the economy remained with the central planning agency.

CENTRAL CONTROL

Socialist central planners create a five-year plan, a one-year plan, and a fifteen-year plan. Among these, the five-year plan is the most important and goes into the greatest amount of detail. The one-year plan interprets the goals of the five-year plan for the current year, while the fifteen-year plan guarantees that inter- and intra-sectoral growth takes place at a balanced rate.

The plans provide for the regulation of individual enterprises through four specific means:

1. Direct means. Since the replacement of plant and equipment is not provided through depreciation, the enterprise must continually seek ministerial approval. Accordingly, the central agency has a strong direct impact on what equipment the enterprise will receive and the research and development it is able to undertake.
2. Indirect means. The central authority, operating through several different agencies, can control both the amount of credit available to a specific enterprise and the amounts of rent and taxes it must pay.
3. Indirect administrative means. Regulation may also be effected through administrative controls. For example, a firm may or may not be licensed to carry on international trade. At a lower level of regulation, a firm may be denied a building permit to carry on required expansion.
4. Direct administrative means. Controls can also be exercised through direct administrative orders. The central agency, acting as the owner of the enterprise, gives specific instructions which are binding on the directors of the enterprise.

The planning agency further affects the ability of individual enterprises to maneuver by controlling such figures as rate of growth, the rate of consumption relative to the rate of growth of the economy, the rate of accumulation (savings) and the productive/nonproductive sector ratio.

Additionally, various incentive schemes have significant impact on the activities of an enterprise. Among these are direct payments, tax rebates, subsidies, and differential rates of profit retention.

Within these centrally determined regulations and in the specific area where an enterprise is permitted to function, the enterprise has some leeway to increase its productive efficiency and hence its profitability. In its attempt to operate efficiently, the enterprise may make use of marketing tools.

MARKETING RESEARCH

It should not be surprising that marketing research plays a large role in a socialist economy. Under planning, the need for marketing research is vital. It is carried out by large national institutions. These agencies service the planning board, the ministries, manufacturing enterprises, and, to an increasing extent, foreign marketers.

The research institutes specialize in forecasting demand for specific goods and in obtaining data for and working with econometric models. Attitude research and various behavioral research is much less important.

The number of studies conducted as well as the sample sizes of specific studies can be quite large. In Hungary, for example, the National Institute of Marketing Research operates six panels of 3,000 families each, with questionnaires mailed every two or three months and with 90 percent cooperation rates. The statistics descriptive of this panel operation are sufficient to cause envy to western marketing researchers.

There are some interesting ways in which marketing research is used in a socialist country. First, the information obtained from consumers may be used in normative as well as descriptive ways. For instance, if it is determined from a consumer panel that a specific family's income has reached the proper level and if, from its inventory of durable goods, it is evident that this family could use, say, a TV set, then the planning authority might decide to build them a television set. The authority would organize TV production in such a way that the family could obtain a TV. Even if that particular family wanted a washing machine more than a TV (provided that washing machines are not manufactured in sufficient quantities), it becomes difficult for the family to obtain one. Therefore, it is quite likely that the TV purchase planned for the family becomes a real purchase by the family.

Marketing research is especially important in a socialist country because the system is less flexible in adapting to wrong market estimates. If, in fact, a plan has been drawn which required the manufacture of a specific number of frying pans, the system is not sufficiently sensitive that frying pan production could be halted prior to the fulfillment of the plan. Accordingly, the cost of a wrong decision is high and the amount of shortages or excess inventory is significant when the research is wrong.

THE PRODUCT

The type of production is regulated by the central planning authority. For example, it was determined that the economic production level of automobiles in Hungary is somewhere between 200,000 and 300,000 units per year. Simultaneously, it was determined that the demand for automobiles in Hungary is somewhere between 20,000 and 30,000 units. Accordingly, Hungary could not economically justify its own automobile production. Rather than build its own automobiles, Hungary has entered into reciprocal agreements with its trading partners whereby Hungary supplies many of the other countries from its large bus factory and in turn buys its autos from the other countries. Similar examples can be found in other areas of production. Each country will attempt to specialize in types of production where it has an advantage and avoid other specific areas.

When demand manifests itself there is no guarantee that demand will be satisfied. A product may emerge to satisfy the demand or certain acts may be taken to temper the demand. For example, there may be a promotional campaign to show that that particular good is not "socially acceptable."

Since products tend to be generic as opposed to branded, lack of competition keeps the level of product quality quite low. There are, however, recognizable differences among products depending on what factory produced them. There seems to be a form of brand competition among products based not on brands, but on the factory of origin.

Service associated with products is also low, especially at the distribution stage. Long lines seem to be the accepted mode of acquiring goods in socialist countries. While there has been some improvement in services they are still far from acceptable to a Westerner.

Products from the West have had a strong impact on product quality in socialist countries. They are freely available in some of the socialist countries and certainly can be seen in all socialist countries. While they are beyond the purchasing ability of most of the population, they do influence their expectations and aspirations. Thus, western goods create strong pressure for improvement of socialist goods.

There are, however, important factors in socialist countries that prevent the emergence of new products. First, it is not clear that an enterprise could charge a higher price for a superior good. If superiority means higher costs but not higher prices, it is evident that an enterprise would not wish to move in this direction. Second, a new product might require changes in the production line. Since managers have learned how to live with their existing production lines and to make a "reasonable profit" with them, they are reluctant to make changes which leave them open to a reassessment of costs by the ministry. If that reassessment is less favorable, they will have a more difficult time earning profits.

PRICING

Initially, prices represented the labor content value and were strictly determined by the central authority. Recently, however, prices are determined on the basis of both costs and social desirability. Socially desirable products, such as drugs, cultural activities, community services, transportation, and housing, are highly subsidized in order to maintain a low price. Others, such as alcohol, tobacco, luxury goods, and jewelry, are deemed socially undesirable and are heavily taxed. In addition to direct taxation, goods also bear a "circulation tax" which is differentiated from product to product. In Hungary, for example, the circulation tax on sugar is 2 percent, on wine 20 percent, and on beer 30 percent. Heating fuels carry a negative circulation tax (i.e. they are heavily subsidized).

If the government fixes prices, it should also insure that the goods are available. It is in this area that the central planners have generally failed. For example, housing is one of the socially desirable goods as defined by the government. It is heavily subsidized and rental prices run as low as $15 per month for an apartment. Nevertheless, people are willing to pay up to $40,000 to purchase a condominium apartment.

How can this phenomenon be explained? The answer is found in the lack of availability of adequate housing in the rental market. Incidentally, one of the reasons governments have permitted the appearance of condominium housing in the socialist countries (which, after all, is private ownership) is that housing prices deviate greatly from building costs. While it was a principle of government that prices on housing should remain low, government could not afford to make additional housing available at these prices. Hence the condominium.

Some countries are experimenting with fully floating prices or with prices that can move within a predetermined range. For example, in Czechoslovakia about 6 percent of commodities have market-determined prices, while in Hungary the figure is 23 percent and in Yugoslavia, 50 percent.

With controlled prices, the profit potential varies widely from industry to industry. Accordingly, the use of profit as a yardstick of industrial performance is open to major difficulties, many of which have yet to be faced by socialist countries. Most of these manifest themselves in capital-intensive industries such as the generation of energy.

Of all the differences between the two systems, price determination is probably the one which characterizes most clearly the fundamental differences in philosophy.

PROMOTION

The level of advertising, point-of-sale effort, and packaging quality is far below that in the western countries. The role of promotion is seen to be educative or informational, not to create competition among nonexistent brands.

Promotion is a seriously underutilized tool in socialist countries. With a generic good like linen, for example, Argunov (1966) reports an interesting experiment in the Soviet Union. Through special promotional techniques including displays, TV advertising, fashion shows, and persuasive advice, the sales of a product during a two-week test period were increased by a factor of 10. Accordingly, it is not unlikely that promotion will play a much greater role in the socialist marketing systems of the future.

Promotion can also be used in the socialist system to harmonize the purchasing patterns of consumers with the "social rationality" of the planners. Instead of producing a good that is in demand, advertising can be used to diminish the demand for the product. If advertising can increase the desirability of a product it can also decrease its desirability. We are just beginning to attempt this in the West, as exemplified by the campaigns against cigarette smoking. When the central agency has virtually unlimited funds, it can sponsor negative advertising as part of its quest to achieve its goal.

Personal selling, as can be expected, is at a low level of development, especially in the industrial area. There are simultaneously few sellers and few buyers. Much of the production of an enterprise is committed, sometimes by plan, for significant periods in advance.

DISTRIBUTION

The distribution system in socialist countries is surprisingly ineffective. "Surprisingly" because there is great potential for organizing socialist distribution systems efficiently. Since all distribution channels are owned by the same agency, many of the optimizing models employed to some extent in the West could have greater impact in socialist countries. For the time being, however, queues, out-of-stock products, and over-stock inventories are common. So are inefficiencies in regional distribution.

Outside the USSR, experiments are being undertaken with privately-owned small retail stores. These can be usually easily identified due to their neatness, cleanliness, longer hours of operation, and generally better service atmosphere.

THE FUTURE OF MARKETING IN THE SOCIALIST COUNTRIES

From the foregoing it can be seen that there has been considerable closure between the marketing systems of the free enterprise countries and the socialist countries. Some of that closure may have come from the free enterprise system moving closer to the socialist system. A good example would be price controls on fuels during the energy crisis. While the technologies of marketing in both systems are moving closer together, it may be misleading to predict that the socialist countries will become more capitalistic through the introduction of the profit motive. Certainly their major differences remain.

It is important to bear in mind that the point of departure for the two systems is totally different. First, while the free enterprise system has concerned itself with developing a sufficient market to clear the goods it is capable of producing, the socialist system still is attempting to continue to increase its productive capability. Hence one system is market-oriented, while the other is still production-oriented. Second, the emphasis in the free enterprise system is on the individual while the socialist system tends to focus on the social aggregate. Third, the goals of individuals are self-determined in the free enterprise system, while they are centrally determined in the socialist system according to "socially acceptable" criteria. Fourth, the free enterprise system is far more responsive to market needs than a centrally planned system.

The socialists are trying to harmonize a philosophy of what is socially desirable with the satisfaction of demand from the market-place. In the free enterprise system, the primary focus has been on responding to those demands from the marketplace. This has caused some problems in the social arena. Many of the problems discussed in the West, such as the use of disposable containers, develop from the fact that the system is market responsive without recognizing the consequences of delivering what may be socially undesirable.

REFERENCE

Argunov, M., "What advertising does," Journal of Advertising Research (December 1966), pp. 2-3.

FURTHER READING – PART THREE

Aikin, Olga, "How the law is tying up the marketer," Marketing (May 1978), pp. 59-62.

Behrman, Jack N.; Boddewyn, Jean J.; and Kapoor, Ashok, International Business - Government Communication (Lexington, Mass.: D.C. Heath, 1975).

Coleman, Kenneth M. and Davis, Charles L., "The structural context of politics and dimensions of regime performance: Their importance for comparative study of political efficacy," Comparative Political Studies (July 1976), pp. 189-206.

Huszagh, Sandra McRae, "Reducing legal risks to marketing in multiple country operations," Columbia Journal of World Business, Vol. XIII, No. 1 (Spring 1978), pp. 50-8.

Litvak, Isaiah A. and Maule, Christopher J., "Anti-corporate propaganda and the multinational enterprise," Management International Review, Vol. 17, No. 4 (1977), pp. 9-19.

Rummel, R.J. and Heenan, David A., "How multinationals analyze political risk," Harvard Business Review, Vol. 56 (January-February 1978), pp. 67 ff.

Schöllhammer, Hans, "Ethics in an international business context," Management International Review, Vol. 17, No. 2 (1977), pp. 23-33.

Simonetti, Jack L. and Simonetti, Frank L., "When in Rome, do as the Romans do?" Management International Review, Vol. 18, No. 3 (1978), pp. 69-74.

U.S. Department of Justice, Antitrust Guide for International Operations (Washington, D.C.: U.S. Government Printing Office, 1977).

Zeira, Yoram, "Ethnocentrism in host-country organizations," Business Horizons, Vol. 22, No. 3 (June 1979), pp. 66-75.

IV

Market Structure: Demand Analysis and Market Resource Base

Introduction to Part IV

The attention in Part Four is on structural market factors. The thrust is first on demand analysis – the most critical aspect of market intelligence – and second on other elements of the local market environment that is broadly termed the "market resource base." It includes the existence of distribution channels, the availability and accessibility of promotional media, marketing research agencies, and other facilitating aspects.

Of most immediate concern to formulating international marketing strategy is the size and nature of markets generally and market segments particularly so that the firm can fully benefit from its differential advantage. The aim is to strategically match, as well as possible, the company's manpower, capital, and technical resources on the one hand to the foreign market requirements on the other. Segmentation analysis in international markets has received relatively scant attention compared to domestic marketing. Reading 15, by Thorelli, examines similarities and differences in multinational consumer market segments. Based on research in Europe and the United States with co-editor Becker and Jack Engledow, the reading develops a profile of cosmopolitan, elite consumers, called the Information Seekers (IS), whose common attitudes and consumption patterns often supersede national differences found among average consumers. The IS tend to be a lot more information-sensitive than the average and apparently represent a powerful influence in the international marketplace. They are found in increasing numbers in industrially advanced countries, raising the interesting proposition that cross-cultural similarities between certain market segments in different countries may outweigh in importance differences between segments in the same local markets. Several strategic implications for the MNC's marketing strategy are discussed.

Reading 16, by Kanter, demonstrates that cross-cultural influences on local consumer values and lifestyles are a two-way flow. As

Europeans were prone to adopt American consumption patterns, particularly during the reconstruction years after World War II, Americans are now reversing the trend. As the standards of living on the two continents have more or less achieved comparable levels, Americans, as Kanter notes, are more ready than ever to accept European values, attitudes, and products. Marketing implications for the MNC would seem obvious. Buying patterns and patterns of symbolic significance among consumer groups in industrially advanced countries are likely to acquire a greater degree of cross-cultural similarity, gradually even beyond that of the IS segment, in the future.

Once countries and market segments in them have been identified and matched to the company's capabilities analytically, they must be assessed quantitatively. Reading 17, by Moyer, introduces some rigorous techniques of market analysis that are useful in estimating demand on the industry, company, and product levels. The article is included in this collection as an example from a large body of writings on the use of quantitative methods in marketing research and analysis. As Moyer indicates, one of the limitations on the <u>international</u> application of such techniques is the limited availability, reliability, and comparability of data in many countries. In the LDCs especially <u>caveat emptor</u> is the rule of prudence in the use of the local data base.

Reading 18, by Mayer, exposes some of the methodological problems that arise in multinational marketing research. These stem from cross-cultural diversity found in different countries, such as in language, education, attitudes, and values. The article contains many real-life examples which could prove invaluable in helping to avoid the kinds of calamities likely to encounter the international market researcher failing to adapt methods to the local market environment and consumer characteristics. As Mayer rightly points out, this involves an imaginative adaptation rather than blind duplication of methods across national, cultural borders.

Reading 19, by Wells, analyzes the "migrations" of industrial and consumer products. The thesis is that a new product typically emerges in the U.S.A. or in some other industrially advanced country. As the product reaches the rapid growth phase of its life cycle in the country of origin, exports begin to build up to country B. Eventually demand abroad is sufficient to justify local production in country B. In a third phase facilities in the country of origin and in country B compete in export marketing into country C. In a final phase, plant facilities in country B or C — prevailing on lower labor costs or other differential advantage — are ready to export back to the country of origin, that is, the international product life cycle is complete. The theme is familiar — as are several variations on it. The strategic implication is that it requires marketers to plan with the international product life cycle in mind. This is desirable both to capitalize on natural opportunities and to predict and forestall competitive inroads.

Though Wells wrote the article some dozen years ago, his premises are as valid today as they were then. A modification may be added, however, in that the international product life cycle today is just as likely (sometimes more likely) to originate in a country <u>other than the</u> <u>U.S.A.</u>, which Wells then assumed to be the principal starter of new product life cycles. Indeed, the U.S.A. may end up as the ultimate net exporter in the final phase of the cycle if the dollar continues losing ground vis-à-vis other major currencies, rendering American labor once again more attractive and competitive in world markets. The latter-day "invasion" of the U.S.A. by German and Japanese companies, establishing a manufacturing foothold in diverse industries ranging from automobiles to consumer electronics, from chemicals to machinery, may well be indicative of such a development.

Reading 20, by Thorelli, draws attention to the unique pool of over 2,000 strategic marketing planning experiences in the PIMS program of the 200-plus company members of the Strategic Planning Institute. The note includes a listing of several data banks of value in strategic planning in international marketing.

15 The Information Seekers: Multinational Strategy Target *
Hans B. Thorelli

INTERNATIONAL MARKET SEGMENTATION – A CHALLENGE

No one can be everything to everybody. This is true even of General Motors. Whether by design or accident, every seller is confined to a part of a broader market (served market vs. potential). When the concentration to a certain sector or sectors is part of a strategic plan we shall call it market segmentation. A viable market segmentation strategy is based on at least four assumptions: the segment is readily identifiable; it calls for a different marketing strategy than the market as a whole; it is large enough to provide a profitable opportunity, alone or with another segment; it can be reached in an economical manner.

Segmentation is practiced in both industrial and consumer markets, but here the attention is confined to end consumers. Segmentation may be based on geographic, demographic, or psychographic variables, or typically, some combination of them such as career-oriented young women in U.S. metro areas.

A key issue in international business is whether to use a strategy of homogenization (standardization) or heterogenization (adaptation, differentiation) when expanding to another country. Clearly standardization is attractive by offering economies of scale in production, marketing, and management time. Homogenization calls for similarity in values and demographics. This is readily achieved in the case of a low-unit-price good catering to a universal drive. The classic example is Coca-Cola. The more expensive, complex, or status-oriented the product, the less likely it is that a unified strategy will reach the mass market in widely different cultures. In these cases management may be faced with a tradeoff situation between possible cost savings in reaching a limited new clientele with the standard strategy and possible cost increases in reaching a broader new market with an adaptation

*Reprinted from California Management Review, Vol. 1980-81.

strategy. The equation is complicated by the fact that it is sometimes feasible – though never costless – to convert local tastes by the strategy of a change agent.

Our research has established an important way in which consumers may be segmented across national borders in the industrialized countries of the West: the search behavior of consumers. It turns out that the Information Seekers of these countries constitute a truly cosmopolitan market, while the average consumers are the prime exponents of variation in local culture. The use of search behavior as a basis of market segmentation strategy is essentially a new concept.

CONSUMER INFORMATION GAP AND THE INFORMATION SEEKERS

In most consumer markets a gap exists between the product information readily available and the data needed not just by the perfectly savvy economic man of classical economics but even by ordinary mortals bent on semi-rational purchasing. Somewhat paradoxically, the prime reason for the consumer information gap is the very richness of our markets, with product and brand proliferation, increasing complexity of the average product, and rapid change. Too, nonmetro areas, due to the narrow selections of local stores, are removed from much of this richness, as much information is lost when the actual product is not at hand. Mass production calls for mass distribution and mass communication, resulting in the growing depersonalization of individual transactions. In addition, commercial information is sometimes misleading. At the same time consumer expectations regarding product performance seem to grow exponentially with the level of affluence. No doubt, a yawning consumer information gap is there – and it is growing.

The average consumer (AC) copes with the gap by adopting an essentially passive strategy: he makes a fairly superficial search limited to the most readily available alternatives. Many AC do indeed perceive themselves as well-informed buyers, while others are aware that continued search might well have resulted in a better buy. They are not willing, however, to spend the time and nervous energy required – or make that sacrifice in the face of the risk that they might not find a better buy after all. Typically, students tend to buy gas and snack foods from outlets closest to campus, often those that charge the highest prices in town.

By contrast, a small but influential group of consumers do their best to bridge the CI gap. These Information Seekers (IS) are distinct from the majority of AC in at least five important respects pertaining to search:

1. IS are more conscious about information than AC. IS will rank availability of information as a much more important buying criterion (next to performance, price, etc.) than will AC.
2. IS are knowledgeable about more information sources than AC.
3. IS consult a greater diversity of information sources than AC.

4. IS consult more systematic and complex sources of information (such as Consumer Reports) than AC.
5. IS make use of a broader range of media, especially with regard to printed matter in various forms.

The IS we have in mind is a generalist, that is, he is interested in in-depth information about a broad range of products. Frequently he wants to know about new products or models even though not contemplating immediate purchase. Demographically, he (or she) tends to be highly educated, have a professional or managerial job, be in the middle or upper middle income group, and 25-45 years of age. There are as yet no hard data as to the size of this segment. We estimate that it comprises 5 to 20 percent of the adult consumer population in the industrial countries. Southern European countries tend to be at the lower end of the range, France, Switzerland, and Austria in the middle, Benelux, Britain, and Germany in a higher tier, and the Scandinavians at the upper end of the range. Canada and the United States are probably in between Scandinavia and Britain-Germany.

The IS group may seem to be a modest one, although their number is in the millions in all larger Western nations. Three major factors lend additional interest to information-seeking as a basis for market segmentation strategy. First, the number of IS is growing in all these countries as the level of education in general (and consumer education in particular) keeps rising, accompanied by greater affluence. Second, it turns out that a great many AC engage in intense information search for a single good (in the U.S. most often autos) or a narrow set of products of special interest to them. When acting in this capacity AC may be labeled Specialty Searchers. Taking the IS and Specialty Searchers together one might speculate that the population of information-conscious is twice as great among camera buyers as among vacuum cleaner buyers, and that even among the latter there is a Specialty Searcher for every IS.

The third factor may well be the most important. It appears that the IS play a role in the marketplace much greater than their numbers (and income) would indicate. At least they perceive themselves as opinion leaders, frequently asked for advice by their AC friends. (The IS are not always early adopters, however, preferring to have reliable information before they plunge.) As opinion leaders they seem in some ways to be acting as proxy purchasing agents for many AC with whom they may never even have been in personal contact. While we do not have data permitting us to isolate the Specialty Searchers it seems plausible that in the markets of special interest to them they act much like the IS do in general.

Before a marketer takes off in hot pursuit of the IS he should be reminded that these consumer professionals are also the vigilantes of the marketplace. They have high expectations and they have the clout and mind to give vent to dissatisfaction. Data demonstrate that they complain a lot more often than AC about shoddy or defective merchandise, misleading advertising, out-of-stock conditions, and any other shortcomings they encounter. More than others, IS take on the often thankless task of blowing the whistle, of filing a complaint, of battling public and private bureaucracy in the perennial struggle to ensure consumer sovereignty.

GERMAN AND AMERICAN CONSUMERS: COMPARATIVE RESEARCH

Before discussing the strategic implications of the IS (and AC) segments for multinational corporations we shall briefly touch on the research on German and American consumers, in which the existence of the cosmopolitan IS group was discovered. The research is reported in agonizing detail elsewhere (Thorelli, Becker, and Engledow, 1975).

The researcher needs tighter and less ambiguous definitions than the marketing practitioner is perforce willing to live with. We defined IS operationally as subscribers to consumer product testing magazines, i.e., Consumer Reports in the U.S. and test and DM in Germany. Operational definitions provide a practical and unambiguous vehicle for research, but rarely correspond on a one-to-one basis with the underlying concept under study. Clearly, one can be an IS as previously defined without being a test magazine subscriber. (There are many other information sources one may borrow; a test magazine copy from the library or a friend.) One may also be a subscriber without being an IS. (The subscription was an unwelcome Christmas gift from my mother-in-law.) Figure 15.1 schematically shows the relationship between subscribers and IS, and how these groups fit into the social structure. The figure makes no pretense of being drawn to scale. Our data show that the vast majority of subscribers are indeed IS — the three "spillover" triangles are small. About 2.5 percent of U.S. households are subscribers to Consumer Reports, and it may well be that as many as 7 to 9 percent of the adult consumer population read it. This is just over one half of our gross estimate of the number of IS in the country.

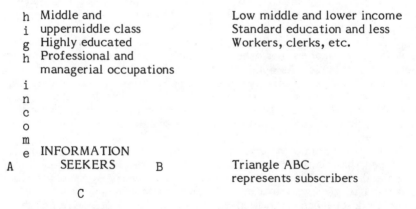

h   Middle and   Low middle and lower income
i   uppermiddle class   Standard education and less
g   Highly educated   Workers, clerks, etc.
h   Professional and
    managerial occupations

i

n

c

o

m

e   INFORMATION
A   SEEKERS   B   Triangle ABC
                                    represents subscribers

         C

Average consumers (AC) constitute the majority of all income and social groups

Fig. 15.1. The information seekers, average consumers and test journal subscribers: demographic characteristics.

Our study used large representative interview samples of subscribers in metropolitan areas in both countries, supplemented for control purposes with national mail subscriber samples. A methodological finesse is worth recounting: our colleague Jack Engledow added another interview sample of nonsubscribers matching the subscribers on demographic variables as well as location and type of dwelling. Not unexpectedly, the great majority of this matched sample were in the AC group.

A general overview of hundreds of detailed findings is presented in Figure 15.2. The figure reflects the basic research carried out in 1970. A selective update in 1976 showed nearly identical results regarding demographics and media use as well as self-perceived planfulness and opinion leadership. There was some change in other attitudes, reflecting the decline of confidence in all institutions, and notably government, business, advertising, and, to some extent, product testing agencies themselves. Interestingly, there was also some further convergence of German and American IS characteristics. The discussion below ties in with the 1970 data, which demonstrated its robustness by our research update.

Figure 15.2 actually presents two levels of comparison: between subscribers and AC in both countries separately and inter-country comparison between these two groups. To achieve this, the information in the cells directly reports on subscribers only. AC are "opposite" to IS, except in the "neutral" case, when there is no statistically significant difference between the two groups. Thus, the least interesting cell is that labeled E.

The most interesting cells are A and I, which in effect profile the cosmopolitan subscriber and, we claim, the cosmopolitan Information Seeker. We have already discussed income and social class, where the IS (as represented by subscribers) tend to be members of the occupational elite. In both cultures over 40 percent of IS were college graduates (as opposed to 11 percent of the total population in the U.S. and 5 percent in Germany), and less than 7 percent had completed grade school only (as opposed to 28 percent of all Americans and 32 percent of all Germans). Little wonder that we find major differences between IS and AC in media use. IS are multi-media types, while AC are lookers and listeners. Though IS indeed do some TV viewing and radio listening, their focus is on reading. It comes as no surprise that IS rank high on ownership of consumer durables; that in itself adds to their store of consumer information.

In the attitude area, we already know that IS consider themselves as planful and opinion-leading consumers. Perhaps surprising to some, a greater proportion of them than of AC have an overall favorable opinion of business as an institution. This does not stop them, however, from being more critical than AC of a variety of specific business practices. IS in both countries wanted more government activity in the consumer affairs area – notably with respect to consumer information and education.

American Comparisons
Subscribers vs. Average Consumers

	Subscribers High	Neutral[a]	Subscribers Low
German Comparisons Subscribers vs. Average Consumers **Subscribers High**	A. Universal "Highs" Demographics: Income Education Social Class Attitudes: Planfulness Business Opinion Leader Newspaper and Magazine Readership Shopping Concern: Available Information Information Source: Product Testing Consumer Activity by Government Ownership of Selected Durables	B. German High-American Neutral Demographic: Age Information Source: Other newspaper or magazine Shopping Concern: Styling	C. German High-American Low Attitude: Increased Government Control of Business Satisfaction Measures: All, including satisfaction with product and shopping activity and available information
Neutral[a]	D. American High-German Neutral Attitude: General Liberalism Shopping Concern: Brand Reputation Increased Consumerist Activities	E. No Significant Difference From Average Consumer Most other variables not listed elsewhere fell into this category.	F. American Low-German Neutral Attitudes: Advertising Student Power Shopping Concerns: Product Availability Economy of Operation Credit Information Source: Personal Observation
Subscribers Low	G. American High-German None	H. German Low-American Neutral Attitude: Welfare	I. Universal "Lows" Television Viewing Radio Listening

[a]No significant difference between Subscribers and Average Consumers

Fig. 15.2. Within and between country comparisons of subscribers (IS) and average consumers (AC) in Germany and the United States.

138

We now come to some relatively modest differences between IS in Germany and the United States, as indicated by cells B, D, F, and H. In these cases IS in one of the countries differed strongly from the local AC while there was no significant difference between IS and AC in the other nation. German IS were significantly older than local AC, and they quoted nontest magazines and newspapers as an information source in their latest purchase of a major durable good more often than did AC, while this difference was not observed in the U.S. Relatively minor differences were also found in shopping concerns (buying criteria) in the latest purchase of a major durable good. Relative to local AC, German IS were more concerned with styling than American, while the latter were relatively more concerned with brand reputation than the former. Among the dozen buying criteria respondents were asked to rank in importance, American IS ranked immediate availability of the product in the store, economy of operation, and availability of credit significantly lower than local AC. Apart from the strong concern for availability of information both American and German IS ranked performance and durability high as buying criteria across the broad range of durables covered by the survey. Although the IS-AC difference as regards these two criteria was not statistically significant, there is some reason to believe IS are better judges of these characteristics than fellow consumers.

American IS were significantly more critical of advertising than AC, while, as shown by cell F, there was no such difference between German IS and AC. However, German attitudes toward advertising were uniformly lower than American. Thus IS in the two countries were actually much closer together in their views than American and German AC.

In only two areas did German and American IS have opposite views when compared to AC in the respective countries. German IS were more in favor of increased government control of business than German AC, while in the U.S. these views were reversed. It would carry us too far to philosophize about the underlying reasons for this discrepancy. More immediately relevant here is the fact that while American IS were less positive in all areas of consumer satisfaction – with the product itself, with the shopping experience, with overall availability of information in the marketplace – than American AC, German IS were more satisfied on all scores than the local AC. We do not believe that these differences are due to better products, distribution, or information in Germany, but rather to a longer legacy of affluence and consumerism in the United States. There is reason to believe the German IS will move closer to the American: our observation from consumer research in some 20 nations around the world is that expectations among consumer sophisticates are highly correlated with affluence. Thus it is that the most affluent countries also have the strongest consumerist movements.

As the research summarized here represents somewhat of a new departure, a number of the findings must be regarded as tentative. In many specifics, however, our results are corroborated by researchers in

Britain, Holland, Belgium, France, Norway, Sweden, and Canada. We are quite confident that a sizeable segment of IS exists in the industrialized nations of the West, and that it is cosmopolitan in the sense that in demographics, media use, and, in some respects, even in style of life the IS in one of these countries are more like IS in other countries than they are like average consumers in their "home" country.

STRATEGIC IMPLICATIONS FOR THE MNC

There are a number of strategic guideposts for the multinational corporation bent on catering to the cosmopolitan IS and deriving the economic benefits of a homogeneous market strategy throughout the industrialized West.

1. Communications. The key role in singling out and reaching a market segment is played by communications. Being voracious users of personal and commercial as well as independent media, the IS can easily be reached in the same manner as consumers in general. However, the IS may be reached more cheaply and more effectively by special tailoring of both media and message. IS read a lot more than AC. Many highbrow periodicals have heavy IS readership. Magazines of general consumer interest, such as Good Housekeeping in the U.S., Britain, and Canada reach many AC as well as IS. A number of auto and hobby magazines will have a concentration of IS as well as Specialty Searchers. Most product testing magazines will not accept advertising. The way to impress readers of Consumer Reports and corresponding publications abroad is to have products good enough to come up with consistently favorable ratings.

Superior information will be an important business strategy in the future as a means of gaining differential advantage in the marketplace. The IS much more than AC are interested in "hard" rather than "soft" information, in fact rather than fancy (though not constitutionally averse to subjective appeals), and in multi-faceted, systematic information rather than simplistic approaches. Point-of-purchase information in the form of labels, educational brochures, and sensible owner's manuals (made available before the transaction) are good illustrations. Comparative ads covering an array of product characteristics, including some where the advertiser's rank is not outstanding, is another.

2. Product mix. IS indicate a concern for what may be termed "quiet quality," as reflected in such product characteristics as performance and durability in cars, appliances, and other durables. It is difficult to generalize beyond this point. As noted, German IS were relatively more interested in styling than American, while the latter were more concerned with brand reputation (possibly as a proxy for incomplete information) than the former. There is, indeed, no reason to assume that IS should have homogeneous preferences regarding all characteristics of all products – even inside any given country. Speaking generally, it seems clear that IS more than AC everywhere are concerned with getting "value for money," but, of course, value in some respects is a subjective matter.

Though the IS often are not in the group of early adopters, they follow hard on its heels. For this reason, and because they tend to be pace-setters, it is advisable to reach them early on in the product life cycle.

3. Pricing. Price is no isolated or dominant concern of the IS. They are bent on value, whether the car they are looking for is a Cadillac or a Chevette. Although many IS take stock in brand reputation, most IS are too savvy to accept blindly the easy decision rule that "you get what you pay for" used by many AC.

4. Distribution. Although not unimportant, dealer reputation and location and immediate product availability do not rank as major buying criteria among the IS. Credit ranked last of all IS shopping concerns. But service aspects in a major purchase loom high on the list of priorities of the IS. We dare say this is why foreign automobile manufacturers have placed such an emphasis on trying to build good service networks in the United States. They may not have realized that at least until the early 1970s the IS were their prime customers, but certainly it was those IS who put the pressure on for good service and availability of parts. Best of all in international marketing, of course, is if the product can be designed in such a way as to require only a minimum of service.

IN CONCLUSION

We have seen that the cosmopolitan Information Seekers constitute a readily identifiable and reachable market segment extending across the industrialized West. Taking the cosmopolitan view, the segment is a large and affluent one, and must offer many golden business opportunities. Basically, each such opportunity may be exploited by a standard strategy (local competition, marketing infrastructure, and government regulations may call for some variation). The attractiveness of this segment is enhanced by the IS' tendency to be opinion leaders and "proxy purchasing agents" for fellow consumers. Incidentally, this fact should serve as a warning against adopting a strategy which might disappoint them.

For the foreseeable future the IS in any given country will continue to be a relatively small, though highly articulate market next to the majority of average consumers. These AC are the prime bearers of local culture and local values. The MNC interested in reaching the AC market must generally be prepared to make significant local adaptations in strategy.

On a selective basis, our discussion may be applied within any single nation as well as in international marketing. A Dutch producer aiming only at the local IS market might find it big enough at least for starters. If he wanted to expand he would have the tantalizing choice of refocusing on Dutch AC, most likely by a different communications mix, or of pursuing the IS segment in other countries. We must, however, warn against extrapolating the argument to either the communist bloc or to the less developed countries. In these cases the local market systems are sufficiently different from those of the industrialized West to make most of our propositions inoperable.

REFERENCE

Thorelli, Hans B.; Becker, Helmut; and Engledow, Jack, The Information Seekers - An international study of consumer information and advertising image (Cambridge, Mass.: Ballinger, 1975).

16 The Europeanizing of America: A Study in Changing Values*
Donald L. Kanter

INTRODUCTION

With American products, fast food franchises, and United States multinational corporations girdling the globe, one has customarily thought in terms of the Americanizing of Europe, not the opposite. Changes, however, in the external conditions in America seem to have occurred producing changes in terminal and instrumental consumer values and attitudes (Rokeach, 1973).

Interestingly enough, this rapid shift in socio-psychological outlook seems to more or less approximate a European mode in terms of behavior as well as Weltanschauung. It should not be startling to say these changes have vast implications for consumer marketing strategy (Katona, 1971).

There will be fewer retreats for Americans to former days of conspicuous consumption. External conditions – technological, psychological, environmental, and governmental – are the constraints.

For instance, government has become an anonymous, regulatory force in American life with all the depersonalization this implies. As the bureaucratic structure has mushroomed, Americans have come to question the immediacy and responsiveness of the democratic process. Recent candidates of both major political parties have campaigned on this point.

Moreover, Americans no longer perceive that they control the world, so to speak. European countries lost their colonies long ago and

*From Donald L. Kanter, "The Europeanizing of America: A study in changing values," in H. Keith Hunt (ed.), Advances in Consumer Research, Vol. V, Proceedings of the Eighth Annual Conference of the Association for Consumer Research (Ann Arbor, Mich.: Association for Consumer Research, 1978), pp. 408-10. Reprinted with permission.

felt the destruction of two world wars. It is only recently, however, that Americans have felt diminished power over world affairs, with all of the concomitant threats to security and potency this implies. Terrorism, along with diminished control, has also become part of the collective unconscious, adding to feelings of general slippage and unrest.

To add to this decline of perceived omnipotence is the realization and acceptance of finite and limited resources. It is, for example, a significant development that American oil companies have undertaken massive advertising campaigns urging consumers to conserve their product, petroleum, not to consume it. The assumptions of unlimited affluence, boundless food, fuel, and productivity, and – most important-ly – a vision of the American consumer as voracious, eager, hungry, and greedy, no longer seem accurate (Webster, 1974).

The future has arrived bringing changed aspirations and new social and sexual roles. Americans will make new attempts to cope with increasing depersonalization and anonymity brought about by over-population and bureaucracy as well as inflation and psychological dimunition. People are seeking different means of achieving equilibrium in a continuously clamorous world, bringing about different ways of consuming and evaluating goods and services.

It is in these differences – the response to a changing total environment – that the Europeanizing of America may be seen. Clearly, the analogy is imperfect; but it may be descriptive of a new values constellation. As conditions of scarcity, bureaucracy, and inflation – recurring European experiences – occur in this country, the modes of adjustment appear to become closer in substance and style.

THE CHANGES

First there is the American loss of innocence. Something very simple is meant by this loss of innocence which goes beyond Mark Twain, Edith Wharton, or Henry James. Americans never before had military and diplomatic defeats approaching the magnitude of Viet Nam. They had not recently come close to a Watergate or an international oil cartel, or known crime and violence to such an unprecedented and televised extent.

What is the significance, however, of loss of innocence to the Europeanized American? It means, among other things, that what is vulnerable and uncertain about life has been brought home to most Americans. Certain mainstream cultural assumptions lost validity in the late 60s and the life of everyday quiet desperation is not so easily tolerated among many people. People feel they cannot manipulate their destinies as much, formerly an article of faith. This contributes to feelings of anomie. Psychologists might say that the locus of control has shifted from the self to external forces (Thornhill, 1975).

America's adult generation was raised to believe that one can be virtually anything he wants to be, including President of the United

States. But Americans are moving towards a more fatalistic attitude, resembling that found in Europe ("que sera, sera"). There is a lowered expectation about the ability to manipulate one's environment. In addition, the parameters have been narrowed in regard to the invincibility of self-help. Boundless optimism in achieving traditional American goals seems inappropriate.

A related aspect of Europeanizing is the enormous growth in skepticism and cynicism. People question other people's motives more than before. The concept of the blunt, open-faced American, a guileless, Candide-like character, is not a valued aspiration. In the current environment this does not help survival.

What does this increased cynicism mean? For one thing, authority figures are suspect. A study conducted at the University of Southern California to examine reactions to public service advertisements about illegal drugs is illustrative (Kanter, 1974).

Star athletes (ostensibly reference group symbols) in effect said: "I can't do my thing if I'm high on drugs." These ads elicited disbelief in 88 percent of the grade school children tested. When questioned further, the students felt one can't play that kind of game without being high and that the revered athletes were lying.

The current American approach to skepticism and cynicism may be characterized in part as trading off. This approach recognizes that things are rarely absolute; ("What do I have to give for what I get?") People appear to have arrived at a certain shrewdness in their dealings with this realistic and cynical approach to life. "Street smarts" have become operative in our society. In a phrase, this is the ability to "aim off" – to take one's time. Don't quite reveal yourself; maintain a facade; feign ignorance. This is the time-honored peasant's protection.

Another basic characteristic of Europeanizing is the changing timeframe of Americans. No longer is immediate response a virtue. From the customary American spontaneity and rapid closure, people tend to feel that it is notoriously unsafe to enter into a situation, to make decisions without waiting for events to clarify. This is an old English technique of negotiation identified by Charles Dickens in Bleak House in the 1860s, when he spoke of "fogging the issue." In other words, conditions change, hence wait, it may even go away – if not, continue to obscure the point and postpone a decision.

But a most crucial element of this phenomenon is that people want time – almost more than things. The marketing implications of this are enormous. Time will be a reward assuming many forms – longer holidays and shorter workweeks; temporal instead of financial bonuses.

The Europeanizing of Americans is also expressed in new levels of aspiration. Not everyone wants to grow up to be President or leader. Many would prefer simply to "play the game," collect time and have fun, being cooler and less hassled. Increasingly, aspirations are not so much power oriented as time oriented: narcissism or self-absorption is the new patriotism, up to a point. This is absolutely crucial to the leisure, automotive, cosmetic, and a multitude of other businesses.

The trade-offs between risk taking and security are also changing. As corporations – including multinationals – grow, loyalty does not tend to keep pace, it is actually quite limited. People prefer to keep their options open. By "hanging loose," to use the argot, one doesn't have to commit all that much of oneself. One may try something, stay detached, then move – a shrewd "street-smart's" way of operating. Literally, take the money and run.

Also, there is a growing appreciation of natural simplicity and a European-type sensuality. Americans have come to realize the existence of basic body truths; that biological man is a very natural entity, smells and sights included.

In terms of sex, for instance, more people wallow less in guilt than in pleasure, no matter how transient or shallow. But discretion, rather than confrontation (I've sinned) is the style of coping with an extracurricular relationship because people accept that simple bodily functions are natural, not perverse.

Along with these simplicities come things like walking out, European promenading. Even in those American cities where inhabitants fear there's no place to walk safely after dark, the urge is transformed as it were into getting away; the Friday afternoon get-away is becoming a mass ritual. People are more pastoral rather than less. Camping is enjoying phenomenal growth in popularity. Clothing for the rugged outdoor life – blue jeans, hiking boots, work shirts – is high fashion.

The natural and simplistic trends have led, among other things, to a reevaluation of the foods one eats. The empty calories of junk foods are now part of the mental geography of most people, not only mothers. "Health" foods, as they were called, are now everyday fare.

Notions of quality and obsolescence have also undergone changes, re-emerging in highly European form. More and more, Americans purchase goods for reasons of durability and repairability not just for the sake of change, even if they pay more initially. Automobiles are expected to last longer; refrigerators are expected to last longer. Things are nurtured, not discarded.

This emerging mentality is an expansion of the idea that less is more. Things and their accumulation bring far fewer rewards than do accumulation of time, leisure, and freedom in being one's self.

Related to simplicity and the downplay of accumulation is a new esteem for physical fitness. Exhilaration for a bike ride or a ski slope are just as important as shopping (with all its psychic transactional satisfactions) for the odd piece of furniture. This means, among other things, new channels for dollars and opportunities to express individuality in even eccentric kinds of ways.

Europeans have lived with scarcity, limited resources, and minimal locus-of-control feelings and have developed other means for asserting their dignity and individuality. As Americans come to face limits on their positions, possessions, and power, their quest for viable modes to assert themselves becomes crucial. This phenomenon of self-assertion under new environmental conditions can impact not only the advertising and product design function. As values change in society, so must the whole marketing approach.

REFERENCES

Kanter, Donald L., The Government Anti-Drug Campaign. A paper presented to the American Psychological Association (Honolulu, September 1974).

Katona, George; Strumpel, Burkhard; and Zahn, Ernest, Aspirations and Affluence - A Comparative Study in the United States and Western Europe (New York: McGraw-Hill, 1971).

Rokeach, Milton, The Nature of Human Values (New York: Free Press, 1973).

Thornhill, Michael A., "A computerized and categorized bibliography on locus of control," Psychological Reports (April 1975), pp. 505-6.

Webster, Frederick E., Social Aspects of Marketing (New Jersey: Prentice-Hall, 1974).

17 International Market Analysis*
Reed Moyer

INTRODUCTION

International market analysis often concerns two basic tasks: (1) assessing the size of existing markets and (2) forecasting the size of future markets. Domestic market analysts also perform these jobs, but international market researchers face two handicaps that make their job more difficult. First, they must analyze many diverse markets. Each has apparently unique characteristics that make generalizing difficult. The second handicap is the paucity of reliable statistical data for many foreign markets, especially in developing economies.

Consider the first handicap. The world is divided into over 100 sovereign nations; each may be a potential market for products of international firms. Several factors – differing customs, tastes, the trade restrictions, and collection of national statistics – require the analysis of individual countries' markets. Even markets within trade blocs, e.g., the European Economic Community, are usually evaluated as individual countries rather than together as a trade group. Most of these national markets are small compared with the U.S. market. For example, Belgium's gross national product (GNP) is less than 2 percent of the U.S. total.

These small fragmented markets pose a problem. The relatively low payout in many markets permits only modest market research expenditures in each. If a firm enters many national markets, the total potential may be great; however, the market research necessary for analyzing the markets will be either superficial and reasonably priced in relation to the benefits or adequate but expensive.

---

*Slightly abbreviated from "International market analysis," Journal of Marketing Research, Vol. 5 (November 1968), pp. 353-360, with permission.

The second handicap, inadequate data, is more severe than the first, especially in markets outside of the Western European/North American region. Many factors contribute to the inadequacy of data: insufficient governmental emphasis on data collection, too few trained market research personnel, respondents' reluctance to divulge information.

Both handicaps require modified research approaches when analyzing the small fragmented markets that constitute the underdeveloped world. They put a premium on discovering economic and demographic relationships that permit demand estimation from a minimum of information. Fortunately for the researcher these relationships exist. This article will point out some of these relationships and indicate a few techniques that permit market evaluation (sometimes crudely) within the limits of available data.

The reader should realize that the analysis and techniques described here are relevant principally for researching markets in the less developed countries. For our purposes, the situation in Western Europe and other relatively advanced areas of the world (e.g., Australia, Canada, Japan) differentiates them from the underdeveloped countries in several respects. First, markets in most of the developed areas are large enough to warrant more refined research techniques than those suggested here. The payout will usually be great enough to justify the kind of detailed research conducted by American firms in their country. Thus, a U.S. tire manufacturer studying the feasibility of establishing a plant in West Germany might use research techniques and methods of analysis similar to those he would use in the U.S. Second – and related to the first – most of the economically advanced countries generate relevant industry statistics on which to base an adequate market research effort. Therefore, the need to resort to the crude measures suggested here is diminished in these countries. It is principally in those countries with nonexistent or unreliable data and with payouts too small to warrant a large research expenditure that I recommend the techniques and analysis described in the following sections.

The reader should also invest the quantitative measures described here with less than divine authority. Quantifying relationships may be a useful exercise, but they often mask overriding qualitative factors that outweigh the numerical relations. This is especially true when macro techniques are used to analyze micro markets.

DEMAND PATTERNS

First we need to learn the industrial growth patterns for representative countries of the world to gain insight into consumption patterns, our principal concern. Knowing trends in manufacturing production aids market demand analysis in several ways. First, besides inventory changes and net imports or exports, goods produced are goods consumed. Thus production patterns generally reveal consumption patterns, and knowing them helps exporters to assess market opportunities (after adjustments for exports, imports, and changes in inventory levels;

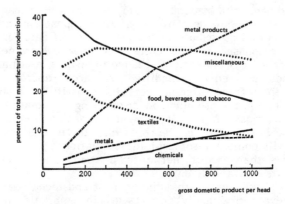

gross domestic product per head

Fig. 17.1. Typical patterns of growth in manufacturing industries (Based on a time series analysis for selected years, 1899-1957, for seven to ten countries depending on commodity; dollars at 1955 prices).

unless there are substantial fluctuations in these three items, production <u>trends</u> will mirror consumption trends even though the <u>absolute</u> levels of each may never coincide). Moreover, knowing trends in manufacturing production is useful because these industries represent potential markets for U.S. exporters of inputs, e.g. raw materials and machinery, used by industries. Finally, growing industries represent investment opportunities for U.S. firms interested in operating abroad.

The figure broadly reveals growth patterns in large industry categories. It relates the percent of total manufacturing production accounted for by major industrial groups to gross domestic product per capita. At early growth stages when per capita incomes are low, manufacturing centers on the necessities, i.e., food, beverages and textiles, and light manufacturing. As incomes grow these industries decline relatively and are replaced in importance by heavy industries.

Economic growth also creates changes in the import composition with important implications for international marketers. As industrialization proceeds, countries generally develop a predictable import pattern; however, a country's resource endowment may modify this pattern. For example, fuel-scarce economies must import increasing quantities of fuel as they industrialize. We see this occurring today in Latin America. However, much of coal-rich Western Europe and the United States launched industrialization without large fuel imports.

Table 17.1 shows the changing relative importance of imports of various commodities for countries at different industrialization levels. Industrialized countries import relatively more food products and industrial materials than manufactured goods, which are more important for the less industrialized countries. Although the percentage of total imports represented by manufacturers is lower for industrialized countries than for the semi-industrial and underdeveloped countries, the <u>dollar volume</u> of manufactured goods imported into industrialized countries far exceeds sales of these goods to poorer countries. In 1965, manufactured imports for the industrialized countries in Table 17.1 totalled $61.3 billion and for the semi-industrialized and nonindustrialized, $19.2 billion.

Table 17.1. Imports of Major Commodity Groups by Representative
Countries Classified by Stage of Industrialization, 1965[a]

Stage	Food	Fuels	Industrial materials	Manu- factures
Industrial countries[b]	19.2%	10.9%	16.1%	53.8%
Semi-industrial countries[c,e]	15.7	6.5	8.3	69.5
Non-industrial countries [d,e]	17.4	5.1	4.5	73.0

[a]Expressed as percentage of total imports.
[b]Belgium-Luxembourg, France, West Germany, Italy, Netherlands, Sweden, Norway, Switzerland, United Kingdom, United States, Canada, Japan.
[c]Australia, New Zealand, Union of South Africa, India, Pakistan, Argentina, Brazil, Chile, Colombia, Mexico, Israel, Turkey, Yugoslavia.
[d]Congo, U.A.R., French Morocco, Nigeria, Southern Rhodesia, Indonesia, Iran, Philippines, Cuba, Peru, Venezuela.
[e]For Chile 1963 data were used; for several of the non-industrialized countries 1962, 1963, or 1964 data were used.

NOTE: The classification of countries follows that used by Alfred Maizels (1963, p. 68) except that the non-industrialized countries have been restricted to a sample of 11.

Source: From Yearbook of International Trade Statistics, United Nations, 1965.

Industrial development affects imports of manufactured goods in two ways: (1) on the demand side and (2) from import substitution (Maizels, 1963, p. 63). Developing new industries increases demand for capital equipment and raw materials needed in the new production processes. Moreover, income growth leads to the substitution by consumers of relatively income-elastic goods, e.g. durables, for such income-inelastic commodities as food.

INCOME ELASTICITY MEASUREMENTS

A useful statistic, the income elasticity of demand, describes succinctly the relationship between the amount demanded (consumed) of various goods and economic progress. Symbolically,

$$\frac{\frac{\Delta Q_A}{Q_A}}{\frac{\Delta Y}{Y}}$$

measures the income elasticity of demand for Commodity A where Q represents the quantity demanded, Y is the income, and Δ refers to quantity changes. The demand for goods with values greater than one is relatively elastic. Goods with values less than one are income-inelastic. The amount demanded of commodities with values less than one rises relatively slower than changes in income levels; as income rises, the demand for goods with higher income elasticity coefficients increases relatively faster than for goods with lower values. This information aids the researcher interested in predicting growth in the demand for particular products or product classes in international markets.

Several cautions should be considered. First, although the usual income elasticity example assumes that income increases, it may also fall in which case the quantity demanded of income elastic goods would fall relatively faster than that of income inelastic products. Second, a high income elasticity coefficient does not necessarily imply high volume markets. On the contrary, greater dollar volume will probably exist in markets for necessities that are consumed in large quantities by the majority of consumers. Nonetheless, the potential for growth in demand as income increases is relatively greater for goods with high elasticity coefficients than for those with low ones. Emphasis on the relative responsiveness of demand changes to income changes cannot be overstressed. Finally, empirically derived income elasticity coefficients are probably subject to measurement errors. Therefore, they should be used only as rough indicators of the responsiveness of demand to income changes.

Table 17.2 summarizes the results of several income elasticity studies that cover both consumer and industrial products and some services and are calculated on a time series and cross section basis. Several conclusions stand out. First, necessities, such as food and clothing, tend to be income-inelastic; the demand for durable consumer goods, purchases of which are postponable and made more frequently by high income groups than by low ones, is income-elastic. Capital goods and chemicals are income-elastic, confirming the impression that these commodities are consumed by more developed (higher average income) countries. Second, different ways of computing the elasticities produce different results. Several factors contribute to this result, including errors in measurement, sampling, and drawing samples at different times.

Table 17.2. Income Elasticity Measurements

Commodity	Cross section	Time series
Food and beverages, excluding alcoholic beverages	0.54^b, 0.53^c	0.8^a
Alcoholic beverages	0.77^b	
Tobacco	0.88^b	
Clothing	0.8^a, 0.9^a 0.84, 0.89^a	0.7^a, 0.8^a
Textiles	0.5^a	0.8^a
Household and personal services	1.19^b	
Communication services	2.03^b	
Recreation	1.15^b	
Health	1.80^b	
Durable consumer goods		2.7^a
Furniture	1.61^c	
Appliances	1.40^c	
Metals	1.52^c	
Chemicals		2.1^c
Machinery and transportation equipment, except passenger cars		$1.5\text{-}2.0^a$

[a]From Kastens 1960, p. 42.

[b]From Gilbert, et al. 1958, p. 66.

[c]From author's calculations.

The income elasticity measurements may not apply equally to all income groups. Figures in Table 17.2 are averages. Another qualification of these elasticity results is that there have been no price change adjustments in the time series calculations. Prices of goods in relatively new industries, such as chemicals and transport equipment, tend to fail as the industries grow. Thus demand increases for these industries' goods result from a combination of price and income factors. This distorts their income elasticity measurements compared with the elasticities for older industries with relatively more stable prices.

Prices affect the elasticities in several other ways. Relative price differences among major consumption categories (food, clothing, services, etc.) should be greatest among countries at different growth stages than for a single country. Thus a low income country's inhabitants may buy relatively more services (having a high labor content) than clothing (relatively more capital-intensive than services) than is true for low income members of a high income country. But this substitution effect in low income countries is overpowered by the income effect, i.e., the low income country's inhabitants have insufficient disposable income to buy many services even though services are relatively cheap. This income effect may therefore result in total expenditure on services in a low income country being less than that in a high income country.

A final impact of prices on expenditure patterns is that, other things equal, the consumption of a relatively low priced good in Country A with per capita income similar to Country B's will exceed consumption in B for the same good at a higher price. The reverse holds with higher priced commodities. Thus Norway with per capita income twice as high as Italy's consumes half as many fruits and vegetables per capita as does Italy, because of different fruit and vegetable price levels in the two countries. Different excise taxes and subsidies will influence prices with consequent impact on consumption levels. Therefore the watchword in using income elasticities is "caution." They are useful guides for consumption estimation but are no substitute for careful and comprehensive demand analysis.

Another use of elasticity measurements is in calculating import substitution elasticities mentioned in the previous section. This elasticity measures the responsiveness of imports to changes in domestic variables such as income and, possibly, population. Chenery (1960) found for example that import substitution is higher in investment goods than in intermediate goods, and in consumer goods it was almost nil.

MULTIPLE FACTOR INDEXES

Those interested in international market research may borrow a technique successfully used in domestic market research, i.e., multiple factor indexes. If conditions prevent directly computing a product's market potential, using proxies to estimate demand may be a satisfactory substitute. A multiple factor index measures potential by indirection, using as proxies variables that intuition or statistical analysis reveal to be closely correlated with the potential for the product under review. (Single factor indexes, also often used, relate the potential of a commodity to the size of a single proxy variable).

In Western Europe the J.W. Thompson Company uses multiple factor indexes to rank markets quantitatively and qualitatively. As factors it uses population, population per square mile, value of imports and exports, private consumption, expenditures, and number of cars, radios, and telephones in use. Weighting the factors equally, it ranks each Western European country quantitatively by computing an average index using gross values of the factors just listed. An index using per capita data for the same factors, again equally weighted, provides a qualitative ranking.

Ordinarily market indexes are constructed not to measure total potential but either to rank submarkets or to assign potential shares of the total market to each submarket. Erickson (1963, p. 23) constructed such an index for Brazil. Using population, domestic income, and retail store sales, all expressed as percentages of national figures, he measured the potential for consumer goods for each of Brazil's 21 states. It has the advantages and disadvantages of Sales Management's Buying Power Index after which the Brazilian index is modelled.

An index of this kind might be used to establish sales quotas and evaluate sales performance, among other purposes. This Brazilian index assigns a potential to the state of São Paulo of roughly 30 percent of the nation's total. If sales for the product under study fall below the level required by the index and if the product's sales are related to the three-factor index, management has reason to question performance in that submarket. Obviously such a tool must be used judiciously.

Gross indicators like GNP, net national income, or total population are useful in constructing an index but, when possible, one should restrict use of factors to variables that closely fit the product. The better the variables serve as sales determinants of the product for which the index is constructed, the more reliable it will be. For example, determining potential for an electric household appliance might require using such factors as private consumption expenditure on durable goods and the number of wired homes. An index determining potential for boys' outerwear might include an income variable, number of young males in the appropriate age range, and a temperature variable, if data are available. If not, the analyst must use substitute variables.

ESTIMATION BY ANALOGY

Estimating market size with available data is difficult and with inadequate data is even more difficult. Scarce data require resourceful techniques, one of which is estimating by analogy. This can be done in two ways by (1) cross-section comparisons or (2) Merritt Kasten's term, by "displacing time series in time" (1960). The first technique estimates the market size of a commodity in Country A by computing the ratio of a gross economic indicator, e.g. disposable personal income, for both A and B (for which market data are available) and using this ratio as an estimate of the consumption ratio of the commodity in question.

The time series device uses as a demand estimate for a product in Country A, the demand level for the product in B when B was at the same level of economic growth as A is today. This technique assumes that product usage moves through a cycle, the product being consumed in small quantities (or not at all) when countries are underdeveloped and in increasing (and predictable) amounts with economic growth.

Obviously these techniques have drawbacks. The cross-section approach assumes linearity in the consumption function. Both assume comparable consumption patterns among countries. The following factors can create errors in estimates using either technique:

1. Nonlinearity of consumption functions.
2. Possible lack of correspondence between potential for a product and its sales because of improper pricing, inadequate credit terms and facilities, defective product quality, inhibiting governmental policies (tariffs, taxes, embargoes), etc.
3. Differences in culture, tastes, and habits that dictate different consumption patterns for two apparently similar countries.
4. Technical factors, e.g., recent inventions that permit a late-developing economy to consume a product earlier in its growth phase than economically more advanced countries.

REGRESSION ANALYSIS

Regression analysis may be a powerful tool in predicting market size in all countries, but especially when data are scarce. It also provides a quantitative technique to sharpen estimates derived by the deduction by analogy method just explained.

Cross-section studies using regression analysis benefit from existing predictable demand patterns for many commodities in countries at different growth stages. Just cited were factors that confound attempts to estimate demand in one country from the experiences of another. Despite these obstacles there are still strong international demand patterns that increase the predictive power of the regression technique.

A use of regression analysis is to derive demand estimates by analogy, i.e., by studying the relationship between gross economic indicators and demand for a specific commodity for countries with both kinds of data. We then transfer this relationship by analogy to the less developed country where, more than likely, only the gross economic indicators are available. If, however, data relating directly to demand for the product in question are available in the less developed country, we would obviously substitute these data for the indirect technique described.

Table 17.3 summarizes regression results that relate the consumption of various commodities to a gross economic indicator. A linear regression model $y = a + bx$ was used where y is the amount of a product in use per thousand of population and x is GNP per capita. The equations explain from 50 percent to 78 percent of the variation in the dependent variable. The simple least-squares slope coefficients are statistically significant at the 0.01 level.

Table 17.3. Regression of Consumption on Gross National Product,
Various Products

Product	Number of observations	Regression equation	Unadjusted R^2
Autos	37	-21.071 + 0.101x	0.759
Radio sets	42	8.325 + 0.275x	0.784
TV sets	31	-16.501 + 0.074x	0.503
Refrigerators	24	-21.330 + 0.102x	0.743
Washing machines	22	-15.623 + 0.094x	0.736

Sources: Statistical Yearbook, United Nations, 1962, and Maizels (1963), pp. 308-9.

Technically, the title of Table 17.3 incorrectly refers to the consumption of the products it lists. The dependent variable, showing the amount of product in use per capita, is a kind of summary of previous consumption.   In effect it records the sum of previous purchases, less withdrawals from use because of obsolescence and other reasons. Data are available, however, for the computation of regressions using consumption as the dependent variable, though often these data are difficult to obtain.   Ingenuity and a diligent search of data sources, however, are usually rewarding.

From the regression results in Table 17.3, we may conclude that an increase of $100 per capita in GNP will result, on the average, in an increase of ten automobiles, ten refrigerators, nine washing machines, seven TV sets, and twenty-seven radio sets per 1,000 population. Undoubtedly there is a saturation point for these and other products. Beyond a point (not reached for the five commodities analyzed here) consumption will increase at a decreasing rate, requiring the use of a different kind of equation to describe the relationship.

Factors other than economic growth also contribute to expansion in product demand. We considered these forces previously. The regression for automobiles would have been improved by excluding a few countries' observations. For example, consumption of cars in Switzerland is far less than its level of affluence permits because of an excellent public transportation system, difficult terrain, and the imposition of heavy import duties on cars. Undoubtedly adding price as another independent variable would improve the fit of the equations, although getting this information makes research considerably more difficult.

Some products do not lend themselves to simple regression analysis. For example, a very poor fit resulted for a regression of cement consumption per capita on gross disposable product per capita. Many other variables, including the prices of cement and its substitutes, would have been necessary to improve the results. For paper, however, a reasonably good fit was derived using only gross domestic product as the explanatory variable (regression results: $0.441 + 0.035x$ $R^2 = 0.66$, statistically significant at 0.01 level). Fortunately the consumption of many products can be estimated reasonably accurately by knowing only the income (or GNP) per capita in the countries studied. The demonstration effect undoubtedly leads to this predictable consumption pattern from one country to another.

To use the regression technique to estimate demand an analyst must first compute the regression, using whatever explanatory variables seem appropriate, and provide a close fit. If the unexplained variation is reasonably low, the analyst may use the results as an estimate of current demand in countries for which no demand data are available. Getting an estimate of demand requires knowing the value of the independent variable, e.g. GNP. Fortunately these data are readily available on a current basis. The United Nations and others also estimate growth rates, permitting calculation of future GNP levels to predict future demand.

Specifically, assume that we want to estimate the consumption of paper in Country X where this statistic is unavailable. Its present GNP per capita is $200. Using the regression equation (see above), we calculate present consumption to be 7.4 tons per capita. We may also want to estimate the consumption of paper in that country five years hence when GNP per capita is expected to be $250. Using the same regression equation, we estimate the per capita consumption to be roughly 9.3 tons. Multiplication of this figure by estimated population (also available in UN reports) provides a total consumption estimate for X. This figure may be qualified by using standard error values to provide a range within which the anticipated consumption may fall rather than to make a point estimate.

Obviously there are limitations to using this technique as a demand estimator. Not the least of the problems is the assumption that the relationship prevailing in countries for which demand data are available can be transferred to the less developed countries lacking these data.

INPUT-OUTPUT ANALYSIS

Input-output analysis was used first to describe a country's economic structure and for economic development planning; analysts now recognize the potential of the analysis in international market research as more countries develop I-O tables (see Faucett, 1960, pp. 4, 59). This is especially true in market research for industrial products that lend themselves better than consumer goods products to I-O analysis.

I-O tables permit several kinds of analysis. One can trace the direct and indirect impact on the demand for one's products of changes in demand for other industries' products. One can also determine the extent to which sales are made to final users and, if so, how much the industry depends on sales to governments, households, export markets, etc. Furthermore, the tables reveal the number of industries consuming another industry's products, a valuable datum from the standpoint of planning distribution channel requirements.

The most valuable use of I-O tables in international market analysis is in predicting future output levels for one's customers. A current I-O table summarizes the structure of today's economy. An analyst may ask how a 30 percent increase in government expenditures would affect the demand for his industry's products. How would doubling the growth rate in vehicle production affect the output of rubber products in Country X? What would be the impact on textile demand of a relative contraction in output of consumers' goods at the expense of capital goods in Country Y (underdeveloped economy)? The possibilities for analysis and prediction from simulating different economic conditions are infinite. I-O's value stems from its being a model that makes it reusable for analytical purposes.

I-O analysis has its disadvantages, too. It assumes that production functions are linear; hence, the technical coefficients are fixed over all output ranges. It thus rules out changes in input-output relationships resulting either from changed production processes or from alterations in output level. Outdated tables for some countries make this drawback even more severe. Unfortunately we know little about the stability of technical coefficients.

Another limitation is the small number of cells in most tables, far fewer than the number of industries in each country. Data may be grouped into so few "industries" that the input-output relationships are meaningless. Moreover, in many underdeveloped countries' tables, lack of interdependence among industries may leave most cells vacant. Thus only twenty-three of the 306 cells in Tanganyika's (in 1957 before becoming Tanzania) I-O table were filled (Peacock and Gosser, 1957, p. 21).

Nonetheless I-O tables are useful to the resourceful analyst. Their shortcomings should diminish as data become more abundant, the technique better refined, and more countries adopt them. By 1966, twenty-one countries plus the OEEC countries as a group were constructing I-O tables on an annual basis or intermittently; another six countries had them planned or under construction but had no announced plan for periodic compilation of future tables (United Nations, 1966, p. 135).

DUAL ECONOMY PROBLEM

In this discussion I categorized countries as underdeveloped as though each had a relatively homogeneous population. Of course, this is fallacious. Every country has regional income differences, which are often quite pronounced in the less developed countries. This condition leads to their being described as dual economies. The dual character is evident from a comparison of poor rural areas accounting for a majority of the population in most underdeveloped countries with pockets of relative affluence in the cities.

The contrast may show up in comparisons of average income or purchasing power for different regions of the country. The Brazilian states of São Paulo and Guanabara, for example, in 1959 accounted for 23 percent of Brazil's population but 46 percent of domestic income earned and 51 percent of retail sales (Faucett, 1960, p. 23). The four poorest states, on the other hand, accounted for 13 percent of the people and generated only 5 percent of domestic income and 3 percent of retail sales. The same pattern prevails in other less developed countries.

The dual economy problem requires analyzing economies by segments rather than looking only at the whole. One might rule out a country with low per capita income as a potential market for an income-elastic product if he were not going to probe for more than the average income figure for the entire country. This average might conceal the existence of one or more desirable regional markets in which incomes would support the product's sale.

SUMMARY AND CONCLUSIONS

This article briefly describes several techniques to aid international market analysis. It is not meant to be exhaustive. Obviously there are many conventional devices, useful in domestic marketing research, that may be used equally effectively in marketing research abroad, especially in developed economies. Thus consumer surveys, panels, store audits, readership studies, and other techniques familiar in the United States are becoming equally familiar abroad. Indeed several methods discussed here are equally applicable to domestic market research. This would certainly be true for using multiple factor indexes and, to some extent, income elasticity measurement and, more recently, input-output analysis.

But the short-cut research methods of deduction by analogy, analysis of import substitution elasticities, and the use of regression analysis discussed in this article are more applicable in the less developed countries than they are in the developed countries. In the latter, the analyst generally has adequate, if not always abundant, data. In the former, however, the data can be pretty scarce.

REFERENCES

Chenery, H., "Patterns of industrial growth," American Economic Review, No. 50 (1960), pp. 624-54.

Erickson, L.G., "Analyzing Brazilian consumer markets," Business Topics, No. 11 (1963), p. 23.

Faucett, J.G., "Input-output analysis as a tool of international market research," Market Research in International Operations, Management report No. 53 (American Management Association, 1960).

Gilbert, M. et al., Comparative National Products and Price Levels (Organization for European Co-operation, 1958).

Kastens, M.L. "Organizing, planning and staffing market research activities in an international corporation," Market Research in International Operations, Management report No. 53 (American Management Association, 1960).

Maizels, A., Industrial Growth and World Trade (Cambridge University Press, 1963).

Peacock, A.T. and Gosser, D.M., "Input-output analysis in an underdeveloped country," Review of Economic Studies, No. 25 (1957), p. 22.

United Nations, Problems of input-output tables and analysis (1966), pp. 135-6.

18 Multinational Marketing Research: Methodological Problems*
Charles S. Mayer

While the literature on multinational surveys abounds in "state of the art" advice on how to avoid traps, very little actual work has been done in this area. For example, Webster states that "One can use the same method or different methods in the various survey countries so long as the method used in each is as good as possible there" (1966). While such advice is certainly important and points in the right direction, it does not solve the problem. In order to have truly comparable data from multinational markets, it is not sufficient to attempt to control sources of error. Since such error will never be completely eliminated, the data, having been collected, have to be adjusted for residual error sources.

However, before such adjustment can be done, much more knowledge is required. Such knowledge is generally obtained at a cost and usually requires some form of experimentation. And here is where one of the major problems arises in the multinational marketing field. First the funds for conducting such research may not be readily available as research budgets are generally controlled at the national level and, at that level, the concern about comparability across nations is not as strongly felt. More important, however, is the general nature of the problem — the subject does not lend itself to experimental design. Respondents in different countries are not assigned to those countries by a random procedure, but happen to occur in their cultures and are affected by their background. There is no possibility for having a full experimental design in which test groups and control groups (the two being comparable before the experiment) can be utilized.

*Slightly abbreviated from Charles S. Mayer, "Multinational marketing research: The magnifying glass of methodological problems," European Research, Vol. 6 (March 1978), pp. 77-83. Permission to reprint this paper has been given by the European Society for Opinion and Marketing Research-ESOMAR, Wamberg 37, 1083 CW Amsterdam, The Netherlands. Subscription rate to "European Research" is ₺ 20 per year. Free to members of ESOMAR. Single copies ₺ 3.70. Subscription address: Kluwer Publishing Limited, 1 Harlequin Avenue, Brentford, Middlesex TW8 9EW, England.

Due to the lack of tightly controlled experimental designs to measure the impact of various cultural and national effects, much of the adjustment of data will have to rely on subjective assessment. Here the researcher more than the manager will be concerned by the entry of such subjectivity into the analysis. Since the alternative is to overlook the problem, however, the introduction of subjectivity is unavoidable. Needless to say such subjectivity is only as good as the insights of the assessor, which is one of the reasons for attempting to avoid it.

A further problem with many of the errors in the multinational marketing field is that they are subject specific. For example, knowing some "true" reporting differences between French and American shopping habits will do very little to clarify reporting differences on vacation habits in these two nations.

ERROR RATIO DECOMPOSITION

One approach to break total research error into its various components is a technique known as Error Ratio Decomposition (ERD), which seems appropriate in the multinational setting.

Essentially, ERD takes the total error and decomposes it into multiplicative components. The researcher or manager is in a better position to make estimates about each term in the ERD than he would be about the total error. Since not much quantitative data is available in this field, a fully quantified ERD at this stage seems unjustified. However, the ERD approach is useful in identifying the following ratios:

- definitional error
- instrument error
- frame error
- selection error
- non-response error
- random sampling error

Each of the error sources identified above will be discussed in greater detail with examples. Before leaving this general section, however, one more crucial point has to be made. The magnitude of each of these ratios is not minimized necessarily by attempting to replicate methodology from country to country. While a mechanical approach to replicating methodology is simple it does not assure comparable results. For example, in different countries it may be desirable to use completely different sampling procedures to arrive at roughly comparable groups. For measuring canned food consumption, for instance, a cross-sectional sample is needed in a developed country, while an up-scale sample could be the most efficient design in a developing country. In the UK a telephone survey may introduce a more significant bias in the results than would changing the survey instrument. The telephone owning population in that country is quite unrepresentative of the total population due to a low penetration of telephones. To a large extent, comparable research results will be obtained through the skillful, creative combination of different research techniques in different market settings, rather than on a blind insistence on the replication of methodology. Multinational marketing research is yet another aspect of marketing that depends on the skillful combination of art and science.

DEFINITIONAL ERROR

The way the problem is defined in each country will clearly have a significant impact on the results. Definition is complicated by the following factors:

Conceptual Equivalence

Concepts range over the whole spectrum from very general issues to culture-specific topics. Concepts like hunger, avoidance of pain, welfare of the family can be assumed to be general and present in all cultures. Other topics like dieting are certainly culture specific – they would not even be understood in some. And still other topics and products are perceived differently in different cultures.

Some examples might best illustrate the conceptual equivalence issue. Hot milk-based drinks are consumed during the evening (just prior to retiring) in the U.K. and are perceived to have restful, relaxing, and sleep-inducing properties. In Thailand, due to the nature of cooking facilities, these drinks are generally consumed not in the home, but in the morning on the way to work and are perceived as having stimulating, energy-giving, and invigorating properties. Unless these usage differences are built into a survey on hot milk-based drinks in these two countries, the results will be totally meaningless.

Other examples can also be cited. For instance, whether a bicycle is viewed as a means of transportation or as a leisure time sports equipment will have a tremendous impact on how a study on bicycles should be conducted. If home-ownership takes on different meaning in the U.K. and the U.S. does it make sense to study the amount of husband/wife decision-making activity and interpret this as being a valid difference in the interaction patterns? (Hempel, 1974) It may well be that the differences arise due to the fact that the "products" are conceptually different.

Definitional Equivalence

In many product categories, great care has to be taken when conducting studies in several countries to ensure that the products are properly defined. Let us take heavy-duty detergents as an example. In the U.K. washing-machines are frequently equipped with a heater coil which enables the wash to be boiled prior to being agitated. Unfortunately, such boiling action will kill the enzymes. Accordingly, in the U.K. heavy-duty detergents will not include enzymes. In Switzerland, a pre-wash is felt to be part of the washing-cycle and often the pre-wash ingredient and the detergent ingredient are sold jointly. In West Germany, the heavy-duty detergents often do have enzyme action. In attempting to compare heavy-duty detergent consumption in the three countries, how would one define the product?

Some other examples will further illustrate the problem. In the Northern European countries beer is considered as an alcoholic beverage while in the Mediterranean countries it is viewed more as a soft drink. In attempting to measure beer consumption, what other beverages should be included in the alternative list? Similarly, in Japan non-carbonated fruit drinks are consumed with great frequency and as alternatives to soft drinks. In doing a soft drink study in Japan, fruit drinks would have to be included in the list of alternatives, while the same would not necessarily be true in the U.S. The way that a product is positioned in a survey − and hence defined − will clearly have an impact on the results obtained. And the same product may have to be defined quite differently in different countries.

An even more fundamental example of definitional equivalence can be given. An attempt to standardize age groupings on an international basis had to be abandoned. It was found that persons in the same age groups in different cultures were at different stages in their life and family cycles. Hence, defining age groups that were chronologically identical did not in fact create comparable groups.

There is clearly an interaction between conceptual and definitional equivalence. In fact, all the concepts considered under the heading of a single error are interrelated. While it may make the exposition clearer to discuss the equivalence issues under different headings, it should be emphasized that only one error − in this case definitional error − would be assessed.

Temporal Equivalence

Research projects could be conducted in several countries simultane-ously, sequentially, or independently. Thus, the time dimension is introduced. Superficially, the simultaneous conducting of studies in several countries (or different regions within a country) would seem to be the methodologically preferred technique. However, if special seasonal factors are present or other events are happening in only some of the countries (such as political elections, special activism on certain product categories, and so on), the simultaneous design may not alleviate the problem. Further, if product or service demand can be viewed as evolutionary and if we accept the international product life cycle as being lagged from the more advanced to the lesser advanced nations (Wells, 1968), then conducting the same study at the same time in different countries will not yield comparable results.

Market Structure Equivalence

Market size, market share, penetration rates, distribution channels, levels of competitive activity, all have an impact on how a particular research question can be framed. An interesting demonstration here is a 1963 Readers' Digest study which showed that French and German customers consume more spaghetti than Italian customers. This strange result was achieved because the question asked about packaged branded spaghetti. While spaghetti is generally sold in this form in Germany and France, in Italy it is sold loose and unbranded. Though the result that more packaged branded spaghetti is consumed in France and Germany than Italy is quite valid, it does not meet the goals of the research if in fact spaghetti consumption is the variable of interest. The consumption pattern, market structure, and channels of distribution differences were not properly taken into account in arriving at this finding.

INSTRUMENT ERROR

In personal interviews, the questionnaire and the interviewer errors are so thoroughly confounded that it is more useful to think of a single instrument error. Such a process is also more general if telephone or mail surveys are also to be considered.

Linguistic Equivalence

If the study has to be conducted in different languages, problems of linguistic equivalence arise. Linguistic equivalence is much more complicated than just straight translation. While many methods are available for translating a questionnaire from one language to another, such as back translation (having the questionnaire translated from one language to the other by one translator, and then having it back-translated to the source language by another), parallel-blind-translation (having several individuals translate the questionnaire independently, and comparing the results), the committee approach (essentially the same as the previous, except that discussion occurs between translators during translation), or the random probe (placing probes at random in both the source and the translated questionnaire during the pre-test period to insure that the respondents are understanding the questions in the same way), none of these is really sufficient to guarantee linguistic comparability. Such comparability may be a fundamentally unobtainable goal. Nevertheless, efforts in this area are certainly necessary and will avoid many of the famous faux pas.

    The method of decentering is another approach to the translation problem. In this process both the source and the target language versions are viewed as open to modification. If translation problems are recognized within the source document, it is modified to be more easily translatable.   Through this process, the source questionnaire itself becomes clearer and more precise. For example, through decentering, the phrase "I like to gossip at times" may become "I sometimes like to talk about other people's business." It should be noted here that there is a link between conceptual and linguistic problems. For example, some concepts just cannot be translated into certain languages or they cannot be asked in a meaningful way in certain cultures. Accordingly, one of the assumptions of ERD, namely independence among ratios, is violated. If this violation is felt to be sufficiently great, the two ratios, definitional error and instrument error, have to be collapsed into a single ratio measurement error. While such a procedure eliminates the problem of false assumption, it replaces it with an equally difficult one – attempting to assess a single ratio that is dependent on many different, interactive components.

Contextual Equivalence

The interviewer/respondent's perception of each other can have a strong and differential impact on the results obtained from different countries. For example, if college-educated interviewers are used to question lower class respondents and if the specific language and expression used has a status reflecting property, the answers will certainly be effected by such mutual perceptions. Status consistency between interviewers and respondents could be one possible solution here. Such status consistency can range anywhere from perceived role (e.g., government agent) to race, class status, and even the particular dialect spoken.

The location in which the interaction between interviewer and respondent takes place and the presence of other parties can also have a strong impact on the results obtained. Moreover, the environment of the interview cannot always be controlled through research design. For example, in Southern Italy it is almost impossible to interview the home-maker alone. The presence of other members of the family, who might be looked to for the "appropriate" responses, cannot be eliminated.

In a slightly different vein, in the Orient and the Middle-East, it may be difficult to conduct in-home interviews. The assumption is that it is rude for the interviewers to invite themselves into the respondents' homes. Interestingly, such "research folklore" did not stand up in an empirical test in Japan (Berent, 1975).

Instrument Equivalence

Not all survey instruments may be usable in all countries. The telephone, for example, may not reach a representative cross-section. Similarly, many countries suffer from an unreliable postal service. Also, the importance of some of the contextual limitations mentioned above could limit the use of personal interviewing. There is enough evidence in the domestic setting to show that the type of instruments used will have an impact on both the responses received and the non-response rate.

The form of instrumentation that can be employed across countries is also at issue. For example, long questionnaires will not be effective in Hong-Kong where the respondents will not tolerate them. In Brazil, on the other hand, even short questions tend to become long as the respondents will try to make sure that they have interpreted every question correctly.

Response-Style Equivalence

Different cultural groups or nationalities may have different response styles. For example, Mitchell (1968) cites that in Malaysia the Chinese are more reticent and more likely to be nay-sayers while Indians and Malaysians are more loquacious and are more likely to be yea-sayers.

In different countries there may also be a different stress on accuracy. For example, the humility of a Japanese may cause him to undervalue certain of his assets or properties, while in the Middle-East the respondent is more likely to exaggerate.

Different cultural groups might also respond differently to open-ended versus closed questions. Even after the translational problems are minimized, a closed question might ellicit opinions in a culture that do not truly exist. On the other hand, open-ended questions can create coding and analytical problems, while also adding to survey costs.

There are several approaches to attempting to create instrument equivalence. First, a conscious recognition of the above problems can go a long way toward eliminating them. Second, the multi-method approach toward measurement attempts to elicit the same basic response to questions posed in different ways. Clearly, such a procedure has the advantage of establishing face-validity, but at a cost. Third, the recognition that total equivalence may not be an achievable goal can motivate the analyst to assess a larger, but more "credible" interval around an estimate.

FRAME ERROR

In different countries, sampling frames are available from different sources. For example, they may come from electoral lists, municipal lists, housing registrations, area probability samples (based on Census Tracts and Block Data) or the frame may consist of assigned quotas. If these frames include different proportions of the population in each country, that can introduce a further error. For example, if one is studying population mobility and if one frame only includes 70 percent of the population while another includes 90 percent of the population, and the excluded proportion tends to be more mobile than the rest of the population, no true measurement of social mobility can be made.

At a lower level of abstraction even specific issues like the definition of a "dwelling unit" will change from country to country and will probably be tied to that country's national definition.

A further problem with frames is their relative accuracy. For example, in one sample of an Asian city, one out of four addresses was found to be non-existent (Mitchell, 1968). This finding was obtained for a frame that had been used in the past for several important studies. Closely related to the accuracy of a frame is its currency. Especially in rapidly growing areas such as African and Middle-Eastern cities, frames tend to get inaccurate very quickly.

SELECTION ERROR

This error refers to the way that the actual sample is selected from the frame. The great advantage of probability samples is that this error can be left out of the analysis. However, even with probability samples, great care has to be taken that the way the sample was in fact obtained is consistent with the initial design. For example, if interviewers are a part of a sample generating process, they could (and often do) create significant sampling errors. In selecting a sample, two issues are of concern, the representativeness of the sample and its scope. Under representativeness the concern is with obtaining a microcosm of the universe. Under scope is meant the domain of inclusion within the sample. For instance, this domain could totally exclude certain components of the population (assumed to be of no interest) or at least under-sample some segments and over-sample others. For example, in a study comparing French and U.S. shoppers, Green and Langeard (1975) restricted the scope of their French sample ". . .to have the French sample bear the same relationship to the French population along the demographic variables of age, income, education and employment status as the U.S. sample had to the U.S. population." In this way they traded-off representativeness for scope and hence comparability.

NONRESPONSE ERROR

There are obvious cultural patterns of nonresponse. For example, in a study of five countries (Almond and Verba, 1963), response rate ranged from 17 percent to 41 percent. Moreover, in one of these five countries (Mexico), females constituted 64 percent of the respondents while the 1960 census figures show that there were only 52 percent women in the population. Conversely, in different studies in India, 80 percent of the interviewed are men.

Individual item nonresponse may also vary significantly among countries. In certain areas there may be political pressures to keep information from strangers. Again in the Almond and Verba study only one percent of the population in the U.S. refused political party affiliation while 35 percent in Italy refused the same item.

Nonresponse is clearly influenced by call-back patterns and by sample replacements (if permitted). How these factors should be controlled from country to country is quite crucial because it is likely that one can achieve equivalent non-response rates by having differential call-back patterns. Whether equivalent non-response rates or equivalent methodology will yield better results is still a moot question.

SAMPLING ERROR

Sampling error is the only "culture-free" error in the decomposition. It depends on the size of the sample and can be computed from theory. Moreover such theory has universal acceptability and is quite objective.

Usually, this is the only error in a total error decomposition that is formally treated by analysts. For example, Green and Langeard (1975), or Hempel (1974), in subjecting their two-nation samples to a chi-square test, implicitly treat only sampling error as the critical source of difference. Clearly such a procedure will underestimate the possibility that the differences between the two results are due to error only. While researchers would clearly be happier with the conclusion that the significant differences hypothesized exist, they are not entitled to arrive at this preferred hypothesis until all other alternatives hypothesis (such as that the differences are due to different reporting errors in the two studies, different survey instruments used, differential non-response, or sampling) can be rejected.

ADMINISTRATION

A large and complex area in multinational surveys concerns the stage of administration. It is through administration that the intended becomes the actual. Depending on the particular position of the reporter, the literature abounds with the benefits of working with centralized or decentralized market research agencies. This issue is sufficiently complex to be ruled outside of the scope of this paper. Nevertheless, it should be pointed out that each and every one of the ratios discussed above can be influenced by the skill of the research administration.

CONCLUSIONS

Comparison is usually at the base of any multinational study. Whether the purpose of such comparison is to emphasize similarities or differences is a question of the researcher's disposition. In either case, however, the credibility of the comparison is strongly influenced by a host of technical and methodological problems. Since such problems do not generally get sufficient recognition, the purpose of this paper was to draw attention to them.

Nonsampling errors of major and unknown proportions influence cross-national comparisons. Among them are definitional error, instrument error, frame error, selection error, and non-response error. Total error, the combination of sampling and non-sampling error sources, has to be computed in order to establish a credible interval. Such an interval is necessary for testing hypotheses. Before the researchers' proposed hypotheses can be accepted, all other alternative hypotheses have to be rejected. Such alternative hypotheses are usually methodological or technical – differences occur due to noncomparability.

Much more data is required prior to being able to reject alternative hypotheses. Cross-national error sources have to be identified, minimized and quantified before they can be eliminated from subsequent analysis. Such experimentation, however, will be hampered by two interdependent obstacles. First is the very nature of the multinational environment. Since differences occur within national (cultural) boundaries, it is very difficult to design experiments to measure them. Individual respondents cannot be assigned randomly to each treatment (country) but fall into a specific group exactly because of their group belonging. The only possibilities of unravelling some of these knotty problems are expensive, multi-method approaches. However, since even in the larger multinational marketing firms the research budgets are controlled at the national level, it is unlikely that expensive methodological multinational studies will be sponsored.

The error sources identified in this paper are certainly important for multinational research. The multinational setting makes their identification and comprehension easier and magnifies their impact on results. However, their systematic study should be of interest not only to the multinational researcher – they are equally present, though better disguised, in all domestic studies. Perhaps the multinational setting could serve as the microscope for the whole marketing research industry. Through its magnification of methodological problems it can permit us to understand more clearly problems common to all research.

REFERENCES

Almond, G.A. and Verba, S., The Civic Culture (Princeton, N.J.: Princeton University Press, 1963).

Berent, B.H., "International research is different," in Proceedings of the 1975 International Marketing Congress (Chicago: American Marketing Association, 1975).

Green, R.T. and Langeard, E., "A cross-national comparison of consumer habits and innovator characteristics," Journal of Marketing (July 1975), p. 36.

Hempel, D.J., "Family buying decisions: A cross-cultural perspective," Journal of Marketing Research (August 1974), pp. 295-302.

Mayer, C.S., "Assessing the accuracy of marketing research," Journal of Marketing Research (August 1970), pp. 285-91.

Mitchell, R.E., "Survey materials collected in developing countries: Obstacles to comparison," in S. Rokkan, ed., Comparative Research Across Cultures and Nations (The Hague: Mouton, 1968), pp. 223 and 217.

Webster, L.L., "Comparability in multi-country surveys," Journal of Advertising Research (December 1966), p. 16.

Wells, L.T., Jr., "A product life cycle for international trade?" Journal of Marketing (July 1968), pp. 1-6. (See Reading 19).

19 A Product Life Cycle for International Trade*
L.T. Wells, Jr.

The lowering of barriers to international trade has resulted in many opportunities for American companies to profit from exports. Clearly, the businessman needs ways of analyzing the potential exportability of his products and, equally important, tools for predicting which products are likely to be threatened by import competition.

Until recently, the manager was dependent on the explanations of trade offered by the classical and neo-classical economists. Their reasoning generally led to the conclusion that each country will concentrate on exporting those products which make the most use of the country's abundant production factors. The economic theory is elegant — it can be stated mathematically or geometrically and it can be manipulated to yield, under certain assumptions, answers to questions such as what is the value of free trade to a country, or what are the costs and benefits of certain restrictions. So long as the problems posed are of a very broad nature, the theory provides a useful way of analyzing them. However, when the theory is applied to the detailed problems facing the businessman it becomes of limited value.

THE TRADE CYCLE MODEL

A new approach to international trade which appears most promising in aiding the business executive is closely related to the product life cycle concept in marketing. The model claims that many products go through a trade cycle, during which for example the United States is initially an exporter, then loses its export markets and may finally become an importer of the product. Empirical studies of trade in synthetic

---

*Slightly abbreviated from L.T. Wells, Jr., "A product life cycle for international trade?" Journal of Marketing, Vol. 32 (July 1968), pp. 1-6, with permission.

materials, electronic products, office machinery, consumer durables, and motion pictures have demonstrated that these products follow a cycle of international trade similar to the one which the model describes.

According to the trade cycle concept, many products follow a pattern which could be divided into four stages:

Phase 1: U.S. export strength
Phase 2: Foreign production starts
Phase 3: Foreign production competitive in export markets
Phase 4: Import competition begins

A brief look at the reasoning underlying each of these stages will give some clues which will help the businessman to identify the stage in which particular products may be. The concept can then be an aid in predicting the product trade performance to come and in understanding what actions the manager can take to modify the pattern for certain products and to profit from different stages of the cycle.

Phase 1: U.S. Export Strength

What kinds of new products are likely to be introduced first in the United States? It can be assumed that American entrepreneurs have no particular monopoly on scientific know-how or on very basic technical ability. What they do have, however, is a great deal of knowledge about a very special market – one which is unique in having a large body of high-income consumers. Products which satisfy the special demands of these customers are especially likely to be introduced in the United States. Moreover, due to a monopoly position of the United States as a supplier of the new products which satisfy these unique demands, they offer the best opportunities for export.

Empirical studies have failed to show a very simple relationship between demand and invention. However, there can be little doubt that certain products are more likely to be developed in America. Automatic transmissions for automobiles promised to be pretty expensive additions to cars. If an inventor considers the chances of his brainchild's being purchased by consumers, a U.S. inventor would be more likely to pursue an automatic transmission than a European. The European inventor would more probably concern himself with ideas suitable to European demands. He might respond to high fuel taxes and taxes on engine displacement by developing engines which produce more horsepower per cubic inch. He might develop better handling suspensions in response to the road conditions. An inventor usually comes up with products suitable to his own market. It is also likely that the final product development leading to commercial production will be achieved by an entrepreneur responding to his own national demand.

Even if an American is most likely to be the first to produce a high-income product, why does he not set up his first plant abroad where labor may be cheaper? At the early stages of a product's life, design is often in a constant state of flux. There is a real advantage which accrues to a manufacturer who is close to the market for his products so that he can rapidly translate demands for design changes into more suitable products. Moreover, these changes often require the availability of close communication with specialized suppliers. Hence, the instability of product design for new products argues for a location in the United States – near to the market and close to a wide range of specialized suppliers (see Hirsch, 1967). The entrepreneur is less likely to be concerned with small cost differences for new products. The existence of a monopoly or the significant product differentiation at the early stage of the product life cycle reduces the importance of costs to the manufacturer. The multitude of designs and the lack of standard performance specifications make it difficult for the consumer to compare prices. Also, in the early stage of the product life cycle the consumer is frequently not very concerned with price. Success comes to the manufacturer who can quickly adjust both his product design and marketing strategy to consumers' needs which are just beginning to be well identified.

At this point, the American manufacturers have a virtual monopoly for the new product in the world market. Foreigners who want the good must order it from the United States. In fact, wealthy consumers abroad, foreigners with particular needs for the product, and Americans living abroad seem to hear about it very quickly. Unsolicited orders begin to appear from overseas. U.S. exports start to grow – initially from the trickle created by these early orders – to a steady stream as active export programs are established in the American firms.

Phase 2: Foreign Production Starts

Incomes and product familiarity abroad increase, causing overseas markets eventually to become large enough that the product which once appealed primarily to the U.S. consumer has a broad appeal in the wealthier foreign countries. Not only does a potential foreign producer now have a market close at hand, but some of his costs will be lower than those of the U.S. producer. Imports from America have to bear duty and overseas freight charges – costs which local products will not carry. Moreover the potential foreign producer may have to invest less in product development – the U.S. manufacturer has done part of this for him. Some measure of the size of his potential market has been demonstrated by the successful sale of imports. Favorable profit projections based on a demonstrated market and an ability to under-price imports will eventually induce an entrepreneur in a wealthy foreign market – usually first in Western Europe – to take the plunge and start serious manufacture. Of course, this manufacturer will, in some cases, be an American subsidiary which starts production abroad, realizing that if it does not, some other company will.

However, the calculations that yield favorable costs projections for competition with imports from the United States in the foreign producer's home market do not necessarily lead to the conclusion that the foreign producer will be a successful competitor in third markets. For many modern manufactured goods he is likely to be at a serious disadvantage due to the small size of his plant in a market where he also must bear the burdens of freight and tariffs. Scale-economies are so important for many products that the U.S. manufacturer, with his large plants supplying the American market, can still produce more cheaply than the early foreign producers who must manufacture on a significantly smaller scale.

During this second stage American exports still supply most of the world's markets. However, as foreign producers begin to manufacture, U.S. exports to certain markets will decline. The pattern will probably be a slowdown in the rate of growth of U.S. exports. The slowdown in the rate of growth of exports of home dishwashers in the last few years as European manufacturers have begun production provides an example of a product in this phase of the cycle.

Phase 3: Foreign Production Competitive in Export Markets

As the early foreign manufacturers become larger and more experienced their costs should fall. They will begin to reap the advantages of scale economies previously available only to U.S. manufacturers. In addition, they may have lower labor bills. Hence, their costs may be such that foreign products become competitive with American goods in third markets where goods from both countries have to carry similar freight and duty charges.

During this stage, U.S. producers will be protected from imports in their domestic market where they are not faced with duty and overseas transportation costs. However, foreign goods will gradually take over the markets abroad which were previously held by American exports. The rate of growth of U.S. exports will continue to decline. The success of European ranges and refrigerators in Latin America points out that these products are in this phase.

Phase 4: Import Competition Begins

As the foreign manufacturer reaches mass production based on his home and export markets, his perhaps lower labor rates and newer plant may enable him to produce at lower costs than an American manufacturer. His cost savings may be sufficient that he can pay ocean freight and American duty and still compete with the American in his own market. This stage will be reached earlier if the foreign producer begins to think in terms of marginal costs for export pricing. If he believes that he can sell above full costs in his home market and "dump" abroad to use up his excess capacity, he may very quickly undercut the U.S. producers pricing on full costs.

During this final stage, U.S. exports will be reduced to a trickle, supplying very special customers abroad, while import competition may become severe. The bicycle is a product which has been in this phase for some time.

The Cycle

Thus the cycle is complete – from the United States as a strong exporter to the stage where imports may capture a significant share of the American market. Figure 19.1 shows schematically the U.S. export performance for an hypothetical product.

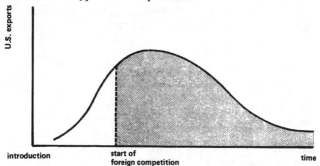

Fig. 19.1. Export cycle.

The early foreign producers – usually Western Europeans – will face a cycle similar to that of the U.S. manufacturer. As still lower-income markets become large enough, producers in these countries will eventually become competitive – displacing the dominance of the early foreign manufacturers. The manufacture of products moves from country to country in what one author has called a "pecking order" (Hufbauer, 1966).

So far, there are only relatively few examples of the less developed countries becoming exporters of manufactured goods. The classic example is standardized textiles. Another interesting example is the export of certain standardized computer components from Argentina. However, the current growth rate of over 12 percent per year for exports of manufactures from less developed countries may indicate they will soon become an important factor for the American businessman.

HOW DIFFERENT PRODUCTS BEHAVE

Obviously, the export patterns are not identical for all products. Three variables were critical to the argument supporting the trade cycle concept: the uniqueness of the appeal of the product to the U.S. market, the reduction in unit costs as the scale of production increases, and the costs of tariffs and freight. Differences in these variables will be very important in determining how a particular product behaves as an export or import – and thus what the profit opportunities or threats will be.

High-Income Products

The advantage of the United States in export markets in certain products was said to be dependent on the uniqueness of the appeal of the product to the American consumer. The cycle would be more "stretched out" if this demand is particularly unique. For such products, the U.S. manufacturer will probably remain an exporter for a longer period of time and can postpone his fears of import competition.

It is possible to categorize some products for which the U.S. demand is "unique":

Luxury function. Certainly products which perform functions people are willing to do without until they are comparatively wealthy have a particularly large demand in the United States. Movie cameras and room air-conditioners come immediately to mind. In fact, a classification of consumer durables into luxury, discretionary, and necessity shows a remarkable correlation with the U.S. export performance of the products. Exports increased 330 percent over a ten-year period for the luxury products, compared to an almost 84 percent increase for the discretionary items and only a 7 percent increase for the necessity products (see Table 19.1).

Table 19.1. Ratio of Value of 1962-1963 Exports to Value of
1952-1953 Exports

Necessity		Discretionary		Luxury	
Refrigerators	0.47	Automobiles	0.99	Movie Cameras	4.14
Ranges	0.87	Electric Clocks	1.04	Freezers	0.74
Radios	1.42	Still Cameras	4.66	Air Conditioners	3.59
Irons	1.56	Washers	1.35	Slide Projectors	4.66
Televisions	1.04	Vacuum Cleaners	1.78	Dishwashers	8.50
		Mixers	1.25	Outboard Motors	4.18
		Record Players	1.81	Recreational Boats	4.40
Average	1.07		1.84		4.32

F=7.0 (Significant at 0.95 level)

Note: Adjustments for freezer exports to Canada and 1963 still camera exports raise significance to 0.99 level.
Source: Classification of products from James Gately, Stephen Gudeman, and George Moseley, "Take-off phenomenon," unpublished paper submitted to Consumer Behavior Research Seminar (Harvard Business School, May 27, 1965). Export data from U.S. Department of Commerce, Bureau of the Census, FT410 Reports.

Expensive to buy. Products that cost significantly more than other products which perform similar functions appeal primarily to a high-income market. Electric knife-sharpeners are an example of this type of product. A study by Time Marketing Service (n.d.) showed that 21.5 percent of households with incomes of over $10,000 (where the heads were white collar, college educated) owned electric knife-sharpeners. In contrast, only 11.6 percent with incomes under $10,000 owned them.

Expensive to own. Similarly, products that are expensive to maintain or to operate compared to alternative products which perform similar functions are uniquely suited to a high-income market. The American automobile provides an example. The disadvantage of its high fuel consumption more than offsets the advantages of more space and higher horsepower for most low-income foreign consumers.

Labor saving. Products which save labor by substituting a relatively large amount of capital are particularly appealing to the American market. The high cost of labor, a function of high American incomes, makes it very attractive to buy items such as heavy road building equipment and computers which substitute capital for labor.

Of course the businessman can influence the appeal of his products through his product policy. For example, he can build larger or smaller cars, automatic record players or simple ones.

Scale Economies

The trade cycle is also influenced by the amount of savings in cost, which can be achieved by increasing the scale of production. If a small plant is equally as efficient as a large one for a given product, a foreign producer will start to manufacture while his market is still relatively small. U.S. exports will not be as successful, and import competition will probably soon begin.

The effect of scale economies is well illustrated by the cases where a product goes through several stages of manufacture. In refrigerator production, for example, low costs can be reached in assembly operations at a much lower volume than in the manufacture of compressors. This difference shows up in the performance of U.S. exports for one period where exports of completed refrigerators fell drastically, but exports of compressors for inclusion in refrigerators assembled abroad held their own.

Tariffs and Freight

If tariffs or other trade barriers overseas are high for a particular product, foreign production is encouraged. Hence U.S. exports will receive early competition from foreign production. Developing countries have frequently raised tariffs to encourage local production while their markets are still small. However, if the American tariff is high, it follows that the United States manufacturers need worry less about import competition.

High freight costs, usually for products which are heavy or bulky compared to their value, tend to discourage trade. Not only will foreign production occur earlier, but foreign competition is unlikely to become a serious threat in the U.S. market. In the extreme cases of very high transportation costs, trade never occurs, or occurs almost entirely along borders where a foreign source is closer than a domestic one. For example, trade in gravel has never been significant because of transportation costs.

Exceptions to the Cycle

Not all products can be expected to follow the cyclical pattern described. For some products the location of manufacture is tied to some particular natural resource – agricultural, to certain types of land; mining and initial processing, to areas containing the mineral. The manufacturing processes for some products such as the traditional handicraft goods have only slightly increasing returns to scale. Moreover, some products appear to remain sufficiently differentiated so that price discrepancies play only a slight role. For example, American cigarettes have continued to command a price-premium in Europe.

There are also manufactured goods for which even the U.S. market is not large enough to allow significant scale economies. Such products tend to be produced in various locations close to market clusters, and no one area achieves a large cost advantage. Trade tends to be more on the basis of product differentiation or specialization. However, as demand in the United States grows, a standard version may be produced in quantity, bringing the cost down so that the product moves into the cycle under discussion.

High-performance sports cars and sail boats may be examples of this type product. Until recently, much of the production for such sports cars was located in various areas of Europe and was based on small production quantities. Recently both of these products have seen some large-scale manufacture in the U.S. and significant cost-reductions. General Motors led the way with mass manufacture of the Corvette. More American manufacturers will probably enter the high-performance sports car market and compete with the virtually hand-produced, expensive European sports cars.

THE TRADE CYCLE AND BUSINESS PLANNING

Obviously, no simple model can explain the behavior of all products in international trade. However, the trade cycle model does appear to be useful for understanding trade patterns in a wide range of manufactured goods. Although no such model should be used by the businessman without a careful examination of individual products, it does provide some very useful hints as to which products might be exportable and which might suffer import competition. The concept can give some clues as to the success of various product policies.

Market Segmentation

The model provides some insights into the role which market segmentation can play in increasing exports and protecting against imports. Design modifications can be made for certain products which can change the appeal of the product to different kinds of customers and thus modify the trade cycle. In fact, the manufacturer often makes such changes for reasons unrelated to international trade but rather as a response to changes in the nature of his home market. As the American consumer becomes wealthier and more sophisticated, and as domestic competition becomes more severe, the manufacturer often makes his products more automatic, more powerful, more luxurious. The marketer may be trying to differentiate his product from those of his competitor, or he may simply be responding to the demands of a wealthier consumer. These changes may make the product more suited to the growing incomes of the American customer, but they will also affect its exportability. The item may become too expensive for the majority of foreign consumers, hastening competition from foreign-produced goods.

This gradual product sophistication may, however, provide some protection against imports in the United States. No doubt the size and automatic features of the American automobile long held a special appeal to the high-income American market and consequently held back the flow of imports. The product design did, however, have another effect: simpler, cheaper foreign cars have been able to capture a part of the U.S. market more concerned with economy of operation and lack of style obsolescence than with luxury, fashion, and automatic features – second cars, student cars, etc.

The American automobile industry initially did not respond to imports by trying to produce a real economy car in competition with the Volkswagen and Renault, but rather produced a middle-range product (the compacts) which competed with Volvo and Peugeot, for example. The move was probably a wise one. No doubt, the producers of the economy cars abroad had reached cost savings from scale economies equivalent to anything the U.S. producers could hope to obtain. Moreover, they had lower labor costs. By choosing to attack the middle range, the American manufacturers chose a market where they could have a scale advantage for a time, until the higher-income segment of the European market was so large that middle-range cars would be more important. Perhaps the U.S. manufacturers simultaneously created a more exportable product for the future.

For products where design sophistication consists of adding special features to a basic model, export versions can be produced simply by eliminating some of the extras. Thus, some producers can extend the exportability of their products while simultaneously satisfying the more sophisticated needs of their home market.

PRODUCT ROLL-OVER AND FOREIGN INVESTMENT

Of course, the point is finally reached for many products where design changes can no longer make the American product competitive abroad or safe from imports. The U.S. firms may follow two strategies for survival: a continual product roll-over, shifting resources to new products more suited to the unique demands of the American market; and manufacturing abroad to take advantage of lower production costs and to save tariffs and transportation charges. The strategies are not mutually exclusive, but both require advanced planning and constant surveillance of the future of individual products and assessments of the company's capabilities.

CONCLUSION

Companies can no longer afford failure to analyze opportunities for profit offered by exports and the possible threats to their own market posed by imports. The trend of international events indicates an increased importance of trade to businessmen. In response to this changing environment, the manager must have a continuing program to analyze the future directions of international trade in his products so that he may plan early enough for appropriate policies. The product cycle model provides a useful tool in this analysis.

REFERENCES

Hirsch, S., Location of Industry and International Competitiveness (Clarendon Press, 1967).
Hufbauer, G.C., Synthetic Materials and the Theory of International Trade (Harvard University Press, 1966).
Time Marketing Services, Selective Mass Markets for Products and Services, Time Marketing Information, Report No. 1305.

20 A Note on PIMS and Strategic Planning Data Banks

Hans B. Thorelli

A theme of this book is that Strategic Planning is crucial in international marketing. A set of strategic planning tools of extraordinary importance has been developed in recent years by the PIMS (Profit Impact of Market Strategies) Program of the Strategic Planning Institute (SPI) (955 Massachusetts Avenue, Cambridge, Mass. 02139; Executive Secretary, Dr. Sidney Schoeffler). At this time PIMS is the only strategic data bank in the world based on data for individual lines of business in a great number of industries. SPI is a cooperative venture open to companies in any part of the world. At the beginning of 1980 it has some 240 member companies reporting well over 2,000 lines of business to the common experience pool. As yet most members are American and Canadian; the majority of overseas members are British. For strategic planning purposes it is, of course, imperative that the bank is based on individual product-market businesses. Corporate data of a diversified company are of marginal interest in planning for a specific operating unit.

PIMS is based squarely on the ecologic view of business set forth in Reading 1. Thus, it does recognize that each business is a unique interaction system of firm and environment. Yet the differences between businesses are differences in degree rather than in kind. Accordingly, we may learn as much – in many cases even more – by benefiting from cross-sectional experience as from learning from competitors in our own market. Currently, PIMS is cross-sectional essentially by virtue of the great number of different industries and markets represented in the pool. It is rapidly becoming more cross-sectional in another dimension of special interest here: a growing number of lines of business are being entered from different countries. Here again differences between countries in any given product market (e.g., automobiles or light bulbs) may be crucial – it is still vital to recognize that these dissimilarities, too, are differences in degree.

PIMS generates results at two widely different (though interrelated) levels. Custom-tailored reports on the performance of a specific line of business relative to all lines of business in the pool, and to the score of businesses most like that particular line on a variety of criteria specified by the user, are reported for each line of a member company, as are reports on the likely degree of success of a battery of alternative strategies for each line. At a more general level, PIMS aims at nothing less than providing the basis for the development of the underlying "natural laws" of business. Indeed, in that area, too, considerable progress is being made, as indicated by the sample of academic writings based on PIMS in the references below.

Of special interest to the international marketer are the Start-Up Business reports generated by PIMS. These reports are based on data and assumptions about a contemplated new market entry (industrial hearing protection devices in Brazil, for example) and alternate strategy assumptions supplied by the user. Again, the performance forecasts of the reports are based on the cumulative experience of scores of start-up businesses facing analogous situations. Clearly, too, the ability of the program to generate objective data about the expected level of performance of businesses operating in widely different environments may be of special interest at the headquarters level of multinational companies.

There are now literally dozens of data bases of interest for specialty purposes in strategic planning in international marketing. Many of these are computerized, as is the case with the import-export trade enquiry system of the World Trade Center in New York. The export associations of many countries maintain similar systems. Some other special-purpose data bases are the following:

World Index of Economic Forecasts (Praeger Publishers, 1979)
Business International Corp., country and regional reports
Business International Corp., BI/DATA (computerized)
Economist Intelligence Unit, London, country and market reports
Derwent, patent and license availability bank
SIMCOST (Arthur D. Little Co.), cost variables world-wide
Predicast, market and economy forecasts
PREDEX, forecasting exchange rates
DIALOG (Lockheed Information Systems, computerized), broad
    range of subjects

REFERENCES

Gale, B.T., "Market share and rate of return," The Review of Economics and Statistics, Vol. LIV, No. 4 (November 1972), pp. 412-23.
Schoeffler, S.; Buzzell, R.D.; and Heany, D.F., "Impact of strategic planning on profit performance," Harvard Business Review, Vol. 52, No. 2, (March-April 1974), pp. 137-45.
Thorelli, H.B. (ed.), Strategy + Structure = Performance (Bloomington: Indiana University Press, 1977).

FURTHER READING - PART FOUR

Berent, P.H. (ed). International Marketing Research: Does It Provide What the User Needs? (Amsterdam: ESOMAR, 1976).

Brasch, John J., "Sales forecasting difficulties in a developing country," Industrial Marketing Management, Vol. 7, No. 5 (October 1978), pp. 354-60.

Brislin, R.W.; Lonner, W.J.; and Thorndike, R.M., Cross-Cultural Research Methods (New York: John Wiley & Sons, 1973).

Carr, Richard P., Jr., "Identifying trade areas for consumer goods in foreign markets," Journal of Marketing, Vol. 42, No. 4 (October 1978), pp. 76-80.

Douglas, Susan and Dubois, Bernard, "Looking at the cultural environment for international marketing opportunities," Columbia Journal of World Business, Vol. XII, No. 4 (Winter 1977), pp. 102-9.

Karchere, Alvin J., "Economic forecasting in international business," Columbia Journal of World Business, Vol. XI, No. 4 (Winter 1976), pp. 62-9.

Kaynak, Erdener, "Difficulties of undertaking marketing research in the developing countries," European Research, Vol. 6, No. 6 (November 1978), pp. 251-9.

Mitchell, Paul, "Infrastructures and international marketing effectiveness," Columbia Journal of World Business, Vol. XIV, No. 1 (Spring 1979), pp. 91-101.

Partanen, Juha, "On national consumption profiles," European Research, Vol. 7, No. 1 (January 1979), pp. 27-39.

Permut, Steven E., "Marketing research: The European view," European Research, Vol. 6, No. 2 (March 1978), pp. 49-56.

Plummer, Joseph T., "Consumer focus in cross-national research," Journal of Advertising, Vol. 6, No. 2 (1977), pp. 5-15.

Samli, A. Coskun, Marketing and Distribution Systems in Eastern Europe (New York: Praeger Publishers, 1978).

Schooler, Robert D. and Ferguson, Carl, "A model to determine the activated potential of foreign markets," Marquette Business Review, Vol. XVIII, No. 3 (Fall 1974), pp. 129-36.

Vogel, Ronald H., "Uses of managerial perceptions in clustering countries," Journal of International Business Studies, Vol. 7, No. 1 (Spring 1976), pp. 91-9.

Weber, J.A., "Comparing growth opportunities in the international marketplace," Management International Review, Vol. 19, No. 1 (1979), pp. 47-56.

V

Marketing Strategy: One-Up on the Marketing Mix

Introduction to Part V

To synchronize marketing strategy and market structure is the key challenge in marketing management. Part Five is addressed to marketing strategy, and so, to varying degrees, are Parts Six to Eight. We ask the reader's indulgence for the fact that while the readings in this part touch on broader issues of strategy, they are focused on the instruments of the marketing mix, i.e., on product, price, promotion, and distribution. This is to make certain that each of these areas is given coherent treatment. The treatment is enriched by a number of case histories, illustrating successful international marketing strategies and not so successful ones for each of the elements of the mix. Again, we emphasize that marketing strategy represents something vastly more significant than a random mix of the marketing instruments. The crux is the holistic effect achieved when the instruments mutually enforce each other as indicated in Part One. In Part Eight, the concluding part of the book, we shall return to the planning of general strategy in international marketing.

Reading 21, by Keegan, is an integrated treatment of product and promotion (communication) in multinational marketing. An array of conceptually different product-promotion combinations is presented with useful practical examples. Reading 22, by Ball, further illustrates the concepts by the real life experience of a French company whose American subsidiary came to dominate the U.S. ballpoint pen market through imaginative product and promotional adaptation strategies.

In contrast to the sophisticated strategic marketing approaches required in the industrially advanced countries, Reading 23, by Stone, provides a down-to-earth discussion of product simplification in marketing to the LDCs. While it is true that products especially adapted for materially primitive conditions are often scorned by the large, poverty-stricken groups in the LDCs (presumably for reasons of pride), it is equally clear that these nations do represent a vast potential market for simplified goods. The article gives some successful examples and suggests that British ingenuity is still abroad. The story on "Budd's do-it-yourself cars" in the short Reading 24 shows convincingly how the simplification concept can help fill real needs in Third World countries.

Reading 25, by Becker, emphasizes the need to align international pricing policies and strategies to company objectives, which in turn must be atuned to the local marketing environment. Various pricing problems are examined in light of different degrees of international involvement and the environmental cost constraints that arise. The discussion on price escalation in international marketing will be particularly instructive to readers not yet experienced in export (or import) operations.

In a less and less stable and predictable world, the international marketing executive should be particularly aware of varying inflation rates and fluctuations in foreign currency markets. In Reading 26, Phatak offers some helpful, step-by-step guidelines on how the MNC can best minimize exposure risk due to currency fluctuations. The story on Argentina's inflation, the world's highest, as recounted by Martin in Reading 27, gives us a glimpse of how consumers and businessmen alike try to cope with an oppressive price spiral. An implication for international marketing strategy is to quote prices and require payments in a relatively stabler currency, where possible.

Reading 28, by Killough, takes a look at the transferability of advertising across national boundaries. The writer makes the important distinction between what is said in an advertisement (i.e., the "buying proposal") and how it is said (i.e., the "creative presentation"). The consensus from interviews with 120 international advertising executives is that the buying proposal has a great deal of transferability where buying motives and standards of living are similar. Examples cited are among the industrialized countries of Western Europe, the United States and Japan. However, the creative presentation likely will need adaptation to reflect local differences in culture, communication, laws, and buying appeals. The most important conclusion is that successful transferability of advertising (and other marketing variables, too) requires careful planning at the headquarters level to allow for central coordination with local adaptation to fully achieve multinational promotional objectives.

Reading 29, by Ahmed, addresses the question of channel selection and control – a perennially difficult problem in domestic marketing, infinitely compounded in the international setting. Using European and Japanese automobile manufacturers marketing in the United States as example, Ahmed demonstrates that the more successful firms tend to exercise a higher degree of control over channel members than the less successful ones in such vital strategic areas as pricing, product, promotional, and service policies. Channel control also plays a role in Reading 30, by Hintz. Using a combination of local manufacturing, exporting and licensing, the experience of Culligan shows that even a relatively small company, originally confined to a domestic, one-market strategy, can become a successful multinational marketer with proper planning and strategic adaptation. Part Six addresses more directly the specific problems encountered in international marketing by the small firm.

21 Five Strategies for Multinational Marketing*
Warren J. Keegan

Success lies in market response to a product offering. Although many companies have highly satisfactory product planning approaches for their domestic markets, very often the multinational product planning is left undone. This lack of planning for international markets is one of the major factors inhibiting the growth and profitability of international operations today.

The purpose of this article is to identify the <u>five strategic alternatives available to international marketers</u> and to show how to decide which strategy to use. Since the communications used to advertise and promote a product are such an integral part of the product itself, we shall include this factor in our analysis. Table 21.1 summarizes the proposed strategies.

STRATEGY ONE: SAME PRODUCT, SAME MESSAGE WORLDWIDE

As a company begins to move into foreign markets, there are good arguments for pursuing a uniform strategy of international marketing. This approach involves offering exactly the same product with the same advertising appeals to each national market. The uniform approach has a number of advantages. Firstly, and by no means the least, is its simplicity. Its demands upon executive and marketing time are minimal. It requires no original analysis or data generation, only execution or implementation. Since the product itself is unchanged, engineering and manufacturing costs that would be incurred by product changes are reduced to zero. In sum, it is the <u>lowest cost international product strategy</u>.

*Slightly abbreviated from Warren J. Keegan, "Five strategies for multinational marketing," <u>European Business</u> (January 1970), pp. 35-40, with permission.

Table 21.1. Multinational Product-Communication Mix:
Strategic Alternatives

Product Strategy	Communications strategy	Product examples	Product function or need satisfied	Conditions of product use	Ability to buy product
1. Uniform	Uniform		Same	Same	Yes
2. Same	Different	Bicycles Recreation Transportation	Different	Same	Yes
3. Different	Same	Gasoline Detergents	Same	Different	Yes
4. Different	Different	Clothing Greeting cards	Different	Different	Yes
5. Invention	Develop new communications	Hand-powered washing machine	Same		No

Another reason for a uniform strategy is the scarcity of good ideas. When a new one comes along, a wise manager tries to exploit it as much as possible. A case in point is Avis Rent-A-Car. They have used their "We Try Harder" theme in America and in Europe – both times with success.

Many companies have followed this approach, with varying degrees of success. There is a story told in a well-known Belgian biscuit company about the company's nineteenth century founder. A relative of the company's founder had shipped some of the company's biscuits to China. The biscuits were very well received, and the relative wrote to Belgium saying that the Chinese liked the biscuit very much and that there was an excellent market for the company's product in China but that one modification would be required. Unfortunately, the company's white package was the color of mourning in China. If the package were changed, he wrote, there would be a substantial market. The founder replied with the hauteur of nineteenth century commercial pride, "If the Chinese wish to eat our biscuits, they will take them in a white package." Needless to say, the uniform strategy failed in this case.

In more recent times, companies such as PepsiCo have employed the uniform strategy. PepsiCo has sold exactly the same product, with the same advertising and promotional themes and appeals used in the United States, in each of the more than 100 countries in which it operates.

Coca-Cola sends to all its local managers a suitcase packed with materials including a bible which gives all the ads to be printed in color, those to appear in black and white, the number of times it can be full page or half page, and so on. The suitcase specifies each photo, every line of copy to be used, the tapes of music to be played over the radio.

The local managers can do nothing on their own without first clearing it with headquarters in Atlanta.

These two companies' outstanding international performances are often cited in justification for this strategy.

Unfortunately, the uniform strategy does not work for all products. One U.S. company spent several million dollars in an unsuccessful effort to capture the British cake mix market with its American-style fancy frosting and cake mixes, only to discover that Britons consume their cake at tea time, and that the cake they prefer is dry, spongy, and suitable to being picked up with the left hand while the right manages a cup of tea. Another U.S. company that asked a panel of British housewives to bake their favorite cakes discovered this important fact and has since acquired a major share of the British cake mix market with a dry, spongy cake mix.

The uniform product-communications-price strategy has an enormous appeal to most multinational companies because of the cost savings associated with this approach. Two sources of savings, manufacturing economies of scale and eliminations of product R and D costs, are obvious. Less apparent, but still important, are the substantial economies associated with standardization of marketing communications. For a company with worldwide operations, the cost of preparing separate print and TV-cinema films for each market is enormous. PepsiCo International marketers have estimated, for example, that production costs for specially prepared advertising for foreign markets would cost them $8 million per annum, which is considerably more than the amount now spent by PepsiCo International for advertising production for its international markets. Still another source of savings of the uniform strategy is its marketing and managerial simplicity. Since a company's whole market department, and much of its general management, is focused on such questions as which product to offer, at what price, and with what kind of advertising appeals, uniform strategy obviates the necessity for rethinking the answers and reduces the need for expensive manpower in each branch.

While the cost advantages of a uniform strategy are unmistakable, cost reduction is not as important as profit maximization. As shown above, the uniform strategy in spite of its immediate savings may in fact prove to be financially disastrous. Furthermore, even companies such as PepsiCo who have had a generally successful experience with a uniform strategy are now beginning to conclude that while they have done well, they can do even better if they adapt their marketing mix.

STRATEGY TWO: SAME PRODUCT-DIFFERENT COMMUNICATIONS

When a product fills a different need or is used differently under conditions similar to those in the domestic market, the only adjustment required is in marketing communications. Bicycles and motorscooters are illustrations of products which often fit this approach. They satisfy needs for recreation in the United States and for basic transportation in many parts of the world. Outboard motors are sold mainly to a recreation market in the United States, while the same motors in many countries are sold mainly to fishing and transportation fleets.

In effect, when this approach is pursued (or, as is often the case, when it is stumbled upon by accident) a product transformation occurs. The same physical product ends up serving a different function or use from its original one. An actual example of a very successful transformation is provided by the U.S. farm machinery company which decided to market its U.S. line of suburban lawn and garden power equipment in less developed countries as agricultural implements. The company's line of garden equipment was ideally suited to their farming tasks and most importantly, it was priced at almost a third less than competitive equipment – especially designed for small acreage farming.

There are many examples of food product transformation. Many dry soup powders, for example, are sold mainly as soups in Europe and as sauces or cocktail dips in the United States. The products are identical; the only change is in marketing communications. In this case, the main communications adjustment is in the labeling of the powder. In Europe, the label illustrates and describes how to make soup out of the powder. In the U.S. the label illustrates and describes how to make sauce and dip as well as soup.

The appeal of the same product-different marketing strategy is its relatively low cost of implementation. Since the product is unchanged, R and D, tooling, manufacturing setup, and inventory costs resulting from additions to the product line are avoided. The only costs of this approach are in identifying different product functions and reformulating marketing communications (advertising, sales, promotion, point of sale material, etc.) around the newly identified function.

STRATEGY THREE: DIFFERENT PRODUCT, SAME COMMUNICATIONS

A third approach to international product planning is to extend without change the basic communications strategy developed for the home market, but to adapt the home product to local conditions. The different product-same communications strategy assumes that the product will serve the same function in foreign markets under different use conditions.

Esso followed this approach when it adapted its gasoline formulations to meet the weather conditions prevailing in market areas but used without change its basic message, "Put a Tiger in Your Tank." Since the tiger is an almost universal symbol of power, Esso was able to use its campaign in Europe, America, and Asia.

There are many other examples of products which have been adjusted to perform the same function internationally under different environmental conditions. International soap and detergent manufacturers have adjusted their product formulations to meet local water conditions and the characteristics of washing equipment with no change in their basic communications approach. Agricultural chemicals have been adjusted to meet different soil conditions and different types and levels of insect resistance. Household appliances have been scaled to sizes appropriate to different use environments, and clothing has been adapted to meet fashion criteria.

STRATEGY FOUR: DUAL ADAPTATION

Certain market conditions indicate a strategy of adapting both product and communications. As a result of different market conditions and the product's serving different functions, this combines strategies two and three.

U.S. greeting card manufacturers have faced this in Europe, where a greeting card provides space for the sender to write his own message in contrast to the U.S. card, which contains a prepared message, or what is known in the greeting card industry as 'sentiment.' The conditions under which greeting cards are purchased in Europe are also different from those in the United States. In Europe, cards are handled frequently by customers, which makes it necessary to package the greeting card in cellophane.

To sell instant coffee in England, Nescafé had to use this strategy. Their traditional instant coffee, developed in Switzerland and sold on the Continent, did not sell well in the United Kingdom. Their local marketing managers made tests and found that most Englishmen prefer a light, almost blond coffee. Their coffee-drinking habits had been developed during World War II, with the presence of American troops; consequently their taste in coffee is similar to the American one.

In marketing the new blend, Nescafé found that coffee is viewed as a non-traditional drink. As is well known, everyone drinks tea; those who choose coffee, like the young, are looking for something different. To reflect this, their publicity spots were made more aggressive.

STRATEGY FIVE: PRODUCT INVENTION

The adaptation and adjustment strategies are effective approaches to international marketing when customer needs and the conditions under which products are used are similar to those in the home market. Unfortunately, this is not always the case, particularly in the less developed countries which contain three-quarters of the world's population. For these markets, the strategy should be invention or the development of an entirely new product designed to satisfy customer needs at a price within reach of the potential customer. This is a demanding, but — if product development costs are not excessive — a potentially rewarding product strategy for the mass markets in the middle and less developed countries of the world.

Although potential opportunities for invention in international marketing are legion, the number of instances where companies have responded is disappointingly small. For example, there are an estimated 600 million women in the world who still scrub their clothes by hand. These women have been served by soap and detergent companies for decades, yet only recently did one of these companies attempt to develop an inexpensive manual washing device.

The effort was launched by the vice-president of Marketing-Worldwide of Colgate Palmolive who asked the leading inventor of modern mechanical washing processes to consider "inventing backwards" — to apply his knowledge not to a better mechanical washing device but to a much better manual device. The device developed by the inventor is an inexpensive (price under $10), all-plastic hand-powered washer that has the tumbling action of a modern automatic machine. It is one of the most efficient converters of mechanical energy to a hydraulic washing action yet developed and is reported to have been very favorably received in Mexican test markets.

HOW TO CHOOSE A STRATEGY

The best strategy is one which optimizes company profits over the long term. Stated more precisely, it maximizes the present value of cash flows from business operations. Which strategy for international markets best achieves this goal? There is no general answer to this question. Rather, the answer depends upon the specific product-market-company mix.

Some products demand adaptation, others lend themselves to adaptation, and others are best left unchanged. The same is true of markets. Some are so closely similar to the home market as to require little change. Other markets are moderately different and lend themselves to adaptation, and still others are so different as to require adaptation of the majority of products. Finally, companies differ not only in their manufacturing costs, but also in their capability to identify and produce profitable product adaptations.

PRODUCT-MARKET ANALYSIS

The first step in formulating international product policy is to analyze each product. How is the product used? Does it require power sources, linkage to other systems, maintenance, preparation, style matching, and so on? Examples of mandatory adaptation are products designed for sixty cycle power going into fifty cycle markets, or products calibrated in metric measures going to the Anglo-Saxon markets. Products that require upkeep should be changed to reflect the different maintenance standards and practices, and products used under different conditions than those for which they were originally designed must be adapted. Even more difficult are the product adaptations which are clearly not mandatory, but which are of critical importance in determining whether the product will appeal to a narrow segment rather than a broad mass market.

European companies frequently neglect adaptation of distribution and communications. Too often, companies believe they have adequately adapted their international product offering when they make mandatory adaptations of the physical features of a product (i.e., converting 220 volts to 110 volts) but extend their home market communications approach and rely upon export channels for distribution. The effect of such practice is to leave excellent products far short of their true market potential. Perhaps the most impressive example of what a company can do if it does commit itself to the full development of advertising and distribution programs is Volkswagen of America. It has developed a one billion dollar plus business basically by <u>taking a given product and exploiting its potential to the limit with a communications program specifically designed for the U.S. market</u>, and a dealer organization whose quality and coverage have been widely admired in the industry.

COMPANY ANALYSIS

Even if product-market analysis indicates an adaptation opportunity, each company must examine its own product-communications development and manufacturing costs. Clearly, any of the product strategies must survive the test of profit effectiveness. The often repeated exhortation that in international marketing a company should always adapt its products, advertising, and promotion is clearly superficial, for it does not take into account <u>costs</u> of adapting products and communications programs.

What are adaptation costs? They fall under two broad categories — <u>development</u> and <u>production</u>. Development costs will vary depending on the cost effectiveness of product/communications development groups within the company. The range in costs from company to company and product to product is great. Often, the company with international product development facilities has a strategic cost advantage. The vice-president of a leading U.S. machinery company spoke recently of this kind of advantage:

> We have a machinery development group both here in the States and in Europe. I tried to get our U.S. group to develop a machine for making eliptical cigars that dominate the European market. At first they said, "Who would want an elliptical cigar machine?" Then they grudgingly admitted that they could produce such a machine for $500,000. I went to our Italian product development group with the same proposal and they developed the machine I wanted for $50,000. The differences were partly relative wage costs, but very importantly they were psychological. The Europeans see elliptical cigars every day, and they do not find the elliptical cigar unusual. Our American engineers were negative on elliptical cigars at the outset and I think this affected their overall response.

Analysis of a company's manufacturing costs is essentially a matter of identifying potential opportunity losses. If a company is reaping economies from large-scale production of a single product, then any shift to variations of the single product will raise manufacturing costs. In general, the more decentralized a company's manufacturing setup, the smaller the manufacturing cost of producing different versions of the basic product. Indeed, in the company with local manufacturing facilities for each national market, the additional manufacturing cost of producing an adapted product for each market is zero.

A more fundamental form of company analysis occurs when a firm is considering in general whether or not to explicitly pursue a strategy of product adaptation. At this level, analysis must focus not only on the manufacturing cost structure of the firm, but on whether the firm is capable of identifying product adaptation opportunities and of converting them into profitable products. The ability to identify possibilities depends to an important degree on the creativity of people in the organization and the effectiveness of information systems in the organization. The latter capability is as important as the former. Nescafé was able to find the right blend of coffee for the English only because of its well-developed marketing departments and their close connection to headquarters. The existence of salesmen, for example, who are creative in identifying profitable product adaptation opportunities is no assurance that their ideas will be translated into reality by the organization. Information, in the form of their ideas and perceptions, must move through the organization to those who are involved in the product development decision-making process and this movement is not automatic. Companies which lack perceptual and information system capabilities are not well equipped to change products, and either should concentrate on products which can be left alone or should develop these capabilities before turning to a product adaptation strategy.

SUMMARY

The choice of product and communications strategy in international marketing depends on three key factors: (1) the product itself, defined in terms of the function or need it serves; (2) the market, defined in terms of the conditions under which the product is used, the preferences and ability to buy of potential customers; and (3) the costs of adaptation and manufacture of these product-communications approaches. Only after analysis of the product-market fit and of company capabilities and costs can executives choose the most profitable international strategy.

22 Entering U.S. Market, Bic Had to Vie with American Brands and also with Japanese*
Donald A. Ball

In less than 20 years Bic Pen Corp., in which Bic France holds a majority interest, has become the leader in the American ballpoint pen market, with a claimed 70 percent share. Furthermore Bic has also been instrumental in more than doubling this market during the same period.

Bic entered the market by buying the Waterman Pen Co., but soon found that this purchase was of little help in obtaining the kind of access it wanted to U.S. trade channels.

Very early, Bic France found that European marketing methods based primarily on price were not applicable in this country. American dealers required point-of-purchase displays, heavy advertising, and attractive packaging as well. Bic USA was so successful in developing these marketing aids that now marketing expertise flows from the American operation back to France.

In addition, Bic USA has moved into other products which can be piggybacked with its pens in American retail outlets – a lighter, a razor, and a line of pantyhose. For all of these, packaging and distribution are the name of the game.

Bic's American strategy for pens was based on serving three market segments: over-the-counter, commercial, and specialty advertising. Up to this time, most American manufacturers of inexpensive pens had concentrated primarily on the consumer market.

It was essential to show the American public that the Bic pen was reliable and rugged. Heavy TV advertising was employed to show Bic pens undergoing all kinds of torture tests and still being able to write. When Bic decided to enter the porous pen market – already dominated by Flair, made by Gillette's Paper-Mate unit – Bic was already known for its aggressive approach, so the Bic Banana campaign enabled the company to capture 30 percent of this market.

*Reprinted from Donald A. Ball, "Entering U.S. Market, Bic had to vie with American brands and also with Japanese," Marketing News (March 10, 1978), with permission.

The pen market, of course, is a rough one — a foreign company entering the American market must not only contend with its U.S. counterparts but also with companies from other countries which may have the same goals in mind. Bic, for instance, not only must do battle with some of the Paper-Mate entries, Scripto, and others but also must meet competition from Pentel and Pilot, Japanese operations which are offering it some of the toughest competition. Bic, however, is staying on top of its markets by its continuous hustle.

Special promotions have been employed not only in the over-the-counter market but also in the commercial segment. Offers of free, high-quality premiums, such as cookware, to businesses which specify Bic pens to their office supply dealers have been eminently successful.

Although Bic USA has become a leader in the worldwide Bic organization with respect to marketing methods, the French parent still decides what products are to be marketed, and new product lines come principally from headquarters.

It was the home office, for example, which directed Bic USA's entrance into the disposable lighter market in 1973. Bic France felt that even though Gillette had an early lead, Bic USA could still get a large share of the market because it already had the distribution channels and the marketing expertise. The assumption was correct, and now Bic USA has a 30 percent share of this market.

23 The Massive Market for Simplicity*
P. Stone

On a scruffy doorway near Covent Garden Market is a sign saying "Intermediate Technology Development Group." What goes on beyond a door on the second floor suggests that all is not yet lost for British enterprise. ITDG is a limited, non-profit making company. Its main product is a catalogue of British companies and their wares, aimed at small scale enterprises in the developing countries.

In some parts of the world, what ITDG is trying to encourage in Britain exists naturally — because it is obvious that it should. For example, in Japan the Toyo Kogyo motor company used to produce a three-wheeled truck for the home market. When Japan began to prosper, the market for the cheap, slow three-wheeler practically disappeared. So the company sought out southeast Asian countries which were at an appropriate stage of economic development and mounted an export drive in those countries. Its three-wheeler still sells.

Halfway between a bicycle and a car, the three-wheeler was an example of "intermediate technology." In the same way, a horsedrawn mower and reaper, representing the halfway stage between a sickle and a combine harvester, might be the ideal thing at a certain stage in a country's economic evolution. One British manufacturer still draws an income from such a machine, thanks to ITDG.

But intermediate technology is not the same thing as old-fashioned technology that we have now abandoned. In agriculture, for example, many machines which gave good service in nineteenth-century England were made by casting metal. Now lighter, stronger versions may be built by welding rolled sections. The design will have been modified to suit modern production methods — but the machine will still be put to the same use.

---

*Reprinted from P. Stone, "The massive market for simplicity," British Industry Week, Vol. 25 (April 1969), pp. 24ff, with permission.

IMMENSE POTENTIAL

The less-developed countries are growing at 5 percent a year on average. Some are growing far more rapidly. They constitute an expanding market in which it is possible to sell a wide range of manufactures without the need to invest in speculative R and D or to adopt sophisticated designs. The potential demand surge from these countries is immense; British exporters should establish themselves now, with a view to future prosperity.

That is only part of the reason why the existence of ITDG is an encouraging sign. The way in which the company came to be formed suggests that the British may not have lost the ability to triumph in spite of their own Government and, more difficult, their own economists.

Such economists as Lord Balogh and Mr. Kaldor have long been active in the field of aid to the underdeveloped countries. Even before economists were employed by the British Government, international organizations like FAO and UNESCO offered challenging jobs to men prepared to help the poor nations. The accepted emphasis was placed on the provision of an infrastructure – steel plants, railways, chemical plants and the like. All these were big projects demanding large amounts of scarce capital and technical resources. The idea of expending capital on lesser things was frowned upon, because capital is generally less productive if dispersed. This "industrialization first" orthodoxy led to the neglect of the agricultural sector.

Commonsense suggested that a slow build-up of agricultural wealth by the introduction of simple technology – moving from sickles to scythes – might be a sensible step. When the British National Export Council was about to send off a mission to sell British agricultural machinery in Nigeria, it was suggested that much of the machinery was too sophisticated for Nigeria's stage of development. With the help of the National College of Agricultural Engineering, a list of hand- or animal-operated agricultural machinery was compiled and dispatched in a hasty three weeks. The response to these machines was far warmer than that accorded to the expensive combine-harvesters which British agriculture considers necessary.

From that time, theoretical arguments on the merits of concentrating capital expenditure rather than frittering it away on intermediate technology became increasingly irrelevant. ITDG simply responded to demands from the developing countries.

ADVERTISING REVENUE

Obviously a much enlarged catalogue was the next logical step, and this provided a way to raise funds. Suitable manufacturers were invited to advertise in the catalogue at the rate of L 10 a halfpage. Butyl Products took four pages to give a handy guide to building your own reservoir; most companies took less. One company now advertises a windmill pump for Ł 120 complete f.o.b. – "remember there are no running costs." One company advertises ploughshares in both French and German, another displays its harrows with a photograph of two superb English Shire horses. There are advertisements for irrigation packs, wheelbarrows, small engines and generators, pulleys, looms, printing machines, and tractors. Animal-drawn tool bars can be bought for as little as Ł 10.

When a response comes, it can be embarrassingly large. By 1950, Bamletts of Thirsk, which appears to have had the distinction of making the last animal-drawn reaper and mower in Britain, was down to making one or two a year. Now that the idea of Britain as a supplier of intermediate technology has caught on, things have changed. Tanzania and Pakistan wanted them too. Bamletts sold a license to a company in Pakistan and is now drawing royalties from a design that seemed obsolete ten years ago.

MOULDING POLICY

Gardening tools form a good part of the equipment requested and such devices as spring-loaded forks and spades ought to sell well. However, ITDG realizes that peasants have profound suspicions of anything too new. Although the spring-loaded spade may be the suburban gardener's answer to digging a small plot with minimum exertion, a peasant used to, say, the mattock, will find the change far too great. ITDG has therefore helped to promote the development of a more efficient mattock, with an extra handle for added leverage.

What does ITDG do next? Again, circumstances are moulding policy. ITDG now gets many enquiries not only for hardware but also for advice and information. What is needed is a clearing house for technical enquiries. That need is now being investigated with a view to establishing "Inter-tech," which would have two functions. One would be as a base for consultancy, in order to promote the field application of low-cost intermediate technologies, the other would be to run a London-based office to handle enquiries from abroad and find British companies, research associations and the like which could provide the answers.

SUCCESSFUL PATH

ITDG treads a somewhat tortuous path between being business-like and being charitable. It is determined, however, to lean as far as possible towards commercial behavior; the "rate for the job" is a firm policy. One interesting pointer to future development is VITA, or "Volunteers for International Technical Assistance," an American nonprofit organization which provides spare-time assistance from a bank of specialists. It also defines key problems for concentrated development effort. The result of one such effort, the VITA solar cooker, is now "in wide demand throughout Africa."

24 Budd: Do-It-Yourself Cars for Third World*
Railway Age

The Budd Co. figures that over the next five years, railroads in the less-developed countries of South America, Africa, the Middle East, and the Far East will need to purchase around 14,000 no-frills railway passenger cars – and to help meet this need Budd on October 26 unveiled what it described as "a revolutionary new stainless-steel passenger rail car with prefabricated components that can be shipped anywhere in the world and assembled by customer countries."

Budd introduced its new "International Rail Car" at a news conference in New York, held, appropriately, in the Dag Hammerskold Room of the United Nations Plaza Hotel. James H. McNeal, Budd's president and chief executive officer, said the car will sell for around $150,000. A prototype of the car has been constructed at Budd's Red Lion plant in Philadelphia and has passed safety and performance specifications.

McNeal said the car "offers low maintenance and operation costs (and) is adaptable for any service – ranging from the sophisticated to the basic – depending upon customer requirements." He added that all components – aside from the basic shell – can be manufactured or furnished by the customer country, or can be supplied in any desired degree of refinement by Budd.

"The concept can become the foundation of any nation's rail car-building industry," said McNeal. "It provides for increasing locally manufactured content of the car consistent with any nation's degree of industrial development."

Rene H. Vansteenkiste, Budd's group vice president in charge of commercial products, noted that the new approach "may revolutionize worldwide passenger car production by using U.S. techniques and materials, and capabilities of customer countries in manufacture of rail transportation equipment."

---

*Reprinted from "Budd: Do-it-yourself Cars for Third World," Railway Age (November 13, 1978), with permission.

The 109-seat coach consists of four major modules that can be shipped in crated units for easy assembly. The interior is equipped with two toilets, fluorescent lighting, and molded fiberglass seats. "When more amenities are wanted," said Vansteenkiste, "the options include full insulation, heating and air conditioning, variations in toilet styles, curtained windows, vinyl-cushioned seats, and other comfort features."

He pointed out that the modular construction permits significant economies in shipping: "The four major subassemblies – sides, roof, floor, and ends – are packaged in a single reusable steel crate, which can be folded for storage or returned. Other equipment – trucks, seats, interior linings, and other parts – is shipped in a standard Sea-Land container. As a result, the International Rail Car needs only about half the shipping space of a conventionally assembled car of the same size."

25 Pricing: An International Marketing Challenge
Helmut Becker

Traditionally, pricing has often been regarded as a routine function that could be relegated to lower management once the general policy had been set at the top. Under this assumption it is likely that pricing is viewed as a static or passive marketing decision variable, routinely executed, as management places greater emphasis on non-price competitive marketing instruments. In recent years, however, the status of pricing has changed to that of a much more dynamic or active marketing element. This switch is due to a number of factors, internal and external to the firm. Internally, probably the strongest force that has propelled pricing to greater relative importance in the marketing mix is the adoption of the systems concept. With it comes the realization that all the marketing tools interact with each other, that each can complement and, at least in part, be substituted for the others. The hallmark of a successful marketing strategy is the specific combination and synergistic effect of all the variables at any given time – including a fitting price. Externally, in a world of increasing competition, government regulation, accelerating inflation, and widely fluctuating foreign exchange rates, management is simply forced to take heed of its pricing policy – especially in the international sphere. Thus, pricing decisions have become far more difficult and, at the same time, more vital to the health of the enterprise than they were even five or ten years ago.

PRICING POLICIES AND OBJECTIVES

Figure 25.1 depicts a well-known approach to the pricing decision process (Oxenfeldt, 1960). It makes the point that logically, the pricing decision process starts with the selection of the target market. It is important to know how consumers perceive low or high prices for a given product and how sensitive they are to price changes. The product/brand image in turn is greatly influenced by the price level and must be matched with the customer perceptions in the target markets. Images such as "luxury" product, "quality" brand, or "economy" model are part of the pricing consideration, just as much as they are a part of the overall marketing plan. For example, a high price strategy, designed to foster exclusivity or a high quality image, frequently must be supported by aggressive promotion.

Pricing policies must reflect the firm's objectives, whether these are to maximize profits in the short or long term, to obtain a certain target return on investment, to maintain a specific market share, to promote customer loyalty and market stability, or to retain control over end user prices. For instance, a firm may have a policy "to meet competition when and wherever possible." A price reduction by a competitor may then lead the firm to lower its prices to the level of the competitor, or by a specified percentage, or to the break-even point, whichever is higher.

STAGE ONE:	selecting target markets
	↓
STAGE TWO:	choosing a brand image
	↓
STAGE THREE:	composing a marketing mix
	↓
STAGE FOUR:	selecting a pricing policy
	↓
STAGE FIVE:	determining a pricing strategy
	↓
STAGE SIX:	arriving at a specific price

Source: From Alfred R. Oxenfeldt, "Multi-stage approach to pricing," Harvard Business Review, Vol. 38 (July-August 1960), pp. 125-33.

Fig. 25.1. The pricing decision process.

Internationally, variations in market conditions, competition, governmental regulations, and all kinds of environmental constraints are much more pronounced than domestically. Pricing objectives and strategy must be adapted to local requirements in foreign markets, and yet they must be consistent with company goals worldwide. Thus, a firm may have a 15 percent return on investment as a corporate objective, while allowing break-even operations in country B, but insisting on 20 percent ROI in country C. Similarly, the company may pursue a profit maximization strategy in country D, while at least 25 percent market share is the pricing objective in country E.

In utilizing pricing as an active marketing variable, management may have to incorporate control over end-user prices into company policy. However, such a policy may prove impossible to implement internationally, particularly in the exporting situation, where the length of the channel of distribution and the number of intermediaries increase. Such a situation may indeed force the firm to abandon some of its price controlling efforts and to concentrate on f.o.b. prices obtained before the goods ever leave the home country. Or the company may have the option to enter the foreign market via licensing, joint ventures, or wholly-owned manufacturing facilities in an effort to regain some degree of pricing control. Of course, in a number of countries antitrust or other legislation does not permit resale price maintenance at all.

INTERNATIONAL PRICING DECISIONS

In the international arena, the complexity and scope of pricing decisions tend to rise exponentially with the number of countries involved, since management must now deal with multiple sets of environmental constraints, market factors, and firm factors. In addition, the firm has to protect itself against risks non-existent in domestic marketing, such as the political and economic conditions in the foreign national market. For example, floating exchange and varying inflation rates add a financial dimension to international marketing that is less relevant for domestic strategy. Phatak lists a number of ways in which it is possible to deal with these kinds of problems in international business (see Reading 26), including quoting of customer prices in another, more stable currency, borrowing, bartering, hedging, and entering into currency swaps.

In general, there are several situations in which pricing decisions must be made: setting price for the first time; initiating a price change; meeting or reacting to price changes by competitors; and multiple product and product line pricing, where demand is interrelated. Internationally, pricing decisions can be classified roughly in terms of the degree or stage of foreign involvement by the firm: export pricing (passive or active); foreign market pricing (from branch or subsidiary); coordinating pricing between the home country and one or several foreign countries; international lease pricing; and intracompany transfer pricing.

The general pricing situation and international pricing dimensions can be related to each other in matrix form as in figure 25.2, indicating the type of pricing decisions that must be made in individual cases. Thus, it may be possible that the firm is confronted in one market with a "first time – exporting" pricing decision and in another with a "multiple products – foreign market sales branch" pricing situation. The difficulty is compounded when the firm or the branch exports to third countries, or has to react quickly to aggressive competition in one foreign market environment while bound by cartel agreements or government controls in another.

PRICING PROBLEMS	INTERNATIONAL PRICING SITUATION EXAMPLES			
	exporting	foreign subsidiary or branch	internat'l leasing	intra-company transfers
first time pricing				
price changing				
competition pricing				
multiple product pricing				

Fig. 25.2. International pricing decision matrix.

Leasing as an international marketing strategy requiring pricing decisions is growing in importance too. Already popular in the United States in such diverse areas as truck and automobile fleets, computers, office copiers, and canning machinery (just to name some examples), leasing is gaining rapidly in other markets as a marketing-financing mechanism. It is applicable in markets where credit tightness does not permit direct purchase or in industries with a fast pace of technological progress (e.g., computers), where customers are reluctant to commit large sums of capital for equipment that may quickly become obsolete. Leasing may also be a technique to market/finance entire plants or other installations in LDCs where scarcity of foreign exchange reserves would otherwise not allow such large-scale investments. With financial support and protection provided, for example, by the Export-Import Bank of the United States to both export lessors and to foreign importers of American equipment for lease to their customers, the attraction of leasing as an international marketing strategy is bound to increase.

International lease pricing decisions are complicated by the fact that they must explicitly include the time value of money invested in the machinery or facilities leased to the foreign customer. In addition, the risk from technical obsolescence and lease cancellation remains with the lessor and must therefore be included in the price, that is, in the periodic lease payments. Inflation and floating exchange rates at home and abroad make the time value and future cost of capital as well as the replacement costs of the leased equipment more difficult to forecast. To minimize these risks in lease pricing may require a price or lease payment escalator clause with remittance in home country currency (assuming it has greater currency stability).

Intracompany or transfer pricing presents a vexing problem to multinational marketing management superbly analyzed by Shulman (see Reading 40). For example, intracompany shipments or "sales" to a foreign branch or subsidiary constitute in fact imports into that country subject to import duties, foreign exchange controls, import quotas, and even possible dumping charges if priced below full cost, in addition to, of course, corporate taxes in both countries. Policies that guide the sales to foreign branches and subsidiaries must therefore fulfill certain intracompany pricing objectives.

DETERMINANTS FOR INTERNATIONAL PRICE SETTING

Beyond corporate objectives, international price setting is determined by (1) costs; (2) customer behavior and market conditions (demand factors); (3) market structure (competitive factors, channels of distribution); and (4) environmental constraints (economic, educational, and cultural). Since all of these factors vary substantially from country to country, the list price, discounts from list, markups, and allowances will often vary between domestic and foreign and between several foreign markets.

1. Costs are frequently used as a basis for price determination, largely because they are easier to measure than some of the other variables. Costs provide the price floor that must be covered for the firm to at least break even. They include manufacturing, shipping, and marketing costs, as well as overhead (administration, taxes, depreciation, and so forth). Obviously, to minimize costs in international marketing, the mode of foreign involvement and country location is of crucial importance. For example, exporting tends to lengthen distribution channels and increase marketing costs, while (hopefully) permitting full capacity operations and manufacturing economies at home. Foreign manufacturing facilities, on the other hand, may reduce some marketing and distribution expenditures, but may increase financial risks due to currency exposure and expropriation.

The key question regarding costs as a price determinant is whether to utilize full or variable costs. In the long run, there can be little doubt that the firm, in order to remain profitable, must recover all costs. In domestic marketing, where continuous operations are naturally presupposed, full cost pricing plus some predetermined markup for profit is the usual practice. A similar approach would be appropriate in the case of foreign marketing from local manufacturing and warehousing facilities. However, variable costs may well be adequate as an export pricing basis where the objective is to relieve the company of a temporary surplus or excess capacity (for example). When more permanent relationships with foreign distributors and customers are sought, total costs must eventually be recovered for profitable exporting. Then too, full cost pricing reduces the risk of dumping charges, particularly where variable cost prices fall below domestic selling prices. Technically, of course, the financial results are improved whenever prices exceed marginal cost even by the smallest of amounts.

2. Demand and market factors are a vital input in determining prices. In a sense, demand sets the ceiling price, an upper limit to what customers are willing to pay for a given product or service. Methods for estimating demand and market potential are fairly well established and are the same domestically as internationally. The difficulty arises in the availability of data within countries and the comparability of data between countries, a theme fully developed in Readings 17 and 18. Despite the sometimes seemingly insurmountable problems in demand analysis and forecasting, the international marketer must make a judgement concerning the quantities that could be sold at different prices for each foreign market. There could also be some cross-over demand from one country to the next where they are in close proximity to each other and where prices differ widely between them.

3. Market structure and competition require the firm to set a "realistic" price bounded at the top by the ceiling price set by demand factors and limited at the bottom by the floor price set by costs. The intensity of competition varies from country to country and from one market to the next. Beyond economics, cultural, legal, and political constraints modify competitive market behavior. A few giant organizations may battle for market share in periodic price wars in one country, mainly because product differentiation may be effectively prevented by overly restrictive advertising regulations. Across the border, strong anti-merger legislation may allow numerous relatively small firms to operate rather unencumbered by government interference, their success only subject to the lively winds of competition in so-called nonprice areas. (Of course, if A charges the same price as B but A has higher quality — or his product carries a warranty while B's does not — A is the low price seller). Failure to assess competition in foreign markets carefully may well lead to low sales volume and/or to prices forced down to the variable cost floor.

4. Environmental constraints and costs in the inter-nation interface and in the competitive position of nations themselves in the global arena are forever changing. This is well illustrated in Volkswagenwerk's decision to start producing the "Rabbit" in the United States in 1978. To remain price competitive in the American marketplace, the company had to increase the dollar content of the car. The decision was made in light of the concern's disastrous year 1974, when it incurred nearly one third of a billion dollar loss worldwide. VW's chief executive, Dr. Toni Schmücker, attributed the loss of a dominant position in the American small-car market and attendant profit problems to the high wages in Germany, increasing shipping costs, and unfavorable exchange rates. With no let-up expected in the continuing deterioration of the dollar's value relative to the deutsche mark, VW's future ability to compete in the American market would have been seriously hampered without local manufacturing facilities.

The combined forces of environmental constraints often also entail cost factors that impact specifically on international (as opposed to domestic) pricing decisions. Included are fees, tariffs and special taxes, additional packaging, labeling requirements, shipping and middleman costs, additional risk, insurance and financing charges, costs arising from varying levels of inflation, and fluctuating currency exchange rates.

Fees, Tariffs, Taxes

Of all the international environmental cost factors, fees, taxes, and tariffs are the most pervasive and sometimes the most disruptive to foreign trade. Tariffs are a form of taxation whose purpose is to raise government revenues, to reduce unwelcome competition from abroad, to conserve foreign exchange reserves, or simply to discourage the country's citizens from consuming certain products thought to be harmful. Tariffs almost always have the effect of raising prices to consumers. They are levied as ad valorem duty or a percentage fee on the value of the imported product (e.g. 18 percent of the declared value or invoiced amount on a down comforter); as specific duty or flat fee for each item imported (e.g. 50 cents per standard bottle of white wine); or as a combination of the two. In addition to tariffs, there may be charges on import licenses, usage of dock facilities and customs handling, and remittance fees – all costs which have to be taken into account in pricing.

International Distribution Costs

International distribution costs affect pricing in foreign markets in several ways. Extra shipping, freight, sea-worthy packaging, and customs brokerage charges can significantly increase price and reduce competitiveness of imported products. Even locally assembled goods can be impacted in their prices, where parts and raw materials must be imported from one or several other countries. The availability and efficiency of local distribution channels and transportation networks play a major role. For example, Italy and (to a lesser extent) France are dominated by small, independent retail business, whereas large chains are common in the United States, Germany, and Sweden. The United Kingdom and the Netherlands are in between. A fragmented retail structure and transportation system tend to reduce order size and increase the layers and numbers of middlemen. The result is a less efficient distribution system and higher prices for consumers, which helps explain the persistent price discrepancies among the EEC nations.

Risk, Insurance, and Financing Charges

Risk, insurance, and financing charges are in principle the same in international as in domestic marketing. However, the length of time between ordering and actual delivery of products and receipt of payments is usually much greater in international marketing, increasing risks due to political and economic instability. Loss from expropriation, riots, restrictions in profit repatriation, inflation, and exchange rate fluctuations, are all examples of possible risks that are aggravated by time lags in international marketing. Though there are some ways to alleviate some of these dangers (for example, the risks to currency exposure are discussed in Reading 26), a skimming strategy – high price with modest volume – is one alternative by which the firm can try to increase its own rewards for assuming unusual risks, at least in the short run.

INTERNATIONAL PRICE ESCALATION

The combined effect of cost factors in the international environment of the types illustrated is often that consumer prices in foreign markets are far in excess of prices for equivalent products sold domestically. This phenomenon is called international price escalation. It occurs frequently in the case of exporting to LDCs, but can also be observed in many instances among foreign products sold in Europe, the United States, Japan, and other industrialized countries.

To be sure, price escalation can have diverse reasons for its occurrence; a product, already at the maturity stage in its life cycle at home, may initially be introduced to the upper social strata in a foreign country as a luxury product at a high price. Kentucky Blended Whisky exported to Germany and Japan and Perrier Mineral Water to the United States are examples. A skimming strategy is appropriate in such cases because the high price will help convey the desired status image of the goods in question. Another reason for high priced export products may be a higher profit goal required because of the greater international marketing risks involved. Then, too, there may on occasion be some price gouging and profiteering by middlemen and others involved in the distribution process, resulting in high prices that would be impossible to sustain in a more competitive market environment. However, more often than not, price escalation is the result of added international cost factors discussed in the previous sections. That is, the ultimate foreign consumer prices are raised by additional packaging, shipping, and insurance charges, by longer, often less efficient distribution channels, higher middlemen margins, tariffs, import license fees, special taxes, and as a result of fluctuating exchange rates. Traditionally, many of these costs are computed on a percentage basis, one on top of the other, and thus in essence compound the price escalation effect.

Illustrations

Table 25.1 illustrates the price escalation principle in international marketing. Four different foreign market cases are compared with a typical domestic pricing situation – say, in the United States – including applicable markups in the conventional manufacturer-wholesaler-retailer marketing channel. While the examples are hypothetical, they are realistic in demonstrating the price pyramiding effect that is frequently encountered in international marketing. The product might be a low-priced, simple consumer gadget (such as an inexpensive electronic watch or calculator) retailing domestically for as low as $12. In all the export cases c.i.f. charges of $2.50 and a 20 percent tariff on c.i.f. value are added, but wholesale and retail margins are assumed to remain unchanged from the domestic situation, so that the true escalation effect can be fully appreciated. It must be realized, however, that foreign distributor margins may well be higher, particularly where channels are more fragmented and less efficient.

The examples in Table 25.1 are arranged sequentially, each succeeding case incorporating an additional pyramiding factor. The first export case parallels the domestic pricing situation, except for the c.i.f. and tariff charges. As can be seen in the Table, the wholesale distributor is at the same time the importer, and the price rises by "only" 70 percent, to the equivalent of $20.40.

More typically, however, the product will be brought into the country via an import distributor. The insertion of the importer into the international marketing channel, as this was done in the second case, has the effect of more than doubling the foreign retail price to $25.50, an increase of 113 percent over its domestic counterpart.

In the third case, the situation is similar to the second, but a "value added tax" (VAT) of 16 percent (as for example in the EEC) is added to the assumptions. VAT is essentially a noncumulative turnover tax that is levied only against the difference between the middleman's selling price and cost. Please note, however, that in the importer's case (Case 3) the VAT is imposed on the full export selling price as this represents the "value added" to or introduced into the country from abroad. The full taxing of imported products is often thought to discriminate unfairly against them. By the same token, the refunding of VAT on exported goods, amounting to an export subsidy in fact, is often considered to allow the exporter an unfair competitive advantage in foreign markets. Such uses of turnover taxes have occasionally called for retaliatory action on the part of the affected countries in the form of higher tariffs and/or import quotas. The VAT causes the export price to rise another 27 percent over case two to $32.41 or 170 percent above the domestic equivalent.

In the fourth case, finally, it is assumed that the distribution channel is lengthened, presumably because it is less efficient than that of other countries. The introduction of an additional channel member raises the price by 39 percent over the third export case or 275 percent over the domestic price to nearly $45. The sales volume is likely to be

Table 25.1. International Price Escalation Effects (in U.S. Dollars)

EXPORT MARKET CASES

International Marketing Channel Elements and Cost Factors	Domestic wholesale-retail channel	Case #1 same as domestic with direct wholesale import cif/tariff	Case #2 same as #1 w/foreign importer added to channel	Case #3 same as #2 with VAT added	Case #4 same as #3 w/local foreign jobber added to channel
Manufacturer's net price	6.00	6.00	6.00	6.00	6.00
+ insurance and shipping cost (c.i.f.)	*	2.50	2.50	2.50	2.50
= Landed Cost (c.i.f. value)	*	8.50	8.50	8.50	8.50
+ tariff (20% on c.i.f. value)	*	1.70	1.70	1.70	1.70
= Importer's Cost (c.i.f. value + tariff)	*	10.20	10.20	10.20	10.20
+ importer's margin (25% on cost)	*	*	2.55	2.55	2.55
+ VAT (16% on full cost plus margin)	*	*	*	2.04	2.04
= Wholesaler's Cost (= Importer's Price)	6.00	10.20	12.75	14.79	14.79
+ wholesaler's margin (33 1/3% on cost)	2.00	3.40	4.25	4.93	4.93
+ VAT (16% on margin)	*	*	*	.79	.79
= Local Foreign Jobber's Cost (= Wholesale Price)	*	*	*	*	20.51
+ jobber's margin (33 1/3% on cost)	*	*	*	*	6.84
+ VAT (16% on margin)	*	*	*	*	1.09
= Retailer's Cost (= Wholesale or Jobber Price)	8.00	13.60	17.00	20.51	28.44
+ retailer's margin (50% on cost)	4.00	6.80	8.50	10.26	14.22
+ VAT (16% on margin)	*	*	*	1.64	2.28
= Retail Price (= what consumer pays)	12.00	20.40	25.50	32.41	44.94
Percent Price Escalation over: Domestic	----	70%	113%	170%	275%
Case #1			25%	59%	120%
Case #2				27%	76%
Case #3					39%

215

curtailed by such a high price, necessitating in turn lower ordering quantities and/or causing low stock turnovers. As a consequence, costs and foreign middlemen margins will probably be higher than the domestic margins as was originally assumed for the illustrations. The escalation problem is further aggravated as a result.

A striking empirical example of international price escalation was reported in the Wall Street Journal in 1972. It concerns a case of Del Monte California peach halves and its distribution. The peaches land in Yokohama at 26¢ a can. Immediately, customs and handling charges add 9¢ to the price. Then the importer sticks on a bit more than a penny. He sells it to a primary wholesaler, who adds another 3¢. The wholesaler then sells it to a secondary wholesaler, who adds a further 2¢. He sells it to a grocery store, which adds on an additional 11¢. The final retail price is 52¢ a can – twice the landed price.

Strategic Implications

The exporter has a genuine interest in the price at which his product is sold in foreign markets. For instance, the price elasticity affects the quantities that can be sold at various price levels. Then, there is the question of whether margins are adequate in inducing foreign middlemen to perform at the desired service level. Further, because of the product/price association, excessive price variations between countries can negatively impact on consumer attitudes and ultimately on international company sales. Large price differentials may also stir up "unauthorized" (and undesired) trade across national boundaries.

Inspection of Table 25.1 provides some clues as to what approaches might be appropriate when the international marketer is faced with price escalation problems:

1. Shorten the international distribution channel wherever possible. While this strategy may not eliminate any marketing functions per se, it will reduce the number of times certain functions are being performed and hence limit the compounding effect of price escalation. Shorter channels also tend to enhance the control that can be exercised over end-user prices.
2. Reduce manufacturer's net price in certain markets abroad, with variable costs as a floor. This strategy cannot be regarded as a permanent solution, however. Authorities of the importing country may invoke antidumping charges and/or countervailing tariffs, thus in fact negating any price advantage that might be gained.
3. Adapt the product to the foreign circumstances, and market it at a lower price abroad. Lower quality, less frequent model changes, reduced options, and simplified designs are some of the strategic alternatives to consider. However, in markets with comparable standards of living and with a lively inter-country trade and tourism, such product adaptation may be of limited applicability.

4. Export only parts of the product for assembly abroad.
5. Establish manufacturing facilities abroad.

Strategies 4 and 5 have the effect of decreasing the import content of labor, materials, and parts in stages such that the export price escalation problem can ultimately be reduced to zero. Such strategies would reduce or eliminate c.i.f. charges, tariffs, and the discriminatory effect of VAT; shorten the distribution channel; and improve the marketer's control over final selling prices. The international marketing problem then becomes largely one of "domestic" marketing abroad. While this may help in some cases, it must be remembered that international marketing is based on the systems concept. Through local manufacturing the company may gain cost and price advantages, but it may lose some of its "foreign" image and prestige, exactly what is often sought after by certain market segments. A case in point is Löwenbräu Beer, originally imported from Germany, but later brewed in Texas and marketed in the U.S.A. by the Miller Brewing Company under a licensing agreement. Once it became accepted among American epicures with a taste for fine beers that Löwenbräu was a rather "ordinary" premium beer from Texas, the mystique disappeared. Relative market share started slipping and Miller began searching for a substitute, "real" import brand. None had been found as of this writing.

REFERENCE

Oxenfeldt, Alfred R., "Multi-stage approach to pricing," Harvard Business Review, Vol. 38 (July-August, 1960), pp. 125-33.

26 A Note on Currency Problems in International Marketing*

Arvind V. Phatak

(Ed. note: Marketing and finance are tightly interlocked – although this is not always well recognized by representatives of either function. The tie is especially close in international marketing, characterized by different currencies and different rates of inflation. Indeed, in times of high volatility in these areas the marketer must be sensitive to the financial implications of his actions, as these fluctuations may greatly affect the profitability of operations in the short run and the relative competitiveness of countries in the longer run.

This excerpt from Arvind Phatak's book, Managing Multinational Corporations, gives a condensed summary of the concept of currency exposure and of measures aimed at minimizing foreign exchange losses due to devaluation. We may add that quoting prices in a reasonably stable currency occasionally may be helpful, notably if payment can also be expected in that currency.)

THE CONCEPT OF EXPOSURE

An asset or a liability is considered to be exposed whenever an alteration in currency exchange rates changes its dollar value. The difference between the exposed assets and the exposed liabilities of a company denotes its exposure. (We are assuming that the U.S. dollar is the home country's currency.)

A company's current assets plus current and long-term liabilities expressed in foreign currencies that are affected by any change in currency conversion rate are termed as exposed. Fixed assets tend to increase in price in terms of the local currency because a foreign

---

*Excerpt from Arvind V. Phatak, "The concept of exposure," Managing Multinational Corporations (New York: Praeger Publishers, 1974), pp. 315-329, with permission.

currency devaluation is usually accompanied or preceeded by rapid domestic inflation. Fixed assets, therefore, generally maintain their dollar value. All items that can be classified as fixed assets such as land, buildings, plant and equipment, and so on are generally considered by a U.S. parent company as not exposed to exchange risk.

"Net exposure" may be defined then as local currency assets excluding fixed assets, less local currency liabilities. A quick method of calculating a company's loss (or gain) due to a change in the foreign exchange rate of the local currency vis-a-vis the U.S. dollar is to calculate its net exposure (as defined above) and divide it by the old and new foreign exchange rate. The difference is the company's foreign exchange loss (or gain).

Suppose, for example, that a U.S. multinational company has a subsidiary in India. This subsidiary has local currency current assets and local currency liabilities amounting to Rs10,000 and Rs5,000 respectively giving it a net exposure of Rs5,000. The multinational company would incur a loss of $500 if the rupee was devalued from Rs5=$1 to Rs10=$1. This is because Rs5,000 at the old exchange rate equalled $1,000 but only equals $500 at the new rate. Conversely, the multinational company would incur a gain of $500 if the Indian subsidiary had a negative net exposure of Rs5,000, that is, its local currency liabilities exceeded its local currency current assets by Rs5,000, in which case it would have to pay $500 less than prior to the devaluation to pay off the liabilities of the Indian subsidiary.

REDUCING LOSSES DUE TO CURRENCY DEVALUATION

A multinational company can take the steps outlined below to minimize its net exposure in the subsidiary that is located in a country whose currency is likely to be devalued.

1. Reduce holdings of local currency, time deposits, and short-term investments.
2. Remit to parent company all funds through dividends, royalties, management fees, and so on, that would otherwise remain idle in the subsidiary (to the extent that this is permitted by local authorities).
3. Reduce or liquidate local currency receivables.
4. Liquidate all foreign currency obligations.
5. Maximize both short-term and long-term local currency borrowing.
6. Prepay expenses designated in stable currencies.
7. Designate accounts payable in terms of local currency.
8. Defer payables in local currency to the latest possible date.
9. Designate payments for goods and services from the parent company in home office currency.
10. Use spare cash, that cannot be remitted to parent company, to buy additional fixed assets or inventory, which may be later sold at higher prices in local currency thus maintaining their dollar value.

11.   Use barter or triangular deals when local foreign exchange regulations do not permit transfer of currency out of the country.

12.   Resort to hedging of current assets if losses due to anticipated devaluation exceed hedging expenses. In practice, hedging consists of meeting future committments or protecting future income by buying or selling a forward contract to offset or minimize the exchange risks of loss on assets or liabilities which are denominated in a foreign currency. (A forward contract refers to the sale or purchase of a specified amount of a foreign currency at a fixed exchange rate for delivery or settlement on an agreed date in the future or, under an option contract, between agreed dates in the future.)

13.   Enter into currency swap contracts to provide working capital to the subsidiary. A swap may be defined as the exchange of one currency for another for a fixed period of time. At the expiration of the swap each party of the swap returns the currency initially received. A multinational company may use a currency swap as follows: a local bank may extend a loan to the local subsidiary denominated in local currency at a certain premium interest rate. Simultaneously the parent company extends an interest free loan to the local bank, the size of which is negotiated between the two parties. On the swap termination date, the local company repays the local bank the borrowed money with interest and the local bank in turn repays the parent company the dollar amount it had borrowed from the latter.

27 Keeping Ahead: Anyone in Argentina Can Give You Lessons on Beating Inflation*
Everett G. Martin

Besides being the world soccer champions, the Argentines can also claim the distinction of having the highest inflation rate in the world — 170 percent in 1978 and 140 percent or so in 1979. Yet they don't seem too disturbed about it. In fact, Argentines take a perverse pride in their inflation. Not only has the individual Argentine devised his strategems for keeping ahead of it, every aspect of economic life is geared to live with it. "It has turned us into an economy of speculation instead of production," an economist says.

Watch any Argentine as he courses through the crowded streets of downtown Buenos Aires and you get some idea of how inflation has programmed his behavior. No matter how urgent his mission, he cannot pass a bank without stopping to check the latest interest rate on savings. At every money changer's establishment, he pauses to note how the peso is doing against other currencies.

THINKING IN REAL TERMS

The foreigner may be completely confused, but Argentines young and old seem able to absorb all the pieces of information and calmly decide what to do next to protect the value of their money. The editor of a business magazine boasts that "the entire Argentine population has a much better knowledge of financial matters than North Americans." To which a banker adds: "We always think in real terms. You give a worker a 20 percent raise when the inflation is 25 percent and he immediately wants to know why you are cutting his salary. And if you want a discussion of the money supply, just ask your cab driver."

*From Everett G. Martin, "Keeping ahead: Anyone in Argentina can give you lessons on beating inflation," The Wall Street Journal, Vol. LIX (July 16, 1979), with permission.

Pensions are indexed so that purchasing power is not lost, and it seems that most retired people own some property anyway. They also have the most free time to go from bank to bank manipulating their money. Argentines watch the banks because interest rates are uncontrolled and banks may change them at any time. "Each day we look at our loan demand," the banker explains. "If we need more capital, we just push the savings rate up a bit. If the other banks don't counter us, within two days you see people begin switching to us."

For all their inflation expertise, Argentines are at a loss to tell Americans, for example, how to deal with their own, much lower inflation rate of 14 percent. "We have financial instruments and special tax provisions to protect us," the banker says. "You have nothing. You put your money in a savings account and you lose because the interest rate is negative compared with inflation, and then your government taxes you as if you had made a profit." Argentine tax laws do not allow that, he points out. Argentine laws also do not allow inflation to push anyone into a higher tax bracket, and they keep business from being taxed on any profits attributable solely to inflation.

Since January 1979, very few savers in Argentina have been rushing to switch banks; the interest rates are only about 6.9 percent a month, which, in effect, is negative. The explanation for this, as anyone on the street can tell you, is that for a variety of economic and political reasons, dollar loans are cheaper than peso loans. Businesses are therefore seeking dollar loans, and the demand for pesos is down. "The minute the people saw our rates become negative," the banker says, "they started buying hard goods like refrigerators, cars, or apartments because they didn't want to hold pesos."

PLAYING THE MARKET

They also started playing the stock market with a vengeance. It looked like a reasonable gamble. And with so many people buying stocks, stock prices did move up. One day in May 1979, 104 stocks climbed and only 25 dropped. The shares of one manufacturing firm tripled that day. Between November 1978, and May 1979, the shares of a paper company went to 300 pesos from 7 pesos, while those of a cement company rose to 1,600 pesos from 300 pesos. The president of a wallboard manufacturing firm said, "We haven't done anything, really, except survive these crazy times, yet the total value of our shares has risen to $27 million from $2 million since January (1979)."

Some sophisticated speculators are wary of the stock market, and they engage in more complex financial maneuvers designed to play on the current difference between the rate of inflation and the rate of change in the relationship between the dollar and the peso. (In July 1979, there were about 1,330 pesos to the dollar). Likening the continual turnover of money to a pedaling action, Argentines give these maneuvers such colorful names as the bicycle, the reverse bicycle, and the tricycle. "If you stop pedaling," a business consultant says, "you fall off."

Right now, with inflation rates higher than the rate of the dollar's rise against the peso, the reverse bicycle is the thing to do. A well-heeled speculator explains how: "You borrow $500,000 today. Use the dollars to buy a peso bond with principal and interest indexed to the inflation rate, hold it for a month, then liquidate to pay off your dollar loan. You can make $14,300 because the inflation has increased the amount of your pesos by 7% plus increasing the real interest on the bond, while the dollar has gone up less than 5%." The bicycle involves the same sort of deals starting with the borrowing of pesos. As for the tricycle, it is an even-more-complex transaction involving a financial instrument that somehow makes everything you have earned tax-free. Despite his efforts, the helpful speculator was unable to make the process clear to the writer.

Retailers, too, have learned to think in terms of speculating instead of selling. "This is a country where retailers will raise prices during a recession to make up for their slower turnover," instead of lowering prices to lure customers, an economist says. "It doesn't matter too much if they sell their merchandise," he says, "because they think they are making money by its increasing value from inflation. One appliance-store owner I know showed a bigger profit, on paper, by closing up and going to the seashore for a month than his competitor who stayed home trying to make a sale."

In Argentina, retailing is done almost entirely through boutiques and corner food stores. "The key thing to remember," says Richard Ahrens, manager of Harrods, Buenos Aires's only department store, "is that people buy those little stores as real-estate investments. Sales don't really matter as long as inflation is pushing property values up." One result is that many little shops display knit sport shirts for $140, cotton pajamas for $90. None of the shopkeepers seem to mind that customers are not coming in.

DOES SKILL HURT?

Economics Minister Jose Martinez de Hoz argues that his countrymen's skill at living with inflation is one of the root causes of its continuing fast pace. Mr. Martinez de Hoz has been guiding the economy ever since the military seized control in 1976 from the populist government run by the widow of the late dictator Juan Peron. The Peronists had kicked off the latest binge of inflation with their spending. The military turned to Mr. Martinez de Hoz, a businessman, because he offered a plan to straighten out the mess gradually without causing widespread unemployment. Such unemployment, the military feared, would help the left-wing guerrillas who were terrorizing the country.

Lest he touch off a severe recession, Mr. Martinez de Hoz could not resort to drastic cuts in the budget, which accounts for 40 percent of the country's gross national product. Instead, he increased the state companies' prices for their services and products such as railroad fares, electricity, telephones, and gasoline, and he tightened tax collections.

He has brought the deficit down to manageable proportions: it could be financed without printing more pesos as the Peronists had done. Critics of the economics minister, however, argue that the size of the budget and of public investment is still so great that it remains a major cause of inflation.

IMPORTS WANTED

Probably the prime cause, Mr. Martinez de Hoz says, is the foreign-exchange problem. When the military took over, the problem was that Argentina had no foreign reserves and faced default on its international debt. Mr. Martinez de Hoz met that immediate crisis: he ended the Peronist policy of holding down farm prices to subsidize city dwellers and of imposing stiff taxes on farm exports. He thereby allowed farmers to receive higher prices at home while holding down the world prices for their exports of grains and beef. The farmers responded with bumper crops, and now the country's foreign reserves total more than $8 billion.

That solved one foreign-exchange problem, but it created another, namely, too few imports. Thus, 1978 exports exceeded imports by some $2 billion. The central bank had to create pesos for Argentines to convert all those dollars into. Mr Martinez de Hoz blames the issuance of all that new currency for 80 percent of that year's inflation. And with a 52 percent increase in the wheat harvest in 1979, the problem could get worse. Mr. Martinez de Hoz's answer is a five-year program to cut tariffs in stages to encourage imports. He wants low-cost imports to force Argentine manufacturers to either produce at competitive prices or go out of business. To give them an incentive to modernize, he has already eliminated tariffs on machine tools. But Argentine companies are so immersed in debt, operating in an inflation, that few can take advantage of these incentives. To make matters more difficult, the government has begun indexing business loans, and many companies face serious problems in rolling over their short-term loans. Says an economist, "We've been conditioned to the old rule for 30 years. People still don't believe that the new rules are going to last."

28 Improved Payoffs from Transnational Advertising*
James Killough

This article focuses on the process of advertising transfer. It tries to answer the questions of what determines success or failure in internationalizing advertising and of how success can be improved through systematic planning. It is based on in-depth interviews with senior managers of multinational companies and advertising agencies whose responsibilities cover 120 product-lines and services.

THE PLANNING PROCESS

The key to success in advertising transfer is a strong commitment to planning per se. Nine out of every ten executives interviewed in this survey are agreed on this point. Without a well-structured strategic planning process, the contribution of the best advertising message to global marketing is marginal. As the chief executive of one of the largest multinational marketers of food products said: "Our success is in our planning. We know going in that 10 percent to 20 percent of the advertising propositions we have will be dogs. Another 10 percent to 20 percent are obvious winners. Success comes from knowing how to sort out the other 60 percent to 80 percent."

Here are some suggestions on how to go about structuring the planning process for getting a better payoff from advertising world-wide.

Step 1: Clarify the Marketing Policy

A coherent advertising strategy should be developed as an integral part of forward planning at the strategic level. Some of the questions to be tied down are these:

- Do global sales represent a substantial opportunity for new franchises? Or do they represent a way to sell existing production? The former is buyer-oriented and argues for a breadth-of-sale approach. It leads to the development of advertising that is primarily concerned with addressing the needs of the local market. The latter is producer-oriented and generally avoids new conditions. It leads to development of advertising concerned primarily with finding the target audience most receptive to the product benefits already established in the home market.
- What is the aggregate of distinctive qualities most characteristic of the corporation? An international facade, even logotypes, can create a false impression if the basic foundation is local.
- How important to the total marketing effort are cost savings on advertising? High-technology marketers are among those who may find that the use of centrally produced material results in savings that can be a significant part of the total advertising appropriation.

Step 2: Organize to Reflect the Needs

Some of the questions to be covered in this planning stage include:

- What degree of management control is required? A single standardized campaign provides strong de facto control. It may also stifle local initiative. What is the similarity of the largest audiences? A large central line organization works well when target audiences are quite similar (i.e., for high-technology products such as ski equipment or industrial products such as Fiat's trucks).
- Can advertising executions as well as concepts be produced and controlled from a central line source? John Deere, for example, has pioneered in this approach, turning out several hundred pieces of advertising in up to 12 languages each year from one central office and one central advertising agency for its European region.
- Can advertising executions and concepts be produced by smaller sized staff operations? This organizational approach is useful in fields such as foods and beverages where local tastes vary so greatly. For example, one of the largest European multinationals sells over 200 products in 85 countries. The evaluation is handled by a small but highly professional staff. The staff role is that of teacher rather than supervisor — ensuring that the constantly accruing advertising knowledge is both available and understood by the local line managements.

- What are the costs involved? Centralized advertising has high-cost factors for the time spent in disseminating information, for making sure it is understood, and for ensuring that it has a fair trial. These elements should be weighed against the time spent locally in redundant activities or in opportunities lost altogether.
- What are the benefits of standardizing key external services? Common research techniques are essential. It does no good at all to have an advertising campaign tested with different techniques. In order to compare either buying proposals or creative presentations, the same methodology must be used in dealing with situations where familiarity with local advertising is presumably a valuable asset.

Step 3: Evaluate the Advertising Inventory

After having sketched out an organizational framework, the next stage is to take a look at the advertising that is currently associated with sales success in a major market. As the survey findings suggest, the idea content, which is the substantive part of the advertising proposition, can usually be transferred intact. The strategic content and the executional form of each face a series of barriers. These barriers are predictable.

The key, then, is to use the knowledge of predictability as the focal point for highly centralized strategic planning within the context of an organizational framework which allows for considerable flexibility of executional interpretation at the local level.

PROPOSITION VS. PRESENTATION

In their professional lifetimes, the executives in this survey have learned that the assignment cannot be tackled without understanding that advertising propositions for international transfer consist of two elements which must be considered separately because the reaction to them is different in different countries.

I call the first element the "buying proposal." It represents the sales points, or those elements of the seller's product or service judged by him to be most persuasive and most relevant to the prospective customer. In the context of an advertisement, the buying proposal is what one says. It is the content, not the form.

Everything that is not part of the buying proposal is part of how one says it. The advertising message is formed when that proposal is developed into a "creative presentation." This starts with the headline idea (e.g., "Esso puts a tiger in your tank") and all the visual and verbal elements which surround that central statement. Some other examples to clarify the difference between the two elements are shown in table 28.1.

Table 28.1. Differences between Advertising Proposition
and Presentation

Product category	Buying proposal	Creative presentation
Leisure-time driving	Off-the-road technology	Jeep's "We wrote the book on 4-wheel drive"
Toothpaste	Cosmetic benefits	Colgate's "Ring of confidence
Bank trust department	Conservative management	Chase Manhattan's "Nest egg"
Laundry detergents	Heavy-duty cleaning	Procter & Gamble's "Tide gets out the dirt kids get into"
Airline travel	In-flight service quality	British Caledonian's "The airline other airlines hate"

Buying proposals and creative presentations are distinct from one another but not independent. This distinction is crucial in looking at international advertising transfer problems. Buying proposals generally have a good chance of acceptance across broad chunks of geography. Creative presentations do not.

The Buying Proposal

The executives surveyed felt that strong buying propositions can be transferred without significant change more than 50 percent of the time. These executives were nearly unanimous in citing the similarity of customer motivations as the most important reason. The target audiences for most products and services tend to be more similar than dissimilar in their buying motivations.

Therefore, if a group of potential customers in a country can be identified as having a set of needs and interests similar to the buyers of the product in established markets, the chances of successful adaptation are good. The converse is also true. If the profiles are very dissimilar, the chances of successful adaptation are reduced more than by any other factor.

The trend is toward further drawing together. The top managers interviewed in this study cited the development of worldwide communications systems. Thus television has joined movies as an important vehicle to create international awareness of new ideas. Also, the strengthening of broad regional economic groupings – in Europe, with the Andean Common Market, in parts of Africa, and in the Middle East

– has generated a flow of information that helps to establish common receptions over wide geographical areas.

Primary benefits

If the target audiences have certain general levels of interest in a product, they must then also be shown to agree on the specific benefits. Very often they do. Industrial or high-technology products normally have target audiences that are quite similar in most countries. This is because, by definition, their needs are so highly specialized that the products are specified accordingly.

Western movies strike the same responsive chord in the imagination of most people worldwide. Other products such as Stuyvesant cigarettes have deliberately chosen to ignore any national identity. Levi's jeans capitalize on the universal appeal of casual, westernized American clothes. Coca-Cola works with the universality of youth. Gasoline retailers are nearly always assured of reaching a large audience with "speed and power," as detergents are with "cleaning."

Another worldwide theme is "top quality" used by John Deere agricultural products in every market. The concept of economy, either as "low price" or as the more sophisticated approach of "value for money," has surmounted the national barriers time and time again for a wide variety of products, as Pepsi Cola has proved. Still another recent example is the Lufthansa Airlines theme of punctuality in arrival that proved appealing to the businessman, regardless of his nationality, who flies frequently.

For many other product positionings, however, the universality of primary benefits cannot be taken for granted. Sales of cavity-reducing fluoride toothpastes flourish in countries where having healthy teeth is of major importance. But in the north of England and in the French areas of Canada, the predominant reason for buying toothpaste is breath control. The basic appeal of fluoride toothpastes is therefore limited.

Similarly, household polishes and waxes are advertised to leave a high shine on furniture. However, most Germans look for a cleaning benefit rather than shininess.

Secondary influences

There is another set of qualitative factors beyond determining the primary benefits that I call the target audience's "frame of mind." Thus a buying proposal has to check out with three reference points – traditional beliefs, contemporary behavior, and product familiarity. Let us briefly consider each of these secondary influences.

Traditional beliefs are deep-rooted. Travelers from northern Europe going to the sun-filled Mediterranean look for clean beaches – and worry about the wholesomeness of the food. Latin tourists visiting their neighboring countries care less about the wholesomeness of the food and much more about its taste. In addition, the availability of clean hotel rooms is more important to Latins than the availability of clean beaches. North Americans touring the cradles of civilization are obsessive about almost any paintings, statuary, or ruins which predate Christopher Columbus and Jacques Cartier.

Contemporary behavior is a variant on traditional beliefs that involves preferences formed by the activities and attitudes of the society. For example, Belgium is a small country of 13 million people, but an important coffee roaster has to provide three separate roasts – and use three different buying propositions in advertising – to please the palates of the northerners who want a mild bean flavor, the southerners who want it strong, and the citizens of Brussels who definitely want it in between.

Product familiarity is another reference point in the buying proposal. Thus DuPont used a different advertising approach in neighboring European countries as a function of familiarity with its brand name of Teflon. General Motors and Ford have wholly unique campaigns for their familiar marquees in the Middle East. Before a brand of air freshener can be sold broadly on an export basis, someone has to advertise what air fresheners are and what they do.

The three qualitative factors just noted determine advertising transfer success or failure per se. They do not determine the size of the market. This information requires quantitative research, a counting of noses once the target audience and the benefits desired have been identified. The original buying proposal may be an excellent "sales in depth" but leaves out the majority of potential customers. In such cases, other product qualities which do have meaning – that is, "sales in breadth" – must be brought forward instead.

Proposition barriers

As I noted earlier, the idea content of the buying proposal can usually be transferred successfully. However, there are two circumstances in which a lot of time and talent can be wasted trying to transfer a good buying proposition to a foreign audience. These are usually:

1. When values are highly personalized. The best example is food. There are only a few examples where a standardized sales argument for a line of food products has been uniformly adopted. People are literally very particular about taste – most of all when nutritional values for themselves and their immediate families are concerned.

2. When products and services truly have independent appeals. In developing the buying proposal of an advertising-supported sales program for commemorative coins of the Royal Canadian Mint, two clear motivations to purchase became obvious. The product had an appeal to the investor; it had another and different appeal to the seeker of intrinsic value. But trying to put the two motivations to purchase together served neither interest. Consequently, a different buying proposal had to be created to fit each important consumer group.

The Creative Presentation

A preponderance of the executives surveyed felt that creative presentations do not travel across geographical boundaries nearly as well as buying propositions. Less than 30 percent of all advertising campaigns are used outside of the market for which they were first produced. At one time such was not true. That was in the great boom of international operations which started after World War II. Universal advertising campaigns were common during that 15- to 20-year period when American companies looked at the world as one big export oyster.

For example, Esso's tiger appeared even in Malaysia where big cats are no joke. The artwork, headlines, photos and films, and typography were developed centrally and used literally worldwide.

But times have changed. Consumers everywhere today are more conscious of their own identity. Sometimes this consciousness comes from a realization of political power. At other times, it comes from an awareness of economic power. And it always means a distaste for feeling patronized by "foreign" advertising.

National obstacles

Again, as noted earlier, the creative presentation usually cannot be transferred intact. That is because the presentational interpretation at the local level faces a series of predictable obstacles. The barriers include cultural, communicative, legislative, competitive, and executional problems. Any one of them is enough to reject an otherwise strong creative presentation.

Cultural barriers can be illustrated with two examples. Sellers of coffee find their task complicated by the traditions associated in different countries with the drinking of coffee. In tea-drinking Britain, a positioning as a tea substitute can optimize market share. Thus campaigns that may have been highly successful in a coffee-drinking culture cannot be adapted in Britain because they are geared to differentiating the product from other coffees rather than as a substitute for a tea-drinking occasion.

From culture to culture, nothing could be more of a profound obstacle than the role of the sexes. Women are accepted without question as authorities and spokespersons in Anglo-Saxon countries. Such acceptance of women is less true in Latin countries – and not at all true in conservative Islamic countries where women neither drive automobiles nor do the shopping.

Communicative barriers are a thicket. Some parts are thornier than others, but all of them must be negotiated successfully. The problem is more fundamental than simple, straight translations. These can always be made. Rather, the problem is one of transliteration. No two people respond quite the same way to an advertising image. For example, an English car manufacturer had to scrap its U.K. creative presentation, which it had planned to use in the American market, built around the promise that its stylish new sports model would "go like a bomb."

Sometimes images just are nonexistent. A major soft-drink company lost time and money with the promise of thirst-quenching rewards based on "glacier fresh" or "avalanche of taste" in high-consuming countries of the Near East where the idea of wintry mountain temperatures is unknown in common local experience.

A large number of advertisers have forgotten the simple fact of illiteracy. Many potential customers – in numbers greater than their governments will usually admit – simply cannot read the presentational message.

Humor and animation must be evaluated carefully. They are based on the assumption of a common general reaction to an exaggeration of some kind. In the case of animation, in fact, there has to be an ability to distinguish fantasy from reality. Some cultures are too literal-minded to routinely make these distinctions. Even in his heyday, the friendly Esso tiger was regarded with some skepticism by the Swedes, who thought that having some kind of cartoon character in the gas tank just did not seem too sensible.

Legislative problems can be formidable. Children may not be used in France to merchandise products. Campaigns which rely on freedom of choice fare badly in countries where a particular political party always dominates at the polls. Such happened to PepsiCo's "feeling free. . ." campaign in one of the world's "democracies."

Censorship organizations can confound the most straightforward statement. How can a leading antidandruff shampoo tell its product story without using the word "dandruff" in its advertising?

In some countries the use of broadcast media is controlled by the government and therefore is available on a very limited basis. Availability of TV is crucial in order to demonstrate the benefits of some products and services. Another factor is strict limitation of the length of episode. This constraint can alter a campaign drastically by cutting out integral parts of a commercial which simply needs a certain amount of time to tell a sequential story from beginning to end.

Competitive positions provide another major obstacle that must be acknowledged. Leading producers can often ignore their competitors of lower station and concentrate on their own virtues. Thus the dominant chewing gum in France can afford to make generic advertising since its name is virtually synonymous with "chewing gum." But in other markets, where the same product has a much smaller share, the advertising approach must overtly provide a rationale of distinctiveness versus competition.

Executional problems are the final barrier. These are the most exasperating because they are small things, such as poor printing reproduction, which can ruin the credibility of an otherwise fine campaign. In one advertisement, a benevolent sun in the background came out as a fireball. Instead of promising a perfect Caribbean vacation day, it unintentionally warned of burning, peeling, and itching. In another instance, a usually savvy U.S. toiletries manufacturer discovered too late that TV viewers in Madrid knew a lot more about bull fighting than did the Chicagoans who made the film.

Landscapes and models, however beautiful they may be, may carry negative connotations if they are not native to the country. For many major corporations, these can be unwelcome ambassadors that remind the target audience of the foreignness of the product and tar it with the brush of the unpopular "multinationals."

All of the foregoing barriers to advertising transfer are real ones. They can also be artificial. Sometimes local executives inside marketing operations erect them to prevent an element of outside control on their activities or to cater to local pride of proprietorship which says that creativity "must be invented here." Consequently, there is a tendency to increase substantially the home office involvement in both persuading and policing the actions of their local advertising executives and agency representatives.

GETTING A BETTER PAYOFF

Although we have seen that there are certain obstacles to the internationalization of advertising, there are powerful reasons to try to make it work. Here are some considerations of how the effort can pay off decisively:

- A common advertising approach helps to support basic business decisions. With the aim of becoming the leading car seller in Western Europe, Ford began in 1967 to achieve this end by integrating its Continental and British activities. The company sees Europe as one market rather than a series of separate national ones. This commonality internationalizes production, parts, and servicing. It also puts a common advertising face on Fiesta, the small car (made in four European countries and assembled in three of them). The buying proposition for Fiesta is the same throughout Europe. The creative campaign is executed just as faithfully.
- Alberto Culver spent considerable time searching for a meaningful way to demonstrate the unique "nonfilming" characteristics of its VO5 hair spray. The company's Italian operation developed such a creative TV property. The Alberto Culver product was shown being sprayed against one-half of a mirror. The mirror was clear. The major competitive product was then sprayed on the other half. The mirror was cloudy. That campaign was subsequently adapted in other major VO5 markets without any significant change being made in the creative presentation.
- Sometimes a single major element of a creative presentation can be used successfully on a worldwide basis even if the other elements of it are not applicable. There is universal conviction in using actual consumers who will not change from their current product even when offered twice as much of a competitor's product. A woman whose skin is so young looking that her neighbors cannot guess her age is an effective salesperson for quality toilet soaps as well as dishwashing detergents.

- Production costs can be a major factor when advertising budgets are low and every penny must be used to buy as much media as possible. Centralized production is therefore important for most industrial or high-technology products.
- Organizational control is improved with centralized advertising. Management knows better what is going on when its subsidiaries either use the internationalized campaign, or justify its modification, or defend the use of a local agency conception. The head of a major U.S. bank mentioned that centralized advertising ranks alongside real estate as a way of keeping him on top of worldwide activities.
- The process of justifying changes from a prototype campaign forces and fosters a greater awareness of how to maximize local impact. The dialogue which flows from that process can be an ongoing source of better understanding between home office and its branches. At the very least, the dialogue helps to establish company-wide some common ways of looking at worldwide advertising problems and evaluating solution choices.

29 Channel Control in International Markets*

Ahmed A. Ahmed

While the question of which member should exercise control over other channel members remains unsettled, there appears to be general agreement that in situations of economies of scale in manufacturing, R and D, and promotion, the manufacturer has a claim to control (Mallen, 1969). Also, where the manufacturers are in an oligopolistic market and the retailers in a more competitive market, a retailer becomes more dependent on and controllable by the manufacturer. These situations are approximated by the United States automobile market. Mass retailers, large enough to counter the manufacturer's control, are practically nonexistent. In fact Stern (1967) maintains that in the American automobile industry the manufacturer's control of the retailers is almost despotic.

This paper focuses on foreign automobile manufacturers who have penetrated the American market with varying degrees of success. It aims to assess the control the foreign firm exerts over its United States affiliate and the affiliate's control over the remaining members of the channel of distribution, namely the affiliate's franchised dealers.

DATA AND METHOD

Channel control is here viewed as the extent to which one member of the channel stipulates policies for the other members handling the same product or brand (Stern, 1967). These include price, product, promotion, and service policies among others. The measure of channel control used in this paper looks for symptoms of control (e.g., product exclusivity and communication) and tries to find out who stipulates policies, if any, and whether those who stipulate policies follow them on to see that they are executed.

*From Ahmed A. Ahmed, "Channel control in international markets," European Journal of Marketing, Vol. 11 (Fall 1977), pp. 327-35. Reprinted with permission.

The information was acquired through interviews with top executives of six U.S. auto importers, augmented by mail questionnaires sent to several others. In all, the 14 responses obtained (of a universe of 18) represented more than 95 percent of the total imports share in the American automobile market (the affiliates included in the study are of these producers: British Leyland Motors Inc., Fiat, Mercedes-Benz, Nissan, Peugeot, Renault, Saab, Subaru, Toyota, Volkswagen, and Volvo; three further companies gave incomplete answers: Lotus Motors, Aston Martin, and Alfa Romeo). Interviews were also conducted with seven foreign car dealers and one regional distributor. The interview and questionnaire surveys were conducted in late 1971 and during 1972.

PARENT-AFFILIATE RELATIONSHIP

Most of the affiliates were legal subsidiaries of their parent-companies. Only two were acting as agencies of their respective manufacturers and none was a branch. A branch arrangement represents the closest form of parental control, whereas an agency arrangement tends to minimize home office control, because an agent is an independent businessman. As compared to either, a subsidiary form represents a more moderate level of home office control, other things remaining the same.

Most of the responses describe the extent of "general control" by the home office as either "light direct control" or "fairly close control." In the first category we find three leading importers: Volkswagen, Nissan, and Volvo. Responses to the question about specific area level of control tended to fall into the category of "little control." These are the areas of: personnel, advertising, customer's services, legal and purchasing decisions. The singular exception to this rule was the area of "financial" control where the majority of the respondents described the level of control as "substantial" with a few calling it "tight." Only three, including the leading importer, replied that home office control over them was "little" in the area of financial decisions. The affiliate of Saab described the level of control as "substantial" in almost all the areas including financial decisions. Most of the companies claimed that the parent-company does not set sales quotas or define a sales price for them. Exceptions to this reply were those of Fiat, Mercedes-Benz, and Aston-Martin. Probably the luxurious nature of the products of the latter two and the nature of their target market dictated that.

All except one of the respondents frequently fed information about operations to their respective parent-company. All these report to the home office on a monthly or a bi-weekly basis, (a rather short period). Finally, most of the executives queried did not feel that the present level of home office control hampered their ability to respond to growth opportunities in the U.S. market. A minor exception to this were executives of two small importers who probably felt that their companies would do better if they were allowed more leeway.

With the exception of financial decisions, the responses lead one to conclude that the majority of the affiliates operate with a substantial degree of independence from their parent companies abroad. Home offices appear to allow their American affiliates considerable room to respond to local market conditions. Parent-companies, of course, retain to themselves the ultimate control as evidenced by their control of the purse. They also have the power to change the affiliate's top management if they are unhappy with the affiliate's performance. However, parent-companies seem to follow the "management-by-exception" principle, allowing the subsidiary a free hand as long as its performance is satisfactory and only intervening in crisis situations.

The data did not reveal a relationship between the control index, as here developed, and the affiliate's sales ratio (in the parent output) and the affiliate's market penetration ratio. Extensive control by the parent-company over the affiliate was not related to success in the American automobile market.

CONTROL OVER DEALERS

Most of the United States importers employ regional distributors, a practice prevalent among domestic producers too. The domestic producers, though, own their regional distributors which is not always the case with the importers of automobiles. A few leading importers own some of their distributorships; but they also rely heavily on independent distributors. Volkswagen and, to a lesser degree, Toyota fell into this category. Nissan, the third largest, owns all its distributorships.

Making the distributorship a part of the company is likely to raise the degree of control over the dealer as the selection, enfranchising and other standards have a better chance of being observed than otherwise. Almost all the importers who do not own their distributorships allow those distributors to enfranchise dealers in their respective regions. Part of the reason that a substantial number of importers employ independent businessmen as regional distributors is historical. When these companies first entered the American market they may have been anxious to gain representation with a minimum of financial risk. Today the tendency among some is to buy out those distributors whenever the opportunity presents itself. Volkswagen of America is a leader in this tendency.

The companies do not own dealerships outright except for one or two model dealerships. Almost all the companies replied that they require their dealers to raise and invest a minimum amount of capital as well as provide after-sale-service and submit periodic reports to the company. About half the respondents claimed that they do not require their dealers to approximate a suggested retail price. Included in this group were the leading four importers. This probably does not reflect the actual practice, as fear of antitrust laws may prevent them from divulging such information.

In the area of product policy, the majority of companies stated that most of their dealers do not carry the company's products exclusively. Exceptions to this rule are the dealers of Volkswagen, Toyota, and, to a lesser extent, Nissan. This implies that control over the dealer in the case of the majority of the companies is not tight. The dealer in this case would be less dependent on any one maker. His bargaining power is increased as he can threaten to give more attention to the other make he carries. Even though most of the companies do not enjoy this product exclusivity with their dealers, almost all companies replied that they set sales goals for their dealers. Without a sales goal the company's control over the dealer would be compromised.

Given those demands on the dealers, do the companies inspect their dealers frequently to find out if the dealers are living up to these demands and to advise them if not? Out of thirteen responses to this question, eleven said that they inspect their franchise holders monthly. As to who carries out the inspection, nine companies said that it is done by a company representative or by a distributor who is part of the company. Two top importers allow distributors they do not own to do some of the job. This is apt to weaken the company's control over the dealer.

One ultimate weapon the company has over its dealer is the renewal of the contractual agreement when it expires. The shorter the period of the contractual agreement, the more power and control the company has over the dealer. In this connection, seven out of twelve respondents said that the average length of the contract is one year. The two leading importers were in this group. Only three other companies said that the period of the contract is indefinite. The remaining two importers had their contracts running two or three years.

To discover the strength of the association between the company's overall control over the dealer and the performance of each of the two (the affiliate and the dealer), a control index was again constructed and rankings were made. The results showed substantial positive rank correlations. The extent of the importer's control over the dealer tends to be associated with the successful penetration of the U.S. market by the foreign importer. Control tends to enhance the performance of both the importing affiliate and its franchised dealers. Market share tends to vary with the degree of the affiliate's control. The dealer, in conforming with the company's policy, benefits from national advertising and the product image created by the importer. Presumably, this is an advantage in a low-priced economy market, where both the manufacturer and the dealer strive for volume. Mercedes-Benz is an exception, having a comparatively large sales volume among imported automobiles, in spite of its high-priced, luxury car image.

CONCLUSIONS

Success for the affiliate and the dealer is a function of other factors in addition to control, such as product, price, and promotion. The products of the majority of the importers happen to be in the same product class (small economy cars) and in the same price range. This fact gives the factor of control more importance than would be otherwise. In an industry with national and regional advertising acting as a pull factor and with huge manufacturing investments, the manufacturer needs to make sure that the dealer generates the required sales volume. History tells us that the successful importers are those who, from the start, placed a great deal of emphasis on the way their franchised dealers conducted business. For example, Volkswagen of America, from the beginning, set rigorous standards for its franchised dealers and saw to it that they were met (Nelson, 1961). Toyota and Nissan, shown by this study to exercise substantial control over their franchised dealers, are also the ones whose market shares are continually rising. A relatively new foreign entrant in the American market, Mazda (not covered in the study), began to increase its market share only after new management became more selective in its choice of dealers and put rigorous demands and standards for its dealers in almost all policy areas (Burch, 1972).

The general conclusions made on the basis of this study are:

1. American affiliates of foreign automobile manufacturers, both successful and unsuccessful ones, operate with substantial degree of independence from their parent-companies.
2. Successful automobile affiliates tend to be those that exercise a substantial degree of control over their respective franchised dealers. Their dealers in turn tend to be ones with a relatively high average sales volume among other foreign car dealers.
3. Even though a high market penetration ratio raises the ability of the affiliate to control its dealers, individual case histories suggest that control over dealers raises the sales of both dealers and the company.

REFERENCES

Burch, C.G., "A car that may reshape the industry's future," Fortune, Vol. 86, No. 1 (1972).

Mallen, B., "A theory of retailer-supplier conflict and cooperation," in L. Stern (ed.), Distribution channels: Behavioral Dimensions (Boston, Houghton, Mifflin & Co., 1969), pp. 176-87.

Nelson, W.H., Small Wonder: The Amazing Story of Volkswagen (Boston, Little, Brown & Co., 1961), pp. 172-203.

Stern, L., "The concept of channel control," The Journal of Retailing, Vol. 43, No. 2 (1967).

30 Culligan Thrives on Hard Water in Overseas Markets*
Donald M. Hintz

How did Culligan, a company which markets the improvement of water quality, make the transition from a business confined to the United States and Canada to the status of a worldwide marketer? The company, in its first 22 years, had given no consideration to overseas business; but now, after 20 years as a foreign marketer, it conducts business in 92 countries through 1,349 local dealers.

The story of Culligan as an international marketer goes back to 1958, when an American living in Switzerland noticed an ad for the company's water softener in Life. Jim McElroy was that man, and he convinced Don Porth, director of marketing, that it would be worthwhile to make a seven-country survey of the European market. Porth and McElroy (who now is executive vice president and director of marketing for Culligan Overseas Co., headquartered in Brussels) did find hard water in Europe – on the average three times harder than the water in North America. In talking with natives of Brussels, Paris, Rome, Zürich, Düsseldorf, and London, they also found that people were aware of their water problem but not of the solution.

These conclusions indicated a fertile new market, which also presented quite a dilemma, because water conditioning products do not lend themselves to simply being added to a line of appliances in appliance or department stores. Being too small a company to consider the establishment of branch offices or sales organizations in each country, management decided to approach the European market by appointing licensed distributors.

Culligan's first licensee was established in Belgium, and the first sales were an automatic commercial water softener for the U.S. Pavilion restaurant at the Brussels World's Fair and another for the restaurant in the top of the Atomium, the Fair's theme structure.

---

*From Donald M. Hintz, "Overseas, Culligan found water hard, marketing easier." Based on talk given before the International Trade Club of Chicago (October 1977). Reprinted with permission.

Establishment of the business in Belgium was not without its frustrations, but the company did reach about 200 customers during the first year, and this "success story" was then used to interest licensed distributors in other countries.

The important thing to do in approaching a foreign market is to find out if there is really a market for the product or service. Culligan found that the commercial attachés of U.S. embassies are very helpful in evaluating prospective markets. Take France as an example. A water softener that sold for $350 in the United States, would have to sell for $500 in France after considering transportation, duty, and taxes. With a per capita income of $462 at that time, the French market did not look promising at first. However, it was determined that, if only 0.5 percent of households were able to afford the $500 device, the potential would be significant. Today, Culligan's French marketing company has one of the largest sales volumes of any of its subsidiary or independent companies outside the United States. This goes to prove that per capita income alone may not be a valid indicator of market potential for a given product or service.

The German market was discouraging too at first. More than 60 competitors existed there in a country approximately the area of the states of Illinois and Indiana. However, upon surveying these competitors, it was found that they were very regional in scope. The one or two national companies did not compete for the household or commercial or industrial markets Culligan was interested in, but directed their sales efforts toward large-scale municipal work.

Another fact surprising to Culligan was the state of the art of that industry in Germany at that time. The process of water softening was discovered in Germany in 1856. However, the products manufactured in Germany in 1956 were 30 years behind those marketed in the United States. Thus Culligan's water softeners had great consumer appeal compared to the regional competitors in Germany. International business, however, has developed tremendously during the past 20 years, and many American competitors are now conducting business overseas. At the same time, some of the competitors in Germany and elsewhere have developed or licensed new technology, so today Culligan faces a very competitive "ballgame."

Culligan soon established licensees in all the countries of Western Europe and a few in the Middle East. All shipments were made directly from the factory in Northbrook to the individual distributors in each of these countries. And after four years of growth, management reached the conclusion in 1962 that the company had to establish manufacturing facilities in Europe or risk the chance of losing some of its more successful distributors. Freight costs varied from 5 percent to 65 percent of the value of the products, depending upon the bulk of the item, and import duties ranged from about 6 percent to as high as 55 percent, depending upon the tariffs in the destination countries.

The company considered locations in France, Italy, Switzerland, Germany, and the Netherlands before finally settling on Belgium as the site of its first overseas manufacturing facility. It was of tremendous help to its licensees in Europe, the Middle East, and Africa. For example, it reduced the shipping time for the company's major licensee in France from 60 days to about three days after the mailing of an order.

Culligan now employs over 700 people in 10 foreign subsidiary companies. Only six of these are Americans. Although the company has factories in Canada, Belgium, and Italy, many specialty molded parts, sophisticated electronic devices, control valves, and similar items are still produced in the United States for export to its foreign factories for further manufacture and assembly. Also, Culligan distributes directly to foreign licensees in Latin America and the Far East.

What has foreign business meant to Culligan? Foreign sales during 19 fiscal years from 1959 to 1977 grew from $47,000 to more than $33 million. Aside from bolstering consolidated sales, the company found domestic and foreign sales operating in differing economic cycles. In the downturn in domestic sales in 1970 and '71, total sales were buoyed up by increased foreign sales. Conversely, when foreign sales flattened in 1972 and '73, the slack was picked up by domestic sales. Again in 1977, domestic sales were healthy, while foreign sales were still struggling. Had the company confined its activities to the United States over the past 19 years, it is conceivable that total sales might have reached $60 to $70 million rather than the over $93 million accumulated at the end of fiscal 1977.

FURTHER READING – PART FIVE

Chakrabarti, Alok K.; Feinman, Stephen; and Fuentevilla, William, "Industrial product innovation: An international comparison," Industrial Marketing Management, Vol. 7, No. 4 (August 1978), pp. 231-7.

Davidson, William H. and Harrigan, Richard, "Key decisions in international marketing: Introducing new products abroad," Columbia Journal of World Business, Vol. 12, No. 4 (Winter 1977), pp. 15-23.

de la Torre, Jose, "Product life cycle as a determinant of global marketing strategies," Atlanta Economic Review, Vol. 25, No. 5 (September-October 1975), pp. 9-14.

Doyle, Peter and Gidengil, Zeki, B., "A strategic approach to international market selection," in Barnett A. Greenberg and Danny N. Bellinger (eds.), Contemporary Marketing Thought - 1977 Educators' Proceedings, Series #40 (Chicago, Ill.: American Marketing Association, 1977), pp. 230-4.

Dunn, S. Watson, "Effect of national identity on multinational promotional strategy in Europe," Journal of Marketing, Vol. 40, No. 4 (October 1976), pp. 50-7.

Hackett, Donald W., "The international expansion of U.S. franchise systems: Status and strategies," Journal of International Business Studies, Vol. 7, No. 1 (Spring 1976), pp. 65-75.

Heskett, James L. and Mathias, Peter F., "The management of logistics in MNCs," Columbia Journal of World Business, Vol. 11, No. 1 (Spring 1976), pp. 52-62.

Leff, Nathaniel H., "Multinational corporate pricing strategy in the developing countries," Journal of International Business Studies, Vol. 6, No. 2 (Fall 1975), pp. 55-64.

Leroy, George, Multinational Product Strategy: A Typology for Analysis of Worldwide Product Innovation and Diffusion (New York: Praeger Publishers, 1976).

McIntyre, David R., "Multinational positioning strategy," Columbia Journal of World Business, Vol. 10, No. 3 (Fall 1975), pp. 106-10.

Oritt, Paul L. and Hagan, Alfred J., "Channels of distribution and economic development," Atlanta Economic Review, Vol. 27, No. 4 (July-August 1977), pp. 40-4.

Peeples, D.M.; Ryans, J.K., Jr.; and Vernon, I.R., "A new perspective on advertising standardization," European Journal of Marketing, Vol. 11, No. 8 (1977), pp. 569-76.

Terpstra, Vern, "International product policy: The role of foreign R & D," Columbia Journal of World Business, Vol. 12, No. 4 (Winter 1977), pp. 24-32.

VI

Small Business and International Marketing

Introduction to Part VI

The special problems encountered by small and medium-sized business firms in international marketing are the province of Part Six. The two most critical problems are seen as whether or not to engage in international marketing (or to enter a new market abroad) and, if the answer is positive, what channels of distribution to use. Small business typically encounters a third major problem in beginning export operations, namely financing. We have not included readings on this latter matter, as institutional conditions (e.g., export banking facilities, government credit, and risk insurance) vary so greatly between countries. Expert advice should be sought in this area in the individual case.

"In unity is strength," is the proverbial idea which underlies the philosophy of the marketing consortium. Based on the concept of cooperation rather than competition in international markets, the consortium is an organizational exporting device that allows the small company to combine its own skills and resources with complementary ones of other small firms. The consortium is then in a position to present a diversified product/service offering to foreign markets not otherwise possible for the involved companies individually.

Reading 31, by Savitt, examines various forms of consortia. Going well beyond the commonly known financial syndicate, the author notes that the innovative marketing consortium may become not only involved in the assembly of a product/service offering, but also in production and the development of market and marketing data, an aspect of particular value for the small firm. Furthermore, the marketing consortium can be equally effective in establishing channels for import as well as for export. Last but not least, a consortium may be able to market entire systems (e.g., of the turnkey variety), going beyond the traditional assortment idea. Reading 32, by Harvey, relates the case history of a small British firm which found the consortium route the only way in which it could successfully break into international markets.

While the consortium concept provides a viable and for some firms the only feasible way to enter foreign markets, others find the idea impractical. For example, they may resent the loss of independence that comes from the cooperation that is required to make the consortium work effectively. Or, they may find the coordination necessary for the assembly of unified, complementary market offerings too difficult. For these and other reasons, many firms, even small ones, decide to "go it alone." Reading 33, from Business International, greatly facilitates consideration of entry into a (new) foreign market by systematically inventorying all types of commitment, from the modest filling of an occasional export order to the most ambitious: the creation of a wholly-owned manufacturing-marketing subsidiary. In between the two there is a vast range of alternatives, arranged in approximate order of financial and/or risk commitment.

Before making any type of commitment decision (beyond the routine filling of whatever export orders that may come in spontaneously), management is wise to keep in mind two important points of experience. First, that going international rarely is a successful escape from domestic problems. In other words, domestic operations should be fairly well "under control" before venturing abroad. Second, to assure a wise decision on when and where to commit what resources to international operations, there is virtually no substitute for the well-prepared personal visit by top management to the foreign market(s) under consideration. This is simply because international commitments tend to be major commitments, and they invariably represent entrepreneurial decisions.

Reading 34, by Beeth, deals with problems of distribution. It is quite a lively piece on the dos and don'ts of finding and keeping good distributors in international marketing. The article is based on the author's many years of personal practical experience in American and Swedish firms marketing all around the world and as head of IMA-Consult in Brussels. Beyond good distributor relationships, foreign marketing often succeeds simply because of entrepreneurial common sense, imagination, nimble responses to varied demands, and plain old courage. This is vividly illustrated by the "off-beat exports" described in the short Reading 35. It does take ingenuity to locate export markets for sycamore hybrids in Hamburg, orange peels in Tokyo, and bull semen in China.

Reading 36, by Bilkey, provides the most complete literature overview on export behavior of firms. Though slightly abbreviated for the purpose of this volume, the compendium includes analyses of export initiation decisions and motivation, perceived obstacles to exporting, management, firm size, and export destination. The author also presents two export models from which he develops sequential export stages and profiles. From these and the concluding governmental and managerial implications it is possible for the executive to draw helpful inferences about his own firm's particular export behavior, evaluate its export performance, develop an export profile, and determine the current export stage. From a thorough understanding of these factors, strategy for future international marketing operations can be formulated.

31 Consortium Marketing for Small Business: Canada and Eastern Europe*

Ronald Savitt

This paper discusses the use of the marketing consortium by small firms in an attempt to help them to develop and compete in foreign markets. Although the discussion focuses on small Canadian firms desirous of entering Eastern European markets, the concepts have general merit for small firms everywhere.

THE CANADIAN ENVIRONMENT

Canada must export to live. Although it is classified among the world's leading industrialized nations, this is as much a result of its proximity to the United States as of the development of its own resources. Canada has a full complement of industries. The problem is, however, that these industries do not form the basis of an active export marketing sector such as are found in France, Germany, and Japan, for example. Because of the limited Canadian industrial sector, the domination of multinationals, and a high agricultural component, there are difficulties for the largest of Canadian firms, let alone the smaller ones, in the development of foreign marketing activities. The major problem is the lack of managerial skills to discover, enter, and exploit foreign markets.

At the same time, there are opportunities for an expansion of exporting. Canada possesses certain technological know-how and skills in agriculture, forest products industry, petroleum, transportation, and communication. Canada also possesses certain economic and political advantages with developing and Third World countries as well as with the countries of Eastern Europe. In order to overcome the lack of

---

*Slightly abbreviated from Ronald Savitt, "Consortium marketing for small business: Canada and Eastern Europe," Journal of the Academy of Marketing Science, Vol. 5 (Special Issue, 1977), pp. 115-8, with permission.

development of foreign markets, present advantages must be translated into forms which can be marketed abroad. The infrastructure needed to undertake such functions is missing within the foreign marketing sphere.

THE EASTERN EUROPEAN MARKET

The Eastern European market would appear to be one of the least promising areas for Canadian firms if one examines the past and current relationships between them. There are two offsetting conditions, however, which suggest that there are substantial opportunities for increasing mutual trade activities. First, as a general policy, the Eastern European nations are interested in spreading their trade among an ever increasing number of countries. Second, they are expressing demand for capital goods which will allow them to develop their raw material and agricultural sectors. These are areas in which Canadian industry has developed expertise through the application of known technology to its own market and environmental conditions.

The opportunities are present because these Eastern European countries have vast natural resources which are ready for development, but they lack the technology for their exploitation. Also, they want to purchase total plants, typically, which are ready to operate. On the other hand, the small Canadian firm is not fully able to meet the needs required by the purchasing organizations of Eastern Europe. Basically, these prefer to deal with large, complex organizations like themselves. This is where the idea of the marketing consortium comes in.

THE MARKETING CONSORTIUM

The concept of the consortium is not new in economic affairs. The marketing consortium developed here differs significantly from the financial syndicate. It is defined in long-run terms rather than short; also, it has different objectives.

The marketing consortium is based on the principle of two-way market search with specific emphasis on the development of product and service offerings. Within this principle is the notion that the consortium will be exerting effort in both buying and selling dimensions to effect transactions. The effort on the buying side is not simply the accumulation of products and services to sell, but the development of products and services to market. This makes it organizationally different from the trading company, for example, which is basically an agency relationship used to collect goods and services. The difference between the trading company and the marketing consortium at the most general level is analogous to the difference between exporting and international marketing. It is an extension of the marketing concept of an organization within the international context, in which the consortium acts much like a traditional merchant wholesaler in domestic markets, who seeks out a wide product assortment within his product line.

The central concern of the consortium is to assemble and integrate the diverse components of several related small manufacturers and produce goods and services which are compatible with the demand conditions found in foreign markets. There may be even instances where the consortium undertakes production as well as assembly activities. This facilitates the matching of demand conditions which require the purchase of "systems" and "turnkey" operations. The consortium is then basically composed of two parts: a trading unit and an assembly unit (see figure 31.1).

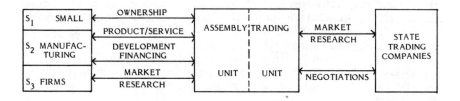

Fig. 31.1. The marketing consortium.

The trading unit will serve much the same function as the trading company in the negotiation of terms with the Eastern European state trading organizations. The assembly unit, however, is the key for the marketing consortium. It is the point at which the offering development takes place. It represents the set of activities which brings together the various products from several firms and integrates them either through production or product integration into the basic offering of the consortium. While some degree of specialization is necessary, flexibility must be a significant concern as demand conditions shift from product to product market across a variety of countries. Part of the flexibility is ensured by the continual development of market data. Other flexibility is built in because of the relationship between the firm and the consortium. It would be reasonable to expect that the consortium in its product development activities will not necessarily use all of the output of all the small firms with which it deals, but only those that relate to what is being developed for the foreign market.

CONSORTIUM FUNCTIONS

1. Service/offering assembly. This function goes beyond the traditional buying activities of wholesale merchants. It more closely approaches the "converters" which, for example, have traditionally been used in the textile industry. These wholesalers are really an intermediate step between production of cloth and the production of garments. They perform the basic wholesaling functions, but additionally engage in the dyeing and cutting of cloth for the many textile

manufacturers. A central element is their knowledge about designs, colors, fabric finishes, and the like. The marketing consortium in a larger perspective would focus on the purchase and preparation of the basic materials which could then be prepared for sale in final goods markets. The functional skills required will go beyond those related to engineering; they must also include those related to applications and design.

2. <u>Production activities</u>. The production activities are more complex than the mere supervision of individual elements. They include three specific subfunctions:

- Production activities, which might be conducted in the home-country (e.g., Canada) or in the foreign country, must be coordinated, depending on the nature of the agreement. For example, the importing country may require joint-ventures between itself and the consortium. The critical issue is that the consortium has the strength from its product-market-assembly activities to influence the location of the production and the choice or combination of factors.
- Transportation and logistics become an important part of the production as well as marketing activities for which the consortium is responsible.
- Technical post-sale service and maintenance are basic parts of all agreements with Eastern European countries. The consortium concept, because of its key role in product development and integration, would offer substantial advantages over traditional trading companies in this area.

3. <u>Market data development</u> becomes the most critical of the marketing functions of the consortium although it is important not to lose track of the other ones. The purpose of the market data is primarily to help in the product planning and development area.

It is quite difficult to develop propositions about the internal structure of the marketing consortium. Based on the conditions established in East-West negotiations, the consortium would have to be structured on a market rather than a product basis. This may be somewhat inefficient in dealing with other economies, where a more promising approach, similar to the brand management used by many large consumer goods firms, could be applied.

The marketing consortium presented here is not without limitations. If it is to be made operational, these limitations must be understood and overcome. There are several areas which need to be considered. One, there may be inter-firm problems arising from the sharing of information which is required in the operation of the consortium. The previous discussion did not deal with copyright, patent, and other proprietary issues which might come into conflict as product offerings are developed. Two, there may be an overlapping of competitive product lines between and among the individual firms and the consortium. Three, there may be problems relating to discrepancies in the size of consortium members, especially since the contribution to any offering may not be proportional to the firm's size. Four, there will be problems as the consortium's market and product offerings change. As was indicated earlier, flexibility is a key concern; when new products are developed and new markets entered, issues concerning the organization's membership are likely to arise. Finally, there may be problems of management. The consortium model may simply be unmanageable because of the diversity of interests which must be served.

CONCLUSION

The small firm is at substantial disadvantage in entering foreign markets. This is especially true within the Canadian environment where the basic conditions for export marketing have not been fully developed. Given certain marketing opportunities for technologically based products and systems, the small Canadian firm is even at a greater disadvantage. If such market opportunities are to be realized, the present approaches to foreign marketing will have to be radically altered in order to correctly work toward a matching of supply and demand conditions. The marketing consortium, based on the concept of product offering assembly, can provide the necessary structure to organize the supply conditions to meet the types of marketing conditions found in East European countries.

32 When a Small Company Blazes a Rich Export Trail*
David Harvey

No one knows better than John Simms that business is tough. As managing director of A.H. Williams, Coventry-based manufacturers of aluminum window frames, he has seen at first hand the carnage that a slump in the construction industry can cause. Many of the company's competitors have joined the ranks of the failed in a period of record bankruptcies. A.H. Williams could easily have gone the same way if it had not been determined to drum up business through a bold, imaginative scheme. This determination led ultimately to a fat Ł 500,000 order from the Middle East.

But it is a success story which transcends the immediate interests of the company's shareholders, customers, and employees. It shows how even small firms with limited resources can win substantial overseas orders. The key to success was a marketing consortium, Unit 6, formed with five other companies from related areas of the construction industry. Its object: to find new markets abroad.

Simms recalls how imperative this had seemed in 1975: "It was a time when we had begun to worry about the future. We had a strong order book, but with the change in the government's economic policy we thought we'd lose what we had in the UK. We felt it was a choice between cutting back or finding new markets."

For small companies with limited manpower, it was clearly impracticable to send salesmen on extended globetrotting tours. With the Middle East identified as a prime target, research had shown that developers there had a strong preference for package deals that enabled them to contract out all aspects of finishing and fitting in one lot. So when A.H. Williams was approached concerning the formation of a marketing consortium, "we went overboard for Unit 6," according to Simms. The other five firms in the consortium were involved in catering equipment, decorative glass and roof lights, joinery, internal partitions, and doors.

---

*From David Harvey, "When a small company blazes a rich export trail," Director, Vol. 30 (October 1977), pp. 84-6. Reprinted with permission.

When Unit 6 was formally constituted in 1976 with two marketing staffs to chase orders, it soon developed into an object lesson in what small firms can achieve when they apply themselves. The research had shown the most promising markets and also what sort of effort was most appropriate. It recommended that Unit 6 should concentrate primarily on countries with an already medium to high GNP to get orders immediately. This was the reason for the attraction of the Middle East, because that area included countries with rapidly expanding economies. Construction and plants are at the top of their shopping lists. With a shortage of homegrown expertise, the field is open to outsiders.

The report also pointed out the necessity of preparing the ground for joint ventures in future years. Joint ventures are for the longer term, but they are needed if companies are not to be penalized by tariff barriers which they may expect the country to throw up once its own industry has gotten under way.

It was later in 1976 that the Ŀ 500,000 order, to provide windows for a bank in the Middle East, came through one of the consortium members. "I've no doubt that if it wasn't for the consortium, we wouldn't have got the order," says Simms.

Although the major order, equivalent to about one quarter of the company's annual turnover, clearly vindicated the consortium project, there had been earlier disappointments. Shortly after Unit 6 was launched, A.H. Williams became involved in tendering for two large contracts in Dubai and the Gulf, neither of which the company won. But the time and effort had been put into the design work just the same. As a consequence, new product development suffered and came to almost a standstill for about a year. Since the design and costing of projects is probably the most crucial and demanding part of the whole bidding exercise, something else had to give. The Middle East is a competitive market with margins lower than those the company would hope to see in the UK, and this makes accuracy in the calculations all the more crucial.

Although the prizes in the Middle East markets are often alluring, they are not to be won easily. Time factors can badly upset pricing calculations. Says Simms, "People want a final price. You can do this up to six months ahead, but it gets much more difficult when you have to wait longer for a decision."

With joint ventures and pricing, A.H. Williams is learning all the time. While the objectives of a consortium are an attractive proposition, the job of devising a legal framework which would enable objectives to be realized without undue risk or favor to any of the parties is not straightforward. Ironically, because problems posed by the size of the order that A.H. Williams won, it was decided to sell the consortium. The main difficulty centered on the joint liability conditions built into the consortium's constitution.

Simms is by no means disenchanted with the principle of joint enterprise. But he feels that there could be improvements in the mix of products and expertise represented. He has already approached a couple of companies with a view of setting up another joint marketing operation. The legal constitution of the group remains the major problem however.

33 Alternative Ways to Penetrate a Foreign Market*
Business International

Whether a company is approaching a foreign market for the first time or has been operating in it for years, periodic reviews of the techniques used in it are necessary to keep ahead of changing conditions and to update corporate objectives in that market.

Factors that call for such periodic examinations include inter-regional shifts, urbanization and suburbanization, technology, transportation, competition, social pressures, local expertise, changing buying patterns and selling outlets, and, of course, government actions and rules and regulations.

Company policies may dictate certain basic operating patterns or preferences, but local conditions and laws may demand important modifications. A company that is rigid in its style of operations, i.e., choosing to invest in a market only as a majority owner or selling only through its own sales force, may be passing up opportunities for great profits. None of the many possible routes to market penetration should be overlooked in a company's periodic review of its approaches. Below is a checklist of the major market routes, from the simplest to the most committed.

DOMESTIC EXPORT SALES

1. Fill unsolicited orders from independent export/import houses that buy and sell for their own customers.
2. Sell to foreign government buying offices, and buying groups of other foreign organizations located in the domestic market (e.g., The Afro-American Purchasing Center Inc. of NY and Amtorg

---

*Reprinted from "Alternative ways to penetrate a foreign market," in 100 Checklists: Decision Making in International Operations (Business International, 1970), pp. 6-8, with permission.

Trading Co.) and qualify for listing on approved government buying lists.

3. Bid on tenders solicited by foreign governments or private organizations (some may be limited to local or regional companies).
4. Sell to foreign subsidiaries in domestic market products for shipment to parent and other overseas subsidiaries.
5. Sell to domestic customers products for shipment to their overseas subsidiaries.
6. Display and take part in trade fairs and exhibitions.

INDIRECT EXPORT SALES

1. Hire the services of a combination export managing (CEM) firm, which in effect becomes your export department. (You get involved only to the extent and with products desired.)
2. Hire the services of an export/import house. It takes over the responsibility for exporting and distributing your product overseas, but leaves you with little control or ability to keep abreast of the market. Can be vital in small and remote markets.
3. Arrange to have another company market your product through its overseas marketing channels, particularly when it is well established abroad and its products are complementary to your own (also called "piggybacking" or "mother hen").

DIRECT EXPORT SALES THROUGH OUTSIDE DISTRIBUTION CHANNELS

1. Join forces with other manufacturers of your product line and export under a group, industry, or association. U.S. companies can do this via Webb-Pomerene Associations (Export Trade Act of 1918), which are designed to enable small firms to engage in foreign trade (cutting costs and competing effectively against overseas cartels) without running into antitrust snags.
2. Organize your own export department, staff it with your own export salesmen, and sell via middlemen in the foreign market. This may be to a commission house or purchasing agent, resident buyer, broker, auction house, export/import merchant, or jobber (takes title to your merchandise); or independent agents and distributors (sells on commission).
3. Negotiate export barter sales via a third party entrepreneur (or direct with foreign purchaser).
4. Form an export consortium with other manufacturers to supply turnkey and large-scale development projects.

DIRECT EXPORT AND SALES THROUGH LOCAL COMPANY SALES ORGANIZATION

1. Create a regional sales branch office and/or subsidiary.
2. If a U.S. company, organize a Western Hemisphere Trade Corporation to engage in export within the western hemisphere; it can obtain concessional tax rates for these activities.
3. Create a national sales branch office and/or subsidiary.
4. Organize a joint selling company with a:
   (a) Local partner.
   (b) Unrelated third-country manufacturer.
   (c) Related third-country subsidiary.
5. Establish own sales force and distributors using:
   (a) Domestic salesmen.
   (b) Expatriate salesmen.
   (c) Third-country nationals.
   (d) All three.
6. Use company sales force as well as "missionary" salesmen for:
   (a) Certain customers.
   (b) Particular areas.
   (c) Particular outlets.
7. Set up regional distribution centers or warehouses.
8. Set up national company distribution centers or warehouses.
9. Hire services and rent facilities of public warehouses.
10. Use combination of company distribution centers and public warehouses.
11. Lease warehouse space in unrelated company warehouses.
12. Organize an overseas franchise system using independent franchises or a combination of company and independents.
13. Team up with another equally strong manufacturer (or several) whereby you each distribute and sell noncompetitive products through company showrooms or dealers in:
    (a) The same country.
    (b) Different countries.

LICENSING, ASSEMBLING, AND MANUFACTURING

1. License patents and/or unpatented know-how in return for:
   (a) Royalty payments and fees.
   (b) Equity.
   (c) Royalty and equity.
2. License patents and/or unpatented know-how for a flat sum payment, e.g., East European deals, and licenses of obsolete processes.
3. Obtain licenses of foreign patents and/or unpatented know-how for use in third countries (and domestic market).
4. Arrange to cross-license equipment of a manufacturer who in turn produces under license your equipment. Each to be sold in respective markets.

5. Contract out manufacture of products to be sold:
   (a) Under your company trademarks and brand names.
   (b) Under private label.
   (c) For small and/or test runs.
6. Operate under a management contract that gives you management responsibility.
7. Set up a consortium with three or more partners, with the company:
   (a) Assuming management responsibility.
   (b) Being passive partner.
8. Purchase an equity interest in an existing manufacturing or assembly operation with:
   (a) 100 percent equity   Cash
   (b) Controlling interest   acquired with   Technology
   (c) Minority interest   Parent stock
9. Set up manufacturing or assembly operations in a free trade zone or free port.
10. Purchase assets of an existing foreign corporation, buying some or all assets for cash, stock, or a combination of the two.
11. Organize a joint venture with a local partner, holding equity through a third-country corporation (a base).
12. Join with a third-country partner in a new manufacturing/assembly operation:
    (a) Unrelated third-country manufacturer.
    (b) Related third-country subsidiary.
    (c) Private financial partner, e.g., Edge Act Corp.
    (d) Public institutional financial partner, e.g., IFC.
13. Create a joint venture with local interests in a new manufacturing/assembly operation:
    (a) Fifty-fifty ownership – with joint management.
    (b) Majority-owned – with management responsibility.
    (c) Minority-owned – with or without management responsibility (i.e., with, if partner is a bank, government).
14. Create a manufacturing/assembly operation wholly owned by a third-country holding (base) company.
15. Create a wholly owned manufacturing/assembly operation.

34 Distributors — Finding and Keeping the Good Ones*
G. Beeth

This article is mainly concerned with distributors (including agents) of industrial equipment. Thus, not all of the conclusions are applicable to distributors in other fields. Generally, we have in mind "sole" distributors, that is, an exclusive distributor for each country.

THE IMPORTANCE OF HAVING THE RIGHT DISTRIBUTOR

Most international companies looking at the actual range of performance of their foreign distributors find that it does not fall within, say, 80 to 120 percent of what they would expect from carefully determined market potential figures. Instead, performance varies from zero to over 200 percent of the expected, and the difference in performance between distributors is enormous. Finding excellent distributors is therefore all-important.

But even with your best efforts, you will never have a group of only excellent distributors. With careful and hard work, you can have a few excellent, many medium, and some mediocre distributors. . .and a few worthless ones whom you are always trying to replace. There is no way to hit 100 percent.

We may take as a rule of thumb, that in most countries with only small markets, there are in each field: zero or one excellent distributors, zero or one medium distributors, one or two mediocre distributors, and the remaining distributors are worthless to you.

In most countries with bigger markets, yet not markets so big that they warrant a subsidiary, there often are in an industrial equipment field: one or two excellent distributors, two or three medium distribu-

---

*Adapted, by permission of the publisher, from International Management Practice: An Insiders View, Gunnar Beeth, copyright 1973 by AMACOM, a division of American Management Associations. All rights reserved.

tors, several mediocre distributors, and the remaining distributors are worthless.

FINDING THE GOOD ONES

Lists of distributors broken down by fields of activity are available for each country from the U.S. Department of Commerce (good), from local chambers of commerce (usually not good), from local classified directories of various kinds (often too all-inclusive), and from other sources. But you don't want a list, you want the name of one distributor – the best one.

One or two firms may have contacted you, but the probability that they are the best is small. Don't waste your time contacting them all by mail and sending them forms to complete. Instead, follow these three steps toward finding a good distributor:

1. Go personally to the country, allowing ample time. Talk to the ultimate users of the equipment to find out from which distributors they prefer to buy and why. Two or three names will keep popping up in the replies you get.
2. Then go to those two or three distributors and see which one or ones you would be able to sign up.
3. But, before making the final choice, look for the distributor who has the key man for your line – as explained below.

Long ago, we used to travel around with a list on which we rated each distributor on a scale from one to ten in each of twenty-four different activities and abilities. Then we weighed these different matters in accordance with the importance of each one and arrived arithmetically at a single over-all rating for each distributor. This was done by taking into account his sales force, his coverage of the market, management ability, service personnel's capability, financial strength, connections, warehouse and service facilities, spare parts stocks, performance in related lines, technical ability to understand the equipment, and several other items.

Unfortunately, the final rating figure for the distributors we were supervising showed no correlation at all to their actual performance.

Then we threw away the list and looked for what was common to the few excellent distributors with which we had the privilege to be working. In this way, we discovered a single new factor which replaced the 24-point list and this new factor bore considerable correlation to success. We started to look for a distributor who had one capable man who would take the new line of equipment to his heart and make it his personal objective to make the sale of that line a success in his country. In some small distributorships, this key man was the owner. In others, he was the sales manager or a salesman. In one company, he was the service manager. In one case, there were two such men instead of one, but that was a rare distributor who somehow did three times what we considered to be the possible volume for his country.

In actual fact, it is not as easy to find a good distributor in some countries, especially in very small, less industrialized nations where you might find that there are: zero excellent distributors; zero medium distributors; one or two mediocre distributors firmly tied to your competitors, and the remaining distributors are worthless to you.

Suppose none of them shows any sign of having or getting the key man you are looking for. What do you do?

First, you can try to find a local businessman in a different field — one who wants to fill the obvious need for a good distributor in your field. If that doesn't work, you can try to get one of the mediocre distributors to switch from the competitor to you. Occasionally you might get to him just when he has become angry at your competitor for some reason or another.

But failing that, you had better forget about appointing any distributor at all in that country — because having a worthless one will cost you time and money every year and possibly prevent a good newcomer in that country from asking for your line.

If everything else has failed, you may want to consider attending a local industrial exhibition in that country to ask further advice from the local prospective end users of your products. If there should be a nearby U.S. trade center, it can help you mount a small exhibition of your products for the specific purpose of finding a distributor.

When you interview distributors, what they tell you is often revealing about them in ways they do not realize. Here is an example. We used to sell compressors and call on distributors in the heavy construction field. For some of them, their prime line was Caterpillar tractors, and for others International Harvester tractors. When asked how their business was, some would answer "great" while others would say that it was impossible to compete against International Harvester or Caterpillar — whichever line they did not have.

Those who said it was impossible to compete raised one warning signal. Is this distributor going downhill? What has happened to him? Why can he not compete?

But those who said that the tractor business was great raised another equally important warning signal. Do they concentrate all of their efforts on their tractor line? Are they great in selling tractors and poor in selling everything else? Signing on distributors who are excellent for another manufacturer in an allied field does not always produce excellent results.

KEEPING THE GOOD ONES

The only way to keep a good distributor is to work closely and well with him, so that he can make money with your line.

View your business from the distributor's side. First of all, he must make money for himself. If that automatically makes him earn money for you, too, then fine. But if he does not make money with it for himself, any good distributor will quickly drop your line.

Even worse, he may put your line away and make it available only if one of his customers insists on getting some of your equipment – but otherwise do nothing for your line.

Thus, you must not only keep the good distributor but also keep the distributor good. And the last part is not always easy because there are many demands on his time from other lines of equipment and from customers with interests and problems outside your field. Somehow, you must arrange through direct mail and visits to keep your line constantly in front of your distributor and among his daily duties and thoughts.

It is best, of course, if you can require that he have one or more full-time persons handling your line. But if the potential sales volume is not high enough to warrant this effort, do not ask for it. If you cause the distributor losses through excessive demands on him, it will backfire on you.

Above all, you must not be stingy in matters such as paying for the training of his men and going beyond your legal warranty obligations to your distributor. He goes beyond his legal warranty toward his customers, and he expects the same from you.

It is important that the rules be spelled out in advance concerning payment of commissions to the distributor or agent. Especially the conditions relating to nonpayment of commissions must be clear. Nevertheless, when an unclear borderline case comes up, you should always rule in favor of your distributor. In the long run, the distributor's goodwill toward your company is more valuable than the commissions paid in borderline cases. The quickest way to destroy a distributor's goodwill is to make him feel cheated – even on a small matter.

Unless your sales volume with each distributor is very large, you cannot afford to run his business or remake a mediocre distributor into a good one.

One American company has an outstanding record of going against the above rule: Caterpillar. They will work so effectively with a distributor that they can make him good in many cases; but for most other companies, this method is too costly.

Instead, if a good distributor changes into a mediocre or bad one, the sooner you can replace him with an excellent alternative, the better. Of course, whether or not the new one will be excellent, you never know in advance. If the new distributor also turns out to be mediocre or worse, then you had better switch again as soon as you have found a third seemingly excellent prospect.

Some people argue that this switching shows a lack of stability and seriousness toward the ultimate users. Don't worry; the ultimate users are probably better aware of the shortcomings of your former distributor than you are. They appreciate your trying to find a good one and your sales figures show it quickly when you succeed. Any good list of distributors is in constant change because the distributors themselves quickly change. It might be that the key man for your line has left his distributor-employer, and your sales drop forthwith to 10 percent of what they previously were in that country. Unless you can get the distributor to replace the departed man with another excellent key man, or switch responsibility for your line to another one of his best men, don't keep that distributor – just hoping that things will improve.

GETTING RID OF THE MEDIOCRE DISTRIBUTORS

When you do change, do it totally, quickly, cleanly, and thoroughly, without worrying about being called ruthless by your old distributor. He will always feel that your cancellation is an affront to him personally, anyway. He will say that you are not loyal. Forget it. An active, aggressive, changing distributor list produces more sales. In addition, your aggressive policies tend to keep the medium distributors on their toes and doing their best.

The lengthy distributor contract has only one important clause: the cancellation clause. The remainder is mainly a listing of who does what, written in legalese. In most light industrial equipment businesses, it should be possible for either party to cancel any time after the first year, upon sixty days' notice to the other party.

What happens to the distributor's stock in case of cancellation by the manufacturer should be spelled out. It will vary considerably from country to country because of local laws, but in no case should the manufacturer be required to take back any obsolete or otherwise unsaleable inventory. If the manufacturer must agree to take back any other inventory, it should be at the net f.o.b., factory price, less a hefty restocking charge, unless local laws force him to do otherwise.

Prior to signing a distributorship contract, the cancellation clause should be checked by a local lawyer to minimize any local indemnification requirements to distributors upon cancellation.

Of course, some distributors may object to a strong cancellation clause, but it is well worth fighting for despite the natural hope that you will never need to use it.

In some countries, the indemnification to distributors upon cancellation depends on just how the business is conducted. In France, if the distributor has certain obligations to report names and addresses of purchasers to you, the indemnification risk increases to compensate the distributor for the market information. In Germany, there is no indemnification to a true distributor, "Eigenhandler," but there is to a commission agent if he has certain reporting obligations.

Since the laws governing a distributor contract vary widely from country to country, their impact on cancellation of distributor contracts must be taken into account when choosing the country from which you want to service and supervise distributors. In an area such as Europe, you may prefer a country with favorable laws which you can invoke for governing the distributorship contracts.

To illustrate the opposite situation, assume that an American subsidiary to France supervises and supplies a distributor for Italy. In this case, the contract must be written so that either French or Italian law applies. Neither is particularly favorable, but Italian law is somewhat better than French law in case the distributor contract has to be cancelled.

But if the same Italian distributor had been supplied from an American subsidiary in Denmark, the contractor should get Danish law to apply, instead, in order to lower the risk of indemnification upon cancellation.

The cancellation of a distributor or licensee agreement can be a somewhat delicate transaction, and it must be handled carefully. If the distributor who is dropped is no good, then the remaining distributors in neighboring countries will understand and support the cancellation. But if the matter is not clear cut (e.g., for some business reason it should become necessary to drop a medium distributor), then the action must be thoroughly explained to the remaining distributors, customers, and others. An excellent distributor is never dropped. Any cancellation must, of course, always be thoroughly prepared under the applicable law.

Contrary to what distributors seem to feel, there is nothing morally wrong in terminating a distributorship which doesn't work out. And in the long run the true interest of a poor distributor will not be served by his representing your business anyway. Typically, the only economical way to improve upon an ineffective independent distributor is to change over to an effective one. Had it been your subsidiary instead, you could have eliminated the specific cause for the "distributor's" ineffectiveness. Unfortunately, this is usually too difficult to do in an independent company.

35 A Note on "Offbeat Exports: Small Entrepreneurs Do Well"*

Time

Under the above heading Time magazine reported some fascinating examples of ingenuity in small business exporting. Willard Clark, founder and president of Worldwide Sires Inc. of California, runs a truly unique operation: he sells bull semen. Acting as a broker for nine artificial insemination cooperatives, Clark exports the frozen semen of prize U.S. bulls (mostly Holsteins) to more than 40 countries, including the Soviet Union. He is now looking to China, where he hopes to hog the market for swine semen. Though his business is only seven years old, he expects sales to reach $5 million this year.

Clark is one of many small, imaginative entrepreneurs successfully pushing a wide variety of U.S. exports. Overcoming problems of language, complex export red tape, and trade barriers, the new entrepreneurs are shipping some unusual products abroad. Trees from the Angelica Nurseries in Maryland are being planted for shade and beauty on the boulevards of European cities. When Europe's nurserymen were unable to meet the demand for the large-leafed, pollution-resistant trees of the London plane variety, Angelica's owners, Mr. Thomas Kohl and his three sons, saw their chance. This year, they sent 5,000 sycamore hybrids to Hamburg from their 1,000-acre tree farm at $24 to $30 each, and they expect to ship as many as 10,000 next year.

Rexton, a small Los Angeles company, buys leftover orange peels from Sunkist and exports them to Japan to be used in making marmalade, whisky, and soy sauce. Katsumi Sato, the Japanese-American owner of the firm, investigated the budding Japanese market for orange peels a year ago, liked what he saw, and went into business. Mr. Sato expects to earn close to $250,000 next year. Meanwhile, he is looking into two other exports for Tokyo: shark fins for soup and jackets worn by the Los Angeles Police Department, popular with teen-agers.

---

*Source material from "Offbeat exports: Small entrepreneurs do well," Time, December 18, 1978, pp. 69-70.

Geraldine Waterbury, also of California, turned to farming after raising a family. She has just produced the greatest crop yield of kiwi fruit in California history – 15 tons per acre. She markets them at $5 per kilo to the Japanese, who consider the kiwi fruit a rare delicacy. Tom O'Toole, a Detroit tinkerer, has designed a single-cup coffee brewer which he has begun to market to the Japanese. Next he will send them production molds, priced at $90,000 and producing up to 15,000 brewers a day. Tolona Pizza Products of Chicago sends more than 500 tons of pizza ingredients per year to Japan and Europe. Anixter Brothers, Inc., of Skokie, Illinois, is supplying Saudi Arabia with $15 million worth of indestructible shelters that do double duty as shipping containers.

These exports will not balance the U.S.'s big trade deficit. But they add up, and they help. More importantly, the sales show that Yankee traders can crack overseas markets – if they show a little of their classic ingenuity.

36 On the Export Behavior of Firms*
Warren J. Bilkey

The export behavior of firms relates to the supply side of international trade. A substantial body of literature has developed on the subject since the early 1960s, but it is so widely scattered and difficult to obtain that few analysts appear to be aware of more than a portion of what has been written. No common model has been developed for the various empirical findings on the export behavior of firms. This article reviews the essential features of that literature and integrates them by topic covered.

EXPORT INITIATION

Analysts concerned with the initiation of the export process have tended to focus on the effects of change-agents, both external and internal. External change-agents include chambers of commerce, industrial associations, banks, government agencies, and other firms. The latter appear to be overwhelmingly the most important and include corporations that buy-out smaller firms and then pressure them to export, foreign firms interested in buying machinery for their own use or components for their manufacturing process, foreign importers, and export agents. The important internal change-agent tends to be a member of the firm's top management who is interested in and enthusiastic about exporting. The determinants of whether or not management takes the initiative in exporting appear to be the following. First is management's diffuse impression of the attractiveness of exporting as an abstract ideal, independently of whatever particular contribution exporting might make to its own firm. The latter cannot be

*Slightly abbreviated from Warren J. Bilkey, "An attempted integration of the literature on the export behavior of firms," Journal of International Business Studies (Summer 1978), pp. 33-46, with permission.

known by management until it explores the feasibility of exporting or gains export experience. Second, is the degree of the firm's international orientation as determined by its background and traditions and by the foreign attitudes of its top management. In Perlmutter (1969)-Thorelli (1966) terminology the latter attitudes are ethnocentric, polycentric, and geocentric. A third determinant of whether management takes the initiative in exporting is its confidence in the firm's competitive advantage (Snavely et al., 1964), involving management's perception of whether or not the firm's product has unique qualities (or is patented); whether or not the firm has technological, marketing, financial, or price advantages, exclusive information about a foreign market or customer, and an efficient distribution network. A fourth determinant of whether or not management takes the initiative in exporting is adverse home market conditions, causing management to explore exporting as a means for the firm's survival (Pavord and Bogart, 1975). The relationship of this initiative to general economic conditions varies greatly among firms, because of the differential impacts that a country's economic condition has at any given time on its various industries.

MOTIVATION FOR EXPORTING

The motivation for exporting is distinct from, though often related to, the initiation of exporting. Some firms are pushed into exporting by an external change-agent (e.g., a foreign customer); some simply take advantage of export opportunities that come their way with no evident objective in mind, while others are motivated to initiate exporting deliberately.

Classical economic theory implies that a firm's probability of exporting tends to vary directly with the profit its management expects from exporting. Hirsch (1971) in a study of 497 Danish, Dutch, and Israeli manufacturing firms concluded that no such relationship existed. However, studies of U.S. manufacturing firms (Simpson and Kujawa, 1974; Bilkey and Tesar, 1977) did yield such a relationship. That is, exporters' attitudes tend to vary directly with the perceived profitability of exporting, and inversely with the perceived intensity of their domestic competition.

PERCEIVED OBSTACLES TO EXPORTING

A considerable number of studies focused on perceived serious obstacles (or barriers) to exporting, the apparent rationale being that a government could stimulate exporting by removing those obstacles, which usually are institutional and infrastructural. Several cross-sectional studies found that nonexporting firms perceived significantly more serious obstacles to exporting than did exporting firms (de la Torre, 1972; Simpson and Kujawa, 1974; Bilkey and Tesar, 1977). Others found either no relation or an inverse relation – meaning that nonexporters perceived fewer obstacles to exporting than did exporters. These seemingly contradictory findings are explicable by differences in the export development of the firms selected for the studies. That is, nonexporters that have not even explored the feasibility of exporting (which will be defined later as firms in export stages 1 and 2) have no basis for knowing their obstacles to exporting; and they, therefore, tend to list fewer than do the exporting firms. However, nonexporters that have explored the feasibility of exporting (which will be defined later as firms in export stage 3) tend to list more serious obstacles to exporting than do the exporting firms. The most frequent serious obstacles to exporting reported by U.S. firms in the empirical studies are insufficient finances, foreign government restrictions, insufficient knowledge about foreign selling opportunities, inadequate product distribution abroad, and a lack of foreign market connections. The type of obstacles perceived tend to vary by industry and by firms' export stages.

MANAGEMENT

Observations have led various analysts to focus on the quality of management as an important determinant of exporting. Three means of measurement have been devised for this purpose. One is peer evaluations as to which firms are most efficient and which firms best perform product planning, advertising, research, and sales administration functions. Exporting firms tend to be evaluated more highly than nonexporting firms. A second measure of the quality of management has respondents evaluate their own managements. Exporters tend to rate their managements as being more aggressive than nonexporters. A third measurement of the quality of management compares (a) managers' attitudes and activities, and (b) the firm's functions and organizational structure with (c) accepted good management practices. Studies using this approach found that exporting firms tended to have better management than did the nonexporting firms (Bilkey and Tesar, 1977).

FIRM SIZE

Many analysts regard a firm's size as critical for its propensity to export, yet empirical findings on this issue have been mixed. Four studies found a positive cross-sectional relationship between firm size and the percent of firms that export and three studies found no meaningful relationship (Snavely, et al., 1964; Bilkey and Tesar, 1977). Two studies concluded that very small firms tend not to export, that beyond some point exporting is not correlated with size, and that between these two points exporting is correlated with firm size (Hirsch, 1971; Cavusgil, 1976). The latter proposition seems capable of reconciling the other analysts' divergent findings; however, the relationship is complicated by a possible intercorrelation of firm size with the quality of management. The extent to which an intercorrelation exists could alone cause firm size to vary directly with a firm's propensity to export.

EXPORT DESTINATION

The Uppsala School argues that exporting tends to begin with the psychologically closest country, and then extends progressively to countries that are psychologically more-and-more distant. (Psychological distance is ". . .the sum of factors preventing the flow of information from and to the market. Examples are differences in language, education, business practices, culture, and industrial development." (Johanson and Vahlne, 1977, p. 24).) This harmonizes with Linder's international trade theory (Linder, 1961) and with empirical findings from studies conducted in the northern part of the U.S. On the basis of Swedish studies, Carlson (1975) concluded that firms producing technology-intensive products are more influenced by psychological distance than producers of other products, and that small firms are more influenced by psychological distance than are large firms.

EXPORT RISK

Portfolio theory suggests that an exporting firm probably faces less total market risk than a nonexporting firm, because of its market diversification, but little empirical work has been done on this issue. Hirsch (1971), in a study of Danish, Dutch, and Israeli firms, concluded that foreign entry is more hazardous than domestic selling. But "light exporters" tend to perceive more risk from exporting than "heavy exporters."

EXPORTING TO FOREIGN AFFILIATES

A survey of 330 U.S. firms with 3,579 foreign affiliates showed that 52 percent of their exports were made to their own foreign affiliates. Of the latter exports 55 percent were for resale without further manufacture; 35 percent were for further processing; 7 percent were for capital equipment; and 3 percent were for all else. The growing relative importance of exporting to affiliates was indicated by a survey of 298 U.S. multinational firms (Barker, 1972). The share of their total exports to their majority-owned affiliates was 44 percent in 1966 and 55 percent in 1970. In 1964, exports to affiliates accounted for 46 percent of all U.S. exports to Canada, for 33 percent to Latin America, for 21 percent to Europe, and 11 percent to Africa, Asia, and Oceania combined. Inasmuch as these studies covered the largest and presumably most advanced U.S. firms, is it possible that exporting to affiliates is the ultimate current stage of a firm's export process?

EXPORT MODELS

A basic modeling question is whether firms' export behavior should be formulated in terms of a multi-activity model, incorporating all alternative activities of a firm (developing exports, expanding domestic markets, increasing product lines, etc.), or in terms of a single activity model (developing exports only). Mintz (1967) illuminated this question by analyzing U.S. export data over the course of several business cycles to ascertain the effects of varying economic conditions on U.S. exports. Her findings imply that, except for very short time periods, a single activity model is adequate because a firm can develop an export program by growing; it need not contract its other activities to export. Consistent with Mintz' findings, all of the following export modeling efforts have been confined to single activity models.

Attempts to formulate export models have tended to focus on three issues: identifying the variables involved, specifying the relationship among those variables at any given time, and specifying the dynamics of that relationship.

Etgar and McConnel (1976) formulated a static cause-and-effect model in the form of an equation, with independent variables on the right:

(i) $$B = \emptyset(E, I, C)$$

where B represents a vector of export related behavioral decisions; E represents a group of internal and external environmental factors (location of markets, technological factors, institutional factors, behavioral forces, economic forces, and legal-political influences); I represents a group of information stimuli (from mass media, personal contacts, and previous experience); and C represents the information processing complex (including learning and choice constructs). The relationship among variables on the right side of the equation, either within groups or between groups, was not indicated, and no empirical test of the model was attempted. However, their model yields inferences that harmonize with observable behavior.

Cavusgil (1976) proposed a static path model composed of both "background" and "intervening" independent variables, as shown in figure 36.1. He calculated the bivariate correlation coefficients for each relationship using Tesar's 1975 Wisconsin data (Bilkey and Tesar, 1977). These are the numbers beside the arrows in figure 36.1.

Welch and Wiedersheim-Paul (1977) formulated a model of the pre-export behavior of a firm as shown in figure 36.2. It is dynamic in that it incorporates feedback loops and interactions and brings into account a substantial number of basic variables. It tries to interrelate those variables in a flow or sequence sense, but does not explain how they relate functionally. It was not tested empirically, but certain Australian case data were provided that tend broadly to support the model.

Carlson (1975) suggested that the internationalization process of firms follows a more-or-less learning curve. Johanson and Vahlne (1977)

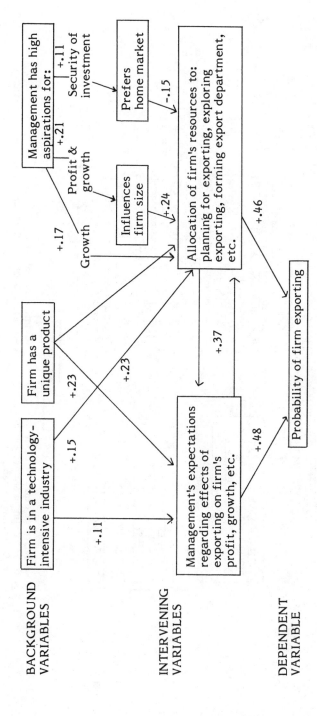

Fig. 36.1. Cavusgil's path model of a firm's export behavior. Numbers are the bivariate correlation coefficients between the variables connected (Cavusgil, 1976, p. 130).

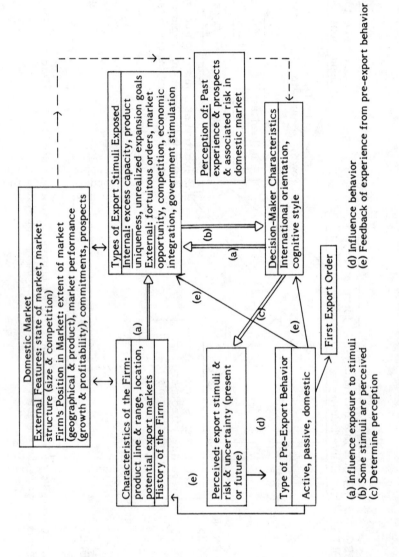

Fig. 36.2. Welch and Wiedersheim-Paul's model of factors affecting the pre-export behavior of a firm (Welch and Wiedersheim-Paul, 1977, p. 4).

Domestic Market

External Features: state of market, market structure (size & competition)
Firm's Position in Market: extent of market (geographical & product), market performance (growth & profitability), commitments, prospects

Types of Export Stimuli Exposed
Internal: excess capacity, product uniqueness, unrealized expansion goals
External: fortuitous orders, market opportunity, competition, economic integration, government stimulation

Perception of: Past experience & prospects & associated risk in domestic market

Decision-Maker Characteristics
International orientation, cognitive style

Characteristics of the Firm:
product line & range, location, potential export markets
History of the Firm

Perceived: export stimuli & risk & uncertainty (present or future)

Type of Pre-Export Behavior
Active, passive, domestic

First Export Order

(a) Influence exposure to stimuli
(b) Some stimuli are perceived
(c) Determine perception

(d) Influence behavior
(e) Feedback of experience from pre-export behavior

274

suggested that internationalization develops from a series of incremental decisions. These propositions are consistent with a stages theory of the export development process. That is, stimuli induce a firm to move to a higher export stage; the experience (learning) gained from that stage alters the firm's perceptions, expectations, managerial capacity, etc.; new stimuli then induce the firm to move to the next higher export stage; and so on. This might be thought of as $S \longrightarrow O \longrightarrow R$ type behavior (where S in the stimuli, O is the organism, and R is the response) with a feedback loop from R to O, which creates conditions for the next stage. (Research seeks to explain why two groups of firms in a given country producing the same product have differing export behavior – one group exports and the other does not. In the $S \longrightarrow O \longrightarrow R$ conceptualization, both groups are subject to the same external stimuli; the difference is in the organism: attitudes, interests, expectations, know-how, etc.) The Uppsala School (Johanson and Wiedersheim-Paul, 1975) conceptualized the export stages as: no permanent export, export via agent, export via sales subsidiary, and, in some cases, production in a foreign subsidiary; and they presented evidence supporting such a model. Bilkey and Tesar (1977) formulated a stages model to which the following generalized multiple regression equation was fitted – the coefficients differed at each stage because of the experience gained from the preceding stages –

(ii) $$A = a + bE - cI + dF + eM$$

where: A is the firm's export activity for the stage in question; E is management's expectations regarding the benefits of exporting after it has been developed; I is the inhibitors (mainly serious infrastructural and institutional obstacles) that management perceives to initiating exporting; F is the facilitators (unsolicited orders, information, subsidies, infrastructural and institutional aids, etc.) management perceives to initiating exporting; and M is the quality and dynamism of the firm's management plus the firm's organizational characteristics that affect exporting. Small case letters are coefficients. The model involves the following export stages, which are derived from Rogers' stages of the adoption process (Rogers, 1962, pp. 81-86).

1. The firm is unwilling to export; it would not even fill an unsolicited export order – because of apathy, dislike of foreign activities, busy doing other things, etc.
2. The firm fills unsolicited export orders, but does not explore the feasibility of exporting.
3. The firm explores the feasibility of exporting. (This stage may be omitted by the receipt of unsolicited export orders.)
4. The firm exports experimentally to one or a few markets.
5. The firm is an experienced exporter to those markets.
6. The firm explores possibilities of exporting to additional markets. And so on.

Questionnaires from 423 Wisconsin manufacturing firms were classified according to the above stages, and step-wise multiple regressions of the type shown in Equation (ii) were calculated for each of three stages. The results differed greatly. Movement from stages 1 and 2 to stage 3 was only partly explained (R^2=.241). The major correlates were directly with whether management planned for exporting, and directly with management's impression of the firm's competitive advantages. No relation was found with management's expectations as to what exporting would contribute to the firm's profits, growth, etc., nor with management's perception of inhibitors (serious obstacles) to exporting. Movement from earlier stages to stage 4 correlated (R^2=.69) directly with whether the firm received an unsolicited initial export order; directly with the quality of the firms' management; and, to a small extent, directly with the firm's size. Again, there was no correlation with management's expectations as to what exporting would contribute to its firm, nor with management's perception of export inhibitors. The percent of sales exported by stage 5 firms correlated (R^2=.70) directly with management's perceptions of the gains from exporting, inversely with the number of perceived inhibitors to exporting, and inversely with the quality of the firm's management.

An important problem in the above models is the huge number of variables that influence the export behavior of firms. One possible solution is to incorporate every variable directly; none of the above analysts did that. A second possibility is to combine the variables into categories, and then to construct a model composed only of those categories; both Etgar and McConnell (Equation i) and Welch and Weidersheim-Paul (figure 36.2) followed this approach. A third possible solution is to combine the variables into nonintercorrelated composites, as Bilkey and Tesar (Equation ii) have done. A fourth possible solution is to relate the variables into background and intervening variables, as Cavusgil did (figure 36.1). The latter possibility seems to be the least ambiguous. Another important problem is to dynamize a model adequately. Both Etgar and McConnell (Equation i) and Cavusgil (figure 36.1) limited themselves to static models which could be dynamized if expanded properly. Welch and Wiedersheim-Paul (figure 36.2) formulated a dynamic model employing feedback loops, but it is vague and could be difficult to implement. Both the Uppsala School and Bilkey and Tesar (Equation ii) formulated dynamic models by employing stages of development. These can be conceived of as sequential alternations in the direction of cause-and-effect equations. Thus, the initial Equation (ii) direction would be from right-to-left, moving the firm to the next higher export stage. The experiences (learning) involved in carrying out that stage would reverse the cause-and-effect flow from left-to-right, affecting the firm's expectations, perceptions, know-how, etc. – i.e., change the coefficients on the right side of the equation. With adequate stimuli, the cause-and-effect flow of the revised equation next would be from right-to-left, leading the firm to a still higher export stage; and so on. Bilkey and Tesar (1977) empirically examined only three right-to-left cause-and-effect flows. Logically, both the feedback loop approach and the alternating cause-and-effect equation flow approach come to the same result. The latter is fairly easy to implement.

EXPORT PROFILES

Two analysts sought to profile both exporting and nonexporting firms as a means for identifying potential exporters among firms that are not yet exporting. Differences in their findings seemingly can be explained by differences in the data they gathered. Snavely, Weiner, Ulbrich, and Enright (1964) found that the most important characteristics in which their sample of Connecticut current exporters exceeded the never exporters were (rank-ordered): one or more of the firm's products were patented; the firm served the entire U.S. market; the firm held sole rights to the patents it used; management was willing to study foreign markets; and the firm utilized a combination of selling techniques rather than only one. The most important characteristics in which the never exporters exceeded the current exporters were (rank-ordered): the firm regarded its small size as a barrier to exporting; the firm sold directly to buyers; the firm utilized only personal selling; and the firm had only a local market. Cavusgil (1976) found that 96 percent of Wisconsin firms with the following characteristics exported: had very favorable expectations regarding the effect of exporting on the firm's growth; planned for exporting; had gross sales greater than $1 million; and had favorable expectations regarding the effects of exporting on the firm's market development. Alternatively, only 5 percent of the firms with the following characteristics exported: had neutral or unfavorable expectations regarding the effects of exporting on the firm's growth; did not systematically explore the feasibility of exporting; and placed a low value on growth.

CONCLUSIONS

The forementioned research findings lead to three major conclusions regarding the export behavior of firms. One is that exporting is essentially a developmental process. This may be conceptualized either as a learning sequence involving feedback loops or as export stages. Second, equation coefficients tend to differ from one stage of the export process to another. This can be illustrated by using the previously listed export stages as a framework for integrating the various empirical findings. The probability of a stage 2 firm entering export stage 3 (exploring the feasibility of exporting) seemingly depends very much on the firm's international orientation, on its management's impression regarding the attractiveness per se of exporting, and on its management's confidence in the firm's ability to compete abroad. The probability of a firm entering export stage 4 (becoming an experimental exporter) is primarily a function of whether the firm receives unsolicited exports, and the quality and dynamism of its management. However, for firms in stage 5 (experienced exporters) the situation changes. Then, the percent of sales exported is primarily a function of management's expectations regarding the effect of exporting on the firm's profit, growth, etc., and on the inhibitors (serious obstacles) management perceives to exporting.

A third conclusion is that export profiles can be formulated; they are potentially very useful, but they should be used in conjunction with export behavior models to achieve their potential. That is, properly developed export profiles along the lines pioneered by Snavely, et al. (1964) and by Cavusgil (1976) could be used by government export promotion agencies, by banks, by export agents, and so on, to identify nonexporters with a high potential for becoming exporters. Limited resources for export promotion — loan funds, export management assistance, export training, foreign market information, etc. — then could be concentrated on the high export potential firms. The considerations (or variables) used for making such profiles must be the same as the operating agencies can obtain from client firms. If certain theoretically important considerations cannot be obtained by operating agencies (e.g., because they involve confidential information), the profiles should be formulated from obtainable correlates of those considerations. However, merely identifying firms with a high export potential would not be sufficient for an export promotion program. The operating agencies still would need to ascertain how much export response during a specified time frame could be expected from alternative export stimulation projects. Behavioral functions would be necessary for this purpose. They should apply to the same type of firms (with respect to export process, type of industry, etc.) as were used to develop the export profiles.

IMPLICATIONS

The research summarized in this paper represents a new development in microeconomics that is completely different in purpose, concept, and methodology from classical and neoclassical economic theory. The conceptual framework of the latter is rational profit maximization. The conceptual framework of the research reviewed here is behavioral consistency. Properly developed behavioral functions and export profiles seemingly could yield insights far beyond those provided by the classical-neoclassical economic models. Even the limited number of export studies to date provided the following useful inferences.

Governmental Policy Inferences

First, for maximum success, export stimulation programs should be tailored to the export development position of the firms to be stimulated. If formulated in terms of the export stages presented this means that: (1) experienced exporters (stage 5 firms) would tend to be stimulated to increase exports by devaluating the currency and by removing perceived obstacles to exporting; (2) nonexporters in stages 2 and 3 would tend to be stimulated to begin exporting (enter stage 4) by being provided with export orders (perhaps by developing Japanese-type trading companies) and with managerial assistance (e.g., export extension programs and export consulting services); (3) firms that have made no export efforts would tend to be stimulated to explore the feasibility of exporting (enter stage 3) by programs propagandizing the attractiveness of exporting (trade association meetings, advertising, public meetings, etc.) and through international education within schools. The latter includes foreign language training, student exchange abroad, international business education, and so on. A second government policy inference is that profile studies can be undertaken to ascertain identifiable characteristics of firms in each export stage. This could help officials of the government programs to target their export stimulation efforts with reasonable precision.

Managerial Inferences

Export management should, first, be keyed to the firm's position in the export development process, which from the firm's perspective is a learning process. A firm that has never exported, logically should, at first, concentrate on gaining basic export experience. The literature suggests that this can be accomplished best by starting with the psychologically closest markets – for most U.S. firms that is Canada; for most Swedish firms that is Norway; etc. As success is achieved in such markets, the firms should extend exporting to the next psychologically closest foreign market, and so on. Then, as adequate experience is gained, the firm should focus on markets that it considers the most attractive and develop them in depth. Eventually this may involve establishing production facilities abroad – a step beyond exporting in the firm's internationalization process. A second managerial inference is that the motivation for exporting probably should be the firm's long-term growth and development rather than short-term profit. A third managerial inference is that management could match its firm's own profile with the profiles of successful exporters as a guide to its export potential. Middle management might find this a useful means for eliciting top management's support for export development. A final managerial inference is that the quality of management probably is the greatest single determinant of a firm's export success.

REFERENCES

Barker, B.L., "U.S. foreign trade associated with U.S. multinational companies," Survey of Current Business (December 1972), pp. 20-28.

Bilkey, W.J. and Tesar, G., "The export behavior of smaller-sized Wisconsin manufacturing firms," Journal of International Business Studies (Spring 1977).

Carlson, S., How Foreign Is Foreign Trade? Acta Universitatis Upsaliensis, Studia Oeconomiae Negotiorum II (Bulletin No. 15 BN 91-554-0289-5) (Uppsala, Sweden, 1975), 26 pp.

Cavusgil, S.T., Organizational Determinants of Firms' Export Behavior: An Empirical Analysis. Ph.D. dissertation (The University of Wisconsin, Madison, WI., 1976).

de la Torre, J., Jr., "Marketing factors in manufactured exports from developing countries," in L.T. Wells, Jr. (ed.), The Product Life Cycle and International Trade (Boston, Graduate School of Business Administration, Harvard University, 1972).

Etgar, M. and McConnell, J.E., "International marketing as decision-making behavior of business organizations," unpublished paper dated November 1976.

Hirsch, S., The Export Performance of Six Manufacturing Industries (New York: Praeger Publishing Co., 1971).

Johanson, J. and Vahlne, J., "The internationalization process of the firm – a model of knowledge development and increasing foreign market commitments," Journal of International Business Studies, Vol. 8, No. 1 (Spring/Summer 1977), pp. 23-32.

Johanson, J. and Wiedersheim-Paul, F., "The internationalization of the firm – four Swedish case studies," The Journal of Management Studies (October 1975), pp. 305-22.

Linder, S.B., An Essay on Trade and Transformation (New York: Wiley, 1961).

Mintz, I., Cyclical Fluctuations in the Exports in the United States since 1879 (New York: National Bureau of Economic Research, 1967).

Pavord, W.C. and Bogart, R.G., "The dynamics of the decision to export," Akron Business and Economic Review (Spring 1975), pp. 6-11.

Perlmutter, H.V., "The tortuous evolution of the multinational corporation," Columbia Journal of World Business (January/February 1969), pp. 9-18.

Rogers, E.M. Diffusion of Innovations (New York: The Free Press, 1962).

Simpson, C.L., Jr. and Kujawa, D., "The export decision-process: an empirical enquiry," Journal of International Business Studies (Spring 1974), pp. 107-17.

Snavely, W.P.; Weiner, P.; Ulbrich, H.H.; and Enright, E.J., Export Survey of the Greater Hartford Area, Vols. 1 & 2 (Storrs, Connecticut: The University of Connecticut, 1964).

Thorelli, H.B., "The multinational corporation as a change agent," Southern Journal of Business (July 1966), pp. 1-9.

Welch, L.S. and Wiedersheim-Paul, F., "Extra regional expansion – internationalization within the domestic market?" Working paper prepared for the Centre for International Business Studies, Department of Business Administration, University of Uppsala, Uppsala, Sweden, dated January 1977.

FURTHER READING – PART SIX

Baylis, Arthur E., "The documentation dilemma in international trade," Columbia Journal of World Business, Vol. XI, No. 1 (Spring 1976), pp. 15-21.

Brasch, John J., "Assessing market potential for exports," Journal of Small Business Management, Vol. 17, No. 2 (April 1979), pp. 13-9.

Brasch, John J. and Crimmons, Joseph, "Some observations on small exporter trade credit risk management," Journal of Small Business Management, Vol. 17, No. 2 (April 1979), pp. 27-32.

Dowd, Laurence P., Introduction to Export Management (Burlingame, CA: Eljay Press, 1977).

Farmer, Richard N., "Thinking small in a multinational world," Journal of Business Administration, Vol. 7, No. 1 (1975), pp. 55-66.

Gordon, David L., "Creating linkages for worldwide development of small and medium enterprise," Journal of Small Business Management, Vol. 17, No. 2 (April 1979), pp. 20-6.

Lee, Woo-Young and Brasch, John J., "The adoption of export as an innovative strategy," Journal of International Business Studies, Vol. 9, No. 1 (Spring-Summer 1978), pp. 85-93.

Newbould, Gerald D.; Buckley, Peter J.; and Thurwell, Jane C., Going International: The Experience of Smaller Companies Overseas (New York: John Wiley & Sons – Halsted Press, 1978).

U.S. Small Business Administration, Export Marketing for Smaller Firms (Washington, D.C.: U.S. Government Printing Office, new editions periodically).

Vesper, Karl H. and Vorhies, Kenneth A., "Entrepreneurship in foreign trade," Journal of Small Business Management, Vol. 17, No. 2 (April 1979), pp. 5-11.

VII

Global Marketing in the Multinational Corporation

Introduction to Part VII

The large, multinational corporation is the subject of Part Seven. The readings deal with characteristic problems of global concern. The first problem is that of achieving coordination of the parts in the interest of the whole. An underlying issue is that of encouraging local initiative without harvesting gross national suboptimization. The second set of problems are those of organization at the national and headquarters levels. Both problems are perennial and call for continuous attention. The reason that no solutions are apt to be permanent is the constant change of the international business environment. As market structures change so do marketing strategies, sooner or later. Systems of coordination and organization will – or should – be adapted to the smooth implementation of whatever strategies are in effect at a given time.

Reading 37, by Brandt and Hulbert, examines the role of headquarters in guiding marketing strategy in the multinational subsidiary. Based on interviews with 63 Brazilian subsidiaries of North American, European, and Japanese MNCs, the authors found varying intensities of headquarters involvement, depending on the type of marketing decisions at stake. For example, a higher degree of headquarters direction was observed in product related areas, whereas promotional and especially pricing decisions tended to allow for greater management discretion at the subsidiary level, making possible a quicker response to changing market and environmental conditions. Incidentally, the setting of export prices from local foreign markets would typically be a rather centralized decision as suggested by Reading 40. A finding with obvious strategic implication in the Brandt-Hulbert article is the fact that subsidiaries with their own marketing research departments necessitated less headquarters guidance. Similarly, subsidiary strategies of market penetration, requiring more local research, generally involved less headquarters interference than did diversification strategies, often considered to be a riskier "growth vector."

It should be added that, other circumstances equal, one should expect a greater degree of home office involvement (directly or at least in the shape of centrally trained local personnel) in a corporation aiming to be a change agent abroad than in one where unilateral adjustment to local environments is the rule. Similarly, a strategy of homogenization will tend to be reflected in greater centralization than one of heterogenization, a topic that will be picked up again in Part Eight.

A global approach and centralization is also the underlying theme of Reading 38, in which Larréché attempts to adapt the Boston Consulting Group's product portfolio model to the task of formulating a competitive international marketing strategy. Each product in the portfolio is analyzed in terms of a "relative market share/market growth" matrix that allows the analyst to determine which product/market combinations are most and least profitable, which ones need development and future commitment, and which ones should be abandoned. The worldwide approach to product strategy is also reflected in Reading 39, by d'Antin. It discusses the product manager organization used in the local operations of Nestlé, one of the dozen most cosmopolitan concerns in the world.   The article demonstrates how the activities of product managers around the world for a given good — say, instant coffee — are coordinated and supported by headquarters services units.

Reading 40, by Shulman, deals with the intricate problems of intracorporate marketing in multinational operations. It is focused on pricing as the single most critical variable, but it must be kept in mind that apart from the tax questions, many analogous issues arise with regard to other marketing instruments (such as product and service) in transactions between foreign national subsidiaries and between subsidiaries and the parent company. A conclusion of the article is that the effects of different intracompany pricing policies on performance measurement and motivation of management of subsidiary operations generally are more critical than any others, including tax effects.

Readings 41 and 42 recount two life experiences, one British and the other Japanese, and the benefits that derive from the global view of international marketing. As the case history of Cadbury Schweppes in Reading 41 vividly illustrates, a company need not be one of the giants to evolve into a truly multinational concern. Recognizing that competition around the world is not locally confined to fragmented markets, but rather stems from "strong, well-organized international brands," the company proceeded to develop a "common marketing language" worldwide that enabled it to achieve involvement and commitment from local managers while gaining centralized, international direction and control. Since then, the "effervescent sound of Schweppes Tonic Water" has become highly popular in upper middle class circles from Australia to the United States.

In dealing with the general Japanese trading companies, Meissner takes us figuratively and literally around the globe in Reading 42. Collectively called "sogo shosha" (SS), these companies signify perhaps the ultimate in global enterprise. Not specialized in any particular trade or industry, SS often act as middlemen, putting together production, finance, marketing, and development deals with and between any company or government in any country on earth. Besides being a catalyst to world trade (Meissner counts 13 ways in which SS are instrumental), SS provide expert advice and service to companies desirous of entering just about any foreign market. In an uncanny way, SS represent perhaps the epitome of what this book is all about, namely the adaptation of strategy to the structure of international and local market environments, wherever and whenever this may be around the globe. Beside their mastery of this strategic concept, the fact that SS are also staunchly Japanese is almost incidental.

37 Headquarters Guidance in Marketing Strategy in the Multinational Subsidiary*

William K. Brandt
James M. Hulbert

Who calls the shots for marketing in the multinational subsidiary? In many firms the marketing decisions rest with the subsidiary managers, with little or no help from the home office. Other companies maintain a tight rein on overseas marketing by developing controls and standardized programs which are implemented around the world. Whatever the current policy, the question of who should make particular marketing decisions remains a point of contention in many multinational firms.

This article addresses the issue by focusing on the marketing decisions of 63 Brazilian subsidiaries of North American, European, and Japanese multinationals. Specific attention is directed at the following questions:

1. How much and what kinds of marketing guidance do subsidiaries receive from headquarters?
2. What characteristics of the parent company or the foreign subsidiary influence the amount and types of guidance received?
3. How do the types of guidance received match with the subsidiary's marketing objectives and strategy?

SUBSIDIARY CONTROLS

Managing a multinational enterprise to achieve corporate objectives requires some degree of integration and cohesion among foreign subsidiaries. The practices adopted by headquarters to attain the desired

*From William K. Brandt and James M. Hulbert, "Headquarters guidance in marketing strategy in the multinational subsidiary," Columbia Journal of World Business, Vol. XII (Winter 1977), pp. 7-14. Reprinted with permission.

level of integration differ dramatically from firm to firm, but two broad patterns of control seem to emerge for marketing decisions.

The first is a pattern of hierarchical authority by headquarters. In these cases, home-office decisions are imposed on subsidiary managers who are responsible for their execution. Centralizing decision-making limits the autonomy of subsidiary management and establishes authority for many day-to-day decisions at the regional or headquarters level.

The second is a pattern of integration of global activities through standardized marketing strategies and programs. Although this pattern is the focus of extensive research in multinational marketing, the use of standardized programs may or may not be associated directly with centralization as defined above.

In some firms, standardization makes unnecessary the direct involvement in decision-making which centralization implies. In others, standardized programs complement the procedures adopted by headquarters to maintain a tight rein over subsidiary decisions.

Subsidiary managers typically enjoy considerable discretion in making marketing decisions especially when compared with their decision-making power in areas such as finance or production. Within marketing, however, the amount of discretion is related to the type of decision being made. In most companies, product-related decisions such as quality and composition, brand name, packaging, and add-delete decisions are tightly controlled by the home office. For distribution, price, and promotional decisions, however, there is generally more autonomy, although this varies greatly by company and industry. Little research is available for industrial or consumer durable products, but among nondurables like cosmetics, soaps, pharmaceuticals, and soft drinks, standardized approaches are quite common. Food products, however, tend to be more culture-bound and therefore less adaptable to standardized programs.

THE STUDY

This article concentrates on the role of the home office in formulating multinational marketing strategy as perceived by subsidiary management. The data were obtained through personal interviews with 63 chief executives and 62 marketing managers of multinational subsidiaries operating in Brazil. Among the subsidiaries where the chief executives were interviewed, 28 had home offices in West Germany, Great Britain, France, Italy, Switzerland, Sweden, Finland, or the Netherlands. This group will be referred to as European. Twenty-four had headquarters in the United States or Canada and will be termed American companies. The remaining 11 were Japanese.

The marketing managers were asked to rank decision areas for which they perceived guidance from the parent company in the form of uniform or standardized directives. These included: sales-promotion ideas, basic advertising message, package design, brand name, product design specification, sales force management methods, and price guidelines. If no guidance was received, the respondent entered a zero in the questionnaire.

EXTENT OF HOME OFFICE GUIDANCE

Multinational subsidiaries in Brazil received most guidance from the parent company in the product-related elements of the marketing mix: product specification, brand name and package decisions (see Table 37.1). In contrast, less guidance was received for promotion and price decisions: less than one-fourth of the companies claimed to receive guidance in these areas. While response bias may have reduced the absolute percentages reported, the rankings and levels of guidance correspond closely with previous research (Aylmer, 1970).

Table 37.1. Subsidiaries Receiving Help from Home Office for
Major Decision Areas

Marketing Decision Area	Proportion Receiving Help
Product	
Product Design Specifications	45%
Brand Name	47%
Packaging Design	32%
Promotion	
Basic Advertising Message	25%
Sales Promotion Ideas	23%
Sales Force Management	13%
Pricing	
Pricing Guidelines	17%
Number of Cases (53)	

INFLUENCES ON EXTENT OF GUIDANCE

The explanatory variables investigated are grouped into two categories: those describing the parent company and those pertaining to the subsidiary.

Parent-Company Variables – These variables including type of industry, nationality of the parent company, volume of worldwide sales, proportion of sales outside the home market, and number of countries with manufacturing subsidiaries.

Although the differences are not statistically significant, the type of industry or product class appears to be associated with home-office guidance (see Table 37.2). Manufacturers of consumer-packaged goods received the least guidance, followed by manufacturers of motor vehicles, and electrical and telecommunications products. Pharmaceutical subsidiaries received much more direction from their headquarters, particularly in promotion and pricing, areas in which other industries tended to be more autonomous.

Table 37.2. Home-Office Guidance by Industry

| Industry | Amount of Guidance[a] | | | No. of Cases |
	None or Little	Mod-erate	Consid-erable	
Consumer Packaged Goods	60%	20%	20%	10
Pharmaceuticals and Chemicals	25%	42%	33%	12
Motor Vehicles and Major Components	47%	40%	13%	15
Electrical and Tele-communications	50%	30%	20%	10
Office Equipment	0	100%	0	3
Textiles	33%	67%	0	3

[a]"None or little" guidance means home-office help was received for none or one of the seven decision areas in Table 37.1. "Moderate" guidance, two or three decision areas; and "Considerable" guidance, four to seven decision areas.

Neither the nationality of the parent company, nor its size as measured by worldwide sales revenues, revealed any important relationship with the extent of headquarters guidance. Europeans provided more advertising assistance and the Americans more pricing guidelines, but the differences were not statistically significant. The proportion of sales outside the home market also had little effect on marketing support from home office.

Another measure of foreign involvement, the number of countries in which manufacturing subsidiaries were located, showed an inverted-U effect in its relationship with headquarters guidance (see Table 37.3). Firms operating in fewer than sixteen countries offered very little assistance, whereas those with sixteen to thirty subsidiaries provided a substantial amount of guidance. Above this number of markets, however, somewhat less guidance was offered. This finding corresponds with the Sorenson and Wiechmann thesis that as firms become truly multinational, they develop standardized processes, for example, planning guides and formats and control procedures, which reduce the need for standardized programs (Sorenson and Wiechmann, 1975).

Subsidiary Variables – Five subsidiary characteristics were cross-classified with guidance measures to determine whether characteristics of the subsidiary itself influenced the type or extent of direction received from headquarters. The variables included: subsidiary sales volume, subsidiary sales volume as a percent of world sales, type of organizational structure, use of product managers in marketing, and presence of an internal marketing research department.

Table 37.3. Home-Office Guidance by Number of Overseas Subsidiaries[a]

| Number of Subsidiaries | Amount of Guidance | | | No. of Cases |
	None or Little	Mod-erate	Consid-erable	
Less than 16	75%	17%	8%	22
16-30	17%	33%	50%	19
More than 30	39%	46%	15%	12

[a]Number of overseas subsidiaries represents the number of countries in which parent company has manufacturing facilities, whole or partially owned.

Larger subsidiaries (sales over one hundred million dollars) tended to receive less guidance than smaller ones. Similarly, subsidiaries whose sales revenues were large as a percentage of worldwide sales (over 6 percent), tended to receive less guidance compared to subsidiaries with less than one percent of world sales. However, none of these variables was significantly associated with home-office assistance in the statistical sense.

The presence of an internal department for marketing research appeared to have some association with home-office assistance. For six of the seven decision areas listed in Table 37.1, subsidiaries without a marketing research department (26 percent) received more guidance from the home office. These results suggest that a marketing research department at the subsidiary reduces the need for guidance that headquarters might otherwise provide. That the presence of a marketing research department is a surrogate for subsidiary sophistication might be a reasonable hypothesis, although the data do not provide a conclusive answer on this point. Almost all subsidiaries in the sample with sales exceeding fifty million dollars had research departments, but as already observed, size by itself was not closely associated with home-office guidance.

HOME-OFFICE GUIDANCE AND SUBSIDIARY STRATEGY

Standardized programs are designed both to aid the subsidiary in achieving its objectives and to be a means of control over its activities. Thus, the types of guidance offered should correspond in some logical way to the marketing strategies pursued by the subsidiary. However, the flow of information from headquarters to subsidiaries is often deficient. In this section we examine the fit between subsidiary objectives and strategies, and the types of marketing assistance received from headquarters.

Marketing managers were asked to describe their primary marketing objective for the coming year as specified in the operating plan. This question was difficult for most respondents to answer, but it was possible to group their statements into three general categories. Nearly two-thirds stated their objectives in terms of penetrating or developing existing markets, a category we labeled "penetration". Although three-fourths of the subsidiaries were evaluated on the basis of profits, only eight percent mentioned profits alone as the primary objective. Another 21 percent, however, mentioned profits in conjunction with some other objective. Both of these responses are grouped as "profit" objectives. The remaining twenty percent claimed that new market or product development was their principal objective, a category we labeled "diversification."

The results in Table 37.4 demonstrate that subsidiaries pursuing penetration objectives received significantly less home-office direction than those following diversification objectives. To achieve penetration objectives, local market information was crucial. It is not surprising therefore that these subsidiaries were also more inclined to have internal departments for marketing research.

Table 37.4. Home-Office Guidance by Strategic Objective
of Subsidiary

Strategic Objective	Amount of Guidance		No. of Cases
	None or Little	Moderate or Considerable	
Penetration	82%	18%	28
Diversification	14%	86%	7
Profit	50%	50%	14

Subsidiaries pursuing penetration objectives significantly more likely to receive less guidance.

$x^2 = 5.01$, d.f., $p < .05$

Diversification objectives, whether they involve developing new products or new markets, represented much riskier growth vectors (Ansoff, 1965). A predictable response to increased risk was greater home-office involvement. Indeed, since many subsidiaries in Brazil lacked adequate facilities for new product development, much of the guidance was essential for introducing innovations.

Subsidiaries with profit objectives were probably under substantial pressure from the home office to increase short-term profits. This concern apparently encouraged greater marketing assistance to insure that the goals were met. The tradeoff between long and short-term profits was a major point of contention in many subsidiaries. Numerous instances were cited to illustrate how meeting short-run objectives to satisfy headquarters had greatly reduced the potential for profits three to five years hence.

In terms of the types of guidance received from the home office, a relationship appears to exist between strategic objectives and the amount of support received. Subsidiaries pursuing penetration objectives received less help in both product and promotional decisions. The firms received more direction with pricing decisions, a crucial element in achieving market penetration. Subsidiaries with other objectives received more guidance from the home office, but there were no material differences among the types of support.

Managers were also asked to rank the strategic decision areas which were most crucial in achieving their objectives. These decision areas corresponded closely with those for home-office guidance. One may hypothesize, for example, that a subsidiary which relied heavily on its sales force was also more inclined to receive guidance in this area. The results did not bear out this expectation. It is plausible that many multinationals have not yet coordinated their home-office guidance with the strategies being pursued by individual subsidiaries. A relationship between marketing objectives and the amount of help received was evident, but this relationship did not carry over to the types of help most needed to reach those objectives.

SUMMARY

Control and integration of subsidiary activities present formidable problems for multinational firms. These problems seem unlikely to diminish as companies expand their international operations and seek the economic benefits of international growth.

This article examined the issue of home-office guidance from a subsidiary point of view. In general, static characteristics of the parent company and the subsidiary appeared to have relatively little influence over the amount or types of guidance provided. A strong relationship was observed, however, between the amount of different types of guidance received and the subsidiary's strategic objective. Consequently, control and information systems should be responsive to the subsidiary's strategic situation. The study also suggests that research on multinational management practices should avoid exclusive focus on the home-office perspective. Unless the subsidiary perspective and situation are considered, important explanatory variables may well be overlooked.

REFERENCES

Ansoff, H. Igor, Corporate Strategy (New York: McGraw-Hill, 1965).

Aylmer, R.J. "Who makes marketing decisions in the multinational firm?" Journal of Marketing, Vol. 34 (October 1970), pp. 25-30.

Sorenson, Ralph Z. and Wiechmann, Ulrich E. "How multinationals view marketing standardization," Harvard Business Review, Vol. 53 (May-June 1975), pp. 38 ff.

38 The International Product/Market Portfolio*

Jean-Claude Larréché

INTRODUCTION

In recent years, a number of product portfolio models have been proposed to guide the formulation of marketing strategies. The Boston Consulting Group (BCG) approach to product portfolio analysis would seem to be the best known of these models, as it has gained wide acceptance among managers as well as academicians. The purpose of this paper is to investigate the potential of the product portfolio approach in the formulation of international marketing strategies. In particular, a critical evaluation is made of the additional problems introduced by the consideration of an international as opposed to a domestic environment in the application of the product portfolio approach.

APPLICATION OF THE PRODUCT PORTFOLIO TO INTERNATIONAL MARKETS

The BCG Product Portfolio

The BCG product portfolio analysis centers on two determinants of marketing strategy, market dominance and stage of the product life cycle, operationally defined for measurement purposes as relative market share (unit sales of the product divided by unit sales of the major competitor) and market growth. Each product in the portfolio is

---

*Slightly abbreviated from Jean-Claude Larréché, "The international product/market portfolio," in Subhash C. Jain, ed., <u>Research Frontiers in marketing: Dialogues and directions, 1978 Educators' Proceedings</u> (Chicago, American Marketing Association, 1978), pp. 276-81, with permission.

represented on a relative market share/market growth matrix by a circle, the diameter of which is proportional to the sales volume of the product. This matrix gives a convenient and explicit visual representation of the relative contribution of each product to the sales volume, growth, and competitive posture of the firm.

According to their positioning on the relative market share/market growth matrix, products are classified into four categories: "problem children" (low relative market share/high market growth); "stars" (high relative market share/high market growth); "cash cows" (high relative market share/low market growth); and "dogs" (low relative market share/low market growth). Research results – mainly the Boston Consulting Group developments on experience effects (Hedley, 1976) and the PIMS project (Buzzell et al., 1975) – on the relationship between market share and profitability, as well as expected competitive behavior over the product life cycle are then used to infer cash inflows and outflows for each of these product categories. "Cash cows" are expected to be cash generators and "problem children" to be cash users, while "stars" and "dogs" should generally break even. To survive in the long-term, the firm needs a balanced portfolio where "cash cows" generate sufficient funds to support "problem children" and "stars," which will eventually become "cash cows" themselves at a later point in time. In this perspective, the objective of the firm's master marketing strategy is the long-term, dynamic development and renewal of a balanced product portfolio. This master marketing strategy will result in the allocation of resources among the various entries of the product portfolio, and in the establishment of guidelines for specific product strategies such as: holding (for "cash cows" and "stars"), building (for selected "problem children"), harvesting, divestment or abandonment (for other "problem children" and "dogs").

Application to International Markets

Although the expressions "product portfolio" and "business portfolio" are generally used to describe this BCG approach, they are unfortunately misleading. Indeed, the structure of the relative market share/market growth matrix requires that the entries be defined not only in terms of products but also of markets. The definition of these entries is a major difficulty in the practical application of the portfolio and may lead to erroneous conclusions. For instance, a product could be globally evaluated as being a "dog," while it may have the position of a "star" in a developing segment of the market. The portfolio entries should then be defined as product/market domains and the BCG approach should more appropriately be termed the product/market portfolio.

There is obviously no clear-cut solution to the selection of a disaggregation level in the definition of portfolio entries. Splitting a product into several product/market entries may clarify some strategic issues and isolate varying growth rates, competitive structures, and emerging trends in different segments. These entries will no longer be independent as they rely on common technology, production, and hence experience effects. This is certainly one of the reasons why portfolio entries in a domestic context have traditionally been defined in terms of products or businesses rather than product/markets.

On the other hand, in international applications of the product portfolio, significant differences between countries in terms of market growth and market structures will generally lead to the consideration of multiple market entries for a given product. To illustrate the particularities inherent in the application of the product/market portfolio in an international as opposed to a domestic environment, we will concentrate here on the case of a given product with markets in different countries.

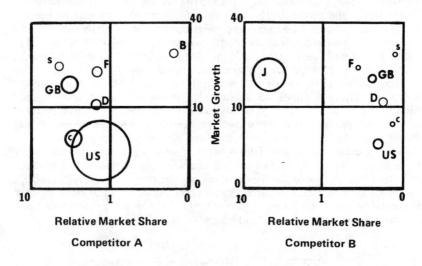

Fig. 38.1. Example of the international product/market portfolio (B = Brazil, C = Canada, D = Germany, F = France, GB = Great Britain, J = Japan, S = Spain, US = United States).

Figure 38.1 represents the product/market portfolio of two competitors, A and B, marketing the same product (or product line) in several countries. Competitor A is a market leader in most countries it operates in. Its largest sales volume comes from the United States, a mature market, where it only has a small market share advantage compared to its closest competitor. Its market dominance is stronger in Canada, also a mature market, and in European countries which are still at a high growth stage. In Brazil, however, the firm has not succeeded in gaining a substantial market share. In terms of the product/market portfolio, the firm has two "cash cows" (U.S. and Canada), four "stars" (Germany, Great Britain, France, Spain) and one "problem child" (Brazil). It should certainly consider diverting some of its revenues from North America to sustain its share of the European countries, to invest heavily in Brazil and possibly in new markets to provide for future growth. A closer look at the product/market portfolio of competitors will, however, provide a more threatening picture of the situation. The total unit sales volume of competitor B is smaller than that of competitor A. Its weak position in the North American and European markets does not represent an immediate danger, but it clearly dominates two fast-growing and potentially large markets. It is thus conceivable that competitor B will eventually generate total unit sales exceeding those of competitor A, and will be able to benefit from lower costs through greater experience effects. This cost advantage may place competitor B in a position to gain shares in mature markets (U.S. and Canada) which may have previously appeared safe from any major competitive disturbance. If competitor A does not take any drastic remedial action, a probable picture of the situation five years hence is represented in figure 38.2.

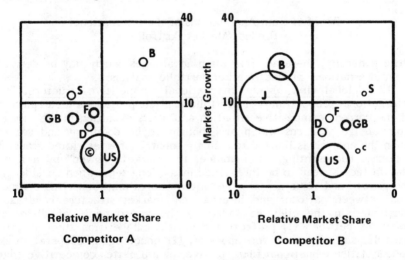

Fig. 38.2. Example of the international product/market portfolio, five-year projections.

This example is indeed representative of the evolution of international competition, in several industries as varied as ball bearings, color TV, shipbuilding, or motorcycles. If competitor A does not perform a product/market portfolio analysis, or limits the analysis to its domestic environment, it will consider its product as a "cash cow" which can easily be protected because of the dominant situation and the cost advantages that it enjoys on the home market. As a matter of fact, the same conclusions will be reached if the analysis is performed globally for the world market, because of the disproportionate importance of the U.S. market at this point in time. Only a detailed product/market portfolio analysis with international markets as entries will give a correct picture of the competitive situation. As illustrated above, the procedure should consider three successive steps:

(a) an analysis of the firm's current international product/market portfolio, (b) an analysis of the main competitors' current international product/market portfolios, (c) a projection of the firm's and competitors' future international product/market portfolios. Such applications of the international product/market portfolio may be particularly helpful for the formulation of a marketing strategy and the allocation of marketing resources across international markets. In the above example, a possible course of action would be to capitalize on the resources and cost advantages stemming from the U.S. market to build market share in Japan, Brazil and possibly other high growth markets. This would ensure future international growth, but would also protect the "cash cow" position in the North American market by keeping a long-term cost advantage compared to competitor B.

Benefits from Applications of the International Product/Market Portfolio

More generally, there are four main advantages which may be derived from international product/market portfolio analysis:

1. A global view of the international competitive structure. The international product/market portfolio analysis provides a clear picture of the current competitive situation and of its evolution in the future. Competitive positions which are thought to be dominant and secure when the analysis is limited to a single country (or a restricted group of countries representing, for instance, the market "served" by a firm) may in fact appear to be threatened in the long term when considering the growth and structure of other international markets. (This distinction between national and international market structure is already illustrated in the dilemma faced by the governments of different countries between (1) protecting domestic competition through anti-trust legislation or, on the opposite, (2) encouraging cooperation or concentration of national firms to give them a better competitive edge in international markets.)

2. A guide for the formulation of a global international marketing strategy. By considering international markets as basic investment units, generators or users of cash, the international product/market portfolio approach places the emphasis on the strategic issue of allocating scarce resources between these investment units in order to attain a stable long-term growth in sales and profits. It provides a framework for analyzing the long term market opportunities, competitive threats, and the flow of resources which have to be considered in the formulation of this global marketing strategy. It thus centers on the longer term and more strategic aspects which have traditionally been neglected in conceptual or empirical research in international marketing. For instance, the issue of standardization-vs-adaptation of marketing policies or the analysis of differences between international markets have been more concerned with the formulation of the marketing mix in different countries. In addition, the international product/market

portfolio analysis provides an opportunity to build on other research areas such as those concerning the clustering of world markets or the international product life cycle.

3. A guide for the formulation of marketing objectives for specific international markets. Without prejudging the respective values of centralized and decentralized organizations in international marketing, imposed or self-assigned marketing objectives for specific international markets may be dysfunctional if the role of each market within the global marketing strategy is not well understood. In some fast-growing markets, management may limit expansion because of limited cash resources or in order to show profits which are more in line with company "norms." In other countries, the high level of cash generated by a mature product may be spent on extensive promotional or product differentiation programs to try to generate some growth. Elsewhere, management may try to keep a small market share product alive in a mature market through expensive price cutting.

The product/market portfolio analysis helps to determine the primary role of each specific market in the international context. This role may, for instance, be to generate cash, to provide growth, to contribute to production volume, or to block the expansion of competition. Once this role has been defined, objectives can be determined for each specific market to ensure that country marketing strategies are coherent with the global marketing strategy.

4. A convenient visual communication goal. There is no doubt that part of the success of the BCG portfolio approach is due to the convenient graphical representation that it provides. The relative market share-market growth matrix allows the integration of a substantial amount of information in a concise, visual way and this advantage is obviously also valid for international applications.

LIMITATIONS OF THE INTERNATIONAL PRODUCT/MARKET PORTFOLIO

In an excellent article, George Day (1977) has investigated the main limitations of the product/market portfolio approach, including: the problem of defining products and markets, and consequently measuring market growth and market share; the use of market share dominance as a proxy for relative profit performance; the assumption that shares tend to stabilize during the maturity stage; the emphasis placed on cash flows; and finally, the problem of implementing strategies derived from the analysis.

Obviously, most of these limitations are equally valid here, but we will primarily discuss the problems more specifically associated with the application of the product/market portfolio to international markets, in terms of four main assumptions underlying this approach:

- the expected patterns of competitive behavior
- the relationship between market share and profitability

- the independence of product/market portfolio entries
- the consideration of cash flow generation as the ultimate marketing objective.

International Competitive Behavior

This product/market portfolio approach relies to a large extent on expected patterns of competitive behavior over the product life cycle. It basically assumes that market share gains are easier to realize in the growth stage than in the maturity stage. This is reinforced by the consideration of experience effects which should give a cost advantage to the market leader in the maturity stage. Heavy marketing investments should thus be expected in the growth stage, while in the maturity stage neither the market leader nor its competitors would benefit from aggressive action which would primarily lower the profit volume.

This pattern of competitive behavior is based on the following three assumptions: (1) cost differences between competitors come uniquely from differences in experience, (2) differences in experience effects between competitors in a given product/market entry depend uniquely on their respective cumulative production in this entry, and can hence be inferred from their relative market shares, (3) the management teams of competing firms share common social and financial responsibilities which impose some boundaries on the realm of acceptable managerial practices. In the international context, these assumptions lose much of the validity that they may have in a closed economy. Differences in wages, sources of supplies, inflation, exchange rates, tariffs, transport, and government subsidies may have a considerable effect on competitive cost advantages. The relative market share of competitors in a given country may be affected by sales volume in other international markets. Finally, a firm may often encounter competitors in world markets who do not obey the same managerial principles as it does. This firm may be used to dealing, in its domestic market, with competitors who have, for instance, similar pressures for profits from their shareholders, similar requirements on capital structure imposed by financial institutions, and similar flexibility to dispose of the labor force in hard times. In addition, because of the educational system, historical practices and managerial mobility, these national competitors may have similar philosophies. On the other hand, the firm's competitors in international markets may have shareholders who favor capital gains and long-term returns over short-term dividends; they may obtain a higher capital leverage from their bankers; they may have stronger pressures to keep their labor force and hence to maintain production volume, even if this is to the detriment of profits; they may be less concerned with profits than with national prestige or the collection of foreign currencies; finally, their management may come from different educational, managerial, and cultural traditions. The successive domination of some European markets by American firms, then of some Western markets by Japanese firms can, indeed, partly be attributed to a misunderstanding by local manufacturers of the competitive behavior of the new entrants.

Market Share and Profitability in International Markets

The BCG product portfolio approach assumes that market dominance, as measured by relative market share, is associated with high profitability. When considering a specific product, this assumption is supported by the existence of experience effects which have been found to reduce total unit production costs by 20 to 30 percent every time cumulative production is doubled, in various industries (Hedley, 1976). A strong relationship between market share and return on investment has also been found across a wide range of consumer and industrial goods in the PIMS project (Buzzell et al., 1975). This evidence indicates that (1) for a given product, competitors with high market shares should have a higher profitability than competitors with low market shares, and (2) a given firm is expected to have a higher profitability on products which have a high market share than for products which have a low market share. This double association between market share and profitability, across products and across competing firms, is one of the main elements to guide the allocation of resources in the product portfolio approach.

There is, however, no empirical evidence yet of an association between market share and profitability across international markets. Obviously, some of the traditional arguments such as market power and economies of scale in marketing operations may still be valid in the international context. However, there may also be a number of reasons why a firm may experience a lower level of profitability in a country where it has a higher market share than in other international markets. Differences in cost arising from disparities in wages, sources of supplies, inflation, exchange rates, tariffs, transport, and government subsidies have already been mentioned. Discrepancies in the efficiency of elements of the marketing system, such as distribution channels or advertising media, may also have an impact on profitability. Because of cultural or income differences, the same product may be addressed to different consumer segments in different countries. Finally, the same product may command different price levels in different countries. Even within the EEC, despite the abolition of tariff barriers, price differences close to 100 percent for some consumer goods such as vacuum cleaners and basic food products can be observed.

Interdependence of International Markets

The product/market portfolio assumes independence of the entries considered, the only link between these countries being their generation and use of a common resource: cash. In particular, there should not be any cost nor demand cross-elasticities between product/market entries. In this way, the decision concerning a single entry, such as the divestment of a "dog," should have no impact on the competitive situation of other entries.

For the international product/market portfolio, this assumption will generally not be tenable, as the entries represent the position of the same product in different world markets. On the cost side, the sales in one market may affect the situation in other international markets, inasmuch as they contribute to total production volume, and hence to experience effects. Depending on the importance of experience effects, transport costs, production adaptations, and restrictions to competition, the degree of cost interdependence may vary considerably. This raises the basic issue of the relative importance to be given to market shares in individual international markets and to world market share. While the product/market portfolio places the emphasis on the market share of specific entries, world market share is certainly a major determinant of international marketing strategy for some products, such as in the case of the motorcycle industry. The trends towards freer international trade and more efficient freight transport play in favor of an increasing interdependence of international markets and a greater importance of world market share.

There are additional reasons on the demand side for interdependence of international markets. Consumer migrations and overlapping of advertising media between countries certainly place constraints on the flexibility that one may have in the implementation of different marketing strategies in different world markets. In addition, disparities in the pricing policy for the same product in various countries may result in the creation by distribution of an uncontrolled secondary trade between these countries. A cursory analysis of the international product/market portfolio could thus lead to marketing strategies in specific world markets which are not implementable or dysfunctional from a global perspective.

Marketing Objectives in International Markets

Present or future generation of cash is considered as the ultimate marketing objective of individual entries in the product/market portfolio. There are, however, other objectives which may be pursued in allocating marketing resources in various international markets. One objective may be the gathering of strategic information about the evolution of consumer needs, competitive moves, or technological developments in leading markets. Different product innovations occur in different countries, and there are clear advantages for a firm to be present in these markets, as in the case of Gillette for disposable lighters. In the car industry, experience in front-wheel drive technology was gained in Europe by Ford and Chrysler before being exploited in the U.S. market.

Another objective in entering a market may be to prevent competition from gaining cost advantages because of unchallenged world expansion, and thus indirectly to protect other international markets. Finally, the development of a good relationship with local government may be a primary marketing objective. It may lead to some specific actions such as keeping a product which does not meet the firm's profitability norms, product adaptations, local production facilities, or exports to a country which was not considered in the international marketing strategy of the firm, as in the case of Ford which accepted to deliver cars from Argentina to Cuba, following a desideratum expressed by the Argentinean government. In all these instances, it is clear that the consideration of a wide range of objectives results in different marketing strategies to those which would have been generated by an analysis of the international product/market portfolio.

CONCLUSION

The product portfolio approach developed by the BCG provides a new tool for the analysis of international marketing strategies. This approach has a number of advantages, the main one being an integrative representation of the current and projected international competitive posture of the firm. There are also a number of limitations to the application of this approach. These limitations do not affect the usefulness of the international product/market approach as a tool for analysis. Indeed, this approach will generally single out issues that may otherwise have gone unnoticed. The main danger of the limitations discussed above is that conclusions may be drawn too hastily in the formulation of marketing strategies.

As adapted from the BCG developments, the international product/market portfolio is of greatest value as a tool for analysis. In this domain, it may even present greater potential for analytical use than applications of the product portfolio to domestic markets. It can build on other concepts which have been well documented, such as the international product life cycle or the clustering of world markets. It should not, however, be used for the design of international marketing strategies without considering other international factors.

REFERENCES

Buzzell, R.D.; Gale, B.T.; and Sultan, R.G.M., "Market share, a key to profitability," Harvard Business Review, Vol. 53 (January-February 1975), pp. 97-106.

Day, G.S., "Diagnosing the product portfolio," Journal of Marketing, Vol. 41 (April 1977), pp. 29-38.

Hedley, B., "A fundamental approach to strategy development," Long Range Planning, Vol. 9 (December 1976), pp. 2-11.

Miller, J.C.; and Pras, Bernard, "The effects of multinational and export diversification on the profit stability of U.S. corporations," Southern Economic Journal (January 1980), pp. 792-804.

39 The Nestlé Product Manager as Demigod*
P. d'Antin

Nestlé marketing management devoted several years of adjustments and readjustments to finding a suitable marketing scheme. Such a painstaking function spends by far the greatest proportion of Nestlé's annual budget. The marketing of a new product, for example, may cost two to three times more than the plant that manufactured it.

Other reasons for Nestlé's organization around the product chief were the following factors in the firm's unique marketing situation:

1. The broad range of food products marketed.
2. The fact that foreign markets account for 97 percent of total turnover.
3. The varying levels of development of the target countries.
4. Country-by-country taste differences – e.g., the French tend to prefer chicory in their coffee, while the Americans drink it straight.

In view of such complexities, it is understandable that Nestlé easily rejected the worldwide standardized marketing (including advertising) favored by such giants as Coca-Cola and Kodak, opting instead for a more intricate, product-oriented approach.

TWO SIMPLE PRINCIPLES

The Nestlé scheme can be boiled down to two basic principles: centralization of method and decentralization of decision making.

In centralizing method, the Swiss company has organized all country subsidiaries along the same lines. Each subsidiary, which lies within the

*Reprinted from P. d'Antin, "The Nestlé product manager as demigod," European Business, No. 28 (Spring 1971), pp. 44-9, with permission.

domain of a regional manager (e.g., for the European region), is headed by a company official who is the equivalent of the Président-Directeur général in France. Under him are three managers – production, finance, and marketing. The marketing department, in turn, is subdivided into sales, market research, and publicity. The marketing manager, who heads the department, is assisted by a staff of product chiefs or managers. In the average Nestlé subsidiary, there is a product chief for Nescafé, milk, chocolate, and soup. For an item like coffee, there are sometimes two associate product specialists, one assigned to ordinary coffee and the other to decaffeinated coffee, which represents a wholly different market, since it appeals to different motivational groups. There are some 500 product managers in the company.

Although the product manager is nearly always a man with a university degree, he is considered to have virtually no practical experience, and must undergo a period of "learning the ropes." The ideal training period lasts at least a year and a half, with six months of selling on the road, six in market research, and six more in publicity. Not every trainee is afforded such extensive training, however, since he may be needed on the job right away. During each of the training periods, the future product chief is an apprentice who actively works rather than merely observes.

When the trainee is considered ripe for product responsibility, he is assigned a particular product in a particular country operation – e.g., coffee in Germany – and presented with the Nestlé marketing "bible." The bible is a loose-leaf volume in five parts:

1. A review of the Nestlé marketing framework and how it works.
2. An information section, subdivided into the general fact book and the product fact book.
3. Space for a provisional budget and a definitive budget.
4. Outline of a system for checking and evaluating marketing activities.
5. Briefing material for advertising agencies.

The product manager's first task is to fill in the information required for the general and product fact books. The general fact book is designed to provide general information on the market of the country to which the manager is assigned – surface area, population and its characteristics, family structure, household budgets, age groups, demographic growth, evolution of the cost of living, competition, income brackets, evolution of commerce, and public communications media, including the press, radio, television, cinema, and display advertising. In other words, the product chief must supply all the facts that apply to the market as a whole, without reference to any specific product. He can of course make use of the reference material available in the subsidiary or at the headquarters in Vevey (Switzerland).

COFFEE AS A SOURCE OF REBELLION

The product fact book contains all the country data concerning the manager's specific product. For coffee in Germany, the product manager must furnish answers to a number of questions: How does Germany rank in the hierarchy of the coffee consumers' market? Is Germany a high or a low consumption market? (These facts alone can be of enormous consequence. In Sweden, for instance, the annual per capita consumption of coffee is eighteen pounds, while in Japan it's half a gram!) How is coffee used – in bean form, ground, or powdered? If it is ground, how is it brewed? Which coffee is preferred – Brazilian Santos blended with Colombian coffee, or robusta from the Ivory Coast? Is it roasted? Do the people prefer dark roasted or blond coffee? (The answer to this question is likewise important: the color of Nestlé's soluble coffee must resemble as closely as possible the color of the coffee consumed in the country.) Do the Germans drink coffee after lunch or with their breakfast? Do they take it black or with cream or milk? Do they drink coffee in the evening? Do they sweeten it? (In France, the answer is clear: in the morning, coffee with milk; at noon, black coffee – i.e., two utterly different coffees.) At what age do people begin drinking coffee? Is it a traditional beverage, as in France, or is it a form of rebellion, as in England and Japan, where the younger generation has taken up coffee drinking in order to defy their tea-drinking parents?

The questions in the product fact book obviously probe much more deeply than those in the general fact book. The product manager hence may not be able to answer them with mere documentary research. He may have to resort to motivational surveys, using non-directive interviews that bring out the consumers' true motivations. Such motivational research pinpointed the identical motivations of young coffee drinkers in England and Japan, and Nestlé now uses practically the same advertising plugs in both countries.

When the product manager has completed both fact books, he must tackle the third part of his bible – drafting the budget, which is also referred to as product planning. First of all, he must draft a six-year budget. Using both past figures and data for the current year, he projects sales for the coming six years in terms of pounds or cases of coffee, and estimates turnover based on probable price increases or decreases due to competition and to estimated contingency factors within Germany. He must also deal with the expense factor, allowing for an evolution in tax rates, social security charges, and labor costs. For this purpose, the production manager supplies him with the necessary information.

Nestlé requires the product manager to make the six-year plan mainly so that he will get into the habit of living in the future. It is considered unimportant if events ultimately contradict his forecast. The important thing is that the product manager – and consequently everyone else in the marketing framework – has had to think far ahead.

When the six-year budget has been presented, the product manager proceeds with his most important report, the one on which he will be judged – i.e., the budget for the coming year. This exercise is not merely a simple bookkeeping forecast, but must include a general review of all the data for mixed marketing – products, brands, packaging and appearance, distribution channels, prices, sales, advertising, market research, and after-sales follow-up. The budget must, of course, contain figures. But the product manager's method of arriving at such figures requires him to ask some rather basic questions: Is the product formula the best? Is the product attractively wrapped? Would there be any advantage in smaller or larger packages? Is this the most suitable brand label? Are the prices too high or too low?

THE DEBATE WITH HEADQUARTERS AT VEVEY

Although the product chief is finally responsible for the annual plan, he must consult the marketing manager and the head of his subsidiary before submitting the plan to Vevey. The plan is written up in two stages: in the spring of the year, he submits to the head office a summary budget or plan containing the main figures. After review, the plan is returned to him, and he is then expected to prepare a detailed budget by October.

The following review at Vevey involves a tripartite discussion among the head office's marketing division, the regional management concerned (in this case, European area management), and a representative of the subsidiary, who may be the product manager himself if he is not located too far away from headquarters. Once the two- to three-day debate is over, the finalized annual plan is accepted.

Headquarters usually manages to review the approximately 500 product budgets or plans of the seventy subsidiaries by the end of November. It then enters on a master sheet a resume of the German subsidiary's total activity for coffee in the coming year. The model for this report is contained in the product manager's bible. Its condensed form makes it possible for the head office to know at a glance, for example, what advertising campaign is being planned for coffee in Germany.

Here is where the centralization of method ends and the decentralization of decision-making begins.

After the final budget has been approved, the product manager alone is the boss. There is no further discussion with headquarters unless some significant change has occurred in the targets. Vevey expects only to receive a monthly report in which the reasons for advances or delays are explained.

Not only is the product manager generally free to implement his product plan, but he has also played a major role in shaping that plan and its objectives in the first place. Vevey officials are quick to point out that planning and budgeting for the entire range of products – even on a six-year scale – are merely the sum total of all the computerized budgets of all the product managers. In both planning and implementation of plans, then, the product chief is the key man in the Nestlé marketing framework.

The product manager is ultimately judged on the success of his product – not just its sales success, but also its profits. It is from the ranks of the product managers that the marketing managers of all subsidiaries are recruited, and very often the president of a subsidiary is a former product chief.

WHERE DO INNOVATIONS COME FROM?

According to top marketing management, one chief advantage of the Nestlé network is its open-endedness, allowing for product innovations to be initiated either through the product manager (from the bottom up) or by Vevey (from the top down). The following case examples based on some facts illustrate the two means by which changes are introduced.

At the outset, a fairly standard Nescafé is released on the English market – i.e., the product in the form in which it is appreciated by the average consumer, but with a few alterations geared to the English market. This particular Nescafé happens to be similar to the one sold in the United States, which is not too astonishing. The English were generally accustomed to drinking only tea, until the presence of American troops led them to discover coffee. The coffee they tried was the Nescafé from the States, with the American taste – a relatively light, almost blond coffee.

A few years pass. Gradually the accumulated data on the market and on consumer attitudes indicate that Britons who have traveled in Italy and France have acquired a taste for a more fully roasted coffee, one that is blacker and somewhat more bitter. A market survey then reveals that a segment of the population – a small but affluent segment – is definitely interested in a product with a fuller-bodied taste made from a darker roasted coffee.

At this point, change is initiated at the product manager level. The product chief queries the subsidiary's production department: "We could sell 100,000 cases of stronger coffee a year. Any suggestions?"

The production manager writes Vevey requesting the manufacturing processes for a coffee that would be more like the Italian and French coffees. By return mail (ideally), he receives the data on roasting temperatures and the blends to use. He and the product chief approve this sample, and write again to Vevey, this time requesting that a pilot plant in Switzerland produce 10,000 jars of one, two, or three varieties of this kind of Franco-Italian coffee. These jars are shipped to England and distributed to 1,000 families, mixed, of course, with other kinds of coffee. In this way, a wide sampling is obtained, which is backed up by a serious market survey.

A decision is then reached – a decision for which the product manager is mainly responsible, though of course with the backing of the English marketing manager and the subsidiary manager. The product chief describes in detail how the new product is to be launched, including the details in his annual budget.

The launching of a special coffee requires greater publicity than ordinary Nescafé. To attract a more affluent segment of the consumer population, a novelty container will be necessary, with a gold-colored top and an engraved label. In settling all these details, the product manager confers with the production department. If he and the production chief disagree on the specifications – e.g., the height of the Nescafé jar – subsidiary management steps in to arbitrate.

WHEN THE TOP MARKETING MANAGER STEPS IN

As stated earlier, one of the duties of the top marketing manager at Vevey HQ is to discuss the figures for all the product budgets during October and November. Once 'this task is out of the way, he has time for reflection. From the reports submitted to him, he may discover, for example, that there is a demand in several countries for a higher quality coffee, possibly more expensive, which would lend itself to being drunk black rather than with cream.

Dropping into his production colleague's office, the Vevey marketing manager presents his findings. The production manager may reply in one of several ways. A better blend may be found. Better coffees may be discovered in Colombia, Venezuela, or Costa Rica or – and this has happened – a new lyophilization technique may be developed, by which a frozen product is dried.

If lyophilization seems the most attractive solution, laboratory tests are undertaken with the various blends and roasts, and also with the various cold temperatures for lyophilization. Such research may take a year or two. It does not end with an ex cathedra verdict. The production manager may produce a number of samples – as actually happened in this case – that are subjected to taste tests before the final choice of the coffee to be launched.

Matters do not end here. The production manager claims that he is going to consider building a new plant, and that this plant will be more expensive than the one that performs the traditional drying process. Hence, the financial manager must be consulted. His reply can be readily anticipated: it will be necessary to fix the price of a jar of lyophilized coffee at 2.50 Swiss francs as against 1.85 Swiss francs for standard Nescafé.

At this juncture, the Vevey marketing manager confers with the European regional manager, and his remarks go something like this: "We have a new and more expensive coffee, for which a market exists. It means building a plant that will cost X deutsche mark. Why don't we try this coffee out in Germany?"

The regional manager may possibly disagree with the marketing manager. In this case, the deputy administration is consulted, and he arbitrates. If he approves, discussions are begun with the president of the German branch, who consults his marketing manager and his coffee product manager, and the machinery goes into motion.

The Vevey marketing manager is not without influence in this machinery. Lyophilized coffee in its initial German version bore no faint resemblance to ordinary coffee. Since people are usually reluctant to change their habits, there was some resistance. Some customers even commented that although they liked this coffee better, it "looked funny." The firm considered processing it differently so that it would look like ordinary Nescafé.

But the head marketing manager gave this advice: "Don't change the processing. Test the market again, taking a different advertising tack. Plug the product as a new coffee produced by revolutionary methods. The proof of its novelty is the fact that it doesn't even look like coffee!"

Retesting was undertaken, with the result that the public declared the coffee to be much better than normal coffee.

Besides contributing much creativity to the development and marketing of products, the head office marketing department is responsible for seeing that the brand name and image are uniformly maintained. It also pays close attention to the uniformity of containers and packaging. The brand image is considered particularly important in an age when many people travel widely. Apart from breaking into the decentralized system to impose its will on such general matters, however, the Vevey marketing department bends over backward to maintain the sovereignty of its product managers.

APPENDIX: SO THIS IS PARADISE?

That "demigod," the product chief, is in an extremely delicate position in the company structure. To recapitulate: the product chief is in neither a line nor a staff position. He must be able to call on all the marketing resources – market research, sales, technical services, advertising, and promotion – and yet he has no authority to demand information or cooperation. His only tool is persuasion. His duty is to determine how each of these functions will contribute to the profitability of his product during the coming year – and even how much money will be spent, for example, on various types of advertising. But, although he may have spent a few months on the publicity side of the business, the product chief is no advertising expert. Similarly, he can request technical innovations for the product, but he is no technical expert, etc.

Further complicating the situation is the rather intricate organizational structures that have evolved as corporations have grown larger and their product ranges wider. Figure 39.1 shows that comparatively Eden-like structure of bygone, simpler times, when the product manager was on a level with the functional personnel he had to deal with every day, and few intermediary levels existed to hamper efficient functioning. However, as figure 39.2 reveals, the product manager in today's more elaborate framework is on a different level from the technical marketing services that he must try to guide and coordinate.

Fig. 39.1. The product manager on an equal level with the functional team.

Another factor not to be overlooked is that if the product chief is given a great degree of autonomy to plan the entire year's activities for his product, he may well begin to believe in his own demigodhood. He may just conceive of himself as a technical expert, an old advertising hand, and sales genius combined.

However outstanding in diplomacy and creativity a product chief may be, he is very likely to become a friction point within the company because of the autonomy granted to him.

Although the structure is described by Nestlé as the perfect solution to many marketing problems, it may well prove to be the source of other, unforeseen difficulties. In figure 39.2, we see that the marketing team has become less homogeneous and that several marketing technicians have moved to different levels. Since work seems to be done less efficiently, the product chief is tending to take into his own hands the duties of the various marketing technicians. Such intrusions can cause tensions (see arrows in figure 39.2 for the "hottest" zones in the organization). For example:

1. The staff technicians bitterly resent the fact that they are rendered powerless by the product manager's usurpation of their tasks.
2. The product chief, who has taken up so many reins of duty, is unlikely to do any job really well, especially since he is not an expert in any of the fields. It is as if an orchestra conductor tried to step down from the podium and play all the instruments at once.
3. Costs and delays multiply.
4. There is a growing threat that an entire sector of marketing activities may become immobilized due to any of the above aggravations or a combination of them. So this is paradise?!

How can these problems be solved or at least minimized so that work gets done with a reasonable degree of efficiency?

1. First of all, the staff services must have enough specialists to adapt to the new, more complex structure and to supply all needed services.

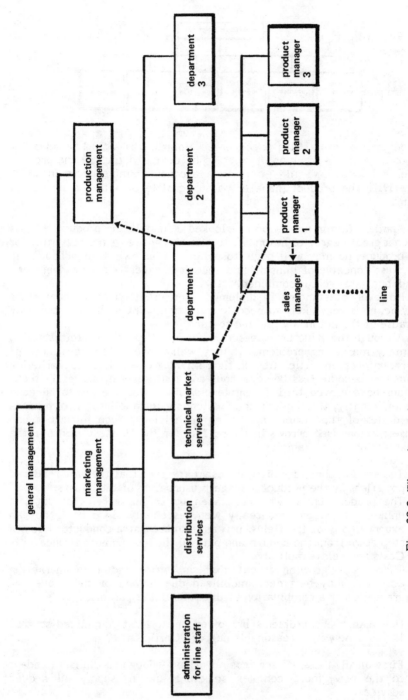

Fig. 39.2. When the product manager functions on different levels.

2. Recourse to staff services must be made obligatory. For example, only a staff specialist (not a product chief) could request outside services.
3. The role of each product manager should be more clearly defined, so that certain limits – ideally, those coinciding with his competence – are placed on his powers.

The strict defining of the product chief's tasks is particularly important, since recruits are usually young men fresh out of business school and bursting with unconcealed ambition. It would be advantageous as well if a work program could be devised by which the product chief would periodically go through another training cycle in sales, advertising, etc.

The company that can keep all its product chiefs happy and maintain a smoothly-running marketing department will be achieving a small miracle. One further way to ease tensions might be to put strong emphasis on the quality of the product manager's management, not just on his product's success, when considering him for company promotions.

40 Transfer Pricing in the Multinational Firm*

J.S. Shulman

The spread of decentralized corporate operations has been accompanied by widespread utilization of the profit center concept to measure, evaluate, and motivate divisional management. As the implications of the profit center idea have been recognized, the need has arisen for rational systems to price intra-company transfers of goods at varying stages of production.

The aim, in general, has been to devise methods that would satisfy the goals of divisional managers to earn adequate profit for their divisions, while simultaneously furthering corporate profit goals. In single country operations, the system is meant to function for this purpose and to provide a foundation for a properly operating control system.

But when a company operates across national borders and exports its practice of decentralized management, with all the accompanying apparatus, new complicating dimensions are added. In international business, there are opportunities to maximize profits that may override the significance of a control system and the transfer pricing mechanism. Likewise, this environment contains threats to international firms, often unforeseen and, even when perceived, seldom factored into control systems.

This article deals with the characteristics which attach to and compound the problem of transfer pricing when a decentralized firm expands its operations into the international environment. It is based upon field interviews with various officers responsible for control, pricing, and taxation functions in the international divisions of several large United States firms.

---

*From J.S. Shulman, "Transfer pricing in the multinational firm," European Business (January 1969), pp. 46-54. Reprinted with permission.

As might be expected, transfer pricing practices vary widely. Each different policy is justified on a reasonable basis – on some special variable which is considered critical by the individual company. Therefore, by looking into the basic argument justifying each specific transfer pricing policy, we may study some of the variables that are critical to transfer pricing policies.

TAXES

It has been observed that the pervasiveness of taxation clouds the entire background of transfer pricing in international firms, and that taxes represent the touchstone by which all transfer pricing is judged. Tax considerations lurk in the background of so many decisions in modern management that the impression of all-importance is understandable.

Evidence indicates that headquarters management often considers international income tax costs in setting transfer prices. But this practice evokes two kinds of problems – one external and one internal. The external problem relates to the counteraction taken by government tax authorities in both the United States and foreign countries. Faced with the minimizing methods practiced by taxpayers, revenue departments throughout the world attempt to take steps which will maximize tax revenues. Despite the fact that international auditing is still relatively new, American government auditors are familiar with corporate tax-minimizing practices. It is also a fact that foreign auditors are expanding their awareness of these problems, and are increasingly taking steps to overcome the long-standing advantages of corporate tax practices. In other words, tax minimization by corporations runs head-on into tax maximizing of government treasury departments.

Internally, pricing for tax savings causes aberrations in divisional operating results. The resulting conflicts in goals lead to dysfunctional decisions. Many control systems in international use do not make allowances for aberrations in price caused by tax minimizing schemes. When allowances are made, they are not always effective or satisfactory. The same problem holds true in other facets of the environment detailed below.

Corporate costs and profits are affected also by import duties assessed by countries of import. A change in a transfer price may cause a change in the duty, both as to amount and as to rate. Therefore, it adds to a company's profit to send goods at low prices into countries with high rates of duty. It may also be advantageous to ship goods at high prices into countries with low import tax rates.

The source of the end product may thus be affected if production processes may be performed on transferred materials equally well, and at no cost differential, in two or more countries with different rates of import rates.

The impact of income and import taxes upon transfer prices leads to additional problems for management, and again one of these problems occurs externally and the other internally. Externally, the goals of income tax administrators and customs officials to maximize revenues for their respective departments are in conflict, because the increased revenue of the one tends to reduce the revenue of the other. The higher the import tax assessed to the importer, the lower the profit remaining as a basis for income taxes. To add to the tax manager's headache, he finds virtually no coordination of the two revenue collecting departments in any country, and a tax-paying firm has to bear the brunt of the two taxing divisions' conflicting goals. Internally, the problems have to do with the effect of import tax pricing upon divisional operating results and upon the motivation of divisional managers. But an added twist results from the attempt of the firm to balance the added cost of duty resulting from a high import price against the lower cost of income taxation in the country of importation as well as the potentially higher income tax in the exporting division.

Notwithstanding the importance of taxation, many firms consider it only one among other factors. One company attitude is summed up in the words of its Vice-President of International Operations." We could connive on taxes, but the savings would be trivial. We prefer to give full attention to operating our company and let the tax liabilities fall where they may." This company considers anything but a straightforward application of tax laws as morally improper. Another company neglects the impact of taxes on pricing entirely, arguing that simple and consistent pricing practices tend to minimize tax investigation problems.

Another reason for neglecting the tax considerations is given by an electronics firm. While this company is aware of the impact of taxes on income, the importance of greater harmony among divisional managers has eliminated tax-motivated transfer price changes. In the past, moves designed to minimize taxes have caused interpersonal conflicts to such an extent as to discourage any further tax-minimizing practices. It is also observed that the narrowing gap among world tax rates makes it less possible to effect significant tax savings, and therefore the sacrifice to greater managerial harmony continually becomes less costly.

CURRENCY FLUCTUATIONS

In most cases, the respondents of our survey use generally recognized practices to mitigate the deleterious effects of inflation in host countries. A preferable method among some firms is to withdraw funds to a safer haven. But, generally, countries that are suffering from rapid inflation are also hard pressed to maintain an adequate balance of foreign exchange. Therefore, in such countries foreign exchange is often restricted by government order to necessary materials purchased, while being withheld from profit transfers.

These problems have triggered apparently opposite pricing practices in two companies operating in Brazil, where excessive inflation is a continuous threat. Because the inflationary condition has made it nearly impossible to show a profit, one firm ships goods in at low prices as a subsidy to its Brazilian division to assist it in profitable operation. Also, the Brazilian government requirement to post a cash deposit equal to six months' projected imports is costly because the cash deposits continually lose value. Resultant side effects of the low pricing practice not only reduce this deposit, but also reduce the inflationary loss of value of the deposit over the six-month period. On the other hand, another company preferred to ship materials into Brazil at extra high prices, in order to remove as much cash as possible to the United States. In this instance, the firm was willing to show a higher profit and pay higher taxes in the United States, but at least, the controller reported, the cash asset, even after taxes and deposit erosion, was safe from further loss of value.

Thus transfer prices can be, and actually are, used as a device to counteract inflationary erosions of assets.

ECONOMIC RESTRICTIONS

Under this heading we include three areas of concern to multinational corporations, the effects of which may be mitigated by adjustments to transfer prices. The first of these has to do with currency rationing. Some countries (notably Israel and several South American nations) have adopted regulations that rigidly restrict conditions under which profits of foreign-owned corporations may be transmitted out of the country. At the same time, governments such as these ration currencies available to corporations' imports. This system provides close supervision by the host country over the outflow of its vital foreign exchange. To some extent, it is possible to circumvent such restrictions by increasing the prices of imports from parent or related companies. High prices paid by a restricted division to related companies can result in a repatriation of profits despite the desires of a host government. Thus, when one avenue is closed alert managements seek other ways to achieve their goals.

Secondly, as a way of increasing manufacturing activity locally, some governments impose restrictions on the number and kinds of components that may be imported into a larger unit. In Mexico, the systematic action of the government in forcing United States parents to ship fewer components, and causing more parts to be manufactured by local sources of supply has had impact on many firms – notably in the automotive industry.

Finally, some governments restrict allocation against local taxable income for expenses incurred and services performed in the country. Thus, for example, head office expenses such as administrative and general, R and D, marketing, and other costs may not be charged to subsidiaries in Venezuela, for example, if the services are performed (as they usually are) elsewhere. In one country, a respondent found himself forbidden to remit royalties, his method of operation in many other countries of the world. In such a case, costs may be recouped by increases in the transfer prices of goods shipped to the foreign subsidiary. At times, the subject foreign government may suspect the compensating use of transfer prices, and local managements are forced to devote time and effort to justify their actions to local government officials.

UNSTABLE GOVERNMENTS

When a company operates in a country in which there has been a tendency for the government to be overthrown (or shaken) with recurring regularity, it is to the interest of the company to keep as little cash as possible in that country. The high feelings of nationalism which often accompany a revolutionary regime further endanger assets of foreign businesses, and expropriation is a risk in such situations.

The fact that a government has been in power for many years does not always call for confidence either. Cuba and Nigeria are two cases in point, in which comparatively stable governments (one of them of long standing) were overthrown much to the shock of managements which were not sensitive to local politics, and were not prepared to deal with the consequences of revolution. In such environments, low prices on transfers out of the country can facilitate transmittal of excess cash, since exports at low prices tend to reduce cash flowing into such countries. High prices on imports may also have the same effect.

COMPETITIVE ADVANTAGES

Transfer prices are used to strengthen the competitive position of a company, or to control or weaken the competitive position of others in a foreign environment. In the case of integrated oil companies, for example, it seems apparent that producers enjoy substantial profit on the raw product. When competing refiners and refining divisions of the producing company enter the market at this stage, raw material costs have already provided a large measure of profit to the producers. The small spread remaining in refining, processing and marketing tends to leave the producers in control of final market prices for finished products throughout the world.

In the firms of our experience this situation does not prevail to any noticeable extent. Some companies do manufacture basic products in bulk (pharmaceutical and chemical firms are cases in point), and they do sell such products to competing manufacturers which process and refine the raw or basic ingredients into competing end products. Attempts are made to maintain resale prices of bulk products at a level which will cause prices of end products to be high enough for competitive advantage. The attempts are not wholly successful. In spite of a limited number of bulk processors, competition at the bulk level keeps the access cost to competitors low enough to cause competition at the level of finished goods.

In another respect, however, transfer prices are used to mitigate the internal effects of outside competition. When competitive forces in a foreign country cause external prices to be lowered by a particular division with resultant damage to the profits, consideration is usually extended to reduce transfer prices into that division. If the local competitive squeeze is beyond the control of the damaged division, the local managers in many countries request the parent – or other divisions – to share its losses by changing transfer prices. It is recalled that in some firms, transfer prices are a function of external prices. In such cases, then, downward changes in external prices beyond local control will, in time, cause changes in transfer prices to strengthen competitive action.

FOREIGN PARTNERS

Incentive exists for companies to charge higher transfer prices to jointly owned than to wholly-owned divisions. At the same time, in counteracting such a tendency, the jointly owned subsidiary has incentive for a directly opposite action. In the field a higher degree of circumspection seems to surround transfer pricing practices where joint ownership exists. In other words, regardless of the locus or the method used to set transfer prices, real arm's length bargaining takes place to a greater extent. Because it also happens, not accidentally we are sure, that jointly-owned subsidiaries are usually more fully integrated, they have a measure of autonomy over outside purchasing and selling beyond the permissible limit for wholly-owned subsidiaries. This freedom is reflected in transfer prices which are acceptable by both sides.

PUBLIC RELATIONS

Under this heading we include several effects of importance which may be attributed to or which accompany transfer pricing systems and concepts. Since external pricing exerts some influence on transfer prices, there is a secondary effect on transfer prices caused by a desire for "good citizenship." The sample companies do consider this effect in their desire to pay a fair share of taxes to host governments.

An overriding constraint to the allocation of income to foreign divisions is a desire to show some measure of good faith to host governments by submitting profits to local taxation.

Along similar lines, we report here the practice of one company with a manufacturing subsidiary in Mexico. In that country the law requires a sharing of profits with employees (currently at the rate of 10 percent of profits with a rise in the offing). As a result this firm sets transfer prices to leave a "reasonable" profit in that country. In addition, an attempt is made to show year-to-year earnings in a gradually ascending amount.

Finally, while possible effects on transfer prices might be brought about by the right of labor unions in Italy to audit company profits and by the right of labor representatives to sit on the boards of directors of corporations in France and Germany, the firms appear to consider the possible consequences too slight to affect their transfer prices.

INTERPERSONAL REACTIONS

The findings discussed so far have been strictly from the point of view of the corporate officers who devise and administer the transfer pricing systems under review. Since interviews were not conducted with overseas managers we cannot report specific personal attitudes or perceived reactions of such individuals. However, it seemed to us that headquarters personnel attempted to consider the perceived needs of overseas personnel. Even if it were intended to ignore managers of foreign divisions, modern management methods coupled with today's speedy communication and easy intercontinental travel make regular interpersonal contacts between management personnel an integral part of corporate life.

In the case of a company whose highly directive transfer pricing system causes a disproportionate share of income to arise overseas, its international managers are sometimes tempted to boast about their "contribution" to corporate profits at periodic meetings of corporate executives. The fact that their profits are in effect allocated rather than earned does not deter their proprietary self-glorification, much to the frustration of domestic managers, not to mention the dismay of headquarters executives.

In all companies whose transfer prices are a function of environmental influence some method of adjustment is used to give appropriate credit to divisions for their real contribution. The method may be credit-backs, or "dual" sets of books, or some other form of memorandum allowance, or compensation in budgets and profit plans. But regardless of the intent, "some things get lost in the wash," and dissensions result in dysfunctional upsets among all such firms at one time or another. It is a rare manager who waits patiently for a headquarters controller to adjust for profit or costs which are put out of line by headquarters directives. In one company, it was reported, the United Kingdom division was directed to lower its price to a new French subsidiary so as to improve startup operating results; but a good deal of ill-feeling was generated when headquarters seemed to forget that the resulting poor performance in the United Kingdom was not at all a reflection of local management.

When freedom to purchase and sell outside is sharply limited, divisional managers chafe for two reasons. First, they feel they are being discriminated against by having to overpay and subsidize a fellow division. Second, they complain about lack of interest for the company as a whole, because higher internal costs may at times reduce total corporate profit. If headquarters seems to be cavalier about corporate

profits, local management frustrations may cause dysfunctional attitudes and action in the field. In those companies which present a
uniform price to the world, the managers of more efficient plants
sometimes complain of having virtually to subsidize less efficient
members by reason of their own economies.

These kinds of reactions are sometimes evident in purely domestic
operations, but for the most part the far-reaching influence of the
multinational environment, when coupled with differences in national
temperament and cultural backgrounds, causes complaints of a more
serious nature to a greater extent than in a single-country operation.

CONCLUSIONS

The establishment and operation of a functional control system to
measure, evaluate, and motivate management in purely domestic sur-
roundings is difficult enough by itself. In the case of multinational
companies, however, the need for feasible control systems is rendered
more urgent by the additional complexities of the larger environment.
An executive has emphasized that the risks in international business are
larger in number and different in kind than in the domestic environment.   He was referring mostly to the problems enumerated here.
Regardless of the risks, however, there is wide recognition among our
sample that the rewards of the international environment – at least to
date – have offered ample incentive to United States firms to expand in
this direction. Nevertheless, any actions which affect the control
mechanism are likely to be more dangerous to the firms engaged in
multinational business; and when adaptations to new conditions cause
alterations to an existing system, management must be careful not
merely to substitute one problem for another.

Accordingly, the first criterion of a transfer pricing method in
multinational business should be that it does not cause destructive
changes in the existing control system, unless adequate adjustments
compensate for the changes, and keep the system operational. In other
words, unless a price change is called for by functional needs of
managers, first attention should be directed at its effect on the control
system. For example, if transfer prices have to be recast in response to
changes in cost of production inputs, the control system, such as it is,
ought not to be changed. If it has been providing useful information in
the first place, it will now reflect the new conditions (the causes, or
inputs) as well as the resultant changes (the effects, or outputs).

But when a transfer price change is introduced in order to counteract, or take advantage of, circumstances external to the usual routine,
then the system will reflect results which are not necessarily the result
of the operations it is designed to measure. And if measurements are
false, then resultant decisions are likely to be wrong. We consider the
three basic requirements of measurement, evaluation, and motivation
to be so vital to the promotion of corporate effectiveness that changes
in the control system should not be tolerated which may react at
cross-purposes to these requirements.

Our recommendation is that the transfer pricing system must primarily be compatible with the operational goals of the control system, and must reinforce its regulatory functions. But when external conditions are of such substance that they either expose the firm to grave threats or make available opportunities for material gains, then the transfer price system may be revamped to accord the greater return to the firm. The magnitude of threat or gain is of relevance to the proposal, since it is not intended to disturb control systems for every minor circumstance. Under such a practice systems would soon cease to operate effectively. In each firm, criteria should be established for selection (or elimination) of matters for consideration.

Quantitative limits would point up the particular relevance in each case. For example, one might use as measures a relative or absolute profit contribution, or a change in market share. Appropriate measures should be apparent in each case. Qualitative rules also have to be established, although they do not lend themselves to precise measurements. For example, one might consider interpersonal effects among managers (at all levels), reaction of public opinion, or changes in attitude of host or parent governments, to mention just a few. And again, the special conditions in each firm and its environment would dictate the criteria.

In proposing what may be thought of as a flexible approach to transfer pricing in multinational business, we are at the same time rejecting a simplistic approach to the problems. There is simply no one easy solution to the problems. We also regard a willingness to tinker incessantly with transfer prices to be equally dysfunctional, because incessant adjustment to the changing world without quantitative or qualitative tests represents too mechanistic and narrow an approach in a complex and changing world.

International business has grown by leaps and bounds, and problems have grown apace; but managers have not always been aware of them. When they have perceived the problems, they have not always responded with suitable solutions. Empirical evidence indicates that interest is high but attention is uneven.

We therefore advise extra care in approaching the concept of transfer pricing in the multinational firm. We recommend a multinational outlook, which includes consideration of regional problems. We suggest that greater effectiveness and, it should follow, greater profit will be the reward for those managements which recognize the multifaced problems, and achieve solutions which reconcile the differences.

41 Cadbury Schweppes Ltd. or: How to Market Successfully Abroad*
Marketing News

Cadbury Schweppes Ltd. of London, England, which markets a wide range of products on five continents, has recently taken a bold step into Bulgaria, and yet only this year began to organize its marketing activities internationally, according to the company's director, John Telford Beasley. "In the absence of sound policies and good planning, we were frankly dependent on good luck providing any form of consistent launch plan for our new products," he said. "And 'good luck' just isn't good enough."

The company had become concerned that its prospects as an international marketer should not be constrained by the poor economic performance and diminishing importance in worldwide status of the United Kingdom. Hence, Beasley and another company executive, Dominic Cadbury, initiated an international brand review that covered established as well as developing markets and included all the company's major product groups: packaged foods, soft drinks, hard liquor, candy, coffee, and health and chemical products. As reflected by Beasley, "It was our overall conclusion that we had no international marketing objectives, policy, strategy, or tactics, but rather a series of domestic or local ones, which, loosely strung together, became a worldwide operation."

Asking whether such a fragmented system was relevant for Cadbury Schweppes in today's conditions, Beasley continued, "Our competition isn't simply local brands, but it is strong, well-organized international brands with all the strength that implies. (In contrast) ... wide differences existed in our marketing approaches and, even more critically, in our marketing standards." He then cited Cadbury's Dairy Milk Chocolate as an example: in New Zealand, the bar appears in a wrapper

---

*From "Beasley tells what Cadbury Schweppes Ltd. did when it found it depended on good luck, had no international marketing objectives," Marketing News (July 16, 1976). Reprinted with permission.

with the Cadbury script logo and a gold panel. In South Africa, the wrapper has a sans serif logo and a white panel, and it shows a glass of milk. Japan's wrapper has a gold panel on a purple landscape. India's has no gold, only white and purple. And France "does its own thing" with pictures.

The situation was equally sad with new product introductions, according to Beasley. Illustrating with another example, he said, "Curly Wurly (a new candy bar)was successfully born in the United Kingdom out of extensive research into children's attitudes to and consumption patterns of confectionary, into their views on value, names, pack designs, and colors. So, in Germany we launched Leckerschmecker and in Australia, Crazy Maze. In neither case were we quick enough off the mark internationally, and our competitors were able to establish versions of Curly Wurly in Germany, Japan, and the United States. . .so a good idea was prostituted on the world market."

Cadbury Schweppes wanted a better approach to protecting and expanding its international brands. It was particularly concerned about advertising campaign standards and the level of support given to them in various markets. There are good reasons why the content of ad campaigns may differ from country to country, but, according to Beasley, "for our major brands – Cadbury and Schweppes – there is a remarkable consistency around the world in their positioning to target groups. Both are generally positioned as: better than average quality, giving value for money, slightly up-market, rather more 'sophisticated', and capable of sustaining premium prices. (Therefore). . . we could not accept that there should be wide variations in our standards of preparing ad strategies, or agency briefings, ad execution, appraisal, and communications research into advertising effectiveness. In short, our ads worldwide should conform to high standards."

"Advertising – other factors being equal – is the key to projecting the desired image, to generating volume and sales, to protecting our brand franchise with consumers from both (major) competitors and private label brands. A brand policy essentially demands a significant and consistent investment in advertising. We decided that one of our international priorities had to be a review of our levels of media expenditures against market share and to remove any imbalance."

That review had revealed that media to sales ratios of Cadbury and Schweppes products varied significantly from country to country, even after adjusting for local conditions and environmental differences. Thus, the ratios ranged from 1.6 to 5 percent for confectionary and from 1 to 4.3 percent for drinks.

In order to achieve a unified branding policy, advertising, budgeting, and product development, Beasley reflected that "we desperately needed a 'common marketing language' as a first step in getting a concerted marketing approach and to lifting our standards around the world." Beasley recognized that there must be a fine balance between setting worldwide standards and maintaining local authority and responsibility. "Our investigations concluded that we should break down the organizational barriers to international cooperation; that we should harness our strengths worldwide behind our two truly international house and brand names; that we should get changes accepted by marketing directors from around the world and not attempt to impose international branding on them; and that together we would lift our standards to equal the best of international marketing organizations."

To obtain agreement and cooperation in achieving its corporate, multinational objectives, Cadbury Schweppes organized its first, company-wide, international marketing conference in February 1976. Said Beasley, "The conference was an unqualified success. Marketing chiefs from around the world agreed to the task of producing a 'common marketing language' for Cadbury and for Schweppes — a common approach to marketing planning, execution, and documentation. International guidelines on the best of our worldwide experience and practices. . . (were subsequently). . . prepared on subjects such as annual marketing plans, ad agency selection, briefing, campaign evaluation and research, sales management, and others more. And, the international marketing directors themselves. . . (provided the necessary) commitment and dedication."

With Messrs. Beasley and Cadbury accepting the responsibility of its execution, the Main Board of Cadbury Schweppes Ltd. approved the overall plan. When it became fully operational, Beasley hoped to achieve through this plan "the benefits of strong local involvement and commitment allied to international control and direction." Successes of Cadbury and Schweppes brands in major markets around the world would seem to indicate that Mr. Beasley's hope was not in vain.

42 Sogo Shosha Hustle to Aid Yankee Traders*
Frank Meissner

Sogo shosha can help American marketers, who are being urged to test their mettle in foreign markets both to increase profits and to help overcome the worldwide weakness of the dollar. Japanese general trading companies — collectively referred to as sogo shosha (SS) — are veteran world traders, and to avail itself of their help, a prospective exporter need not be exclusively interested in the Japanese market. At a time when the spirit of the legendary Yankee traders seems to evaporate, an outright "hustler" spirit pervades these general trading companies which include such names as Chori, Itoh, Itoman, Kanematsu-Gosho, Kinsho-Mataishi, Marubeni, Mitsubishi, Mitsui, Nichimen, Nissho-Iwai, Nozaki, Okura, and Sumitomo. They all go under the designation of sogo shosha, and American manufacturers who wish to poke their noses beyond U.S. borders can use these SS companies to facilitate their efforts.

No other world group has the trading expertise, operational versatility, and overall influence of the sogo shosha. Active in practically every nation around the world, sogo shosha aim at facilitating and developing trade and industrial activities at both international and domestic levels. To do that they provide services in finance, engineering, construction, communications, transportation, marketing, natural resources development, and many other areas.

SS are neither user-nor. maker-oriented, but problem solvers in a supply-demand oriented world. They identify ways to supply goods and services by acting as intermediaries in simple or complex trade deals. They create demand for products in specific markets. They boost trade flows towards existing markets. They look for weak spots in existing trade flows and industrial development and help shore them up. In short,

---

*From Frank Meissner, "Sogo shosha skill, hustle can aid inexperienced U.S. exporters," Marketing News (March 9, 1979). Reprinted with permission.

SS offer a network of international and domestic services that catalyze trade.

Sogo shosha work in at least 13 different ways to stimulate world trade:

1. In acting as trade intermediaries, SS perform virtually every task necessary to assure smooth sale of one country's goods to another country.

2. SS provide access to major distribution networks both internationally and domestically. They have their own distribution centers, in addition to usual channels, through which are handled a variety of important foodstuffs, raw materials, and other products.

3. The role of organizer for business projects, in Japan and overseas, is relatively new. SS are well suited for it. Because of their wide capabilities and talents in dealing with complex trade problems, SS are able to bring together interests and resources of interrelated business and government agencies. They can organize individual firms into a cohesive group for specific projects, ironing out differences among group members.

4. The financial operations of SS have branched out in many directions, assisting client firms by providing extensive credit as well as through purchase of equity. Direct loan guarantees for client obligations help secure financing from other institutions. Many financial institutions will make loans alone on the strength of SS involvement.

5. SS focus their investments in areas of resource development, industrial production, marketing, investment intermediaries, and in some cases even participate in management of the company. SS also assist foreign host countries in locating other foreign firms suitable to each country's business environment, and invite them to invest.

6. SS have often helped Japanese firms become joint venture partners with overseas manufacturers and suppliers, often participating with equity in such ventures.

7. In order to supply future needs of the steel industry, SS organized major international raw materials development projects and assumed some of the risk inherent in such arrangements by signing long-term contracts. Other development operations have resulted in procurement of coal, copper, zinc, crude oil, natural gas, salt, fish, lumber, pulp, and other materials.

8. On construction projects, SS tend to act as general contractors. Thus engineering firms can combine their technical resources with financial and other commercial functions of SS. Working together, the two provide unified leadership for the several companies usually involved in such projects.

9. The SS represent a communications network without parallel in the private sector. Quotes on various ores, political analyses, results of all kinds of research are all made available to clients.

10. Research of all kinds is part of SS facilitating activities: demand studies for goods in overseas markets, identification of appropriate marketing channels, feasibility studies from both local and Japanese points of view, mobilization of available financial resources, and many others.

11. SS are capable of planning and executing virtually every facet of international trading projects: creating new companies, acting as intermediaries for transactions between existing companies, providing financing, marketing research, and a host of other facilitating services.

12. SS arrange for prompt and inexpensive transportation of products from suppliers' delivery points to final destination, varying according to type of shipment and logistics involved.

13. A vast communications network feeding research and market information helps keep abreast of trends, so that SS can help expand marketing activities for numerous products worldwide.

Rather than seek quick profits on single deals, SS like to build long-lasting relationships based on high volume. Thus Japanese trading companies typically realize profits of 1.7 percent-2 percent on total revenue, which in 1977 ran to around $219 billion.

Sogo shosha are the backbone of Japan's commercial success. In 1977 the foreign trade of Japan totaled $156 billion, and SS were responsible for about 55 percent of it. SS handle about 20,000 different items – general merchandise, steel products, ferrous materials, nonferrous metals and materials, electronics, machinery, cars, airplanes, foodstuffs, textiles, fuels, chemicals, forestry products, marine products, various forms of technology, and many more. As uniquely Japanese institutions, SS would seem to work most comfortably with other Japanese companies. Serving them was their original purpose, and hence they can operate with them on a basis of mutual loyalty. Yet SS are willing to extend loyalty to foreign firms as well, and today a substantial part of their activities is import and export of goods on behalf of manufacturers and buyers of commodities in other nations.

A few examples will illustrate the SS mode of operations:

● Importation to Japan of liquified natural gas from Indonesia illustrates how SS go about creating a demand for a product needed in the domestic market. After clearing their plans for a LNG project with the government of Indonesia, SS signed 23-year contracts with major electric power companies, steel mills, and gas companies. Then they brought together an international engineering firm and construction and manufacturing companies and assisted in negotiations between the Indonesian state oil company and Japanese users. By drawing on a strong position with banks and financial institutions worldwide, SS arranged financing for a $4 billion investment. Much of the equipment was provided by Japanese suppliers.

● Many SS have become active organizers of food distribution within Japan. Thus, Yamazaki Baking Company made a joint venture with

Nabisco of the United States. In addition to bringing the two firms together, SS supplied raw materials, wheat flour, potato flakes, sugar, and shortening as well as distributing resulting products through nationwide distribution channels, serving as sales agent for the venture.

- Due to rising production costs in the late 1960s, Japan's aluminum industry was losing its competitive edge. SS established a new source of supply via Alumax, a joint venture with AMAX, one of the world's leading producers of nonferrous metals. SS financial commitment to the venture was $135 million. Japan was provided with stable and competitive sources of primary alumina to supply domestic marketing activities for a full range of aluminum products.

- Through a Canadian subsidiary, an SS learned that foreign investment was sought for promoting development of a pulp industry for export. A meeting was arranged between Honshu Paper and the principals of a medium-size Canadian company, Crestbrook Timber, operator of lumber and plywood mills. Crestbrook was amenable to adding pulp operations to its line of business to allow full use of residual products from sawmill operations. Two Japanese companies agreed to participate by constructing the pulp mill. The joint venture increased employment from 700 to 1,200 in Canada. The plant output is exported to the United States, Japan, and other countries.

- In 1976 SS won a $77 million contract to build a million-ton-capacity cement plant in Algeria, the fifth such plant undertaken in an Arab country. Japan's Kawasaki Heavy Industries provided overall supervision of design, material and equipment procurement, construction, and engineering. Kajima designed the plant, with engineering done by a local Algerian firm. Onoda Cement of Japan was contracted to supervise the plant's operation and train local engineers. Financing was provided by the Export-Import Bank of Japan, payable on a 10-year deferred basis.

- Another SS catalyzed a consortium of foreign firms for building a power plant for Bangladesh. The project included participation of AEG of West Germany (gas turbine generators), General Electric of England (electrical equipment), and SOFRELEC of France (consultants), plus other firms.

- The same SS played a key role in putting together interests of the government of Iran, Nippon Electric, and KDD (International Telephone and Telegraph) for construction of a 4,000-kilometer microwave communications relay system connecting Iran's principal cities.

Herman Kahn (1970) maintains that, "Given the unique character of (general). . . trading companies, charges for their services are a small price to pay for hundreds of years of marketing experience that even a large company could not hope to gain without. . . trial and perhaps costly error."

"The enormous size of the companies is a great asset. It permits them to create superb private communications networks based on satellites and computers, further backed by a business intelligence operation that rivals even those of governments. As a result, these trading companies can keep tabs on global marketing conditions and match up sellers and buyers all over the world as quickly as anyone. This gives Japan a great advantage in dealing with the rest of the world. As the Japanese economy has grown bigger, these same advantages are shared with countries buying from and selling to Japan."

Sogo shosha are not a panacea for any sagging small or large American business looking abroad for its salvation. Chances for success with SS increase, of course, if the company offers a revolutionary product or has new technology for sale. Sogo shosha are easy to contact. The Sogo Shosha Committee of the Japanese Trade Council lists more than 200 representatives all around the world, with no less than 33 in North America, eager to resolve foreign trade problems. Fluent English is spoken in all offices.

REFERENCE

Kahn, Herman, The Emerging Japanese Superstate: Challenge and Response (Englewood Cliffs, N.J.: Prentice-Hall, 1970), p. 274.

FURTHER READING – PART SEVEN

Alpander, Guvene G., "Multinational corporations: Homebase-affiliate relations," California Management Review, Vol. 20, No. 3 (Spring 1978), pp. 47-56.

Alsegg, Robert J., Control Relationships between American Corporations and their European Subsidiaries (New York: American Management Association, 1971).

Kilmann, Ralph H. and Ghymn, Kyung-Il, "The MAPS design technology: Designing strategic intelligence systems for MNCs," Columbia Journal of World Business, Vol. 11, No. 2 (Summer 1976), pp. 35-47.

Kim, Seung H. and Miller, Stephen W., "Constituents of the international transfer pricing decision," Columbia Journal of World Business, Vol. 14, No. 1 (Spring 1979), pp. 69-77.

Liotard-Vogt, Pierre, "Nestlé - at home abroad," Harvard Business Review, Vol. 54, No. 6 (November-December 1976), pp. 80-8.

Malmstrom, Duane, "Accommodating exchange rate fluctuations in intercompany pricing and invoicing," Management Accounting, Vol. 59, No. 3 (September 1977), pp. 24-8.

Picard, Jacques, "How European companies control marketing decisions abroad," Columbia Journal of World Business, Vol. 12, No. 2 (Summer 1977), pp. 113-21.

Ronstadt, Robert C., "International R & D: The establishment and evolution of research and development abroad by seven U.S. multinationals," Journal of International Business Studies, Vol. 9, No. 1 (Spring-Summer 1978), pp. 7-24.

Ryans, John K., Jr. and Woudenberg, Henry W., Jr., "The MNC bribery question," Atlantic Economic Review, Vol. 28, No. 6 (November-December 1978), pp. 28-33.

Wiechmann, Ulrich E., "Integrating multinational marketing activities," Columbia Journal of World Business, Vol. 9, No. 4 (Winter 1974), pp. 7-16.

Wills, J.R., Jr. and Ryans, J.K., Jr., "An analysis of headquarters executive involvement in international advertising," European Journal of Marketing, Vol. 11, No. 8 (1977), pp. 577-84.

Wind, Yoram; Douglas, Susan; and Perlmutter, Howard, "Guidelines for developing international marketing strategies," Journal of Marketing, Vol. 37, No. 2 (April 1973), pp. 14-23.

VIII

The Marketing Plan: Marketing and Economic Development

Introduction to Part VIII

In the final part of the book an attempt is made to pull the threads together. The object of the marketing plan is seen as harmonizing market structure and marketing strategy while retaining a requisite minimum of international coordination.

Reading 43, by Buzzell, provides a backdrop by an incisive discussion of the extent to which it is feasible − or advisable − to standardize strategy in multinational marketing. The exhibit of structural factors which may place limits on attempts at homogenizing strategy is particularly instructive. The conclusion that both the pros and cons of standardization in multinational marketing programs should be considered is very much in tune with the ecologic approach of this book.

Reading 44, by Ayal and Zif, considers alternative international expansion strategies in terms of concentration on a limited number of national markets or diversification into a broader range of such markets (given a certain resource package and time frame). In each case, the merits of concentration or diversification within each national market are also discussed. In analyzing the determinants of strategy choice, this reading has several points of contact with others, notably those by Buzzell and Larréché. A lesson from Buzzell, for instance, is that a strategy of diversification is more likely to succeed if marketing strategy may be standardized across countries. Larréché emphasizes the helpfulness of portfolio analysis in resolving the type of strategic issues analyzed by Ayal and Zif.

In Reading 45 we have tried to apply the ecologic view to the task of strategic as well as tactical planning in international marketing. A step-by-step procedure is sketched out, comprising the original commitment decision as well as an initial plan of operations.

It is befitting that a book on international marketing strategy should end with some thoughts on the broader social and economic significance of the marketing process. Ecology teaches us that marketing institutions and practices as we know them will survive only as they serve a useful purpose in the broader environment. As indicated in Part One, the development of affluent society and customer-oriented marketing have gone hand in hand — and surely not by accident. Reading 46, by Thorelli, is germane in this context by outlining an approach to evaluation of the performance of the MNC in the LDC, with stress on the multiple goals typical of host countries. The building of mutual trust in this sensitive relationship is stressed throughout the reading as a supercritical element of performance.

Reading 47, by Drucker, points to the vast and sadly neglected contribution potential of modern marketing to economic development in the LDCs. In reading Drucker, one is reminded of Paul Hoffman's statement about the most important lesson he learned during his thirteen years as head of the UN Development Programme: "One illusion is that you can industrialize a country by building factories. You don't. You industrialize it by building markets." Ten years later neither the UN nor most LDCs have absorbed this lesson. Here is indeed a challenge for the Third Development Decade: a challenge for planners at the national governmental and international technical assistance levels to make room for, and prevail upon, the greatest change agent as yet devised in nondictatorial cultures, and a challenge to international marketers to demonstrate the power of their tools.

Looking beyond the LDCs, we note that international marketing is the vehicle by which is implemented the international division of labor based on the differential advantages of countries and firms, and it is the means of bringing economies of scale to bear in such incredibly resource-demanding industries as petroleum, drugs, computers, and aircraft. What is more, in our age the multinational corporation has proven a far more effective torch-bearer of a global outlook and intercultural understanding than either national governments or the United Nations. Many have reasons to envy the mission of the international marketer.

43 Can You Standardize Multinational Marketing?*
Robert D. Buzzell

Is it practical to consider the development of marketing strategy, in terms of <u>all</u> of its elements, on a multinational scale? The conventional wisdom suggests that a multinational approach is <u>not</u> realistic, because of the great differences that still exist – and probably always will exist – among nations. For example, George Weissman, president of Philip Morris, Inc., has concluded that "until we achieve One World there is no such thing as international marketing, only local marketing around the world" (1967). Apparently most other marketing executives agree with this view. Thus, Millard H. Pryor, Jr., Director of Corporate Planning for Singer Company, writes:

> Marketing is conspicuous by its absence from the functions which can be planned at the corporate headquarters level. The operating experience of many international firms appears to confirm the desirability of assigning long-range planning of marketing activities to local managers (1965).

The prevailing view, then, is that marketing strategy is a local problem. The best strategy for a company will differ from country to country, and the design of the strategy should be left to local management in each country.

TWO-SIDED CASE

But is the answer this simple? The experiences of leading U.S.-based companies in recent years suggest that there may indeed be something

*Slightly abbreviated from Robert D. Buzzell, "Can you standardize multinational marketing?" <u>Harvard Business Review</u> (November-December 1968), pp. 102-13, with permission.

to be said in favor of a multinational marketing strategy. This article is intended to outline some of the possibilities – and limitations – of an integrated approach to multinational marketing. My thesis is that although there are many obstacles to the application of common marketing policies in different countries, there are also some very tangible potential benefits. The relative importance of the pros and cons will, of course, vary from industry to industry and from company to company. But the benefits are sufficiently universal and sufficiently important to merit careful analysis by management in virtually any multinational company. Management should not automatically dismiss the idea of standardizing some parts of the marketing strategy, at least within major regions of the world.

BENEFITS OF STANDARDIZATION

As a practical matter, standardization is not a clear cut issue. In a literal sense, multinational standardization would mean the offering of identical product lines at identical prices through identical distribution systems, supported by identical promotional programs, in several different countries. At the other extreme, completely "localized" marketing strategies would contain no common elements whatsoever. Obviously, neither of these extremes is often feasible or desirable.

The practical question is: which elements of the marketing strategy can or should be standardized, and to what degree? Currently, most multinational companies employ strategies that are much closer to the "localized" end of the spectrum than to the opposite pole. If there are potential benefits of increased standardization, then they would be achieved by incorporating more common elements in a multinational strategy. Each marketing aspect of policy should be considered, first, in its own right, and second, in relation to the other elements of the "mix."

Let us examine the most important potential benefits of standardization in multinational marketing strategy.

SIGNIFICANT COST SAVINGS

Differences in national income levels, tastes, and other factors have traditionally dictated the need for local products and corresponding local marketing programs. The annals of international business provide countless examples, even for such apparently similar countries as the United States and Canada. Philip Morris, Inc., for example, tried unsuccessfully to convert Canadian smokers to one of its popular American cigarette brands. The Canadians apparently would rather fight; they preserved their traditional preference for so-called "Virginia-type" tobacco blends. Examples of this kind suggest that to attain maximum sales in each country, a company should offer products, as well as packages, advertisements, and other marketing elements, which are tailored to that country's distinctive needs and desires.

However, maximizing sales is not the only goal in designing a marketing strategy. Profitability depends ultimately both on sales and costs, and there are significant opportunities for cost reduction via standardization. The most obvious, and usually the most important, area for cost savings is product design. By offering the same basic product in several markets with some possible variations in functional and/or design features, a manufacturer can frequently achieve longer production runs, spread research and development costs over a greater volume, and thus reduce total unit costs.

The "Italian Invasion"

The lesson of mass production economies through standardization, first demonstrated by Henry Ford I, has been dramatically retaught during the 1960s by the Italian household appliance industry.

In the mid-1950s, total combined Italian production of refrigerators and washing machines was less than 300,000 units; there were no strong Italian appliance manufacturers. In 1955, only 3 percent of Italian households owned refrigerators, and around 1 percent owned washing machines.

Starting in the late 1950s, several companies began aggressive programs of product development and marketing. Ironically, some of the Italian entrepreneurs were simply applying lessons learned from America. One member of the Fumagalli family, owners of the appliance firm, Candy, had been a prisoner of war in the United States and brought back the idea of "a washing machine in every home."

The Italian appliance firms installed modern, highly automated equipment, reinvested profits, and produced relatively simple, standardized products in great numbers. By 1965, refrigerator output was estimated at 2.6 million units, and washing machine output at 1.5 million units. Much of this volume was sold in Italy; home ownership of the two appliances rose to 50 percent and 23 percent respectively. But the Italian companies were aggressive in export marketing, too; by 1965 Italian-made refrigerators accounted for 32 percent of the total French market and for 40 percent to 50 percent of the Benelux market. Even in Germany, the home market of such electrical giants as AEG, Bosch, and Siemens, the Italian products attained a 12 percent market share. The export pattern of washing machines has followed that of refrigerators; by 1965 Italian exports had accounted for 10 percent to 15 percent of market sales in most other Western European countries (from Castellano, 1965, and Marketing in Europe, 1966 and 1967).

The success of the Italian appliance industry has been a painful experience for the traditional leaders – American, British, and German – as well as for the smaller French companies that had previously had tariff protection. Whirlpool Corporation, which acquired a French refrigerator plant in 1962, subsequently leased the facility to a French competitor. Even Frigidaire decided, in mid-1967, to close down its refrigerator production in France.

In competition with other European appliance makers, the Italian companies have benefited from some natural advantages in terms of lower wage rates and government export incentives. But mass production of simple, standardized products has been at least equally important. And, according to Fortune, "refrigerators have begun to look more and more alike as national tastes in product design give way to an international 'sheer-line' style."

Turnabout at Hoover

To compete with this "Italian invasion" in appliances, some of the established manufacturers have tried new approaches. An interesting example is the recent introduction of a new line of automatic washing machines by Hoover Ltd., the market leader in the United Kingdom. Hoover's previous automatics, introduced in 1961, were designed primarily for the British market. The company's new "Keymatic" models featured:

An exclusive "pulsator" washing action.
A tilted, enamelled steel drum.
Hot water provided by the home's central hot-water heater.

In contrast, most European manufacturers, including the Italian producers, offered front-loading, tumble-action washers with stainless steel drums and self-contained water heaters. Either because these features were better suited to continental needs, or because so many sellers promoted them, or perhaps both, Hoover saw its position in the major continental markets gradually decline.

When the Hoover management set out to design a new product line, beginning in 1965, it decided to look for a single basic design that would meet the needs of housewives in France, Germany, and Scandinavia as well as in the United Kingdom. A committee including representatives of the continental subsidiaries and of the parent company, Hoover Worldwide Corporation (New York), spent many weeks finding mutually acceptable specifications for the new line.

The result, which went on sale in the spring of 1967, was a front loading, tumble-action machine, closer in concept to the "continental" design than Hoover's previous washers, but with provisions for "hot water fill" and enamelled steel drums on models to be sold in the United Kingdom. By standardizing most of the key design elements in the new machine, Hoover was able to make substantial savings in development costs, tooling, and unit production costs.

Other Economies

The potential economies of standardization are not confined solely to product design decisions. In some industries, packaging costs represent a significant part of total costs. Here, too, standardization may offer the possibility of savings. Charles R. Williams cites the case of a food processor selling prepared soups throughout Europe in eleven different packages. He observes, "The company believes it could achieve a significant savings in cost and at the same time reduce consumer confusion by standardizing the packaging"(1967).

Still another area for cost savings is that of advertising. For some of the major package goods manufacturers, the production of art work, films, and other advertising materials costs millions of dollars annually. Although differences in language limit the degree of standardization that can be imposed, some common elements can often be used. To illustrate: Pepsi-Cola is bottled in 465 plants and sold in 110 countries outside the United States. Part of its foreign advertising is done by films. According to one of the company's top marketing executives, "We have found that it is possible to produce commercial films overseas in one market, if planned properly, for use in most (but not all) of our international markets." According to company estimates, the added cost of producing separate films for each market would be $8 million per year (Heller, 1966).

All of these examples illustrate the same basic point: standardization of product design, packaging, and promotional materials can offer important economies to the multinational marketer. Even if these cost savings are attained at the expense of lower sales in some markets, the net effect on profits may be positive.

CONSISTENCY WITH CUSTOMERS

Quite apart from the possibilities of cost reduction, some multinational companies are moving toward standardization in order to achieve consistency in their dealings with customers. Executives of these companies believe that consistency in product style, in sales and customer service, in brand names and packages, and generally in the "image" projected to customers, is a powerful means of increasing sales.

If all customers lived incommunicado behind their respective national frontiers, there would be no point in worrying about this matter; only diplomatic couriers and border-crossing guards would ever notice any inconsistencies in products, services, or promotion. But in reality, of course, this is not the case. The most visible type of cross-border flow is international travel by tourists and businessmen. Especially in Europe, with its relatively high income levels and short distances, the number of people visiting other countries has reached flood proportions in the 1960s, and shows no sign of abating. If the German tourist in Spain sees his accustomed brands in the store, he is likely to buy them during his visit. More important, his re-exposure to the products and their advertising may strengthen his loyalty back home or, at least, protect him from the temptation to change his allegiance to a competitor.

Then there is the flow of communications across boundaries. Magazines, newspapers, radio and television broadcasts – all including advertising – reach international audiences. For example, according to estimates by Young and Rubicam International (1966):

German television broadcasts are received by 40 percent of Dutch homes with TV sets.

Paris Match has a circulation of 85,000 in Belgium, 26,000 in Switzerland, and substantial readership in Luxembourg, Germany, Italy, and Holland.

On an average day, over four million French housewives tune to Radio Luxembourg; the same broadcast reaches 620,000 Belgian housewives, 30,000 in Switzerland, and 100,000 in Holland.

The possibility of reaching multimarket audiences with common advertising messages, and the risk of confusion that may result from reaching such audiences with different brand names and promotional appeals, has led some of the major consumer goods producers to explore ways and means of standardizing at least the basic elements of their European campaigns. For instance, the Nestlé Company, Inc. and Unilever Ltd, probably the most experienced multinational consumer goods firms, have both moved in the direction of more "unified" European advertising during the 1960s. When Nestlé launched "New Nescafé" in 1961-1962, for example, the same basic theme "fresh-ground aroma" and very similar creative treatments were used not only throughout Europe, but also in other markets such as Australia. The value of this approach is, perhaps, reflected in the fact that several years ago Nescafé was the leading brand of instant coffee in every European country.

BALANCED APPRAISAL NEEDED

To summarize, then, many companies have found real benefits in a multinational approach to marketing strategy. The gains have included greater effectiveness in marketing, reduced costs, and improved planning and control. Moreover, especially in Western Europe but also in some other parts of the world, social and economic trends are working in favor of more, rather than less, standardization in marketing policies. Tourism, international communication, increased numbers of multinational customers, and other forces are all tending toward greater unification of multinational markets.

But this is just one side of the story. It would be a mistake to assume, as at least a few companies have done, that marketing programs can be transferred from one market to another without careful consideration of the differences which still exist. Let us turn next to that side of the picture.

COMMON BARRIERS

Despite the potential benefits of standardization, the great majority of companies still operate on the premise that each national market is different and must therefore be provided with its own, distinctive marketing program. For instance, after a careful study of the marketing policies of U.S. appliance and photographic manufacturers in Europe, Richard Aylmer concluded: "In over 85 percent of the cases observed, advertising and promotion decisions were based on <u>local</u> product marketing objectives" (1968).

Why is diversity still the rule of the day in multinational marketing? In many cases, differences simply reflect <u>customary</u> ways of doing business which have evolved in an earlier period when national boundaries were more formidable barriers than they are today. But even if tradition did not play a role, it must be recognized that there are and will continue to be some important obstacles to standardization.

A comprehensive list of these obstacles would fill many pages, and would include many factors that affect only one or two industries. The most important and generally applicable factors are summarized in Table 43.1. The rows of this table represent the major <u>classes</u> of factors which limit standardization in multinational marketing strategies. The columns correspond to different elements of a marketing program, and the cells in the table illustrate the ways in which the various factors affect each program element. In effect, each cell represents a condition or characteristic which <u>may</u> differ sufficiently among countries, and <u>may</u> require variations in marketing strategies. As we shall see presently, the experiences of multinational companies afford numerous examples of these barriers to standardization. Let us look briefly at each of the four major factors limiting standardization that are listed in Table 43.1.

MARKETING CHARACTERISTICS

Perhaps the most permanent differences among national markets are those arising from the physical environment – climate, topography, and resources (see the top left of Table 43.1). Climate has an obvious effect on the sales potential for many products, and may also require differences in packaging. Topography influences the density of population, and this in turn may have a strong influence on the distribution system available to a manufacturer.

The cell in Table 43.1 labeled "Product use conditions" includes a wide variety of environmental factors affecting marketing strategies. Differences in the size and configuration of homes, for example, have an important bearing on product design for appliances and home furnishings. European kitchens are typically small by U.S. standards, and there is seldom any basement space available to apartment dwellers for laundry facilities. As a result, there is a great emphasis on compactness of design in automatic washers, for they must somehow be

Table 43.1. Obstacles to Standardization in International Marketing Strategies

Factors limiting standardization	Elements of marketing program				
	Product design	Pricing	Distribution	Sales force	Advertising and promotion, branding and packaging
Market characteristics					
Physical environment	Climate		Customer mobility	Dispersion of customers	Access to media; Climate
Stage of economic and industrial development	Product use conditions; Income levels; Labor costs in relation to capital costs	Income levels	Consumer shopping patterns	Wage levels, availability of manpower	Needs for convenience rather than economy; Purchase quantities
Cultural factors	"Custom and tradition"; Attitudes toward foreign goods	Attitudes toward bargaining	Consumer shopping patterns	Attitudes toward selling	Language, literacy; Symbolism
Industry conditions					
Stage of product life cycle in each market	Extent of product differentiation	Elasticity of demand	Availability of outlets	Need for missionary sales effort	Awareness, experience with products
Competition	Quality levels	Local costs; Prices of substitutes	Desirability of private brands; Competitors' control of outlets	Competitors' sales forces	Competitive expenditure messages
Marketing institutions					
Distributive system	Availability of outlets	Prevailing margins	Number and variety of outlets available; Ability to "force" distribution	Number, size, dispersion of outlets; Effectiveness of advertising, need for substitutes	Extent of self-service; Media availability, costs, overlaps
Advertising media and agencies					
Legal restrictions	Product standards; Patent laws; Tariffs and taxes	Tariffs and taxes; Antitrust laws; Resale price maintenance	Restrictions on product lines; Resale price maintenance	General employment restrictions; Specific restrictions on selling	Specific restrictions on messages, costs; Trademark laws

fitted into a small and already crowded area. As noted in the example of Hoover Ltd. washing machines must also be equipped with self-contained water heating systems to compensate for the lack of central hot-water heaters in most continental homes.

Industrial goods manufacturers also frequently encounter differences in product use conditions. To illustrate:

1. A U.S. producer of farm equipment found that one of his pieces of machinery could not be moved through the narrow, crooked streets of French and Belgian farm villages.
2. Concluding that there is more dissimilarity than similarity in industrial markets in Europe, a chemical industry marketing researcher writes: "(A factor) which would severely affect the market for surface coatings is the fact that materials used in building construction are vastly different in various parts of Europe. Brick, mortar, and tile are used predominantly in Southern Europe, whereas this is not the case in Northern Germany and in Benelux" (Gerunsky, 1967).

Many similar examples could be cited of differences in the environment which call for variations in product design and other aspects of marketing policy.

Development Stage

Differences among countries in stages of economic and industrial development (second item under "Market characteristics" in Table 43.1) also have a profound influence on marketing strategies. Because of the wide gaps in per capita income levels, many products or models which are regarded as inexpensive staples in the United States or Western Europe must be marketed as "luxuries" elsewhere. Even among the industrialized countries income differences are substantial: appliance manufacturers such as Philco-Ford Corporation and Kelvinator of Canada, Ltd. find themselves with little choice but to position their products as deluxe, relatively high-priced items. This, in turn, implies a very different marketing strategy from that used in the United States.

For industrial products, differences in economic development are reflected in variations in relative costs of capital and labor. Thus, General Electric Company and other companies have sold numerical controls for machine tools to U.S. factories primarily on the basis of labor cost savings. The same approach may be suitable in Germany, where there is a critical shortage of labor. But in most other countries it would be far more difficult to justify numerical controls on the basis of labor substitution.

Cultural Factors

This category is a convenient catchall for the many differences in market structure and behavior that cannot readily be explained in terms of more tangible factors. Consider, for example, the figures in Table 43.2, which are taken from a recent survey made by the European Economic Community's Statistical Office. Why do French households consume more than fifty times as much wine as Dutch households, but only two-thirds as much milk? No doubt these differences could be explained historically in terms of variations in water, soil, and so on. But for practical purposes, it is usually sufficient and certainly more efficient simply to take differences in consumption patterns and attitudes as given, and to adjust to them.

Table 43.2. Average Household Consumption
of Beverages, 1963-1964 (in liters).

Country	Milk	Wine	Beer
France	103	116	28
Germany	100	7	46
Holland	153	2	11
Italy	87	95	2

Source: Le Monde, 15-21 February, 1968, p. 7.

There are many examples of cultural differences that have affected marketing success or failure. One cultural factor is the attitude of consumers toward "foreign" goods. To illustrate: Princess Housewares, Inc., a large U.S. appliance manufacturer, introduced a line of electric housewares in the German market. The company's brand name was well known and highly regarded in the United States, but relatively unknown in Germany; and the brand had a definitely "American" sound. The company discovered that the American association was a real drawback among German consumers. According to a survey, fewer than 40 percent of German individuals felt "confident" about electrical products made in the United States, compared with 91 percent who were "confident" of German-made products.

Lack of brand awareness, coupled with suspicion of the quality of "American" products, required the company to adopt a very different marketing strategy in Germany than that employed in the United States, where both awareness and a quality image were taken for granted.

INDUSTRY CONDITIONS

A convenient framework for comparing industry and competitive conditions in different national markets is that of the "product life cycle."

The histories of many different products in the United States suggest that most of them pass through several distinct <u>stages</u> over a period of years, and that marketing strategies typically change from stage to stage.

Some products are in different stages of their life cycles in different national markets. For example, in late 1965 the Polaroid Corporation introduced the "Swinger" Polaroid Land camera in the United States. The Swinger, with a retail list price of $19.95, was Polaroid's first camera selling for less than $50. The introductory promotion for the new model in the United States placed very heavy emphasis on price; there was no need to explain the basic concept of "instant photography," since millions of Polaroid Land cameras had already been sold over a seventeen-year period. Surveys indicated that over 80 percent of U.S. consumers were aware of the name "Polaroid" and of the company's basic product features.

The Swinger was introduced in Europe during 1966. Prior to that time, Polaroid cameras had been extremely high-priced, owing in part to high tariffs, and the company's sales had been at a very low level. Distribution of Polaroid cameras and film was spotty. Most important, fewer than 10 percent of consumers were aware of the Polaroid instant photography concept.

Under these circumstances, a very different marketing strategy was needed for the Swinger in Europe. Polaroid advertising had to be designed to do a more basic educational job, since awareness of the instant picture principle could not be taken for granted. The promotional program also had to be aimed at building retail distribution, which was also taken for granted in the United States.

If products are in different stages of their life cycles in different countries, then it is tempting to conclude that marketing strategies used in the past in the more "advanced" countries should be used in other "follower" nations. There is some evidence to support this conclusion. For instance, as described earlier, the Italian appliance manufacturers have successfully employed strategies similar to those of Henry Ford in the early 1900s; similarly, Polaroid in the 1960s in Europe can profitably use many of the same approaches that it employed in America in the early 1950s. However, history does not repeat itself exactly, and past marketing strategies cannot be reapplied without some modifications.

Competitive Practices

Another important industry condition, partly but not entirely related to the product life cycle, is the extent of competition in each national market. Differences in products, costs, prices, and promotional levels may permit or even require differences in the strategies used by a multinational company in various markets. Even within the European Common Market, there are still substantial variations in prices of many products, reflecting in part traditional differences in the degree of competition. A survey made in 1967 by the European Economic Community's Statistical Office showed that price variations are still substantial even with the Common Market. Typical prices were compared for some 125 different consumer products by country; on the average, the difference between prices in the countries with the highest and lowest prices was 58 percent. Even the price of a staple item such as aspirin varied from a high of 38 cents in Germany to a low of 22 cents in Holland.

The growth of multinational companies in itself has tended to reduce traditional differences in competitive practices. For example: advertising expenditures have traditionally been lower in France than in the United States and other European countries; on a per capita basis, total French advertising outlays are around one-eighth those of the United States and one-third those of Germany. However, according to M. André Bouhebent, a top French advertising agency executive, the entry of foreign competitors is changing the situation: "When German advertisers sell in France, they have the habit of spending at the same rate (as at home), which is three times that of their French competitors. . ." (Advertising Age, 1966). As an example, it was noted that the German Triumph bra and girdle company spends three to four times as much as a French undergarment company to promote its products.

MARKETING INSTITUTIONS

The combination of continued differences in marketing institutions now with the prospect of greater similarities in the future creates some difficult problems for multinational marketers. One such problem may be timing. The experience of Princess Housewares in Germany, previously mentioned, is a case in point.

When Princess Housewares went into the German market, the company had a basic choice to make regarding channels of distribution. In the early 1960s, the predominant system of appliance distribution was independent wholesalers selling to retail stores. Small specialty retailers still dominated the market. However, department stores, mail-order firms, and discounters were growing in importance. Most of these large retailers were able to obtain Grosshändler (wholesaler) discounts from manufacturers, and many of them sold at substantial discounts from "suggested" retail prices. The suggested prices, in turn, were often set at artificially high levels (so-called "moon" prices) to permit the appearance of large price cuts at retail. At the same time, because of public confusion and discontent over artificial list prices and equally artificial discounts, the resale price maintenance law was under increasing attack.

Princess Housewares, as a relatively unknown brand, felt that its first task was to obtain distribution. To do this, the company decided to establish maintained prices and enforce them, so that small retailers' margins would be protected. But this put the company at a disadvantage in selling to the large discounters. It also meant that the company had to sell direct to retailers, since wholesalers could not be relied on to enforce resale prices.

In some ways, the Princess Housewares case boils down to a choice between a traditional distributive system, similar to that used in the United States in the early 1950s, and an emerging but still undeveloped system. U.S. experience suggests that the emerging system will become the dominant one. But can a manufacturer afford to be ahead of the trend?

LEGAL RESTRICTIONS

Different countries require or permit very different practices in the areas of product design, competitive practices, pricing, employment, and advertising. They also impose differing taxes and tariffs, and multinational companies often follow devious paths in the attempt to minimize the total cost effects of these levies. Obviously, such practices can be stumbling blocks for the would-be standardizer.

Some product standards, though ostensibly designed for purposes of safety, are used by governments as a device for protecting home industries. A notable case in point was the imposition of new regulations for electrical appliances by France in 1967, along with delays in issuing approvals. This was generally regarded as a deliberate move to slow down the onslaught of competition by the Italian companies and thus give the domestic industry a breathing space.

CONCLUSION

Traditionally, marketing strategy has been regarded as a strictly local problem in each national market. Differences in customer needs and preferences, in competition, in institutional systems, and in legal regulations have seemed to require basically different marketing programs. Any similarity between countries has been seen as purely coincidental.

There is no doubt that differences among nations are still great, and that these differences should be recognized in marketing planning. But the experiences of a growing number of multinational companies suggest that there are also some real potential gains in an integrated approach to marketing strategy. Standardization of products, packages, and promotional approaches may permit substantial cost savings, as well as greater consistency in dealings with customers. The harmonization of price policies often facilitates better internal planning and control. Finally, if good ideas are scarce, and if some of them have universal appeal, they should be used as widely as possible.

All of this adds up to the conclusion that both the pros and the cons of standardization in multinational marketing programs should be considered.

REFERENCES

Aylmer, R., "Marketing decision-making in the multinational firm," unpublished doctoral thesis (Harvard Business School, 1968).

Bouhebent, A., quoted in Advertising Age, August 29, 1966, p. 218.

Castellano, C., L'Industria Degli Elettrodomestici in Italia (Universita Degli Studi di Genova, 1965).

Gerunsky, W., "International marketing research" in N.H. Giragosian (ed.), Chemical Marketing Research (Reinhold Publishing Corporation, 1967), p. 258.

Heller, N., "How Pepsi-Cola does it in 110 countries," in J.S. Wright and J.L. Goldstucker (eds.), New Ideas for Successful Marketing (American Marketing Association, 1966), p. 700.

Le Monde, weekly overseas edition (15-21 February, 1968), p. 7.

Marketing in Europe (October 1966 and September 1967).

Pryor, M.H. Jr., "Planning in a worldwide business," Harvard Business Review (January-February 1965), p. 137.

Weissman, G., "International expansion," in L. Adler (ed.), Plotting Marketing Strategy, A New Orientation (Simon and Schuster, 1967), p. 229.

Williams, C.R. "Regional management overseas," Harvard Business Review (January-February 1967), p. 89.

Young and Rubicam International, "When is a frontier not a frontier?" (pamphlet, May 1966).

44 Market Expansion Strategies in Multinational Marketing*
Igal Ayal
Jehiel Zif

THE MAJOR STRATEGIC ALTERNATIVES

The choice of a market expansion policy is a key strategic decision in multinational marketing. To develop such a policy, a firm has to make decisions in the following three areas:

1. Identification of potential markets and determination of some order of priorities for entry into these markets.
2. Decision on the overall level of marketing effort that the firm is able and willing to commit.
3. Selection of the rate of market expansion over time, and determination of the allocation of effort among different markets.

This paper concentrates on the third area, assuming that decisions in the first two areas have already been made. In practice, the process will be frequently iterative, whereby analysis of the third area will be helpful in reviewing the first two. Thus, analysis of the third area, market expansion policy, requires identification of some markets with sufficient potential for entry and a preliminary idea about available budget. This may lead, in turn, to reevaluation of the order of market entry priorities and provide more definite budget guidelines. The major strategic alternatives for multinational expansion within this third decision area are market concentration versus market diversification.

A strategy of market concentration is characterized by a slow and gradual rate of growth in the number of markets served. On the other hand, a strategy of market diversification is characterized by a fast rate of growth in the number of markets served at the early stages of

*From Igal Ayal and Jehiel Zif, "Market expansion strategies in multinational marketing," Journal of Marketing, Vol. 43 (Spring 1979), pp. 84-94. Reprinted with permission.

expansion. It is, therefore, expected that a strategy of concentration will result in a smaller number of markets served, at each point in time, relative to a strategy of diversification. Expected evolution of the number of markets served, for a strategy of concentration versus a strategy of diversification, is presented graphically in figure 44.1.

In the long run, a strategy of diversification will frequently lead to a reduction in the number of markets, as a result of consolidation and abandonment of less profitable markets. A fast rate of market expansion is usually accomplished by devoting only limited resources and time to a careful study of each market prior to entry. The firm is, therefore, bound to make a few mistakes and is more likely to enter unprofitable markets and drop them later.

The different patterns of market expansion are likely to cause development of different competitive conditions in different markets over time. The profitability of a late entry into new markets is affected by these competitive conditions and by the length of the product life cycle. As a result, the optimal number of markets served in the long run is not necessarily the same for both strategies.

Strategies of concentration versus diversification lead to the selection of different levels of marketing effort and different marketing mixes in each market. Given fixed financial and managerial resources, the level of resources allocated to each market in a strategy of diversification will be lower than with concentration. The size of the budget gives an indication about possible selection of means or marketing mix. Specifically, a lower level of marketing effort implies less promotional expenditures, more reliance on commission agents, and a stronger tendency for a skimming approach to pricing. A strategy of concentration, on the other hand, involves investment in market share. This implies heavy promotional outlays, a stronger control of the distribution channel and, in some cases, penetration pricing.

DETAILED STRATEGIC OPTIONS

A strategy of market expansion is characterized not only by the rate of entry into new national markets. Two additional considerations are of particular importance for more detailed identification of optional strategies: (1) market segments within national markets and (2) allocation of effort to different markets (and market segments).

Market segments within national markets. Four major market expansion alternatives can be identified when market segments are examined. These alternatives are presented in Table 44.1.

Table 44.1. Market Expansion Strategies Based on Countries and Segments

		Segments	
		Concentration	Diversification
Countries	Concentration	1	2
	Diversification	3	4

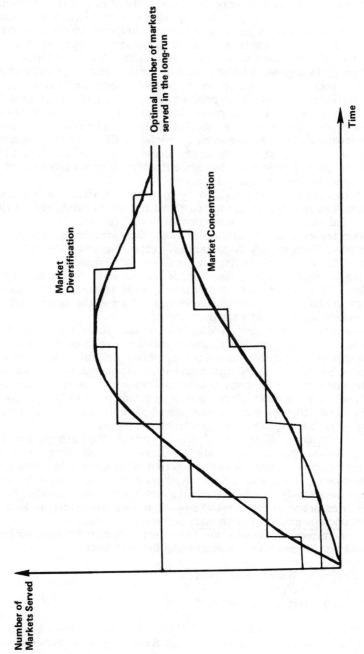

Fig. 44.1. Alternative market expansion strategies over time.

Number of Markets Served

Optimal number of markets served in the long-run

Market Diversification

Market Concentration

Time

355

Strategy 1 concentrates on specific market segments in a few countries and a gradual increase in the number of markets served. This dual concentration is particularly appropriate when the product (or service) appeals to a definite group of similar customers in different countries, and the costs of penetration into each national market are substantial in relation to available resources. To be successful with this strategy, the segments served must be sufficiently large and stable.

Strategy 2 — characterized by market concentration and segment diversification — requires a product line which can appeal to different segments. The strategy is particularly effective when there are significant economies of scale in promotion (e.g., umbrella advertising) and distribution, and when the sales potential of the home market and other national markets served is large. Under such conditions, a firm can achieve growth objectives by concentrating on many submarkets within a limited number of national markets.

Strategy 3 — characterized by market diversification and segment concentration — is suitable for firms with a specialized product line and potential customers in many countries. With this strategy, a firm frequently can use a similar product and promotion strategy in all markets. The strategy is particularly effective when the cost of entry into different markets is low relative to available resources. For strategy identification, it is important to note that two firms may follow different expansion strategies with respect to countries and segments (strategy 2 versus strategy 3) yet serve the same total number of market segments at each point in time.

Strategy 4 is based on dual diversification in both segments and markets. This aggressive strategy can be employed by firms with a product line appealing to many segments, and sufficient resources to accomplish a fast entry into many markets. Large international firms with sales offices in many countries frequently use this strategy when they introduce a newly developed or acquired product line. A poorman's version of strategy 4 can sometimes be employed by small firms with limited resources, based on superficial coverage.

Allocation of effort to different markets. Marketing expansion can be achieved by different means. Even a small firm with limited resources can achieve market diversification quickly by using independent commission agents in each market, with little or no investment. In order to identify a specific strategy of market expansion it is, therefore, necessary to specify the overall marketing effort as well as the allocation of effort to different markets.

A sequence of three stages demonstrates successively larger commitments of resources and marketing involvement:

- Export by independent agents
- Sales subsidiary
- Manufacturing subsidiary

The marketing expansion of Volvo into 20 countries between 1929 and 1973 presents an example of all three stages of resource commitment, with two periods of relatively fast diversification occurring prior to and after World War II (Johanson and Wiedersheim, 1975).

The first two stages above specify an essential element of distribution strategy in market expansion. Extensive use of independent agents is frequently associated with market diversification; and a resource commitment to sales subsidiaries is a more likely strategic element of market concentration. Many firms like Volvo prefer to employ independent agents in some markets and sales subsidiaries in others. The relative share of each distribution method is an important strategic option of market expansion.

Distribution strategies do not always portray a correct picture of effort allocation. A firm may invest the same resources in two markets using a different marketing mix and distribution setup. In one market the firm may employ an independent agent backed by substantial promotional activity. In another market the firm may establish a sales subsidiary with a limited promotional budget. A quantitative measure of effort allocation would be more precise for analytical purposes.

Managers inside the firm can determine the overall marketing investment in each market, based on internal accounting. With this information, it is possible to calculate a diversification index that takes into account both the number of markets served and the uniformity of effort distribution.

An effort diversification index for period t, D_{et}, is given by:

$$D_{et} = 1/ \sum_{i=1}^{n_t} ME^2_{i,t}$$

where:

$ME_{i,t}$ = Marketing effort in market i and period t, expressed as a fraction of the firm's total marketing effort for period t.

n_t = total number of markets served in period t.

This index is equal to the total number of markets served $D_{et} = n_t$ when efforts are equally distributed; it approaches a lower bound $D_{et} = 1$ when the firm concentrates most of its effort in a single market.

CONSIDERATIONS AFFECTING THE CHOICE OF MARKET EXPANSION STRATEGY

The selection of market expansion strategy is influenced by characteristics of the product, characteristics of the market, and decision criteria of the firm. Table 44.2 summarizes 10 key product/market factors affecting the choice between market concentration and market diversification. The following discussion explains the effect of each factor on the adoption of market expansion strategy.

1. Sales response function. Two alternative classes of sales response functions – a concave function and an S-curve function – are common in the literature (Kotler, 1971). Graphic examples of these functions are

Table 44.2. Product/Market Factors Affecting Choice Between
Diversification and Concentration Strategies

Product/Market Factor	Prefer Diversification if:	Prefer Concentration if:
1. Sales response function	Concave	S-curve
2. Growth rate of each market	low	high
3. Sales stability in each market	low	high
4. Competitive lead-time	short	long
5. Spill-over effects	high	low
6. Need for product adaptation	low	high
7. Need for communication adaptation	low	high
8. Economies of scale in distribution	low	high
9. Program control requirements	low	high
10. Extent of constraints	low	high

presented in figure 44.2. If the firm believes that it faces a concave response function, there will be a strong motivation to follow a strategy of market diversification. On the other hand, when the response function is assumed to be an S-curve, a market concentration strategy usually is preferred.

The concave response function implies that the best return on marketing effort is at lower levels of effective effort (see figure 44.2). This is based on the assumption that the markets under consideration include a number of clients or submarkets which are particularly interested in the firm's products. Such interest is frequently generated by a unique product or marketing program, possibly the result of substantial investment in R&D. As additional effort is spent, market share increases, but the firm faces stiffer resistance, more skeptical buyers, and increased effort by competitors. Therefore, market response is characterized by diminishing marginal returns and diversification of effort is more productive.

The S-curve response function assumes that small-scale efforts of penetration to a new market are beset by various difficulties and buyers' resistance and will not count for much. Increases in market share and profitability will be achieved only after a substantial concentration in marketing effort is made. This type of response function is likely for products that do not enjoy obvious advantages — which is, of course, the case for most products.

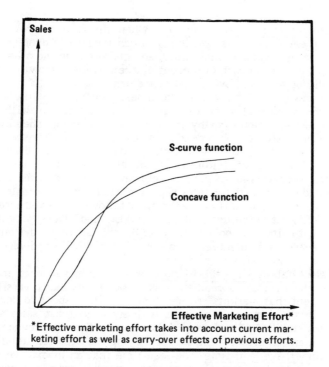

Fig. 44.2. Alternative market share response functions.

A quantitative example of the choice of market expansion under the two sales response assumptions is presented.

Let us assume that the functional form of figure 44.2 is expressed quantitatively, in the following table.

Marketing effort-$	Concave function. Sales-$	S-curve function. Sales-$
100,000	1,000,000	600,000
200,000	1,800,000	1,200,000
300,000	2,400,000	2,400,000

What is the preferred market expansion strategy for a firm which is planning to invest $300,000 of marketing effort in three identical markets? Under consideration are two strategic alternatives: (1) Concentrate all marketing effort in one market; (2) Diversify marketing efforts equally among the three markets (invest $100,000 in each). The outcome of each strategy, depending on the assumed sales response function, will be the following: (preferred strategy indicated by *)

Expansion Strategy	Concave function	S-curve function
1. Concentrate on one market	$2,400,000	$2,400,000*
2. Diversify into three markets	$3,000,000*	$1,800,000

2. Growth rate of each market. When the rate of growth of the industry in each market is low, the firm can frequently achieve a faster growth rate by diversification into many markets. On the other hand, if the rate of market growth in present markets is high, growth objectives can usually be achieved by market concentration.

When the rate of growth of the industry in many markets is high, there are occasional opportunities for diversification with limited resources. Penetration to many markets can be accomplished by relying on marketing efforts of independent sales agents and licensees who are interested in promoting the firm's products in their own growing markets. The case of Miromit, an Israeli producer of unique solar collectors, serves as an example. Following the energy crisis, the firm was flooded by requests for sales representation from interested parties in many countries. In this case, the firm followed a mixed strategy by concentrating its resources in a few markets and diversifying to other markets with little or no investment. By this strategy the number of markets served would increase rapidly, but the effort diversification index would show a slow rate of growth.

3. Sales stability in each market. When demand in each market is unstable, the firm can spread the risk through judicious diversification. To the extent that markets are independent with respect to demand, an increase in the number of markets is likely to increase sales stability. When sales stability in each market is high, the firm can concentrate its market expansion effort while still satisfying the need for stability.

4. Competitive lead-time. The lead-time that an innovative firm has over competitors and potential imitators is an important consideration in selecting a market expansion strategy. When competitive lead-time is short and there is a major advantage to being first in a market with an innovation, there is a strong motivation to follow the route of diversification. In this situation, the firm faces a favorable response function for a limited period. The urgency to enter many markets quickly is diminished if the innovative firm has a long lead-time, or when there is no innovative advantage.

5. Spill-over effects. Spill-over of marketing effort or goodwill from present to new markets is another factor favoring diversification. This spill-over effect can be the result of geographical proximity, cultural influence, or commercial ties. It is common in TV and radio coverage of close national markets. There is obviously a strong motivation to take advantage of spill-over effects by diversifying into new markets which are influenced by current and past effort in presently-served markets.

6. Need for product adaptation. The experience curve phenomenon of systematic reduction in variable cost with an increase in accumulated production volume has a major impact on international market share strategy (Rapp, 1973). Firms that grow faster than their competitors are able to reduce production costs faster and as a result enjoy a major competitive advantage. When the same product is sold in different international markets, market expansion is not only a vehicle for diversification and new profit opportunities, but it also can increase profits by reducing costs in currently-served markets.

Frequently, a company cannot sell the same product in all international markets. There is a need to adapt the product to the standards and regulations of a new country, as well as to the special tastes and preferences of new consumers. The magnitude and nature of the adaptation costs are an important consideration in choosing an expansion strategy. In particular, a firm should assess whether adaptation to new markets requires only a small fixed investment or whether a major change is necessary. If entry into new international markets requires major changes in the production process, the company will not only have to invest a significant amount before entry, but will probably be unable to enjoy the full cost advantage of accumulated experience. In this case there will be a lesser motivation to expand geographically than in the case of an investment that has positive effects on potential economies in production.

7. Need for communication adaptation. Adaptation may be necessary not only for the product, but also for the marketing or communication program. In many situations, the communication program is more important than the technical specifications of the product. In a recent study of international expansion of U.S. franchise systems, 59 percent of the 80 respondent firms indicated alteration in strategy upon entry into international markets (Hackett, 1976). Twenty-five percent of the firms reported a change in product (or service) to fit local tastes, while all other changes were related to communication adaptation. If communication adaptation requires a large investment in consumer and advertising research and in production of new programs, the temptation to follow a diversification strategy is diminished.

8. Economies of scale in distribution. When distribution cost is a significant expense and there are economies of scale with increased market share, there is motivation to follow a concentration strategy. A strategy of rapid expansion into many new markets can frequently increase distribution costs substantially as a result of increased transportation distance and a low level of sales over a large territory. Efficient distribution can, however, be achieved in different ways depending on the product and specific channels. For example, it is possible that diversification with respect to countries and concentration with respect to segments (strategy 3 in Table 44.1) can lead to an efficient distribution system.

9. Program control requirements. Extensive requirements for control are typical of custom-made and sophisticated products and services which require close and frequent communication between headquarters (R&D, production, marketing) and clients. The cost of managerial communication with clients and agents, per unit of sales, is likely to increase with the number of markets served. A comparison of average contact costs in concentrated and diversified markets suggests that the difference in favor of a concentrated market is increasing with the number of contacts (Bucklin, 1966). We can, therefore, expect that when the program control requirements are extensive, a concentrated strategy of market expansion will have an advantage.

10. Constraints. There are a number of constraints on management action in international markets. External constraints include import and currency barriers created by government authorities in the target markets. There may also be difficulties in finding or developing an effective sales and distribution organization. Internal constraints are based on the availability of resources in order to function in new markets. Trained managers and salesmen may be limited, financial resources may be scarce, and production factors may be in short supply.

In the previously mentioned study of international expansion of franchise systems, respondents were asked to rank problems encountered in international markets (Hackett, 1976). The five most important problems were: (1) host government regulations and red tape, (2) high import duties and taxes in foreign environments, (3) monetary uncertainties and royalty retribution to franchisor, (4) logistical problems inherent in operation of international franchise systems, and (5) control of franchisees. The spectacular rate of international market expansion, and the reported plans for further expansion by the respondent firms, indicate that these obstacles were surmountable in most cases. This was partly due to a strategy based on franchisee-owned outlets, which is a form of diversification with limited resources.

External or internal constraints place a limit on the capability or the profitability of market diversification. While some constraints can be overcome, extensive barriers in many markets will lead to market concentration.

APPLICATION

Selecting a market expansion strategy based on the product/market factors of Table 44.2 is bound to raise a few application questions. These questions can be clarified by reviewing the case of a leading electronics manufacturer in Israel (name withheld at request of company executives). The firm is a subsidiary of a large and internationally known American firm. Two relatively sophisticated product lines are being exported: communication equipment and control systems. The communication equipment was developed by the parent company while the control systems were developed in Israel. Table 44.3 and figure 44.3 present, for each product line, a summary analysis of the product/market factors and market expansion graphs.

One question of application is illustrated by Table 44.3. The 10 factors do not point in one direction; some imply market diversification, while others imply market concentration. To clarify the dilemma: (1) Management must weigh the relative importance of the product/market factors in selecting a strategy. Although some factors such as the sales response function will be important in all cases, the relative importance of other factors such as distribution cost are likely to change from case to case. (2) The concepts of market concentration and market diversification should be viewed in relative terms. Occasionally, the choice between concentration and diversification is not

Table 44.3. Case Study: Analysis of Product/Market Factors
by Product Line

Product/Market Factor	Communication Equipment		Control Systems	
	Direction	Implied Strategy	Direction	Implied Strategy
1. Sales response function	Concave	D	S-curve	C
2. Growth rate of each market	High	C	High	C
3. Sales stability in each market	Low	D	High	C
4. Competitive lead-time	Long	C	Long	C
5. Spill-over effects	High	D	Low	C
6. Need for product adaptation	Low	D	High	C
7. Need for communication adaptation	Low	D	High	C
8. Economies of scale in distribution	Low	D	Low	D
9. Program control requirements	High	C	High	C
10. Extent of constraints	High	C	Low	D

clear-cut in absolute terms and a middle course should be selected. In comparison with extreme alternatives, however, the strategic choice is clear.

In the case of control systems most factors point to a concentrated strategy (Table 44.3); the firm followed this strategy with respect to both markets and segments. The direction implied by the factors for communication equipment is more mixed, and the firm followed a middle of the road strategy of "prudent" diversification, or fairly rapid concentrated expansion. The strategy was diversified with respect to segments. Figure 44.3 demonstrates that the expansion of the communication equipment is much more diversified relative to the concentrated expansion of the control systems.

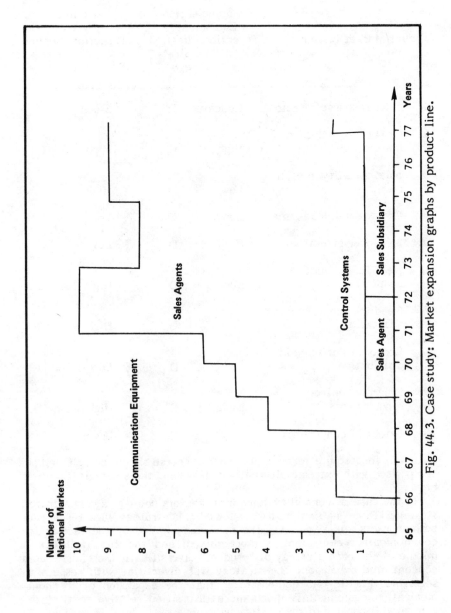

Fig. 44.3. Case study: Market expansion graphs by product line.

A second question of application also can be clarified by reference to the case. A summary analysis like Table 44.3 assumes that the markets under consideration are quite similar and that the effects of the product/market factors can be estimated prior to entry. This is not always the case, as can be seen by the withdrawal from two communication equipment markets in 1973 (figure 44.3).

A few points should be made in response to this question: (1) A summary table, like 44.3, is applicable to a group of similar markets. When different groups of markets are being considered, it is advantageous to analyze each group separately, since a different expansion strategy may be appropriate for each group.

(2) An investment in market research prior to entry can reduce uncertainty, but not eliminate it. Penetration into international markets which are politically and economically unstable is liable to produce surprises with changing events. This was the case with the communication equipment that was introduced into developing Asian and African markets.

(3) A firm may prefer to acquire information by actual testing in the marketplace, rather than by costly and prolonged market survey prior to entry. This policy is particularly applicable when quick entry is important, or when market diversification with limited resources is employed. Abandonment of some markets, following testing, is quite likely under this policy.

(4) Market expansion is a discrete process based on a market by market entry. It is therefore possible and desirable to view it as a learning process, and to correct strategic decisions as more information becomes available. Thus, after three unsatisfactory years in one market, the firm decided to switch from a sales agent to a sales subsidiary, and a second market was penetrated only after eight years of international experience with the product line.

In spite of necessary corrective action, a different and distinct long-term strategy for each product line was pursued, but each was consistent with the evaluation of the product/market factors.

CONCLUSION

The framework for planning and evaluating market expansion strategies presented in this paper focuses on the rate of entry into new markets and the allocation of effort among these markets. It can be used in national or regional marketing, but has special relevance for international expansion. As such it can aid multinational marketing in several ways:

● It helps management specify market expansion alternatives for decision making purposes. In addition to the comparison of the two major and opposing strategies – market concentration and market diversification – the paper aids in defining additional strategic options. By considering market segments within national markets, four viable market expansion strategies are identified (see Table 44.1). By considering resource commitments to new markets, three strategic options are specified and many more are implied.

● It helps management to systematically analyze the problem of choice among the major alternative strategies. Ten key factors affecting this choice are summarized in Table 44.2, discussed in some detail in the body of the paper, and illustrated by examples and a case study. In each application it will be necessary to separately assess each factor and its relative importance for comprehensive evaluation of the alternatives.

● It offers guidance for measuring market expansion. Two specific measures suggested are the number of countries and market segments served, and an effort diversification index, both as a function of time. Measuring market diversification can be used not only for evaluating the firm's own expansion policy, but also for evaluating competitive moves. The factors affecting the choice of strategy can be used to interpret competitive assumptions.

A systematic approach to identification of alternatives, analysis of choice, and performance evaluation will clarify managerial planning and help reduce mistakes and disappointments in expansion to new markets.

REFERENCES

Bucklin, L.P., A Theory of Distribution Channel Structure, IBER Special Publications (Berkeley, CA: Graduate School of Business Administration, University of California, 1966), pp. 49-50.

Hackett, D.W., "The international expansion of U.S. franchise systems: Status and strategies," Journal of International Business Studies, Vol. 7 (Spring, 1976), p. 71.

Johanson, J. and Wiedersheim, Paul F., "The internationalization of the firm – four Swedish cases," The Journal of Management Studies, Vol. 12 (October, 1975), pp. 306-7.

Kotler, Philip, Marketing Decision Making - A Model Building Approach (New York: Holt, Rinehart and Winston, 1971), pp. 31-7.

Rapp, William V., "Strategy formulation and international competition," Columbia Journal of World Business, Vol. 8 (Summer, 1973), pp. 98-112.

45 Strategic Planning in International Marketing

Helmut Becker
Hans B. Thorelli

In the orderly pursuit of any worthwhile endeavor, one requires a plan. While planning involves some inherent risks (one could be proven wrong by subsequent events), it is surely more risky not to plan; a plan forces one to focus on tomorrow. It provides the guideposts for future action toward one's goals, and it serves as a benchmark for evaluating performance. Indeed, without a plan that specifies <u>objectives</u> and provides for the <u>means of getting there</u>, an activity loses much of its purposefulness and direction. One is reminded of the meanderings of <u>Alice in Wonderland</u>, who was advised by the rabbit upon reaching a cross-roads, "If you don't know where you want to go, it really doesn't matter which way you turn."

Few marketing managers would compare themselves with <u>Alice</u>, though some may be "wandering" just as aimlessly. Business firms can be found at any position on the planning continuum, from simply "muddling through," to highly formalized planning, from relying on intuition to utilizing sophisticated simulation models, from "seats-of-the-pants" judgments to detailed tactical and strategic projections for the short and long term.

Not to underestimate its complexity, the planning <u>process</u> in international marketing is nevertheless rather similar to its domestic counterpart. A course of action is drawn up which incorporates all the aspects of deploying the instruments connected with the marketing of a product or service. According to J.A. Howard, the typical marketing plan has these elements:

1. description of the situation: where are we? (situation analysis).
2. identification of problems and opportunities in the situation.
3. definition of objectives of the plan: where do we want to be?
4. forecasting sales and estimating cost and profit contribution.
5. designing the marketing program (strategic planning).
6. estimating the necessary appropriations (budgeting).

While some may consider the determination of objectives as the first step and perhaps at the heart of the planning process, as in "management by objectives," others believe that strategy aspects are the most important. Regardless of which has the greater appeal, the important point to remember is that planning is an iterative process that requires constant monitoring, redefinition, adaptation, and re-evaluation of objectives and strategy, implementation and control in an effort to obtain maximum payoff from ever-changing marketing opportunities.

Despite the parallels to domestic marketing, planning in the international sphere is both more difficult and indispensible. For effective marketing there is a need for organizational coordination between all the firm functions. Though this may sound like a trifling truism at home, coordination is an absolute must in international marketing that can only be achieved through a well-thought-out plan. This is so because international markets are a lot more heterogeneous, and they contain far more unknowns. Only at the risk of courting disaster would the international marketer enter a foreign country without a well-laid plan. While the plan does not guarantee anything, it does increase the likelihood of success and it does help pinpoint pitfalls to avoid in the future.

This is not a Reading on "how" to plan. Rather, the approach taken here is to condense a large number of writings into summary matrix and checklist form. This is done to assist the busy executive in deciding "what" to plan for when entering international markets. There are five international marketing decisions that must be made and planned for:

1. The commitment decision: Given the firm's home market position and resource base, are foreign market opportunities attractive enough to mobilize an international marketing effort?
2. The country-selection decision: Which of several country alternatives is (or are) most attractive for selection as potential international target markets?
3. Mode of entry and operations: Which is the best way of entering the foreign market(s) chosen and conducting the firm's operations in them?
4. Marketing mix decision: Which of the various marketing instruments are most effective in the foreign market environment and in which combination?
5. Marketing organization decision: What is the best way for coordinating multinational marketing decisions, to retain centralized control with maximum local flexibility?

Strategic planning in international marketing comprises these five decision areas. As in marketing in general, international marketing planning is an iterative process. That is, the commitment decision cannot be made in isolation without reference to the possible target countries and the mode of entry, and vice versa. The specific combination of marketing tools being planned for, in turn, depends on the mode of entry and operations, as well as on the country or countries involved. The appropriate marketing organization to coordinate international decisions is greatly influenced by and interactive with all the other planning steps. In each case the major requirement is that objectives and strategy are fused with market structure in the local environment, all the while being coordinated globally.

The way in which the international marketing plan is approached in this reading is by combining the general planning steps with the major international decisions that must be made. This has been done in the international marketing planning matrix in figure 45.1. Each cell in the matrix represents a step in the overall planning process. While some of the planning steps or cells may seem redundant, they in fact should be looked at as being part of the iterative review process between all the planning stages that should be continued until the final planning document is completed. The matrix, then, is designed to provide the planning framework for international marketing strategy. The detailed planning variables for each international marketing decision are listed in Checklists A through E constituting the balance of this Reading.

Besides offering a planning framework, the Reading serves the dual purpose of integrating the materials in this volume. Thus it is natural that we shall apply the ecologic view in presenting our checklists. For a detailed restatement of the ecologic concept of marketing the reader is referred to Reading 1. Briefly, it admonishes the planner to look at the firm's resources ("what are we good at?") and objectives ("what do we want to become?") and to analyze the environment for opportunities and restrictions ("what current or potential customer needs could our firm most effectively satisfy?"). The means of relating the environment (and in it notably the market structure) to the firm's objectives and resources is marketing strategy. Along with this volume's central theme, the key challenge in business planning is to harmonize market structure and marketing strategy.

It should be clear against this background that the checklists are illustrative, not normative. They make no pretense of restating "principles of international marketing management," but they should serve well as bases of reference to practical decision-makers. In any given business situation some of the factors referred to will almost surely seem irrelevant, and some variables not even mentioned here may be highly important. The checklists are not substitutes for executive judgement and experience.

Three comments about the checklists are in order. First, while there is hopefully a logical ordering among the various steps indicated on the lists we are not implying that they should necessarily be handled in numerical order. For example, in a given case it may be preferable to begin by an examination of objectives rather than of resources. Second, while the order between the steps is not so important it is indeed vital that there is feedback among all of them. For instance, it would clearly be suicidal to define a set of objectives without any reference to the operating environment. Third, it will be desirable at many junctures in the planning process – especially if it relates to an LDC – to include an estimate of the reliability and likely error margins of data employed.

INTERNATIONAL DECISIONS	Situation Analysis	Problems-Opportunity Analysis	MARKETING PLANNING VARIABLES			
			Objectives	Marketing Program	Marketing Budgets	Sales Vol. Cost/Profit Estimate
A. Commitment Decision						
B. Country Selection						
C. Mode of Entry						
D. Marketing Strategy						
E. Marketing Organization						

Fig. 45.1. International marketing planning matrix.

Of the five checklists presented, Checklist A relates to the international commitment decision. Before a serious planning effort for an operation in any given country can be undertaken it seems logical to assume that a commitment decision of some kind has to be made, based on a preliminary analysis of various candidate countries. Assuming this has been done, Checklist B provides guidelines for selection of target markets among several alternative countries. Given the commitment to enter one or several specific countries, Checklist C helps specify the mode of market entry and operations. Checklist D details the instruments that comprise the initial marketing program. The marketing mix must obviously be tailored to a chosen country and the mode of local market entry. Checklist E, finally, summarizes some of the aspects of organization and coordination that are so important to success in international marketing. Important ingredients of an effective performance audit are included as well.

The first-time marketing program that evolves should be flexible and regarded as preliminary. Due to the rapidity of change in international markets, an opportunity today may quickly turn into a problem or liability tomorrow. The appropriate time horizon will depend, of course, on such additional factors as the type of product, extent of commitment, the country involved, the financial strength of the firm, predictability of the local market environment, and other variables.

CHECKLIST A: THE INTERNATIONAL COMMITMENT DECISION

This Checklist summarizes the factors to be considered when making the international commitment decision. The decision should be based on sound reasons for entering foreign markets. The firm's own resource base needs to be examined as do the company's objectives and philosophy. A preliminary analysis of various candidate countries and the type and extent of the commitment round out this decision area.

A.1. Reasons to enter markets abroad
    11. Enquiries received from abroad
    12. Domestic market saturation
        (follow international product life cycle. See Reading 19)
    13. Greater profitability
        (margin greater and/or strong demand)
    14. Preempt competition
    15. Excess liquidity
    16. Going international as means of growth preferable to product diversification, acquisitions, market expansion, etc., at home
    17. Better utilization of current resources and differential advantage (capitalizing on synergy)
    18. Temporary overcapacity or excess or obsolescent inventory
    19. Opportunity for barter (see Reading 7)
    20. Securing sources of supply

A.2. Own resources
    21. Domestic operations "under control"
        (going international rarely a good escape from domestic problems)
    22. Sources of differential advantage
        221. High quality image
        222. Cost leadership
        223. Manpower skills
        224. Patents
        225. High liquidity
        226. Marketing know-how

A.3. Own objectives and philosophy (see also Reading 1)
    31. Growth rate
    32. Means of growth (growth in current products vs. unrelated products, finance growth from within, attitude toward acquisitions and mergers)
    33. Desirable sources of differential advantage
    34. Profitability, return on investment required
    35. Risk preferences
    36. Liquidity preferences
    37. Market share desired, etc.

A.4. Type of country preferred
    41. Industrialized West, Japan
    42. LDC
    43. East Bloc

A.5. Type and extent of commitment (see Reading 33)

As to the type of country preferred, predictability, relatively low risk, excellent infrastructure, firm-to-firm transactions, relative absence of government intervention in individual transactions, stiff competition and moderate to good profits are signposts of the industrialized democracies. The LDC's typically evidence lower predictability; fairly high risk, poor infrastructure, high rates of inflation, a dual economy (large primitive, smaller modern sector), frequent government intervention in individual transactions, an environment of regulations which is somewhat flexible (negotiated concessions, tariff exemptions, etc.), modest competition, good to excellent profit perspectives to firms really understanding local conditions, and the challenge of contributing to human welfare more than elsewhere. East Bloc countries are highly unpredictable until a contract is signed but thereafter traditionally very reliable trading partners; they offer low after-sales risk, poor infrastructure (but distribution is the buyer's problem), firm-to-state transactions, no contact with end consumers, great demands for credit, a highly legalistic bureaucracy, typically either very heavy or almost no competition (you are the chosen instrument), somewhat unpredictable profitability (especially due to impossibility of predicting pre-contract selling costs), at least in the past high risks of piracy or grossly insufficient compensation for patents, designs, and other industrial property rights, interest thus far essentially in industrial products, and technical know-how.

Some firms prefer to limit their initial search to countries where English or some other world language is widely spoken in business circles.

CHECKLIST B: THE COUNTRY-SELECTION DECISION

Assuming the commitment to go international has been made and the preferred type of country has been identified, specific country analyses must be performed. Unless there are special reasons or circumstances pointing to a given country, several candidate countries of the favored type should be separately examined by means of a comparative framework that comprises both the international and local environments. At the local level the country analysis includes the government, business culture, marketing infrastructure, and demand analysis. Finally, the country-specific financial requirements and time dimensions must be considered.

B.1. International environment
    11. Relationships between home office country and country X
    12. Tariffs in country X
    13. Nontariff barriers in country X
    14. Currency stability and currency controls
    15. Transportation costs

B.2. Local marketing environment
    21. Government stability
    22. Predictability of public policy
    23. Economic development, growth rate, development policies
    24. Sensitivity to business cycles, rate of inflation
    25. Government controls and regulations
        251. Regulation of competitive practices, antitrust enforcement
        252. State marketing bodies
        253. Health and safety
        254. Product labeling, standardization, consumer information, and disclosure requirements
    26. Local business culture
        261. Philosophy of competition and cooperation
        262. Extent of cartelization
        263. Respect for contracts
        264. Business ethics
    27. Marketing infrastructure
        271. Data availability and reliability
        272. Marketing research agencies

273. Literacy
274. Advertising media
275. Advertising agencies
276. Public warehousing facilities
277. Extent and reliability of postal and telephone systems
278. Transportation facilities and costs

B.3. Market structure and demand analysis (for additional details see Readings 1 and 17)
31. Consumer behavior (buying and usage patterns and patterns of symbolic significance, life styles, distribution of household expenditures)
32. Distributors and margins
33. Price range
34. Product variations
35. Competitors by size and type
36. Competitive strategies
37. Potential competition
38. Local stage of product life cycle
39. Market potential, short and long term

B.4. Financial estimates
41. Short term
411. Investment need
412. Sales volume forecast
413. Profitability estimate, return on investment
42. Long term

CHECKLIST C: MARKET ENTRY AND OPERATIONS

This checklist helps determine the appropriate mode of market entry, the first part of the international operations plan. It is essential that the plan incorporate the general assumptions and specific forecasts on which it is based and that it be prepared in written form, especially if it is a first or "initial" plan. Without these essentials there is no built-in signal system for if and when the plan needs to be revised, nor can a plan lacking in these prerequisites rationally be used as an instrument of delegation, coordination, and evaluation of managerial performance.

If there is anything behavioral science has proven it is that, in Western cultures at least, enthusiastic execution of decisions presupposes some degree of involvement in the preceding decision-making process. Thus, planning cannot be simply delegated to a staff specialist in an obscure corner of the organization. Line executives will rarely have the time to do much of the data-gathering job; however, it is essential that they regularly partake in the actual shaping of the plan.

For the sake of simplicity we shall assume that the decision has been made to begin marketing operations in an LDC on a modest scale (no local production). Once an ongoing operation has been established the preparation of a marketing plan would be similar to that of making a domestic marketing plan; the main difference would be the incorporation of matters involving relationships with headquarters and any operations in third countries.

C.1. Objectives
11. Sales volume expected during initial period
12. Profitability, return on investment (note: the larger the scale of operations, the more likely negative profits during a build-up period.)
13. Permissible risk exposure
14. Going in for a fast profit and then leave vs. aiming for a lasting commitment
15. Philosophy of ownership vs. joint ventures, etc.
16. Complete adaptation vs. acting as local change agent
17. Data feedback for future decisions:
Test marketing or other marketing research, acquisition of data to determine desirability and form of long-term commitment – all the while keeping costs of data generation and analysis in mind.
18. Justification of local objectives in terms of overall company objectives (e.g., role in "portfolio" of businesses, Reading 38)

C.2. International environment
See Checklist B, item B.1.

C.3. Local marketing environment
31. See Checklist B, item B.2
32. Local government view of our kind of product
33. Could we – and should we – obtain favored treatment from government?

C.4. Market structure and demand analysis
41. See Checklist B, item B.3. (see also Readings 1 and 17)
42. Detailed industry and company sales forecast

C.5. Resources
51. Expected sources of differential advantage
(see Checklist A, item A.2.22)
52. Local validity of own patents and trademarks
53. Availability of company personnel with prior local experience
54. Tasks to be performed by company, tasks to be contracted out: marketing research, advertising, distribution may all be contracted out, if desired, given sufficient local infrastructure.
55. Available sources of supply relative to expected sales volume. Supply from headquarters or from other subsidiaries or from outside firms. Adequacy of sources and their ability to adjust to possible fluctuations in demand.

C.6. Mode of market entry (see Reading 33 for additional details)
    61. Domestic exports
    62. Direct exports through outside distribution channels
    63. Direct exports and sales through local sales branch
    64. Licensing, assembling, or basic manufacturing at local level
    65. Joint venturing
    66. International leasing, etc.

CHECKLIST D: MARKETING STRATEGY AND PROGRAM

Assuming the international commitment decision has been made, the country or countries selected, and the most likely mode of entry determined, this checklist numerates the strategic aspects in the overall marketing plan. These include the underlying strategic concept, rationale, general thrust, and consideration of appropriate and matching marketing mix variables.

D.1. Strategy
    11. Overall concept (Gestalt) of our international marketing strategy. Strategy should be explicitly related to local objectives and to our notion of differential advantage. Include definition of market niche, if nichemanship is sought. Deluxe image vs. mass marketer; low profile vs. beating the drum, etc.
    12. Rationale for contemplated differentiation from domestic strategy, if any. Such deviations are often desirable or even inevitable. As they do lessen synergy their justification should, however, be made explicit.
    13. Homogenization or heterogenization of local demand

D.2. Marketing mix implications of strategy
    21. Product: options, models to be marketed, modifications for local market, if any. Product simplification, invention (see also Readings 21 and 23).
    22. Price: skimming vs. penetration. Price relative to current and potential competition; price relative to our policies elsewhere. If price very high compared to domestic due to tariffs, freight, high distributor margins, etc., justify belief that it will be accepted locally. If planned local price is very low, contemplate side-effects on company operations elsewhere (see also Reading 25).
    23. Promotion and intelligence: budget, theme, media, timing. If major resources to be committed, include plan for measurement of promotional effectiveness. Feedback from the marketplace, marketing research (see Readings 21 and 28)

24. Distribution channels
    241. Mode of market entry, see Checklist C, item C.6.
    242. Functions to be performed by channel members or distributors
    243. Margins, promotional allowances (if any)
    244. Short term vs. long term commitments. Note possible need for future flexibility.
25. Post-transaction service
    251. Service and warranty system
    252. Spare parts: locally manufactured or procured vs. imported from home country or subsidiary
    253. Handling of customer complaints
26. Trust: plan for the build-up of goodwill and customer confidence. The larger the operation and the longer its time perspective the more important is trust (see also Reading 1).

CHECKLIST E: INTERNATIONAL MARKETING ORGANIZATION

To bring the plan into fruition requires adequate marketing organization. Checklist E includes among organizational factors the type and nature of coordination between headquarters and international units, scheduling, performance evaluation (audit), and preview of subsequent planning periods.

E.1. Headquarters services and coordination
    11. Manpower allocation at headquarters (HQ) and overseas
    12. Organizational adjustments at HQ, if any
    13. Identification of areas of HQ direction, assistance and consultation. Areas of local autonomy.
    14. Reporting arrangements
    15. Pricing and other policies for intra-company transfers

E.2. Schedules
    21. Step-by-step timing of activities and the attainment of subtargets. PERT or flow diagram techniques may be helpful here.
    22. Budgeting
        221. Master budget
        222. Projected profit and loss statements for each reporting period
        223. Proforma balance sheets for each reporting period
        224. Cash flow projections in each reporting period

E.3. Action potential at the end of the planning period.
    This is an advance audit of operational performance, assuming full realization of the plan. At the end of the period a post-audit should be undertaken, including re-evaluation of the commitment decision and its future implications. These management audits should comprise items of the type indicated below:

31. Resource profile, including personnel skills
32. Differential advantage
33. Data about the market structure and demand
34. Trust and goodwill
35. Patents and trademarks
36. Standing arrangements with local suppliers and customers
37. Competitive position
38. Performance relative to budget
39. Performance relative to other aspects of objectives and plan
40. Impact on host country (see Reading 46)

E.4. Contingency plan: contingency planning is the standby plan for emergencies. It may be a strike, an import prohibition, a currency devaluation, failure to obtain local financing if planned for, or simply the fact that some vital assumption about the future might be mistaken. Take a cue from the military and put down some ideas on how to meet likely contingencies.

E.5. Long term plan: assuming that the substance of the initial plan will be realized, the long term plan should at least present a sketch of the next three to five years. In abbreviated form the framework suggested above would be equally suited to the long term plan.

46 Performance Audits: The MNC through the Glasses of the LDC*
Hans B. Thorelli

The multinational corporation, MNC as we know it today, is essentially a product of the twentieth century. Young as MNCs are, many of them have had time to experience an entire life cycle from birth to death in one or several less developed countries (LDC), a drama proceeding from princely welcome to ignominious expulsion – with or without reasonable compensation (Table 46.1). It should be clear that nobody really "wins" from this outcome of the contest. The mutual interests of the participants call for not a drama but a partnership.

It has become customary to talk about the desirability of such a partnership in the last two decades. Yet it must be stated frankly that during that same period the ante has been "upped" considerably on the MNC wishing to operate in the spirit of partnership. The prime factor has been the proliferation of nations (from about 100 in 1945 to about 150 today) and the concomitant intensification of nationalism, especially (and perhaps inevitably) in the new nations. Today more than ever before in modern times the world political scene reminds us of medieval Europe. A second factor has been the proliferation of MNCs themselves, a factor which has enhanced competition and further reduced the bargaining position of the individual MNC relative to any given host country. Naturally, the competition within its borders of scores of MNC subsidiaries is generally highly beneficial to an LDC, a fact completely forgotten in contemporary discussions in United Nation circles. We are just beginning to see the force of a third factor changing the climate of MNC operations perhaps even more drastically; namely, the emergence of the Third World as a bloc of nations ready to assert its will relative to both the industrially advanced countries and the MNCs, viewed as the offspring of the industrialized world.

---

*Based on the author's article, The Multinational Corporation: Accounting and Social Implications (Urbana, Ill.: Center for International Education and Research in Accounting, Department of Accountancy, 1977).

Table 46.1. Classical Drama of Multinational Business

Country Measures	Role of Country	Role of Company
Tax lures, concessions	Supplicant	Dictator
Import privileges on machinery, import restrictions on competitive goods	Junior partner	Master
"Strict" law enforcement	Arms-length	Arms-length
Discriminatory law enforcement, changes in concession contracts in favor of government	Master	Junior partner
Regulation, restrictions on remittance of profits or capital	Dictator	Supplicant

Note: The final state might be expulsion – with or without reasonable compensation.
Source: Hans B. Thorelli, "The multinational corporation as a change agent," Southern Journal of Business (July 1966), pp. 1-9.

Whatever the nature of the partnership or accommodation of the future, a periodic revaluation of the relationship is most likely to become a standard operating procedure. Interestingly, Cummins Engine Company, Inc., is one of the concerns which even now conducts an annual internal corporate responsibility audit for each overseas operation.

This paper will deal with the evaluation of the MNC from the viewpoint of the LDC. It almost goes without saying that the MNC would be remiss if it did not also evaluate the LDC. Naturally, there are also many other stakeholders interested in evaluating the MNC, such as third-party LDCs, the home country, stockholders, customers, employees, creditors in various countries, competitors, and so forth. The discussion will be directed first to economic performance and practices, the area of almost exclusive interest in classic evaluation of managerial prowess. The "social indicators movement" suggests that the idea of a management audit must not be thus narrowly confined. This is certainly true in the LDCs. Thus, a second part of the paper is devoted to externalities and social performance.

ECONOMIC PERFORMANCE AND PRACTICES

Earnings and Remittances

Consolidated earnings per share or a statement of consolidated return on investment (ROI) as a measure of performance might satisfy a Milton Friedman but almost certainly not an LDC. Its authorities would naturally like to know about the profitability of operations of the local subsidiary stated in accordance with local accounting practice. But this is not nearly enough. First, it might look askance at very high rates of profit as presumed evidence of undue exploitation rather than of superior performance, especially so if most of the surplus has been remitted to the home country. Admittedly, nowadays this kind of a showing would be confined largely to companies using the strategy of FIFO — that is, "Fast In, Fast Out!" For better or worse, such firms literally may be able "to get away with it" before the ex-host country even becomes aware of what went on, much like some fly-by-night operators do inside every country.

Second, the LDC is apt to be more impressed by a stable than by a great growth in earnings. In this respect they are more like Europeans than Americans. Clearly, such an attribute may have implications as to inventory evaluation and the creation of hidden reserves of a distinctly un-American character. Third, the LDC will tend to evaluate earnings data relative to the extent of local participation in ownership of the MNC subsidiary. Too, remittances to the home country tend to be a good deal more palatable if local owners are also getting a share of profits.

Minimum Performance Specified by Host Country

In most industrialized nations there are few, if any, minimum requirements as to economic performance imposed by government on the great majority of companies operating in the "private" sector. Many LDCs, on the other hand, take the view that companies — or, at least, companies of foreign origin — should meet certain minimum performance requirements in areas of special interest to the host country in return for local operating privileges. As is typical of LDC approaches to regulation, such requirements usually are not applied in a uniform manner, the prescriptions varying not only on an industry-by-industry but also on a company-by-company basis.

Requirements of this kind involve such matters as minimum (occasionally maximum) level of physical output, minimum quotient of exports of processed goods, maximum quotient or quantity of exports of non-processed raw materials, and minimum percentages of local materials and labor used in end products. The host country is increasingly concerned also with some of the multinational business practices which in large measure influence the result of the local subsidiary. We are thinking primarily of a variety of corporate tax, currency translation, transfer, and pricing policies. Taken together, these are some of the principal everyday means by which the MNC tries to apply a global perspective of coordination in order to avoid country-by-country sub-optimization in its far-flung operations. These are areas where the interests (at least, short-term) of the MNC and any single host country could be – and frequently are – at odds. The practices involved are sufficiently important to warrant separate comment.

Taxes

Barring undue political risks and constraints on remittances the natural preference of the MNC is to so regulate its internal relations and transactions that it shows high profits in countries with low tax rates and vice versa. This is a frequent empirical observation. Indeed in our own International Operations Simulation – a sophisticated MNC strategy exercise in the management game form – the attention of participating student teams is generally quickly drawn to the possibilities inherent in the differences in local tax rates, loss carryover provisions, and so forth, without any prodding from the administrator of the simulation.

Be it in real life or in the context of a strategy exercise, what seems to the MNC like conservative management of resources, to an LDC with a relatively high tax rate may appear as tax evasion. Clearly, there is room for legitimate differences of opinion as to what are reasonable tax behaviors and policies. The point is that the MNC is well advised not to take undue advantage of the possible naivete of the tax people in an LDC host country. Sooner or later the truth will come out, at which time it is only too easy – in the world in which we find ourselves – for the government to exercise its wrath.

Exchange Rates

European as well as American MNCs in recent years have had ample experience of the hazards of exchange rate fluctuations. To take but one European example, the Ericsson Telephone Corporation of Sweden in 1974 reported $29 million and in 1975 some $18 million "exchange losses charged to operations," principally to the Brazilian subsidiary. These large figures should be seen in relation to consolidated earnings before taxes for this MNC, which in each of these years hovered around $100 million. Clearly, the LDC will have an interest in how the MNC deals with currency fluctuations.

Let us first recognize the distinction between translation and conversion. Translation refers to the process of restating financial accounts from one currency to another. Conversion is the actual sale of one currency for another. Being simulated rather than actual exchange of currency, translation is inherently a matter of judgment. Several conventions exist as to how translation may be executed, each with its set of advantages and disadvantages. Of special concern to the LDC should be the fact that unfavorable translation rates may impede the ability of the local subsidiary to obtain future allocations of MNC resources, at least in the short term.

Involving actual exchange, conversion may be less controversial. However, when conversion has taken place at black market rates — typically with the implicit acquiescence of the local government — the LDC may have an interest in the actual rate not being disclosed.

Intracompany Transfers

The conditions surrounding the transfer of materials, components, and finished products across national borders between various units of the MNC are in principle — though often not in practice — a matter of internal discretion, whether it be exercised centrally or locally. Too often we tend to think of absolute price as the only relevant variable here. But as in all other marketing activity -- and this is what we are talking about in such transfers — there are other considerations. Income, value added and sales taxes, and tariff duties are examples.

The price of materials relative to components and final products, and of components relative to final products, is another important variable affecting local performance as well as the balance between global optimization and local suboptimization. However irrational it may be from a global or even long-term local viewpoint, the pressure from LDCs is invariably in the direction of maximum local processing. MNCs in the future may expect increasingly to have to back up demonstrations of the reasonableness of relative prices with formal and sophisticated make-or-buy analyses in cases of imports of less than finally processed goods. Even so, we all know that strictly economic concerns will not always prevail.

Related to price is the use of accounts receivable (or, conversely, of prepayments) as means of extending intracompany credit, or to delay or advance international remittances and conversion of currencies. Here again, a strategy prompted by global considerations may not be viewed by an individual LDC as in its best interest.

Another aspect of intracompany marketing involves applications engineering, installation work, and the provision of patents and know-how. Such transfer of technology may obviously be of great value to the LDC. Sometimes the services involved constitute part of the purchase of goods; sometimes, they are paid for separately. This brings us to the general area of services payments.

Beyond the examples just mentioned payments are often made between units of an MNC (as indeed between units of many large domestic companies) for general management services, for marketing research, for executive development programs, for intracompany loans, and other services. Many an LDC may wish to establish whether such payments really are for bona fide services, or merely represent means of withdrawing funds and/or avoiding local taxes.

Accounting and Financial Reporting Systems

The financial reporting systems of the MNC must respond to at least three related but distinct sets of needs. There are the needs of conforming to the accounting practices and the reporting expectations of host countries. There are the needs of the MNC headquarters for standardization in reporting systems in order to "really" know what is going on and to ensure comparability between subsidiaries. Finally, there are the needs of the MNC for its own sake and for that of tax authorities in the home country to issue consolidated reports.

Without for a moment questioning the need for the development of international accounting standards one may safely predict that for the foreseeable future the variegated needs and stages of economic development among nations will mitigate against any single-system approach to financial reporting in MNCs. Multiple systems are here to stay, although perhaps not for as long as death and taxes! Yet, in any given case, outside parties have a legitimate claim to know just <u>what</u> system has been used. For instance, if there be hidden reserves, we want to know the why and how.

EXTERNALITIES AND SOCIAL INDICATORS

We now turn to social indicators and externalities, that is, areas of social costs and benefits occasioned by corporate action. The last ten years have witnessed a lively discussion of social indicators, externalities, the quality of life, and the associated "social responsibilities of business." The intensity of the debate has been directly correlated with the industrialization and per capita wealth of individual nations.

Beyond a few United Nations documents, surprisingly little of tangible import has been written about social indicators relevant to the LDCs in general and to locally harbored subsidiaries of MNCs in particular. Yet there is a virtually endless range of possible "social performances" of business from the macro to the micro level, from social aspects of the very core of business operations to the grant-in-aid of an art exhibit. Although some issues have been clarified by legislation, there are generally no hard and fast rules regarding accountability and responsibility here. Neither is there any consensus as to what <u>ought</u> to be. Short term, at least, management is typically at liberty to lead or to lag relative to the actual or perceived needs of host countries in many of these areas.

We have chosen two such areas for discussion, both of which are relatively close to the "core" of business operations. One of them may be labeled loosely as "corporate citizenship" (or the MNC as resource transformer and employer) and the other "the MNC as a change agent." It almost goes without saying that there are no distinct borderlines between them.

CORPORATE CITIZENSHIP

Communications

The provision of information to local stakeholder groups is an important means for the MNC to build trust among these publics. In addition to annual reports, governments increasingly require confidential data from all areas of corporate activity. It is a miracle that Washington has not disappeared under the thousands of tons of forms it has commandeered from business. Even so, under the partnership concept it is often a good idea in the LDC voluntarily to furnish the government data that go beyond the requisite minimum. This is especially true in the area of future plans. Voluntary information programs should be directed also to stockholders, employees, the plant community, the press, and so on. Indeed, the more authoritarian and/or unstable the local government the greater the desirability of building rapport with other groups in society. The prudent MNC will increasingly undertake attitude surveys on a regular basis as a means of gauging how well it stays in tune with various publics.

Value Added

Conventionally, the value added is reflected in the difference between the value of the company's sales and that of its purchased inputs on the income statement. This is definitely of interest to the LDC. However, the host country also might well take an interest in how much of all purchases were local in origin. A Nestlé Alimentana S.A. publication provides an example, as indicated in Table 46.2. This kind of tabulation could easily be broken down further by categories of expenses (and sales) and by individual countries.

Employer Practices

The creation of employment opportunities is vital in literally every LDC. Number, compensation, training, promotion, and stability of employment are matters of concern, as is the proportion of local relative to foreign management and professional personnel. Beyond working conditions and health and safety provisions many companies, notably in the extractive industries, face the challenge of providing schools, hospitals, stores, housing, and transportation facilities. In some of these areas the MNC must tread gently in order to avoid charges of paternalism.

It is also important not to forget the employment multiplier effect of many overseas operations. In 1976 Ford España had 244 Spanish suppliers, who had hired 11,000 new workers to handle the Ford business.

Table 46.2. Nestle's Contribution to the Local Economy 1974
(in percentages and millions of Swiss francs, SF)

	Latin America	Africa	Asia	Total
Local expenses				
Purchases (goods and services)	59.3%	38.0%	31.0%	53.1%
Salaries and labor (including social charges)	11.2%	4.2%	4.4%	9.5%
Taxes	10.7%	7.5%	8.5%	10.1%
Total Local Expenses	81.2%	49.7%	43.9%	72.7%
External expenses				
Imports	15.1%	46.6%	51.5%	23.4%
Dividends, interests, and royalties	3.7%	3.7%	4.6%	3.9%
Total External Expenses	18.8%	50.3%	56.1%	27.3%
Grand Total Expenses, SF (100%)	2303.8	212.1	508.9	3024.9
Exports, SF	49.7	81.8	16.4	147.9

Source: Nestlé in the Developing Countries (Vevey, Switzerland: Nestle Alimentana S.A., 1975), p. 14.

Ownership

To some companies, such as Caterpillar Tractor Company and Ford Motor Company, control associated with full ownership of overseas subsidiaries appears as a practical necessity. It well may be. In such instances, local participation in ownership may be stimulated by offering for sale shares in the MNC itself, rather than in the subsidiary. Verily, this is in the spirit of a truly transnational enterprise. Realistically, however, most MNCs encounter strong pressure to provide local capital an opportunity to participate in ownership of local operations. This may take the form of shares in the local subsidiary but also in joint ventures of different types.

Pollution

At the United Nations Conference on the Environment in Stockholm in 1972 many spokesmen for the LDC – warmly applauded by Communist delegates – declared that environmental protection was for the rich and filthy (not necessarily the filthy rich), while development must have priority in the LDC. To the jester this would suggest that the MNC subsidiary generate as much smoke and effluent as convenient, as tangible indicators of industrial progress. Seriously, as the Union Carbide Corporation has noted,

> Responsibility to the environment involves the selection of raw materials and manufacturing processes that have minimum polluting effects, the control of materials and processes to see that prescribed standards are met, and the installation of pollution abatement equipment.

It must be clear, nevertheless, that the constellation of tradeoffs between economy and environmental protection may be different in an already highly industrialized country and in an LDC. Differences in climate, flora, and fauna may also well justify the use of more potent herbicides and pesticides in some LDCs than in the home countries of MNCs. In situations like this the challenge to the MNC is to overcome by educational programs local suspicions that the pursuit of profits is more important to it than the welfare of host countries.

THE MNC AS A CHANGE AGENT

Value Structure

The cosmopolitan corporation should view itself as an agent of change, an agent of progress in LDC host countries. If it fails in this regard, it is likely to become the victim of nationalism. Yet to become an effective change agent the MNC must be a learner as well as a teacher, able to strike the delicate balance of constructive interaction.

By far the most important contribution the MNC can render to the host country is to contribute to a change in attitudes, a change in value structure among all the interest groups it encounters in the course of doing business. This is particularly true as regards consumers. Nothing could be more vital than introducing, and reinforcing, a customer oriented marketing concept. A basic prerequisite to economic development, at least in non-dictatorial nations, is a strengthened individual need to achieve. Modern marketing and merchandizing, by stimulating the individual to set specific goals in the area of property accumulation, and by dramatizing the relationship between effort, savings, and consumption, is a powerful vehicle in the creation of a climate of values conducive to growth.

Local stockholders frequently have to be educated to see the merit of long term corporate perspectives and of some sacrifice in payout for corporate citizenship measures. Employees must be induced to learn new skills, respect the discipline of industry, be concerned with quality as well as quantity of output, respond to economic incentives, and so on. To object that this is the "imperialism of values" is utter nonsense: as all LDCs want economic development they had better adopt some of the values which have proven conducive to such growth.

Corruption

A perennial issue in MNC-LDC relations is corruption. There is no way this huge topic can be given adequate treatment within the confines of this paper. What follows is a brief review of arguments pro and con and a tentative conclusion as regards subsidiaries of MNC operating in the LDC.

Arguments in favor of accepting the practice of corruption:

1. "When in Rome do as the Romans." This implies an abdication of the role of the MNC as a change agent insofar as ethics are concerned.
2. We should not practice "ethical imperialism," not "shove 'our' values down other people's throats." This argument is based on the questionable assumption that a majority of the population in the host country are in favor of corruption. Not only that: the argument also conveniently overlooks the fact that – for better or worse – the MNC brings pervasive changes in values in many other areas of life in the LDC.
3. We should simply be "neutral" relative to local values. Unfortunately, this argument is untenable. The average MNC subsidiary is a sufficiently major factor on the local scene that a neutral "going along" with the bribery system in effect means actively reinforcing it.
4. Corruption can play a positive role by building an invisible "web of trust" among participants. Maybe so. But the question is whether this is preferable to a visible web of trust based on functional merit.
5. Corruption can play a positive role as the "grease that lubricates" (German Schmiergeld) the local Establishment. Again we have the question whether a bureaucracy cannot be made to run along functional lines.
6. We can not afford to walk the straight and narrow as long as competitors bribe their way through the local bureaucracy. At the level of everyday realities this is probably the strongest reason in favor of accepting corruption as "a fact of life." (A feature article in the Wall Street Journal (February 28, 1977) does suggest, however, that at least in the short run American MNCs have not suffered by discontinuing corrupt practices.) Of course, it does have a little of the flavor of the argumentation of several cadets in the recent West Point scandal: "You cannot get through here unless you cheat," or "Why should I be Simon pure when lots of my buddies are cheating?"

Arguments against corruption:

1. Corruption removes the causal relationship between honest effort and due reward. Thus the system is fundamentally counterproductive.
2. Corruption reinforces fatalism among the "little people" outside the bribery network.

3. Corruption reinforces existing inequalities and by definition involves discrimination. Thus, it tramples equal rights and is antidemocratic.
4. Corruption is a serious block against consumer emancipation in the LDC, as long as bribes can let you get away with selling imitation or fraudulent products, forget about quality control and the health and safety of your products, pollute the environment, use false weights and measures, and neglect warranties and consumer complaints.

Our own view is that while rich countries such as the United States can possibly absorb corruption as just another questionable business practice (and, indeed, we seem to have plenty of it), the LDC can ill afford the luxury. The dysfunctional effects of bribery are simply too great relative to the objectives of economic development. There is plenty of room for both individual and, not least, collective initiatives among the MNCs active in a given host country to contribute to the gradual eradication of corruption.

Technology Transfer

The emphasis on transfer of product and production technology (patents and technical know-how) has been dangerously one-sided. From the viewpoint of balanced development, the transfer of marketing, accounting, and general management technology is at least as important. High time it is that the MNC and the business professions make use of every opportunity offered by the LDC to get on with the enormous task of technical assistance in these fields.

Building Infrastructure

A great challenge of the local MNC is to foster the development of indigenous business infrastructure, such as marketing research and advertising agencies, freight handlers, suppliers, and distributors. Clearly, this may also be viewed as an aspect of technology transfer. We have referred to Ford stimulating local sources of supply in Spain. Twenty years earlier Sears, Roebuck and Company did a truly pioneering job in Latin America by developing, training, and, frequently, financing hundreds of local suppliers and by introducing consumer credit on equitable terms. Unilever in Africa has provided booklets and advisors to local businessmen, showing them how to improve their operations in the key areas of marketing, finance and accounting.

Reducing Dualism

Nowhere is the coexistence of a metropolitan growth sector and a rural stagnation sector as prevalent as in the LDCs. A striking and unfortunate fact of life is that typically both the government and the business community of the LDC pay little more than lip service to the crying need for integration of the rural population into the general thrust of development. Yet, sustained growth of the national economy usually calls for heroic effort to develop agriculture and associated processing activities as well as rural trading and small local manufacturing establishments. Unilever in Africa and, to some extent, Sears in Latin America are representative of MNCs which have accepted the need to bring the two halves of the dual economy together. The LDCs would be well served by many more examples of this kind.

Consumer Protection, Education, and Information

Paradoxically, consumerism is strictly an affluent-country phenomenon. You will not find a Ralph Nader in the Third World. Yet the average consumer is the true underdog of the LDC. Shoddy locally made goods are the order of the day in every nation where sellers' markets, import substitution, and producer unconcern with quality prevail. Unconscionable interest rates and credit arrangements frequently create a buyer dependency that is more like serfdom than consumer sovereignty. Imitation, fraudulent, and unsafe products galore permeate the marketplace. Their minds set on cement plants and heavy industry, LDC governments generally have no interest in consumers. The key to consumer emancipation is consumer protection, education, and information (in that order).

As consumer emancipation is as much a cause as an effect of economic development, and as substandard competition is clearly not compatible with the modern MNC, it is difficult to imagine an area where the long term interest of the MNC and that of the local population are more closely united. What we have here is the ideal area for voluntary action by such corporations, proceeding singly or in unison.

THE CHALLENGE OF THE MNC IN THE LDC

Our thesis is that the mutual interests of the LDC and the MNC call for a partnership or entente. The keystone of such an alliance is mutual trust and respect. One means of assuring that local operations are conducive to trust is a management audit ranging over the wide territory of managerial performance illustrated by our discussion. This audit may be an internal one, as is the case in Cummins Engine, or it may be carried out by consultants. The time may come also when host countries wish to undertake such audits under their own auspices, although this may be less likely where MNCs are already doing it on a voluntary basis.

In some instances it may be in the best interest of the parties to spell out the performance expected by the MNC in some detail in what might appropriately be called a social contract. This may, for example, be desirable when an MNC becomes engaged in a socialist country in a major way. It is true that the overall objectives of growth do not differ much between free enterprise and socialist countries.   However, they frequently differ as to the means appropriate to reaching the ends. This implies that an MNC going into a socialist country had better bargain for maximum acceptable discretion and other rules of conduct at as early a stage as possible. Once the ground rules are spelled out it may be easier in some respects to operate in a socialist country, as the authoritarian power of the state will be behind you.

But when all has been said and done at the local level, it is the mission of the MNC to retain and extend the global perspective. Never should we lose sight of the fact that it represents a more successful instance of international cooperation and a closer approach to global thinking than we have thus far encountered among governments. The MNC is the torchbearer of One World, and here in the end lies its lasting service to humanity.

47 Marketing and Economic Development*
Peter F. Drucker

Marketing is generally the most neglected area in the economic life of developing countries. It is manufacturing or construction which occupies the greatest attention in these economies. Yet marketing holds a key position in these countries. Its effectiveness as an engine of economic development with special emphasis on its ability to develop rapidly much-needed entrepreneurial and managerial skills needs hardly any elaboration. Because it provides a systematic discipline in a vital area of economic activity it fills one of the greatest needs of a developing economy.

MARKETING AS A BUSINESS DISCIPLINE

A distinguished pioneer of marketing, Charles Coolidge Parlin, was largely instrumental in developing marketing as a systematic business discipline: in teaching us how, in an orderly, purposeful, and planned way, to find and create customers; to identify and define markets; to create new ones and promote them; to integrate customers' needs, wants, and preferences, and the intellectual and creative capacity and skills of an industrial society, towards the design of new and better products and of new distributive concepts and processes. It is in marketing that we satisfy individual and social values, needs, and wants – be it through producing goods, supplying services, fostering innovation, or creating satisfaction. Marketing has its focus on the customer, that is, on the individual making decisions within a social structure and within a personal and social value system. Marketing is thus the process through which economy is integrated into society to serve human needs.

*Excerpt from Peter F. Drucker, "Marketing and economic development," Journal of Marketing, Vol. 22 (January 1958), pp. 252-9, with permission.

THE ROLE OF MARKETING

Marketing occupies a critical role in respect to underdeveloped "growth" countries. Indeed marketing is the most important "multiplier" of such development. It is in itself in every one of these areas the least developed, the most backward part of the economic system. Its development, above all others, makes possible economic integration and the fullest utilization of whatever assets and productive capacity an economy already possesses. It mobilizes latent economic energy. It contributes to the greatest needs: that for the rapid development of entrepreneurs and managers, and at the same time it may be the easiest area of managerial work to get going. The reason is that, thanks to men like Parlin, it is the most systematized and, therefore, the most learnable and the most teachable of all areas of business management and entrepreneurship.

INTERNATIONAL AND INTERRACIAL INEQUALITY

For the first time in man's history the whole world is united and unified. This may seem a strange statement in view of the conflicts and threats of suicidal wars that scream at us from every headline. But conflict has always been with us. What is new is that today all of mankind shares the same vision, the same objective, the same goal, the same hope, and believes in the same tools. This vision might, in gross over-simplification, be called "industrialization."

It is the belief that it is possible for man to improve his economic lot through systematic, purposeful, and directed effort — individually as well as for an entire society. It is the belief that we have the tools at our disposal — the technological, the conceptual, and the social tools — to enable man to raise himself, through his own efforts. And this is an irreversible new fact. It has been made so by these true agents of revolution in our times: the new tools of communication — the dirt road, the truck, and the radio, which have penetrated even the farthest, most isolated, and most primitive community.

This is new, and cannot be emphasized too much and too often. It is both a tremendous vision and a tremendous danger in that catastrophe must result if it cannot be satisfied, at least to a modest degree. But at the same time we have a new, unprecedented danger, that of international and interracial inequality. What we are engaged in today is essentially a race between the promise of economic development and the threat of international worldwide class war. The economic development is the opportunity of this age. This class war is the danger. Both are new. Both are indeed so new that most of us do not even see them as yet. But they are the essential economic realities of this industrial age of ours. And whether we shall realize the opportunity or succumb to danger will largely decide not only the economic future of this world — it may largely decide its spiritual, its intellectual, its political, and its social future.

SIGNIFICANCE OF MARKETING

Marketing is central in this new situation. For marketing is one of our most potent levers to convert the danger into the opportunity.   To understand this we must ask: what do we mean by "underdeveloped"?

The first answer is, of course, that we mean areas of very low income. But income is, after all, a result. It is a result first of extreme agricultural overpopulation in which the great bulk of the people have to find a living on the land which, as a result, cannot even produce enough food to feed them, let alone produce a surplus. It is certainly a result of low productivity. And both, in a vicious circle, mean that there is not enough capital for investment and very low productivity of what is being invested – owing largely to misdirection of investment into unessential and unproductive channels.

The essential aspect of an "underdeveloped" economy and the factor, the absence of which keeps it "underdeveloped," is the inability to organize economic efforts and energies, to bring together resources, wants, and capacities, and so to convert a self-limiting static system into creative, self-generating organic growth. And this is where marketing comes in.

LACK OF DEVELOPMENT IN UNDERDEVELOPED COUNTRIES

First, in every "underdeveloped" country, marketing is the most underdeveloped – or the least developed – part of the economy, if only because of the strong, pervasive prejudice against the "middleman." As a result, these countries are stunted by inability to make effective use of the little they have. Marketing might by itself go far toward changing the entire economic tone of the existing system – without any change in methods of production, distribution of population, or of income.

It would make the producers capable of producing marketable products by providing them with standards, with quality demands, and with specifications for their product. It would make the product capable of being brought to markets instead of perishing on the way. And it would make the consumer capable of discrimination, that is, of obtaining the greatest value for his very limited purchasing power.

In every one of these countries, marketing profits are characteristically low. Indeed the people engaged in marketing barely eke out a subsistence living. And "mark-ups" are minute by our standards. But marketing costs are outrageously high. The waste in distribution and marketing if only from spoilage, or from the accumulation of unsaleable inventories that clog the shelves for years, has to be seen to be believed. And marketing service is by and large all but nonexistent.

What is needed in any "growth" country to make economic development realistic, and at the same time produce a vivid demonstration of what economic development can produce, is a marketing system: a system of physical distribution; a financial system to make possible the distribution of goods; and actual marketing, that is, an actual system of integrating wants, needs, and purchasing power of the consumer with capacity and resources of production.

This need is largely masked today because marketing is so often confused with the traditional "trader and merchant" of which every one of these countries has more than enough. It would be one of our most important contributions to the development of "underdeveloped" countries to get across the fact that marketing is something quite different.

It would be basic to get across the triple function of marketing: the function of crystallizing and directing demand for maximum productive effectiveness and efficiency; the function of guiding production purposefully toward maximum consumer satisfaction and consumer value; and the function of creating discrimination that then gives rewards to those who really contribute excellence; and that then also penalize the monopolist, the slothful, or those who only want to take but do not want to contribute or to risk.

UTILIZATION BY THE ENTREPRENEUR

Secondly, marketing is also the most easily accessible "multiplier" of managers and entrepreneurs in an "underdeveloped" growth area. And managers and entrepreneurs are the foremost need of these countries. In the first place, "economic development" is not a force of nature. It is the result of the action – the purposeful, responsible, risk-taking action – of men as entrepreneurs and managers. Certainly it is the entrepreneur and manager who alone can convey to the people of these countries an understanding of what economic development means and how it can be achieved.

Marketing can convert latent demand into effective demand. It cannot, by itself, create purchasing power. But it can uncover and channel all purchasing power that exists. It can, therefore, rapidly create the conditions for a much higher level of economic activity than existed before, can create the opportunities for the entrepreneur. It then can create the stimulus for the development of modern, responsible, professional management by creating opportunity for the producer who knows how to plan, how to organize, how to lead people, and how to innovate.

In most of these countries, markets are of necessity very small. They are too small to make it possible to organize distribution for a single-product line in any effective manner. As a result, without a marketing organization, many products for which there is an adequate demand at a reasonable price cannot be distributed; or worse, they can be produced and distributed only under monopoly conditions. A marketing system is needed which serves as the joint and common channel for many producers if any of them is to be able to come into existence. This means in effect that a marketing system in the "underdeveloped" countries is the creator of small business, is the only way in which a man of vision and daring can become a businessman and an entrepreneur himself. This is thereby also the only way in which a true middle class can develop in the countries in which the habit of investment in productive enterprise has still to be created.

DEVELOPER OF STANDARDS

Thirdly, marketing in an "underdeveloped" country is the developer of standards – of standards for product and service as well as of standards of conduct, of integrity, of reliability, of foresight, and of concern for the basic long-range impact of decisions on the customer, the supplier, the economy, and the society.

Rather than making theoretical statements let me point to one illustration: the impact Sears, Roebuck and Company has had on several countries of Latin America. To be sure, the countries of Latin America in which Sears operates – Mexico, Brazil, Cuba, Venezuela, Colombia, and Peru – are not "underdeveloped" in the same sense in which Indonesia or the Congo are "underdeveloped." Their average income, although very low by our standards, is at least two times, perhaps as much as four or five times, that of the truly "underdeveloped" countries in which the bulk of mankind still live. Still, in every respect, except income level, these Latin American countries are at best "developing."

It is also true that Sears in these countries is not a "low-price" merchandiser. It caters to the middle class in the richer of these countries, and to the upper middle class in the poorest of these countries. Incidentally, the income level of these groups is still lower than that of the worker in the industrial sector of our economy. Still Sears is a mass-marketer even in Colombia or Peru. What is perhaps even more important, it is applying in these "underdeveloped" countries exactly the same policies and principles it applies in this country, carries substantially the same merchandise (although most of it is produced in the countries themselves), and applies the same concepts of marketing it uses in Indianapolis or Philadelphia. Its impact and experience are, therefore, a fair test of what marketing knowledge and marketing techniques can achieve.

The impact of this one American business which does not have more than a mere handful of stores in these countries and handles no more than a small fraction of the total retail business of these countries is truly amazing. In the first place, Sears' latent purchasing power has fast become actual purchasing power. Or, to put it less theoretically, people have begun to organize their buying and to go out for value in what they do buy.

Secondly, by the very fact that it builds one store in one city, Sears forces a revolution in retailing throughout the whole surrounding area. It forces a different attitude toward the customer, toward the store clerk, toward the supplier, and toward the merchandise itself. It forces other retailers to adopt modern methods of pricing, of inventory control, of training, and of window display.

The greatest impact Sears has had, however, is in the multiplication of new industrial business for which Sears creates a marketing channel. Because it has to sell goods manufactured in these countries rather than import them (if only because of foreign exchange restrictions), Sears has been instrumental in getting established literally hundreds of new manufacturers making goods which, a few years ago, could not be made in the country let alone be sold in adequate quantity. Simply to satisfy its own marketing needs, Sears has had to insist on standards of workmanship, quality, and delivery — that is, on standards of production management, of technical management, and above all of the management of people — which, in a few short years, have advanced the art and science of management in these countries by at least a generation.

I hardly need to add that Sears is not in Latin America for reasons of philanthropy, but because it is good and profitable business with extraordinary growth potential. In other words, Sears is in Latin America because marketing is the major opportunity in a "growth economy" — precisely because its absence is a major economic gap and the greatest need.

MARKETING THE CATALYST

Marketing is obviously not a cure-all, not a paradox. It is only one thing we need. But it answers a critical need. Indeed without marketing as the hinge on which to turn, economic development will almost have to take the totalitarian form. A totalitarian system can be defined economically as one in which economic development is being attempted without marketing. Indeed as one in which marketing is suppressed. Precisely because it first looks at the values and wants of the individual, and because it then develops people to act purposefully and responsibly — that is, because of its effectiveness in developing a free economy — marketing is suppressed in a totalitarian system. If we want economic development in freedom and responsibility, we have to build it on the development of marketing.

In the new and unprecedented world we live in, a world which knows both a new unity of vision and growth and a new and most dangerous cleavage, marketing has a special and central role to play. This role goes beyond "getting the stuff out the back door"; beyond "getting the most sales with the least cost"; beyond "the optimal integration of our values and wants as customers, citizens, and persons, with our productive resources and intellectual achievements" — the role marketing plays in a developed society.

In a developing economy, marketing is, of course, all of this. But in addition, in an economy that is striving to break the age-old bondage of man to misery, want, and destitution, marketing is also the catalyst for the transmutation of latent resources into actual resources, of desires into accomplishments, and the development of responsible economic leaders and informed economic citizens.

REFERENCE

Thorelli, H.B., and Sentell, G.D., Consumer emancipation and economic development: The case of Thailand (forthcoming).

FURTHER READING – PART EIGHT

Gladwin, Thomas N., "Environmental policy trends facing multinationals," California Management Review, Vol. 20, No. 2 (Winter 1977), pp. 81-93.

Hoyt, Ronald E., "East-West trade growth potential for the 1980s," Columbia Journal of World Business, Vol. 13, No. 1 (Spring 1978), pp. 59-70.

Sachdev, Jagdish C., "Disinvestment: A new problem in multinational corporation host government interface," Management International Review, Vol. 16, No. 3 (1976), pp. 23-35.

Sethi, Prakash S., "Advocacy advertising and the multinational corporation," Columbia Journal of World Business, Vol. 12, No. 3 (Fall 1977), pp. 32-46.

Steade, Richard D., "Multinational corporations and the changing world economic order," California Management Review, Vol. 21, No. 2 (Winter 1978), pp. 5-12.

Wiedersheim-Paul, Finn; Olson, Hans C.; and Welch, Lawrence S., "Preexport activity: The first step in internationalization," Journal of International Business Studies, Vol. 9, No. 1 (Spring-Summer 1978), pp. 47-58.

General Readings in International Marketing

The journals and books from which our Readings were selected and the works referenced in them are recommended to gain further insights into the growing field of international business and marketing. The sources listed at the end of each Part are provided for the reader who wishes more in-depth coverage of various aspects of international marketing. The writings listed below are suggested as reference material for the reader desiring to broaden general understanding and background of international trade relationships.

Bartels, Robert, Comparative Marketing: Wholesaling in Fifteen Countries (Homewood, Ill.: Richard D. Irwin, 1963). Sponsored by the American Marketing Association, this classic study still has relevance today.

Fayerweather, John, International Business Strategy and Administration (Cambridge, Mass.: Ballinger Publishing Co., 1978). Provides wider perspective on international business as well as marketing's role in it.

Kindleberger, Charles P., International Economics, 5th ed. (Homewood, Ill.: Richard D. Irwin, 1973). One of the best known texts explaining international economics and trade with a macro orientation.

Kolde, E.J., The Multinational Company: Behavioral and Managerial Analysis (Lexington, Mass.: Lexington Books, 1974). For marketing related aspects, see especially chapters 2, 3, 6, and 8 to 10.

Liander, Bertil; Terpstra, Vern; Yoshino, M.Y.; and Sherbini, Aziz A., Comparative Analysis for International Marketing (Boston: Allyn and Bacon, 1967). A sophisticated methodology for classifying and comparing countries.

Miller, Joseph C. and Pras, Bernard, "The effects of multinational and export diversification on the profit stability of U.S. corporations," Southern Economic Journal (January 1980), pp. 792-804. Geographic diversification often more profitable than product diversification is the message.

Moyer, Reed and Hollander, Stanley C., Markets and Marketing in Developing Economies (Homewood, Ill.: Richard D. Irwin, 1968). American Marketing Association sponsored, this book contains a number of useful marketing articles on LDCs.

Terpstra, Vern, The Cultural Environment of International Business (Cincinnati, Ohio: Southwestern Publishing Co., 1978). Excellent analysis of cultural aspects and adaptation requirements in international business and marketing.

Thorelli, Hans B. and Thorelli, Sarah V., Consumer Information Handbook: Europe and North America (New York: Praeger Publishers, 1974). Comprehensive survey of consumer information programs and organizations in the North Atlantic community of nations.

Thorelli, Hans B.; Becker, Helmut; and Engledow, Jack, The Information Seekers: An International Study of Consumer Information and Advertising Image (Cambridge, Mass.: Ballinger Publishing Co., 1975). Report on cross-cultural surveys on consumer attitudes and use of product information.

Vernon, Raymond and Wells, Louis T., Manager in the International Economy (Englewood Cliffs, N.J.: Prentice-Hall, 1977). Addresses managerial problems arising in the multinational enterprise, including marketing.

Wiechmann, Ulrich E., Marketing Management in Multinational Firms: The Consumer Packaged Goods Industry (New York: Praeger Publishers, 1976). An in-depth study of an industry.

INTERNATIONAL MARKETING TEXTS – A SAMPLING

Hess, John M. and Cateora, Philip B., International Marketing, 4th ed. (Homewood, Ill.: Richard D. Irwin, 1979).

Kahler, Ruel and Kramer, Roland L., International Marketing, 4th ed. (Cincinnati, Ohio: South-Western Publishing Co., 1977).

Keegan, Warren J., Multinational Marketing Management, 2nd ed. (Englewood Cliffs, N.J.: Prentice-Hall, 1980).

Livingstone, J.M., International Marketing Management (London: MacMillan, 1976).

Majaro, Simon, International Marketing: A Strategic Approach to World Markets (New York: John Wiley and Sons, 1977).

Terpstra, Vern, International Marketing, 2nd ed. (New York: Holt, Rinehart and Winston, 1978).

Yarker, Ken A., International Marketing (London: Business Books, Ltd., 1976).

Much additional practical information for more specific purposes is available that should be consulted for individual international marketing problems: Business International (12-14 Chemin Rieu, Geneva, and 757 Third Avenue, New York) is a high-quality source of many publications. Excellent surveys of international markets are continually prepared by the Economist Intelligence Unit (27 St. James' Place, London SW1). Such organizations as the UN, UNCTAD, IMF, OECD, EEC, EFTA, and GATT have a great variety of useful publications, most of them for the asking. The ministries of commerce (in the U.K., the Department of Trade and Industry) and the embassies or consular services of most countries furnish advice about governmental services and information sources and may also help in handling particular trade enquiries. International organizations such as EVAF (European Association for Industrial Marketing Research, 39-40 St. James' Place, London SW1) and ESOMAR (European Society for Opinion and Marketing Research, Wamberg 37, Amsterdam) provide information on marketing consultants and research agencies or firms available in different countries. Though no complete list appears to be in existence at this time, the annually published ESOMAR Handbook does contain information on facilities and organizations in numerous countries. The reader who is interested in assembling a still greater variety and specificity of international market and marketing information resources should refer to the "International Marketing" section in Robert Ferber, ed., Handbook of Marketing Research (New York: McGraw-Hill, 1974). He or she will find source listings on individual countries or regions, industries, companies, products, organizations, international surveys and directories, and so forth.   Finally it should be remembered that for major transactions and commitments even seasoned executives request the advice of commercial banks and international consulting or accounting firms.

Thousands of executives and students in some 20 countries on all five continents by this time have participated in the International Operations Simulation (INTOP). This international business strategy exercise in the management game form is the most widely used strategy game of the sophisticated variety among American Business Schools, according to the Computing Newsletter. Directors of executive development programs in MNCs as well as professors teaching international business may wish to consult the administrator's handbook: Hans B. Thorelli and Robert L. Graves, International Operations Simulation (New York: Free Press-MacMillan, 1964). For information concerning availability of program tapes for various types of computer equipment, please contact Professor Thorelli, Graduate School of Business, Indiana University, Bloomington, IN 47401, U.S.A.

Glossary

AID	Agency for International Development (United States)
ANCOM	Andean Common Market (1967)
ASEAN	Association of South East Asian Nations (1967)
CACM	Central American Common Market (1960)
CARICOM	Caribbean Common Market (1973, succeeded CARIFTA free trade group)
C.I.F.	Price includes cost, insurance, and freight
CMEA, COMECON	Council for Mutual Economic Assistance (1949 Soviet-dominated East European trade and development group)
DISC	Domestic International Sales Corporation (United States)
EAEC	East African Economic Community (Kenya, Uganda, Tanzania)
EC, EEC	European Community (1958: European Economic Community)
ECOWAS	Economic Community of West African States
ECSC	European Coal and Steel Community (now part of EC)
EFTA	European Free Trade Association (1960)
F.O.B.	Price free on board in seller's port
FTO	Foreign Trade Organization (export-import monopolies in East Europe)
GATT	General Agreement on Tariffs and Trade (1947)
GNP	Gross National Product
GOSPLAN	Central Planning Agency in the Soviet Union
IBRD	International Bank for Reconstruction and Development (World Bank)
IDA	International Development Association
IFC	International Finance Corporation
IMF	International Monetary Fund
ISO	International Standards Organization
LAFTA	Latin American Free Trade Association (1960)
LDC	Less Developed Countries

MAGHREB	Maghreb Common Market (Algeria, Tunisia, Morocco, Libya. Defunct)
MNC	Multinational Corporation
MFN	Most Favored Nation
NATO	North Atlantic Treaty Organization
OAS	Organization of American States
OCAM	Afro-Malagasy Economic Union (1965)
OECD	Organization for Economic Co-Operation and Development (The "club" of highly industrialized Western countries and Japan)
OPEC	Organization of Petroleum Exporting Countries
OPIC	Overseas Private Investment Corporation (United States)
SDR	Special Drawing Rights (the "currency" of IMF)
UDEAC	Central African Customs and Economic Union (Congo, Gabon, Cameroon, Central African Republic)
UNCITRAL	United Nations Commission on Trade Law
UNCTAD	United Nations Conference on Trade and Development (1964)
UNIDO	United Nations Industrial Development Organization
VAT	Value-Added Tax
WHO	World Health Organization

Country Index

Company Index

AEG, Germany, 331, 341
The Afro-American Purchasing
    Center, Inc., of NY, USA,
    256
Airbus Industry, Europe, 38
Alberto Culver, USA, 233
ALCOA, USA, 93
Alfa Romeo, Italy, 236
Alumax, USA, 331
AMAX, USA, 331
American Commercial Solvents
    Corporation, 85
Amtorg Trading Company, 256
Angelica Nurseries, USA, 266
Anixter Brothers Inc., USA, 267
Aston Martin, UK, 236-237
Avis Rent-a-Car, USA, 192
Bamletts, UK, 203
Bavarian Motor Works (BMW),
    Germany, 89-91
Beatrice Foods Company, USA, 26
Bechtel Corporation, USA, 31
Bic France, 199-200
Bic Pen Corporation, USA, 199-200
British Caledonian Airline, UK, 228
British Leyland Motors, UK, 236
British Oxygen, UK, 82-83
British Petroleum, UK, 82-83
Boeing, USA, 18
Bosch AG, Germany, 341
Budd Co, USA, 204

Burmah Oil, 83
Cadbury Schweppes Ltd, UK,
    225-229
Caterpillar Tractor Company, USA,
    262, 386
Chase Manhattan Bank, USA, 228
Chilean Copper Trust, Chile, 38
Chori, Japan, 328
Chrysler Corporation, USA, 72, 304
Coca-Cola, USA, xvi, 13, 24-25,
    133-134, 191-192, 229, 306
Colgate Palmolive, USA, 195-196,
    228-229
Continental Can Corporation,
    USA, 88-89, 93-94
Crestbrook Timber, Canada, 331
Culligan Company, USA, 240-242
Cummins Engine Company, USA,
    380, 390
John Deere, USA, 226, 229
Dresser Industries, USA, 31, 41
DuPont, USA, 230
Ericsson Telephone Corporation,
    Sweden, 17, 382
Esso, Europe, 227, 231-232
Fiat, Italy, 226, 236
Fisons, UK, 92
Ford España, Spain, 385
Ford Motor Company, USA, 13,
    71, 93, 229, 233, 304, 386,
    389

Name Index

Subject Index

About the Editors

HANS B. THORELLI is the E.W. Kelley Professor of Business Administration at Indiana University. Over the past 12 years he has been the Project Leader of the International Consumer Information Survey sponsored by that University. The following books resulted from this Project: Consumer Information Handbook: Europe and North America (co-authored with his wife, Dr. Sarah V. Thorelli), The Information Seekers (with Professors Helmut Becker and Jack Engledow), and Consumer Information Systems (also co-authored with his wife). A forthcoming product from the Survey is Consumer Emancipation and Economic Development: The Case of Thailand (with Professor G.D. Sentell).

His prior books include The Federal Antitrust Policy: Origination of an American Tradition, International Operations Simulation, and Strategy + Structure = Performance. He is a member of the Consumer Advisory Committee of the Federal Energy Administration and the Consumer Council of the U.S. Chamber of Commerce. He is a former Vice-President--Public Policy of the American Marketing Association and a consultant to major U.S. and European multinational corporations and the Swedish Government. Dr. Thorelli holds a Ph.D. and an LL.B. degree from the University of Stockholm.

HELMUT BECKER is Professor of Marketing and International Business at the University of Portland (Oregon). On the team of the International Consumer Information Survey at Indiana University, he is the co-author of the book The Information Seekers. He authored or co-authored numerous articles on consumer information and advertising image that have appeared in such journals as Decision Science, Journal of Marketing Research, Journal of Advertising Research, Journal of International Business Studies, as well as in German publications. He is a member of the editorial review Board of the Journal of Marketing and the co-editor of the 1972 Combined Proceedings of the American Marketing Association.

Dr. Becker received his basic education in Germany. He is a graduate magna cum laude of the University of Portland, has an MBA from the University of Oregon and a DBA from Indiana University. He is active in the Academy of International Business and the American Marketing Association and teaches in the marketing, international business, and business and society areas.